The Lesbian and Gay Book of

Love and
Marriage

The Lesbian and Gay Book of

Love and Marriage

Creating the Stories of Our Lives

Paula Martinac

A Seth Godin Production

Broadway Books   New York

BROADWAY

Library of Congress Cataloging-in-Publication Data
Martinac, Paula, 1954–
    The lesbian and gay book of love and marriage : creating the stories of our lives / Paula Martinac. — 1st ed.
      p. cm.
    "A Seth Godin production."
    Includes index.
    ISBN 0-7679-0162-2 (paper)
    1. Lesbian couples—United States—Interviews.   2. Gay male couples—United States—Interviews.   3. Dating (Social custom)—United States.   4. Same-sex marriage—United States.   I. Title.
    HQ75.6U5M39   1998
    306.84′8—dc21
                                         97-43996
                                           CIP

Listed below are short biographies for contributors to the following pieces:

page 24: "Cyberpals/Cyberlove: What Does It All Mean?" by Martha Pearse, Ph.D., a licensed clinical psychologist in private practice in Denver.
page 43: "A Boyfriend by Any Other Name" by Mubarak S. Dahir, an award-winning journalist.
pages 132–33: "Marriage: The Ultimate Perk" by Patricia Nell Warren, a widely published commentator and the author of *The Front Runner* and other bestselling novels.
pages 168–69: "Out to the In-Laws" by E. J. Graff, whose commentary on lesbian and gay issues has appeared in the *Boston Globe,* the *New York Times Magazine,* the *Nation, Out,* and other publications. Her book, *What Is Marriage For?* will be published by Beacon Press.
page 190: "Breaking Up Under Glass" by Judy Nelson, author of the autobiography *Choices: My Journey After Leaving My Husband for Martina and a Lesbian Life.*
"Green Card Blues" (pages 54–55) and "Same-Sex Domestic Violence" (pages 186–87) have appeared in different forms in Paula Martinac's column "Lesbian Notions."

Designed by Ralph Fowler

FIRST EDITION

98 99 00 01 02 10 9 8 7 6 5 4 3 2 1

To Katie, for the five best years ever

Contents

Foreword by Roberta Achtenberg   ix

Acknowledgments   xi

Introduction: The Reality of Lesbian and Gay Love and Marriage   xiii

1 Meeting Mr. or Ms. Right   1

    An Imposed Difference   1

    Same-Sex Love in the "Good Old Days"   9

    Brief Encounters, Lasting Love   17

    The Personal Is Still Political   26

    Give Me That Old Time Religion   31

    The Next Time Around   36

    "Type" Casting   38

2 Seriouser and Seriouser   41

    Making It Up   41

    Bringing the U-Haul   46

    Rings and Things   56

    Popping the Question   64

    "The Most Natural Thing in the World"   71

3 I Do! I Do!   75

    The Many Meanings of "Marriage"   75

    A Private Affair   81

    Tradition! Tradition!   85

    Right in Your Own Backyard   99

In the Public Eye 110
So "Domestic" 116
Shaking It Up 119
"Just Two Guys in Love" 125
"In a Heartbeat" 129
A Very Old Desire 134

4 "For Better or Worse, For Richer or Poorer . . ." 139
Our Own Kind of Marriage 139
Settling Down 143
Out in the World 153
"Outlaws" and In-Laws 161
Making It Last 168
D-I-V-O-R-C-E 188
"Till Death Do Us Part" 192
Unexpected Transitions 194
When I'm Sixty-Four 197
Partners in Life and Love 200

5 The Family Way 205
Toward a Broader Concept of Family 205
Chosen People 208
Out of Our (Straight) Past 213
Boom Time 218
Maybe Baby 220
And Baby Makes . . . 224
The Adoption Option 233
Religious Aspects 242
Are Grandma and Grandpa Onboard? 245
Facing the World 247
Role Models 250
When Families Change 252
Smashing Stereotypes 257

Appendix: An Annotated List of Organizations and Resources for
Lesbian and Gay Couples and Families 261
Index 281

Foreword

by Roberta Achtenberg

It is Sunday evening and I am home with Mary and Benjie. Mary and I have been together more than fifteen years. I adore her more than love could compel or convention prescribe. We are as committed to each other as we could possibly be. We have been there for each other through joys and sorrows, in lust and love, through death and birth—and we hope it will always be so.

Our son, Benjie, is twelve. He is rapidly approaching his young adulthood: This year we will celebrate his bar mitzvah. He is a loving, talented, delightful child and we consider him the most extraordinary blessing in our lives.

It has been a wonderful weekend. Saturday we got up early to begin the day-long process of assembling the ingredients for Mary's world-famous Louisiana gumbo. I drove Benjie to religious school, and on the way we talked about his homework, baseball, and the rock concert we had taken him to the night before.

Sunday was devoted to reading the *San Francisco Chronicle* and the *New York Times,* housecleaning, and paying bills. In the afternoon, we took a stroll on the beach, had Sunday dinner with friends, and prepared ourselves for the demands of the coming week.

We are a family, and this is the texture and rhythm of our family life.

We are also a lesbian-headed family, which means that we have faced some extraordinary circumstances. But we've not been alone. As it turns out, thousands, tens of thousands, hundreds of thousands of America's lesbians and gay men have found a way to meet the unique challenge of creating families. It was not always so.

Beginning in the late seventies, the Lesbian Rights Projects (now the

National Center for Lesbian Rights) litigated lesbian mother and gay father custody cases. We answered thousands of calls a year from women and men who stood to lose custody of their children if it became known that they were gay. Despite this daunting hurdle, there arose an enormous drive to create more families than the legal system and the social system could possibly negate. By 1980, hundreds of women started considering alternative parenting: adopting, foster parenting, and giving birth to children as openly gay people. In 1982, the issue became the rights of gays and lesbians to protect their partners, and a few workplaces were successfully organized.

Today, only fifteen years later, we have large numbers of lesbians and gay men publicly proclaiming their coupledom. They are joyously announcing the creations of their families, and privately, publicly, or intimately, before parents, friends, and religious officials, professing their love.

Thanks to the book you hold in your hands, we now have a snapshot in time of lesbian and gay love and marriage. With talent and insight, Paula Martinac tells our stories of courtship, commitment, wedding planning, and parenthood. All of us can find inspiration and comfort in the inventiveness, fortitude, and joy of these families. I know I do.

San Francisco, California
December 1997

Acknowledgments

This book was a massive undertaking, and many people contributed to making it happen. My greatest thanks go to the many individuals and couples who agreed to be interviewed, who let me snoop into their personal lives, and who didn't flinch at my intimate questions. They understood that by sharing their stories they were helping other lesbians and gay men and also the general public to understand the strength, vitality, and lasting quality of same-sex relationships. Their stories were by turns funny and sad, dramatic and ordinary, but always inspiring. I'm sorry I couldn't use all of them, but they enriched my understanding of lesbian and gay marriage just the same.

Thanks also to the lawyers, activists, clergy, and psychotherapists who gave me their insights on lesbian and gay relationships, often willingly discussing their own lives and loves. Many of them, along with other people, were helpful in locating individuals and couples to be interviewed. Special thanks in this regard to Terry Boggis of Center Kids, Ellen Ensig-Brodsky of Pride Senior Network, Jan Flecher, Noemi Masliah, and Lavi Soloway of the Lesbian and Gay Immigration Rights Task Force, and Ben Munisteri.

At Seth Godin Productions, Julie Maner and Leslie Sharpe first conceptualized a book about lesbian and gay marriage, and Julie and Lisa DiMona were in charge of much of the behind-the-scenes work that made the book possible: creating and maintaining the database, calling participants, collecting reprint permissions and photos, to name just a few. Julie Maner also spent long hours interviewing individuals and couples. Thanks also to Susan Kushnik for research assistance with the sidebars and appendix, and to Julie Pophal for her lightning-fast transcription of dozens of interview tapes.

Janet Goldstein, my first editor at Broadway Books, provided guidance and vision from the start of the project and understood the importance of this book to the growing literature on lesbian and gay relationships. Thanks to her and to her team—especially Daisy Alpert and Layla Hearth—for their hard work and commitment. Thanks also to Tracy Behar, my second editor, for seeing the book through to completion.

Finally, my greatest thanks to my partner of five years, Katie Hogan, for her love, humor, and support, and for letting me share so many of our own stories in this volume. If anyone had told me before we met that I would someday write a book about happy, long-term lesbian and gay relationships, including my own, I would have thought they were talking about science fiction. Thanks, Katie, for changing my life.

Introduction

The Reality of Lesbian and Gay Love and Marriage

Unless you've been hibernating, with no access to the mass media, it's been almost impossible to avoid the topic of legalizing lesbian and gay marriage. It doesn't matter if you're gay or straight—you've most likely had to think about the potentiality of same-sex marriage and exactly where you stand on this issue. And if you live in Hawaii, you're actually living and breathing it, with headlines in the local papers almost every day about the pending court decision that would permit same-sex couples to legally marry.

The debate engendered by the litigation brought in Hawaii by three same-sex couples who applied and were rejected for marriage licenses has been enormous. It's not only been the focus of media attention, it's been discussed and fought over in almost every state legislature across the country and in the U.S. Congress. Lawsuits have also been brought in the states of Vermont and New York by same-sex couples seeking the right to marry legally.

There are a number of intriguing legal questions raised by this historic civil rights struggle. Will same-sex couples win the right to marry in Hawaii? In all probability, according to Evan Wolfson, director of the Marriage Project at Lambda Legal Defense and Education Fund, a national nonprofit law firm that works for lesbian and gay civil rights. Will couples go to Hawaii, marry, and then return home to face enormous court battles when Pennsylvania or Montana or the federal government refuse to recognize their unions? That's what Wolfson and other same-sex marriage activists anticipate.

But there are also underlying social questions, which are even more significant for their immediacy to lesbian and gay lives. What effect has the same-sex marriage struggle in Hawaii and all the debate surrounding it had on lesbian and gay relationships and the community? Are all gay people simply dying to go out and get hitched? Are we just trying to mimic straight people, or are we standing on the brink of a radical transformation of the institution of marriage?

For me, the most interesting element of the Hawaii case is the attention it has drawn to lesbian and gay relationships. The fact is, lesbian and gay couples have for generations been "marrying." I don't mean simply that they've been having ceremonies or weddings to celebrate their unions, though they've been doing that, too, and with greater and greater frequency. But what I mean is that lesbian and gay couples have been creating and enjoying lasting relationships that don't usually get much space in the mainstream media or in popular culture.

That's an amazing feat. Think about it. Lesbians and gay men are essentially without legal rights, except in a handful of jurisdictions. Twenty states still criminalize sodomy. In many cases we can lose our jobs, kids, families of origin, homes—just for being open about who we are. We can't legally marry, and even if we've been with a partner for twenty or thirty years, we still have to check "Single" on official documents and our partners aren't entitled to our Social Security benefits. Not only does the government refuse to accept our relationships as valid, but our chosen partners, in many cases, may not even be acknowledged or welcomed by our families of origin. Many clergy members call our love relationships "abominations" and encourage us to either change or to "sin no more" by leading celibate lives. And until very recently, we saw almost no positive depictions of ourselves and our relationships on television or in the movies.

Yet despite these injustices, same-sex couples have found each other and built lives and families together. It makes me angry that we've had to face so many barriers just to be together, but it also makes me enormously proud that many of us have triumphed against the odds.

This book is a celebration of lesbian and gay marriages and a reclaiming of that word to describe our unions. It's a chronicle of the ways in which lesbians and gay men have negotiated and maintained relationships without the benefit of societal recognition or legal marriage. It investigates what the words "love" and "marriage"—portrayed all around us as the exclusive territory of heterosexuals—mean in a lesbian and gay context. "There are more lesbians and gay men in long-term relationships than people realize," says New York–based therapist Vanessa Marshall. "They're just not visible." Though there's no reliable way to count how many lesbian and gay couples there actually are in the United States, one 1992 survey found that 56 percent of gay men and 71 percent of lesbians were in steady relationships.[1]

In this book, we'll explore how lesbian and gay couples have traditionally met and "courted" and how that has changed with the evolution of a more visible gay community. We'll talk about how same-sex partners choose each other as lifelong mates, and we'll trace the markers that move our relationships from casual to committed. We'll look at our rituals of commitment, from moving in together, to exchanging rings, to the private and public ceremonies that some couples have held. We'll investigate how same-sex couples negotiate daily life—everything from being out as a couple in the neighborhood to having holidays with the "in-laws"—and we'll talk about whether or not same-sex couples perceive the need to marry legally. And finally, we'll discuss the myriad ways lesbians and gay men have created families of choice, which may include kids, stepkids, ex-lovers, or platonic friends.

A tall order! But a job made easier and more enjoyable by more than one hundred lesbian and gay individuals and couples all around the country who either took the time to answer a lengthy questionnaire or participated in e-mail, phone, or in-person interviews that delved and pried into their private lives. Almost without exception, lesbians and gay men were eager to tell me about their experiences and to document their relationships for posterity, and you'll hear their voices here. They invited me into their homes for lunch and dinner, even if they'd never met me before; they wrote me moving letters to explain the importance of the topic to them or to thank me for undertaking the project.

To my knowledge, unless otherwise noted, the majority of couples interviewed for this book are still together. The relationships range in length from eighteen months to thirty-six years. In what suggests a turning point in the visibility of lesbians and gay men and a move toward ending the stigmatization of homosexuality, many people allowed me to use their real names.

For all these couples, same-sex love and marriage were not hot new media topics but what they'd been living through every day. If marriage rights are never achieved in Hawaii or any other state, if the Defense of Marriage Act remains on the books for a thousand years, lesbians and gay men will still fall in love and "marry," in the truest sense of the word. As one woman in Tennessee poignantly wrote to me, "They can keep us from being legally married, but they can't change the reality of it."

Notes

1. *Overlooked Opinions,* "The Gay Market," Chicago, January 1992. It should be noted that this survey was heavily biased toward white, middle-class participants, so its results do not give a real picture of the community.

The Lesbian and Gay Book of

Love and Marriage

Meeting
Mr. or Ms. Right

An Imposed Difference

"The world," writes gay novelist Christopher Bram in his latest book, *Gossip*, "is divided between those who want to live in couples and those who prefer quick hits of lightning." A common stereotype of lesbians and gay men that many people hold, particularly the very religious, is that all gay people fall into the "quick hits" category. Homosexuality in the public imagination has often connoted sex, sex, and more sex. ("I wish!" a lesbian friend of mine once joked.) Many people incorrectly assume that lesbians and gay men don't look for mates, just sex partners. And even if we do acquire mates, all we're doing is rolling around in bed with them all day.

What I particularly appreciate about the coming out of TV character Ellen Morgan is that the scripts for the show have taken aim and fired at stereotypes like this one. In an October 1997 episode, for example, Ellen's parents came to visit and found their daughter busily gardening in her backyard, up to her elbows in dirt. Her mother glanced quickly and nervously toward the house, as if expecting a throng of sweaty, naked lesbians to emerge from it. "Did we interrupt anything, dear?" she asked timidly. "No," Ellen quipped, "the stewardesses just left."

It's funny when we see it on television, but it's an image of lesbians and gay men that damages our ability both to be viewed and to view ourselves as whole individuals. Lesbians and gay men have full lives, not "lifestyles," and those lives include sex but don't necessarily revolve around it. While some of us are indeed "quick hitters" and should have the right to conduct our consensual sex lives any way we choose, recent studies suggest that many more lesbians and gay men are actually in what they describe as committed relationships. So, just as heterosexuals aren't defined entirely by the single people among them, neither should we be.

What makes lesbian and gay people "different" from straight people is that we're *perceived* as different and have suffered on account of other people's prejudices by being treated unfairly—for example, by being denied the right to legally marry or to adopt children. The "difference" that the majority has imposed on us colors everything in our lives, from dating to creating families. In fact, our "difference" has forced us to create a distinct lesbian and gay "survivor" culture that allows us to meet and fall in love and also to fill in the gaps of what we have not been able to find in the mainstream.

It's hard enough for straight people to find partners, but when lesbians and gay men have looked for lovers, they have always encountered the added burden of desiring a love that is not supposed to "speak its name." We're surrounded by what poet Adrienne Rich back in the 1970s dubbed "compulsive heterosexuality." We hear complaints about us "flaunting" our sexuality, when, in fact, you can't turn on the TV or open a magazine without being smacked in the face by heterosexuality, much of it quite sexual in nature. Just think about those ubiquitous Cadillac Deville commercials, for instance, with the background music of "Making Whoopee" blatantly promoting hetero-sex.

In contrast, lesbian and gay romantic experience has been erased, ignored, invalidated, or viewed as "adult" (that is, pornographic). Until very recently, most of the gay people depicted on television were single, seemingly adrift and without lovers or friends. The character Carter, an African American gay man on the popular *Spin City,* is a remnant of this. He's supposedly an out activist, but he only hangs around with straight people and he's never given a viable love interest, though all the straight characters take their turns at romance.

Even when lesbians and gay men in mainstream popular culture are allowed relationships, anything vaguely sexual has traditionally been taboo. Only a few years ago in the Academy Award–winning *Philadelphia,* screen lovers Tom Hanks and Antonio Banderas were allowed only a brotherly hug. Finally, the 1997 hit *In and Out* broke through this, at least for gay men, by showing a full frontal kiss between two men. But when, at the same point in time, the lesbian hero of *Ellen* playfully and jokingly kissed her straight woman friend Paige on the mouth, the television show began running an advisory warning about its "adult content."

It's little wonder that we created a subculture in which we could read about and see ourselves being in love—we were starved for it. Because we couldn't find a place for ourselves in the mainstream culture, we fashioned an alternative one, replete with movies, books, and magazines. It doesn't

THE CENTER OF EVERYTHING

Since the early 1970s, lesbian and gay community centers have sprouted up across the country. Though many have folded over the years, others—like those in Albany, New York, and Los Angeles, California—have been serving the community for more than twenty-five years. And in the last few years, the community center movement has really taken off, with new centers opening all the time in areas of the country where lesbians and gay men have often been most isolated.

There is now a national network of community centers that facilitates the founding and growth of new centers, and the Lesbian and Gay Community Services Center in New York (which has been around since 1984) produces and regularly updates a directory of all the centers nationwide. The directory has listings by state and gives both general and contact information for each center.

Community centers are a wonderful place to meet friends and lovers. When I was single and looking for companionship, I found a home-away-from-home at the New York center. A number of my friends and acquaintances met their partners at community center dances and events or while volunteering or working on staff. Besides meetings and cultural events, these centers also provide needed social and legal services or referrals for lesbian, gay, bisexual, and transgendered people.

The Lesbian and Gay Community Services Center in Greenwich Village.

© 1994 Rich Gerharter/Impact Visuals

To find the lesbian and gay center nearest you, you can access the national directory online at http://www.gaycenter.org/ or contact the New York Lesbian and Gay Community Services Center at (212) 620-7310 for information.

---

surprise me that the oldest and most successful lesbian press is Naiad Press, which has survived for twenty-five years while other houses have failed, primarily because it has published lesbian romance novels with happy, girl-gets-girl endings.

We have also slowly but surely built a community of organizations and support groups to help us find each other and connect with friends and lovers. Community centers, in particular, are now the fastest growing lesbian and gay organizations, with new ones cropping up all the time. (See the sidebar, "The Center of Everything.") In addition, a network of lesbian- and gay-owned businesses has emerged, one that includes places like our own restaurants where we can hold hands without being stared at and our own bed-and-breakfasts where we won't be questioned about why two men or two women require a double bed and not twins.

Building community is slow and incremental, and there is still much work to be done. Much of the core work facing lesbians and gay men, however, is internal—combating our own ingrained negative attitudes about our sexuality. Not surprisingly, after years of being told we're "abnormal," many lesbians and gay men have bought society's vision of us as flawed, pathetic creatures doomed to go through life lonely and unhappy. "Many of my clients have internalized this idea," says Michael Shernoff, a gay therapist in private practice, "and believe their single status is inevitable and a result of something inherently wrong with them."[1] Too many lesbians and gay men continue to accept that, even if they find someone special to love, the relationship probably won't last for long. The underlying assumption is that there's something "bad" or "inferior" about the way we love and that we don't deserve anything more than a lifetime of "quick hits," even if we desperately want something different.

The Hawaii same-sex marriage case is significant for a lot of reasons, but what has interested me most about it is that it has brought into sharp focus the fact that lesbians and gay men have created and sustained lasting, loving relationships for many years. Because of homophobia, very few studies have actually looked at the prevalence of long-term relationships in the lesbian and gay community, and those studies that exist are biased toward thirty-something white middle-class participants. But they do suggest that committed relationships are more common in our community than stereotypes would like us to believe.

> "*I think I was always really hungry to be partnered. I spent seven years living alone. There are nice things you can do living alone. Privacy is nice, and freedom is nice. But I've always felt better partnered.*"

The most thorough study to date was done by Partners Task Force for Gay and Lesbian Couples (see also pages 44–45) in 1988 and 1989, in a survey of 1,266 lesbian and gay couples. The average length of relationship for all the couples was six years, though the average age of respondents was just thirty-five. More than 100 couples had been together longer than fifteen years, and four had actually lasted for over forty years—incredible, given the odds against our relationships lasting even a few months.

Lesbians and gay men have created relationships without the benefit of legal marriage and with many strikes going against them. And we've done this for the same reasons that straight people have: for sex, for companionship and love, for creating families. While there are a lot of people, gay and straight, who remain steadfastly and happily single, many of us have a strong desire to have a relationship. If we're not already involved, chances are we're looking for Mr. or Ms. Right. We are, after all, strongly influenced by the mainstream culture all around us, and that culture is one of couples.

"I think I was always really hungry to be partnered," relates April Martin, a New York–based psychotherapist and author of *The Lesbian and Gay Parenting Handbook,* of her own experience as a single person. "I liked being partnered. I spent seven years living alone. It's okay. There are nice things you can do living alone. Privacy is nice, and freedom is nice. But I've always felt better partnered."

What Is a "Date" (And Are We on One?)

In the straight world, girls and boys are indoctrinated from a young age about partnering off and are socialized in certain rituals of heterosexual behavior, like dating. When my teenage niece went on her first date with a boy last year, the occasion was described to me in great detail by both my mother and my sister, even down to what my niece wore. My entire family got caught up in what was actually a rather minor event in the grand scheme of things—a fourteen-year-old girl and boy going to a

Lesbian dating in San Francisco.

school dance together. My niece's first date took on, as it does with other adolescents, almost mythic proportions—it was a heterosexual rite of passage from childhood to young adulthood, an event that garnered great family support and approval.

The ritual of dating, however, wasn't created to include lesbians and gays. No one teaches us how to "homo-date" as kids. Unlike heterosexuals, "lesbians and gay men have almost no . . . experience of coupling until they are adults," points out Reverend Michael Piazza, pastor of a large lesbian and gay congregation, the Cathedral of Hope/Metropolitan Community Church in Dallas.[2] In fact, lesbians and gay men who experience their first same-sex desire in adolescence have generally been socialized to think that homosexuality is abnormal and to hide their feelings. Their families have been unlikely to view a homosexual first date as any sort of rite of passage—except as a passage down the "wrong" road. (See the sidebar, "Resources for Lesbian and Gay Youth.")

"Dating?" snickers Karin Kaj, the author of seven popular lesbian novels *(Paperback Romance, Car Pool,* and *Wild Things,* to name a few) pub-

RESOURCES FOR LESBIAN AND GAY YOUTH

The teen years can be hard enough, but when a young person realizes that she or he is gay, there are added hurdles to get over. How can you be yourself in a world that, for the most part, wants you to disappear? Though studies have shown that lesbian and gay teens can be more isolated and more at risk for substance abuse and suicide, many are leading the way in being visible and in-your-face about their sexual orientation. A number of resources and Web sites are now available to help lesbian and gay teens come out and connect to the community.

BOOKS

Ellen Bass and Kate Kaufman, *Free Your Mind: The Book for Gay, Lesbian, and Bisexual Youth* (HarperCollins, 1996).

Kurt Chandler and Mitchell Ivers, eds., *Passages of Pride: Lesbian and Gay Youth Come of Age* (Times Books, 1995).

Linnea A. Due, *Joining the Tribe: Growing Up Gay and Lesbian in the 1990s* (Anchor Books, 1995).

Tony Grima, ed., *Not the Only One: Lesbian and Gay Fiction for Teens* (Alyson Publications, 1995).

Adam Mastoon, *The Shared Heart: Portraits and Stories Celebrating Lesbian, Gay, and Bisexual Young People* (Lothrop Lee & Shepard, 1997).

Rachel Pollack and Cheryl Schwartz, *The Journey Out: A Guide for Lesbian, Gay and Bisexual Teens* (Puffin, 1995).

WEB SITES

- http://www.oasismag.org—An online magazine, featuring profiles of lesbian and gay activists, writers, and other role models, as well as monthly columns by lesbian and gay youth from around the country.

- http://www.qrd.org—The Queer Resources Directory has a large subdirectory devoted to lesbian and gay youth, including articles, mailing lists, and links to organizations.

- http://www.yahoo.com/Society_and_Culture/ Lesbian_Gay_and_Bisexual—At this site, you'll find an extensive subdirectory on lesbian and gay youth, including information, hot lines, and links to organizations.

- http://www.qworld.org/friends/toqp/ youthres.html—Called "The Other Queer Page: Youth Resources," this site provides links to lesbian and gay youth online magazines, organizations, hot lines, mailing lists, and pen pals.

- http://www.sappho.com/yoohoo/youth/ index.html—This site for the lesbian community includes a subdirectory of links for lesbians under age twenty-five.

- Youth on Q—On Q, one of the gay and lesbian forums of America Online, has a subdirectory under "Communities" for lesbian and gay youth (keyword: on Q).

lished by Naiad Press under her pen name, Karin Kallmaker. She and her partner, Maria, met as sophomores in high school, and though they spent every minute together in what was clearly a form of courtship, "everyone knows girls can't date each other," Karin says. "We had no idea what we were doing, and it never occurred to me to call it dating."

The negative ideas we learn as kids about desiring members of our own sex can unconsciously prevent us from forming lasting relationships as adults. Having to hide erotic feelings for fear of parents' or friends' rejection can also take a toll that persists into adulthood. Though some brave gay teens have recently been standing up for their rights to date each other openly—taking their same-sex partners to their school proms, for example, or creating proms just for gay youth (see also the sidebar, "Out of the Closet and onto the Dance Floor")—the time when teenage homo-dating will be viewed as completely normal and not a cause for great parental and societal concern is still somewhere off in the future.

Because dating is a ritual created by and for heterosexuals, there have been no clear-cut paths for lesbians and gay men who are looking for partners. We've had to make them up along the way. As a result, there isn't even any consensus in our community about what a lesbian or gay date actually is. For lesbians, "we rarely if ever know if we're having [a date]," writes poet and M.S.W., Sylvia Cole, "or if we're just going out 'as friends.'"[3] Girls aren't socialized to be sexual aggressors, the ones who initiate dates, and that can cause real confusion when two adult lesbians who don't know how to make the first move try to get together.

"I didn't understand that she was asking me out, so I brought all my friends along on the date," laughs Linda Villarosa, former executive editor of *Essence* magazine, when she remembers her first evening with Vickie, her lover of more than six years. But as it turned out, Vickie's ability to "go with it" impressed Linda and made her want to get to know her one-on-one.

Lesbian and gay dating can also have extra baggage attached to it because the homophobia we face from the outside world makes many of us overly eager to be in a supportive relationship. Some of us get seriously involved too soon, starting a cycle of quick relationships that last only a few months, just until the first blush of romance has faded. A woman I dated many years ago told me that when we first met, she didn't realize that I was single because I didn't seem as desperate as all the other lesbians she knew, herself included.

For many gay men, the whole idea of dating each other is fairly new. Unlike girls, boys are socialized to be competitive, unemotional, strong, and aggressively sexual. When you add to that the long-held stereotype of gay people as sexually compulsive, it's not surprising that many of the gay male seniors whom author Keith Vacha interviewed for his book, *Quiet Fire: Memoirs of Older Gay Men*—men who came of age in the pre-Stonewall era—fondly remembered sexual conquests and exploits instead of "courtships," even if they had had lengthy relationships.

After the Stonewall riots of 1969 and the sexual revolution of the 1960s, gay men felt freer to explore the sexuality they had had to keep under wraps in the more oppressive previous era. Richard Burns, executive

"I didn't understand that she was asking me out, so I brought all my friends along on the date."

"Out of the Closet and onto the Dance Floor"

BY BRENT CALDERWOOD

"BRENT CALDERWOOD, SEVENTEEN, plans to take a male date to his Senior Prom," read the lead to an Alameda [California] Newspaper Group story on lesbian and gay youth. The next day, I was barraged with threats from my Livermore High School classmates: "If you bring a fag to the prom, we'll kill you."

Every day that week I rushed home after school to clean graffiti and rotten apples from my father's house. I had just come out to him, and I knew too many gay kids living on the streets to take any chances on becoming one of them.

I rationalized my exclusion from the prom by telling myself that proms were silly, superficial, and expensive—not worth the time or money. But this summer, I attended the first ever gay prom in Northern California (and one of the first anywhere), sponsored by the Lambda Youth Group and held in Hayward. Between dancing and flirting with other boys my age, I got a chance to speak to some of the promgoers. Those who had gone to their high school proms said they'd had to either remain closeted or risk violence to do so. In this context, tonight's opportunity to be silly and superficial meant a lot.

Ken, nineteen, grew up in Orange County. He didn't go to his prom, he says, "because I knew I wouldn't belong there. I would not have fun." In high school, Ken explains, "being gay was something I couldn't talk about. I probably would have been killed by the football team." Ken says he came to the Lambda Youth Gay Prom '95 because he needed to: "I missed out on the whole high school experience, and something was missing inside me. I wanted to resolve something, to be able to say 'I know I couldn't have it this way in high school, but now I can have fun.' "

Ken looks down for a moment, contemplating the buttons on his tuxedo. Suddenly he brightens, and looks around Hayward's Centennial Hall in amazement, as if he's just woken up from a few years of amnesia. "I don't see many bored faces," he remarks. "My straight friends said at their high school proms the decorations were bad and the music was cheesy. But this isn't cheesy at all. It's like the straight proms you see in movies. What straight prom could you go to where the mayor speaks—or where there's an espresso bar?"

By the time the evening ends I've interviewed many more people: two of the four protesters

director of New York's Lesbian and Gay Community Services Center, came out in the early 1970s, when he was in college. When I asked him how it felt to date again after the recent break-up of his thirteen-year relationship, he corrected me. "In the seventies and early eighties, prior to the advent of the AIDS crisis," he observed, "I'm not sure that 'dating' existed in the gay world in the way that we use that word today. . . . The idea of calling someone up on a date that would not result in getting laid was not really on the radar screen, at least not among the people I knew."

While there are both differences and similarities in the mating styles of lesbians and gay men, one thing remains clear for our community in general. Despite years of oppression, we've built a culture that allows us to

standing outside with JESUS SAVES posters in their rubber-gloved hands; a handful of smiling parents who are volunteering as chaperones; some of the twenty-six on- and off-duty police officers patrolling the premises; and a dozen teenagers who've already talked to the lady from the Associated Press and don't understand why there's all this fuss just because they want to dance with each other.

The next week I visit the Lambda Youth Group, a weekly rap session in Hayward. At the meeting, the kids are still reeling with postprom excitement. One of the most surprising prom attendees, they tell me, was Brian Morris's mother. Brian, twenty, grew up in San Lorenzo. Once Brian's parents found out their son was gay, they began locking the door earlier than usual, and Brian began sleeping in his car. "If my sister is doing anything, even cheerleader practice, my mom is there!" notes Brian. "But the Lambda Prom is the first gay thing I've ever gotten her to go to. She even took two pictures of me in my tux. I don't think my mom will ever support me, but she's starting to accept me."

After the meeting, the thirty or so kids spill out of the family counseling center and drive to a coffee shop in Castro Valley that serves as their regular postmeeting hangout. I find myself sitting across from Rachel, an eighteen-year-old from Hayward. Like Brian, one of the prom highlights for Rachel was the support she got from her family.

Rachel recalls how her grandmother, with whom she lives, drove to the South Hayward BART stop to pick up Rachel's girlfriend Alaire. Rachel blushes and giggles as she describes the couple's preparations for the prom. "My grandmother helped me get into my dress, because I had to suck my fat in. Alaire got ready in the bathroom, and my grandmother helped fix the bow on her dress. Then she took pictures of us."

In the morning, Rachel recalls, her grandmother asked her why she'd gone to the prom. "I said 'to have fun,' and she just smiled at me and said 'okay.' I was happy that she supported me." So the Lambda Youth Gay Prom turned out to be not only the prom the kids never got, but the prom many of their parents never got. Despite protesters, pickets, and petitions—or maybe because of them—a lot of parents seized the occasion of Gay Prom '95 to let their kids know they loved them. In a nation where one in four homeless youth are gay kids who ran away or were kicked out by their families, this kind of solidarity is anything but silly and superficial.

Reprinted with permission from YO! (Youth Outlook).

find each other and fall in love. Though that culture has grown and changed over time, our ability to love each other has remained constant. In this chapter, we'll take a look at how lesbian and gay couples have met and fallen in love, even while getting the insidious message from mainstream society that they shouldn't or couldn't.

Same-Sex Love in the "Good Old Days"

Years ago, I was at a fund-raiser for the lesbian and gay community center of New York City, talking to two older gay men who proudly

LOVE NOTES

Gay author Eric Marcus has published two editions of *The Male Couple's Guide: Finding a Man, Making a Home, Building a Life* (HarperPerennial, 1988, 1992), a comprehensive, easy-to-read guide that offers practical advice and extensive resources for gay men who are either looking for or are already involved in long-term, committed relationships. A similar volume for women, *The Lesbian Couples'* *Guide: Finding the Right Woman and Creating a Life Together* by lesbian poet and novelist Judith McDaniel (HarperPerennial, 1995), is a warm, witty exploration of the world of lesbian relationships. Through interviews, anecdotes, and resource lists, McDaniel offers plenty of common sense ideas on everything from finding a lover to making it work.

informed me that they had been together for thirty years. Since at that time I hadn't had a relationship that lasted longer than an average health-club membership, I was duly impressed and inspired. "How did you meet?" were the first words out of my mouth after I congratulated them on their longevity.

The men looked at each other and exchanged grins. They hesitated, as if they weren't sure they should tell me. "In the park," one of the men offered, more than a little embarrassed. "He sat down next to me on a bench—" he paused for effect "—and the rest is history!"

I'm a little slow on the uptake, so it didn't register with me for several minutes that, of course, they had met while cruising for sex in Central Park. Their embarrassment probably stemmed from wondering what I—a stranger, a lesbian—would think of them. What I actually thought was that, because I'm from a younger generation, I had never personally known a gay couple who'd met cruising for public sex. Most of my gay male friends met at parties or through their political work.

> *"I was into homophobic jokes because that's a reflection of self-hatred and I hated that part of me."*

But those two older men met in 1960, another world almost, when there were many fewer ways for gay people to meet sexual or life partners than there are today, and hanging out in public spaces like parks and piers (for men) and bars (for both men and women) provided one of the major ways to do so. Though some gay men continue to cruise in public spaces, they do so more for casual sex than for potential relationships.

In these days of the Hawaii marriage case, *Ellen,* and the Tom Selleck–Kevin Kline movie kiss, it would be easy to forget how much things have changed for lesbians and gay men in the last few decades. Just eighteen years ago, my first lesbian lover and I were totally closeted about our relationship. Though no one ever sat us down and said homosexuality was bad, we simply *knew* that it was. We snuck around to tawdry motels, careful to keep our secret even from her roommates. The shame and fear the two of us felt as young lesbians has dissipated over time, as the lesbian and gay community has become stronger and more visible.

It is, however, important to remember our history. Though the overall climate may have improved for lesbians and gay men, we continue to be told—particularly by religious fundamentalists—that we shouldn't have relationships, children, or the rights everyone else has. Though not everyone wants to see lesbians and gay men return to the days of shame and invisibility, there are still plenty of people who think we should somehow be content with second-class status. Fifty-six percent of the heterosexuals polled by *Newsweek* magazine in the summer of 1997 still believed that lesbians and gay men should not be allowed to marry their same-sex partners.

Public display of affection.

We deserve the full lives that heterosexuals claim for themselves. That includes courtships, sex, love, relationships, families. By remembering our stories of struggle and survival we're better able to say no to those who want to control us, our sexuality, and our relationships and deny us the rights that should be ours.

"You Weren't Allowed to Be Gay"—Martin and John

In 1961, when Martin and John first met, it was much harder to find same-sex partners than it is today, especially if you aspired to something lasting. As young men first recognizing their sexual desires in the 1940s, Martin and John experienced a fair amount of self-loathing. Martin remembers sadly that his first gay sexual encounter made him feel "filthy, just filthy." John recalls that, in college, "I was into homophobic jokes because that's a reflection of self-hatred and I hated that part of me." Publicly, John dated a number of women and thought his homosexuality would "go away" when he got married. But privately, he sought out men.

By the time Martin and John met, they had both been involved in emotionally abusive gay relationships for several years and wanted something better for themselves. Their meeting took place at a gay house party, which was a popular way for gay men and lesbians to socialize in the days when gay meeting places were limited largely to bars and public cruising places—a culture that both men had sampled and quickly tired of.

Though they aren't sure exactly how it happened, Martin was invited to a party at the home of John's lover at the time. They both remember it as if it were yesterday. "When I first saw him, my knees turned to water," Martin says with a shy smile. "Oh my God, I really fell." But because they were both in other relationships, though unhappy ones that wouldn't last much longer, nothing happened between them for several months.

At Christmas, mutual friends called to invite Martin to another house party. He was in the dumps about his soured relationship and didn't feel like socializing. But then the friends offered a carrot: "John will be there."

"And I thought, okay, *I'll* be there," Martin says. "That was more or less it. Then, we started calling each other. It was a courtship of about six months."

Did "courtship" for them mean what it traditionally meant for heterosexuals at that time? "Yes, it was a real courtship," Martin confirms. "We would meet once a week for dinner or a movie and we looked forward to it." Their relationship didn't become sexual until after almost six months, though "I wanted it to be," Martin smiles. "I was really hot. But we just didn't."

Finally, they spent their first weekend together, planning a dinner at a romantic inn. But they found to their disappointment that all the rooms were booked. So they drove in the pouring rain to a memorable place called the Skyline Motel. "It was so tacky," John laughs. "It had a bed we put a quarter in."

Though they had both been in gay relationships before, their new romance felt decidedly different to both of them. When I ask why, John has a simple conclusion. "Well, it was love," he says. "This time it was really love."

For Martin, the relationship was distinct because the sexual guilt that he had felt in earlier gay encounters was nonexistent. When he began his sexual relationship with John, "I didn't feel guilty. I felt good. It was just being with him."

Their relationship, however, experienced a number of outside pressures because the repressive times required that many gay men and lesbians hide their sexual orientation and their relationships. Neither Martin nor John felt free to come out to his family of origin. "I should have been able to share our lives with my mother," Martin says with regret.

The fact that they were teachers added another reason to be completely closeted. "There were no [visible] gay teachers," Martin says sadly. "You were not allowed to be gay. We cut out anything that was gay."

"Prior to the advent of the AIDS crisis, I'm not sure that 'dating' existed in the gay world in the way that we use that word today. . . . The idea of calling someone up on a date that would not result in getting laid was not really on the radar screen."

Amazing as it seems for two men who live just a short drive from New York City, "We were so closeted and naive, that we didn't know Stonewall had taken place until about ten years later!" Martin laughs. Mostly because of their long years of isolation, Martin and John are now actively involved in their local gay community.

Both men are relieved that times for gay couples are much better now than when they first met and that there are more ways to get together. Martin notes that the mere possibility of same-sex marriage in Hawaii in his lifetime is astounding. "When I think back to when the word 'gay' was a secret word," he says, "and now there's Hawaii—well, it blows my mind."

Trying to Be "Normal"—Liz and Judi

Lesbian and gay teens have always been more vulnerable than adults because they have fewer defenses against rejection by their peers and repudiation by their families. Having to hide their sexual feelings can take an enormous toll. Statistics show that lesbian and gay teens are more prone to commit suicide, are at higher risk for alcohol and drug abuse, and often have to live on the streets when they're kicked out of their homes. Fully a third of all the homeless in Los Angeles, a recent report by ABC News found, are lesbian and gay youth.

At the same time, there are many inspiring survival stories. Liz and Judi, two women now in their thirties, met as very young, "at-risk" teens in the 1970s, when there was even less visibility for or acceptance of lesbians and gay men than there is today—when there were absolutely no queer youth groups, no movies with positive images of lesbians and gay men, and no Ellen Morgan coming out proudly on television.

The two girls first got to know each other at a New Jersey youth center for "troubled" kids. "For some reason," remembers Liz, "the counselors at the center decided that we wouldn't like each other, and their mission was to keep us as far away from each other as possible. They were afraid that if we even got in the same room together, we would get into a fight."

"We were both kind of hardheaded and willful," Judi adds.

"We had heard the rumors that we were mortal enemies," says Liz, "and we didn't even know each other!"

One evening, there was a scheduling snafu, and the two "enemies" found themselves face-to-face. The girls decided to go upstairs at the center and just talk. "As we talked," Liz recalls, "we discovered that we were different from each other, yet somehow the same." In true teen-rebel fashion, they determined to defy the adults who wanted to keep them apart and be friends.

But the more they hung out together, the more time Liz wanted to spend with Judi. "It was a confusing period in my life," she says. "I knew that I had always been attracted to women, but I also knew it wasn't 'natural.' I was supposed to be like everyone else on the planet, grow up, get married, and raise a family." So when the boy Liz had been dating proposed marriage right after high school, she said yes, even though she knew she didn't love him. "I had to prove I was 'normal,'" she explains.

"I knew that I had always been attracted to women, but I also knew it wasn't 'natural.' I was supposed to be like everyone else on the planet, grow up, get married, and raise a family."

But Liz was smart and had a plan so that she could enjoy the pretense of being "normal" while still being with Judi. "I persuaded my boyfriend to join the service," she laughs, "and start on a career before we got married. With him stationed in another state, I would have more time to spend with Judi!"

Still, she didn't have any positive role models or any context for her feelings. Dating other girls wasn't a picture anyone had drawn for her. As far as she knew, she was the only girl who had ever felt this way about another girl. Liz's confused and conflicted emotions and sexual desires exacted a price. She used drugs more and more to fight her feelings for Judi. "Nothing could make me numb enough to stop thinking about her," Liz says sadly. Eventually, she knew she had to tell Judi she was in love with her or else explode.

One day they drove to a park, and Liz announced that they "needed to talk." She was terrified that Judi would be completely repulsed and that she'd jeopardize their friendship. "The words got caught in my throat," Liz remembers of the painful experience. "I lit one cigarette after another. I didn't smoke them, I just kept stalling for time. I could not take my eyes off her. The electricity in that car was so intense, I couldn't breathe."

It got darker and darker; Liz went through a couple of packs of cigarettes. She was visibly shaking, and her palms were sweaty. Why wouldn't Judi say something, she wondered? Finally, Judi avowed that they weren't going anywhere until Liz told her what she was thinking.

"I said, 'I'm thinking that I love you,'" Liz says. "And she just said, 'Hell, it took you long enough!'" Liz leaned over and kissed Judi for the first time, "and then I knew there was a God in heaven."

But it was far from smooth sailing after that. When Judi went to spend the summer in Israel with an older sister, Liz was miserable. She confided their relationship to Judi's other sister, who she thought would be sympathetic. To Liz's surprise, "her advice was that I should stop seeing Judi because we both had our whole lives ahead of us. She told me that I wasn't being fair to Judi, that she deserved to live a normal life and see other people and one day marry and raise a family." Liz also told her parents about her relationship with Judi. Though they weren't outright rejecting, they pronounced that the girls needed to experience "more" in life and persuaded Liz to let Judi go—a common response of straight family members who mistakenly think that lesbianism is just an adolescent phase.

"Well, I knew that I loved Judi and felt that it would be best to let her live her life as a normal person," Liz sighs. "So I enlisted in the Marine Corps and gave Judi and myself a chance to decide if we were meant to be together."

It would be ten long years before Liz and Judi were able to start really dating, this time as mature adults. By then, Liz had had several relationships, one with an emotionally abusive woman who threatened to "out" her to her Marine Corps commanding officer if Liz left her, and one with a man, who disappeared when he found out Liz was pregnant. When Liz and Judi met up for round two of their romance, Liz had a four-year-old son whom Judi welcomed as her own.

As the saying goes, the heart wants what the heart wants. "Over the years I tried to make the best of things," Liz recalls, "but my heart wasn't in it. I was always in love with Judi."

The Cubby Hole,
a New York lesbian bar
in the 1980s.

© 1990 T. L. Litt/Impact Visuals

"A Different Way of Being Loved"— April and Susan

Too often, lesbians and gay men have been conditioned to think it's their "fault" that they don't respond sexually or emotionally to the opposite sex, and they just keep knocking their heads against the wall, trying. In the mid-1970s, Dr. April Martin, a psychotherapist in private practice in New York, thought her feelings for Susan were just an indication of an oncoming bout of the flu. "I was that heterosexually identified," she laughs. Like many lesbians, April had a long history of relationships with men. At the time a mutual friend introduced her to Susan, April was involved with one man and was considering dating another, though something had always been missing from those relationships.

She and Susan, she thought, were "just friends." April didn't get an inkling of what her feelings for Susan really were until she ran all over New York looking for the perfect birthday present for Susan. "I had something in mind for her that I knew she would love, and I just had to get it,"

April recalls. When April told a friend what pains she'd taken to find Susan's gift, the friend asked pointedly, "Are you sure Susan's just a *friend?*" And the first lightbulb clicked on over April's head. For her, the sudden realization was "dizzying." How could she be a lesbian?

"I knew nothing about the lesbian community," she observes, "but I'd heard a lesbian I knew mention The Duchess." The Duchess was a seedy New York lesbian bar in Greenwich Village from the seventies to the early eighties, when it was closed by the State Liquor Authority on trumped-up charges that amounted to outright harassment. In the grand old tradition of lesbian bars (long before lesbians became "chic"), The Duchess was an uninviting place, dark and dirty and more than a little depressing. But it was also a community hangout, a place to be together in an atmosphere that passed for "safe."

April located the bar's name and address in the phone book and left work one day to head down to the Village. She was terrified of running into someone she knew and jeopardizing her budding career as a psychotherapist. And sure enough, as she was about to open the door to the bar, one of her particularly conservative clients strolled by. April broke out in a sweat, nodded to the woman, and proceeded to walk around the block seven or eight times before she could actually work up the nerve to go inside The Duchess.

"I had four glasses of wine," she remembers, laughing. "And I don't drink, so I was totally tipsy! I danced with half the women in the place. I flirted. I was totally outrageous." She even gave her phone number out, and then, after she sobered up, faced a classic case of homosexual panic, living in fear of what she had done, sure that this new turn in her life could ruin her career and everything she'd been trying to build for herself.

> "*I'd get up in the morning, and realize that Susan had put out the teacup I liked most. I had never said I liked that teacup. She just noticed.*"

"I thought I was about to step off the planet," April recalls of the moment, a few days after going to The Duchess, when she and Susan finally declared their feelings for each other. "It was this blur of both being in love and also realizing that I had altered my life irreparably. . . . Gay relationships didn't work back then. That was the press on them. I felt like I was throwing caution to the wind and risking my career for something that had no future."

But at the same time, April was very aware that she passionately wanted it to have a future. "I knew that I had never been in love in that way before," she says. For April, as for many lesbians who've had heterosexual pasts, the emotional differences between being involved with a woman and with a man became clear very quickly. "I'd get up in the morning," April explains, "and realize that Susan had put out the teacup I liked most. I had never said I liked that teacup. She just noticed. And I realized how much time I had spent noticing those little details about the men I was involved with. Nobody had ever done that for me. This was an entirely different way of being loved."

Brief Encounters, Lasting Love

One of the great challenges of being a stigmatized minority is that finding one another has often been difficult. We're supposed to stay hidden so that heterosexuals don't have to think about us, even though we have to think about them constantly. Some homophobia training sessions for heterosexuals require that the participants not make any references to their sexuality (mention of boyfriends or wives, for example), so straight people can learn how restricting and draining it is when they're expected to conceal a big part of their lives.

Oppressed minorities always develop ways to connect with each other. Over the years lesbians and gay men have resourcefully used our "gaydar" to, as one woman told me, "smell each other out." Queer culture created clues so that we could locate "our people"—everything from pinky rings and red handkerchiefs in former times to pink triangle buttons and rainbow rings today.

Especially in the past, it wasn't just hard to find each other, it could be dangerous, too. In certain circumstances, mistaking someone for gay who isn't can still get you arrested. Many gay men have been entrapped by undercover police officers in public cruising areas. So, for many in our community, meetings in bars and through personal ads became "safe" ways to find potential lovers and mates.

Bar None

Bars have, for at least the last fifty years, provided one way for queers to socialize. Bars served up not only drinks but community—they fostered friendships and a sense of belonging to a defined culture. That was very important to the birth of the lesbian and gay liberation struggle. In fact, the movement officially got its start when the police raided the Stonewall Inn, a gay bar in New York City.

Even just a few years ago, a study showed that 40 percent of the gay men surveyed had met their lovers in bars. Despite the development of

THE LESBIAN AND GAY RECOVERY MOVEMENT

Despite its historical significance, there's also a downside to lesbian and gay bar culture—socializing so much in bars has made alcoholism a significant problem for lesbians and gay men. But it's a problem that the community itself has attempted to take control of by starting social service programs and educating people about the connections between alcohol abuse and unsafe sex.

"There was a time when gay culture was so focused on bars that getting drunk and being in a bar was very closely equated with sex," says Richard Burns, executive director of New York's Lesbian and Gay Community Services Center, which runs an award-winning alcohol and substance abuse program called Project Connect. "And I think that connection was unhealthy. But that's evolving and changing today."

A few resources for lesbians and gay men in need of help with substance abuse include:

- Pride Institute at Solutions is a leader in mental health and addictions treatment for lesbians and gay men, with locations in Los Angeles, New York City, and Washington, D.C.; phone (800) DIAL-GAY or (800) 54-PRIDE.

- Many lesbian and gay community centers across the country offer social services for those in recovery and/or twelve-step groups geared toward the community. The Lesbian land Gay Community Services Center can steer you to a center in your region. See the sidebar, "The Center of Everything" for contact information.

alternative meeting places, bars continue to function as ad hoc community centers, especially in areas without a large or visible lesbian and gay community. (See also the sidebar, "The Lesbian and Gay Recovery Movement.")

When I first came out, I often heard, "You'll never meet anyone you like in a bar!" but that wisdom doesn't seem to have held true for many lesbians and gay men, who have built lasting relationships out of brief initial encounters in bars. One lesbian couple I know met at a bar eighteen years ago and have been together ever since.

Robert Woodworth and his late lover, Noli Villanueva, met thirteen years ago in what Robert fondly remembers as a sort of "forties movie plot." "It was in the balcony of The Saint," he recalls. The Saint, for those of you who aren't familiar with the "fabulous clubs that used to be," was a cavernous, multilevel dance club for gay men in the East Village in New York City. The Saint opened and peaked at the exact same time that the AIDS crisis was first hitting the gay community in the early 1980s. By 1984, when Robert met Noli, The Saint was already in decline as the place to go in New York.

"The Saint was doing these various promotional things to keep attendance up during the summer," Robert remembers. "You could buy a short-term summer membership. It was a time when, because of my work, I was making very little money, so that was all I could afford." But the summer came and went, and Robert found that he never got around to going. "And then it was Labor Day weekend, and I said, 'Well, I guess I ought to do this once!' "

It was a hot Saturday night, and Robert went up to the balcony, "because that's where all the cruising happened." He smiles. His relationship of several years had wound down and was ending. In what seems like kismet, Robert considered leaving the balcony, but something made him stick around for five more minutes. And in that short interlude when he stayed in the balcony, he met Noli, an event he calls "total happenstance."

"We met up there briefly and then went back downstairs," Robert says. "And then we met up again." Like movie lovers, it was as if they were supposed to get together that night. "We had this instant rapport and ease at that point," Robert remembers. "We immediately started dating." Within a few short months, "I knew that I was going to live with him for the rest of my life." But, as for so many gay men, Robert and Noli's relationship was cut short by AIDS. Following a number of debilitating illnesses, Noli died in late 1995.

Like Robert and Noli, Lynne and Esther's meeting sounds a bit like a movie plot, complete with movie dialogue. In 1986, at a lesbian bar called The Pub in West Hollywood, California, Lynne, a Jewish woman who grew up in L.A., was hanging out and relaxing after work. Esther, a Chicana who is also a native Angeleno, walked into the bar. The place was almost empty "all the way down to where I was sitting," recalls Lynne. "Esther walked over and said 'Is this stool taken?' But she didn't do it as a pick-up line. She wasn't even thinking that way. We just talked."

Lynne immediately liked Esther and thought she was someone she'd like to go out to dinner or a movie with, not necessarily on a date but as friends. So she handed Esther her phone number on a scrap of paper.

Though Esther was very attracted to women, "I thought I was straight all my life," she says. "I was nearly married twice to men and engaged three times." Whenever she found herself being sexually drawn to a woman, she'd say to herself, "Oh, that's just an indecent thought. I'll let it pass and won't even think about it."

Esther had had one brief and unsuccessful relationship with a woman at the time she worked up her nerve to walk into The Pub and plop down next to Lynne. But she claims she had to have a few drinks in order to go in by herself and do that.

"While we were sitting there, Lynne told me, 'It is so refreshing to meet a lesbian.' And for a second I thought, 'Huh, who are you calling a lesbian? Just for a second. Then, there was this huge mirror behind the bar where you can see yourself, and I looked at myself and thought, 'Look where you are. I guess you're a lesbian.' " And that was the first time Esther really acknowledged her sexual identity.

The two women continued to talk, had a few drinks, and danced. They enjoyed each other's company, but Esther mistakenly thought Lynne was "too young," even though there was only five years between them. When Lynne gave Esther the piece of paper with her phone number, "I put it in my pocket and kind of forgot about it," Esther says. "A couple of weeks later I was taking clothes to the laundry and I found the paper." It turned out to be a lucky break for both of them. Esther worked up the courage to call Lynne that day, and eleven years later they're still together.

Getting Personal

In the 1970s, a host of lesbian and gay publications started springing up across the country, affording people another way to locate a community, even if they lived in a small town and wouldn't risk showing up anywhere near the local gay bar. It isn't surprising that personal ads quickly became a part of those publications, a popular way of seeking out lovers and friends. In them, you could openly dream about that perfect mate and sexual partner, both boldly and anonymously.

Because personal ads first started in countercultural publications of the sexually explosive 1960s, they have always had the reputation of being about hot, wild sex. In fact, gay men's classifieds have been notoriously steamy, one-handed reads, featuring personal ads extolling "size" and "length."

For lesbians, things were noticeably tamer. *The Wishing Well* (an alternative to "The Well of Loneliness"), for example, billed itself as a "discreet correspondence club" when it began in the mid-1970s. Several other similar services got started later. While the magazines were not sexually explicit (let's face it, a "discreet club" sounds more like it's serving up cucumber sandwiches, not sex), lesbians who made use of them were often engaging in a kind of safe cruising. "I wanted sex," admits Loree, explaining her membership in a lesbian pen pal service in the early 1980s. "I did *not* want another relationship." But she ended up falling for Marcelle anyway. The fact is, many lasting couples have resulted from "GF"s and "GM"s "looking for same," whether for sex, companionship, or a wonderful combination of both. As one woman told me, she fell in love "at first write."

Back in 1976, Steve got a hold of a friend's copy of *The Advocate,* and one ad in particular caught his eye. "I hadn't ever considered a personal ad before, and who knows what I thought I was doing," he says. But he remembers the exact wording of the ad to this day. "Not into one-night stands, but my heart and mind are open." In the mid-seventies, Steve explains, "that was one of the best ads I'd seen."

Steve was twenty-three years old and "still in the process of working out for myself how I could be true to my own principles and live as a gay man, too." He admits that he didn't like much of what little he had seen of gay life in bars and clubs, and so the mystery man of the personal ad, who was "not into one-night stands," intrigued him. He decided to take the chance and respond to the ad, mostly because "it seemed to me like quite a feat to keep one's mind and heart open. I wanted to know more about the man who could."

Ric, who had placed the ad, was three years older than Steve and also didn't cotton to the gay casual sex scene. They liked what they learned about each other in their mailbox courtship, which lasted about six months. Then Ric agreed to drive from Los Angeles to San Diego so they could meet face-to-face. Unlike many correspondents who immediately exchange photos, neither Steve nor Ric had any idea what the other looked like.

"There are a lot of memories from those first two days we spent together," Steve says. "Ric stood in the doorway with the light coming from behind him, and all I could think of was how broad his shoulders were. . . . I still remember my reaction!" So, even though Ric didn't advertise for sex, the two had instant sexual energy.

They spent the summer commuting up and down the coast, in what Steve refers to as their own round of "shuttle diplomacy." "It just seemed to work," Steve says, "though I think we were both a little frightened by the speed with which it moved." By August, Steve had located a job in L.A. because Ric was adamant about not wanting to pursue a long-distance relationship. "It all happened so fast," Steve recalls. "We caught our breaths and went for it."

Decades after Steve and Ric fell in love, personal ads continue to flourish in lesbian, gay, and alternative newspapers and magazines across the country and even in cyberspace. It's a relatively safe way to put yourself out there in a (dating) space that can sometimes be scary and make you feel vulnerable. And in the case of Tim, who is legally blind, an ad provided him with a way to negotiate a social ritual geared toward the sighted population.

"I've never been good at navigating the bar scene," Tim observes wryly. His preferred method of meeting men has always been through the personal ads, where he could reveal more about himself than in casual encounters. By 1990, he had run a total of seven ads in *Chicago Gay Magazine,* but had no luck with the first six, encountering negative responses to his disability.

Mario answered Tim's seventh ad because it wasn't, as Mario puts it, "typical." "It was a lengthy, poetic ad," Tim explains. "I found it difficult to express myself within the confines of an ad, so I wrote a poem." Tim included his phone number, and Mario, who figured he fit the description in Tim's ad, called him up to make a date. "I had answered ads before and had been very disappointed," Mario says. "But I thought it looked like a different ad."

Tim insists that Mario sounded preoccupied and spacey when he called, and so Tim didn't take the date seriously. Even though they set a meeting time for the following weekend, Tim doubted Mario would show up. So he didn't even bother to get dressed.

"I went out and bought new clothes for the date," Mario says of the evening. "I went to his house, and when I got there, I was surprised because he was barefooted and had no shirt on and was in some really ugly shorts. I was disappointed." But not because of Tim's physical disability. Instead, it was because "I had killed myself to try to look nice, and here's this slob," laughs Mario. Fortunately, Tim got another chance to dress for dinner.

In the past, Tim had had a lot of disappointments in relationships and dating because of his blindness and other health problems. "I went beyond that," Mario says of Tim's disability. "I found him very interesting, and I liked that fact that he was so educated."

"I suppose the seventh time is the charm," Tim says.

F2F—Casey and Dakota

As the millennium approaches, a new dating frontier has opened up in cyberspace. While the hazards can be considerable (see Dr. Martha Pearse's thoughts and warnings in the "CyberPals/CyberLove: What Does It All Mean?" sidebar), I met a number of same-sex couples who had found each other online and were making their relationships work. Two women had even held their commitment ceremony online.

One busy gay man, a single father in Oregon, speculates that he would have never found his partner if he hadn't placed a personal ad through the Internet. "Being a single dad definitely restricted my social life," says David, "and I found few opportunities for social interaction without my son. Contacting people over my computer was one way I could 'get out' without leaving my apartment!"

Chat rooms, too, provide a space where people can safely get to know each other before they commit to actually meeting F2F (that's cybertalk for face-to-face). As someone who mostly uses the Internet for work and research, I have to admit a certain ignorance of Netiquette and chat room shorthand. But luckily, Casey and Dakota, who virtually met on a local lesbian and gay bulletin board in Seattle, were fluent in it.

"Casey was the one who used the board all the time," Dakota notes, "and I was just on it occasionally for fun." The two women ended up chatting. "We just clicked so well, we were cracking each other up."

After a couple of virtual encounters, they decided to meet in person at a local bar. At that first meeting, Casey and Dakota talked for three hours until they were both hoarse, and ended up making the rounds of a few places.

Dakota was a little concerned at first about Casey's age. "She looked *really* young," she recalls worrying. "She was wearing braces at the time and I thought, 'Wow, this is a young one!' " But as it turned out, Casey was actually a year older than Dakota.

A few days later, Casey sent Dakota a message through the bulletin board: "Hey, things went really well . . . do you want to go out on a date some time?" Cautious about Casey's age, Dakota wrote back that she wanted to move more slowly, maybe start out as friends and see what happened. So they made a plan to go out with a group of Casey's friends in a low-key, no-pressure kind of way.

That night, Dakota says, "I guess the chemistry was just right. . . . We started talking and playing darts together, teasing and flirting and having a good time. Things were just clicking really well." And though she had adamantly insisted on being "just friends," Dakota found that her mind changed over the course of the evening.

"We ended up at a country dance bar," Dakota explains. "We closed down that place and didn't want to say goodnight to each other, so we went to an after-hours bar and were out until three or four." They went home alone, but neither one of them could sleep. The next morning, Casey called and invited Dakota out to a local park.

"We spent the entire day together," Dakota recalls, "and we were too stupid and wrapped up in each other to put on sunscreen. We both got horrible sunburns." A few days later, they spent their first night together and "pretty much haven't spent a night apart since."

"Being a single dad definitely restricted my social life, and I found few opportunities for social interaction without my son. Contacting people over my computer was one way I could 'get out' without leaving my apartment!"

"CyberPals/CyberLove: What Does It All Mean?"

BY MARTHA PEARSE, PH.D.

FOR THOSE OF YOU who may be wondering, there is a new class of Haves and Have Nots in the world: Those who have or do not have . . . a life online.

For the uninitiated or unaddicted, a life online means . . . you have friends/lover(s)/playmates or even business in cyberspace. Let's do business another time. For now, let's talk about the fun stuff. . . .

Whether you are the snootiest of intellectuals or the earthiest of basic folks, or anything in between, there is a family for you online. Within days, perhaps minutes, you will be able to find a cybersoulmate or two. Ask and you shall receive.

This feeling of family/community is perhaps the most powerful attraction of all. We may call ourselves a community, but the truth is we are a loosely connected network of small clusters of people, or individuals whose only commonality is that we are 1) gay/lesbian/etc.; 2) outside the mainstream heterosexual majority. Community is the organizing system that protects us. Online there are real voices, real names of real people, serious discussions of important issues. It's also playful, flirtatious, and often raucous. In other words, it is a community, a gathering of people who come back day after day to participate in the headiest or most trivial of discussions with others in the community.

Time is compressed. This community costs money. Small talk is limited, unless that's all one intends to do in the first place. Everything seems more intense. Words are compressed, feelings can be very open, and connections are made with more ease than in 3D. People who make strong attachments online learn to love/connect from the inside out, from the basic self, not from a persona that society has constructed.

Do you want to check out someone you've met online? Most people have profiles where you can get some 1) basic data, or 2) a feel for what they might be like, lacking vital statistics. This can be totally fictitious, of course, but often reveals much about a person by virtue of the chosen fiction. You can also watch them interact with others in groups, discussions, or chat rooms. You don't often get that opportunity IRT [in real time]. Does the person listen? Is she rude? Critical? Sensitive? Respectful?

Now, this is all positive so far, but that's not the big picture. There are big downsides of online connections.

First, we are all just as vulnerable to mistakes in relationships online as we are in 3D. The same rules apply. We can pick the people most likely to hurt us just as easily online as off. Chemistry, across a crowded chat room, is just as powerful as across any other room. The equation goes something like this: The more powerful the chemistry, the more dangerous the situation/person. When it comes to chemistry, a little goes a long way. Finding your soulmate after two days is a bad sign.

When there are no visuals, or IRT cues, we all tend to make reality out of fantasy. We create what

---

Though they had both been in relationships with women before, they noticed the difference in this one right away. "There was never any magic in my last relationship," Dakota observes. Casey describes the pattern of her own romantic involvements, which is a common one in lesbian coupling. After the honeymoon is over (what my former therapist used to call "the

we want/need. It may have no bearing on reality at all. In addition, the other person(s) may not be as honest or straightforward as we'd like, and we will never know if we've been flimflammed until it's too late. So, if we need someone to be nurturing, we will find nurturing, whether it's there or not.

Some people present selectively, some downright dishonestly. There is no way to check. Talk can be very, very cheap. A few years ago in Denver in a mixed gender workshop with Dr. Warren Farrell, the male sexuality expert, the participants were asked to reverse traditional dating roles. By the end of the lunch break, the women were supposed to have "scored." It was amazing how many millionaires, senators, and otherwise very accomplished people were born out of a group of rather ordinary folks, in just a couple of hours. Online lines can be just as embellished, just as seductive, just as phony.

For some people, online connections are a way of being close without being close. Carefully avoiding any of the real work of a relationship/ friendship/playmate, one can say all the right things, mean them temporarily, then shut off the machine and go back to the safety of isolation. Never online does one have to put up with someone else's (or our own) mistakes, broken promises, human failings, bodily functions, messed up priorities, or dirty laundry. It can be the illusion of love/ palship without any of the responsibilities of the same.

Because the vulnerability factor can be so high in online relationships, the interactions can become extremely intense. Add a communication problem—that messages carry no tonal qualities or inflections—the potential for misunderstanding is great. There are the emoticons—those little smiley/frowny faces like :-) and :-(complete with at least 200 variations. There is online shorthand—LOL (laughing out loud), ROFL (rolling on the floor laughing), and an equal number of variations. These little embellishments simply aren't effective as voice and facial expression. And since facial/ body language feedback is nonexistent, people often feel free to shoot off their mouths in a manner totally foreign to them in 3D. Sometimes the result is a flashback of junior high drama.

A few words for the cybernewbie: Enter the world of lesbian cyberrelationships with caution. Unless you are a determined and committed recluse, or have a very jealous F2F (face-to-face) lover, you will get caught up in this. It is a safe (mostly), alluring playground full of bright, caring, playful women, as well as a place for friends to meet and share a worry or a sorrow. Just remember these little reminders:

- Don't: be stupid, respond to blatant sexual approaches, accept gifts (pictures) of people soliciting sex partners, say anything you wouldn't want your lover to see, or give up your real life.

- Do: make frequent reality checks, meet any online loves F2F as soon as possible, open your heart a little and get to know some really fine women, take little risks, and keep your day job.

Excerpted from "CyberPals/CyberLove,: which appeared in Circles: Celebrating Colorado's Lesbian Community, *vol. 1, no. 1. Reprinted with permission of the author.*

yummy part" of the relationship), one partner or the other (or both) is itching to hit the road. "I mostly had gone through two-year relationships," Casey says, "where after the second year you are just dying to get out of them. With all those relationships, I never came even close to feeling like what this one, immediately, off the top, felt like. It was totally different."

The Personal Is Still Political

In the last decade, the community that lesbians and gay men have built has provided us with more options for meeting each other than the traditional ones of introductions, bars, and ads. It's now common to meet a potential partner through a queer group or political organization or at a community event.

As a lesbian with a history of community activism, I have to admit a bias toward this way of meeting. I met one ex-lover while working long hours at a lesbian-feminist newspaper, and my partner Katie and I first connected at a lesbian conference sponsored by the local community center. To me, introductions by friends or meetings in bars won't necessarily tell you if you have anything in common with another person except being gay—and that's not going to be enough to sustain a relationship. Personal ads and cyberspace connections can be easily misleading, with luck figuring in heavily with both of them.

But if two people show up at the same political meeting or community event, they know they've got at least one mutual interest and passion. At the very least, they might become friends. The couples profiled here started with a shared political outlook and then realized they had a lot more going for them.

Celebrating Gay Pride.

© 1990 Robert Fox/Impact Visuals

Dancing for the Cure— Shawn and Robert

Since the onset of the AIDS pandemic in the early 1980s, numerous community organizations have formed to protest and advocate for government involvement in finding a cure and to raise money for research. But even in the midst of crisis and death, many activists found partners through their AIDS work. A gay male couple I know met when, as part of an ACT UP action in Washington, they were chained to the White House fence right next to each other. At the memorial service of my friend David, his surviving lover encouraged gay people to cruise each other there, saying that David would have loved the idea.

In recent years, people have walked, danced, and biked to raise money for AIDS organizations. Shawn Walker-Smith lives in San Francisco, the heart of gay America, and he has had an active involvement in this kind of AIDS fund-raising for several years. In 1994, he volunteered to work for the annual AIDS Dance-a-thon in San Francisco, having been both a volunteer and a dancer in the past. That year, he was assigned to the food detail and found his life suddenly changed by—of all things—mayonnaise.

"I was down at one end of the huge center, the Moscone Center," recalls Shawn. "There was another food table at the other end. We were all preparing food for the dancers. I was furiously making turkey and chicken sandwiches, and we were running out of mayonnaise. People were asking for it. We sent a distress call to the volunteers at the other end of the hall, 'We need mayonnaise!' " Shawn marvels at the idea of health-conscious Californians demanding mayonnaise. "I could not believe it!"

Within a short time, a volunteer from the other end of the arena strolled over to Shawn's table with a box of mayonnaise packets. "Did somebody say mayonnaise?" the man asked.

Barely glancing up from his work, Shawn took the mayo and continued making sandwiches, thanking the volunteer who had delivered it.

"Not a problem," the man replied. "I'm always happy to help out my fellow volunteers . . . especially one as cute as you are." Shawn threw his head back and laughed, *"You can come back!"* he encouraged the man.

When their shift was over and the volunteers had broken down the food service tables, Shawn was talking to a friend, "and back comes the mayonnaise guy," he laughs. They chatted briefly, and then the man, whose name was Robert, handed him a flyer for The Brothers Network, an organization for African American men in the Bay area.

"Here's something I thought you might find of interest," Robert recalls flirting. "Especially what's on the back. . . ."

"On the opposite side was his name and phone number," Shawn relates. The subtle, classy come-on got Robert "big style points," says Shawn. "He did very, very well. And I gave him my business card and said, 'Yeah, we'll talk sometime.' "

What Shawn didn't know was that Robert had noticed him long before the call for mayonnaise went out. During a break, Robert had strolled around the room and noticed a tall, attractive man with broad shoulders, a big smile, long legs, "and shorts!" he adds. So, when the cry for

"Robert lost his previous lover to AIDS, so we have this perspective of, well, life isn't permanent and if there's something that's important to you, you work for it, you fight for it."

extra mayo went out, Robert had eagerly volunteered to be the one to bring it to Shawn's table as an excuse to meet him.

The week after the Dance-a-thon, Shawn called Robert and invited him to go out to dinner with him and a few of his friends, who were visiting from out of town. "A no-pressure kind of thing," Shawn explains. The evening went well, and the two men agreed to have a real date a week later—a movie and lunch. Lunch, however, lasted well into the evening, and they spoke on the phone every day after that.

At that point, Shawn says he still had no clue that his relationship with Robert would continue. He considered Robert "fun" and "nice," but also thought that if he didn't see him again, it would be okay. It was three of Shawn's best friends who individually announced that they thought Robert was "the one." They told Shawn they could hear it in his voice and in the way he talked about Robert and the time they'd spent together. "And all three of them love to remind me about that on a regular basis," Shawn notes slyly.

But more than what his friends thought, what was most important in convincing Shawn about Robert was that it felt incredibly easy to be with him. "It just sort of grew out of nowhere," Shawn says. "It seemed like from the very beginning I was very comfortable with him and we were really very comfortable together." After their first dates, they quickly began seeing more and more of each other. The shared experience of witnessing many people in their community die young had an impact on the decision to try to make their new relationship work.

"Robert lost his previous lover to AIDS," Shawn explains. "So we have this perspective of, well, life isn't permanent and if there's something that's important to you, you work for it, you fight for it."

"She Must Have Been on Two Mailing Lists"— Liza and Louise

Lesbians' experiences of community activism have often been very different from gay men's. In the 1970s and 1980s, lesbians, turned off by the sexism they experienced in mixed gender groups, built a movement of their own for specifically lesbian concerns. Many others volunteered their time and energy in the feminist movement, working for the cause of women's rights.

Liza Fiol-Matta has a long history of involvement in the lesbian and feminist movements, starting with her work as a young woman in a lesbian collective of the 1970s. She has redefined her feminist commitment

CANDACE ON KRIS

One of the more visible lesbian couples in Washington, D.C., these days is Candace Gingrich, the half-sister of Newt and author of the memoir, *The Accidental Activist,* and Kris Pratt, a community organizer for the Human Rights Campaign (HRC), a national gay lobbying group. Like many other lesbian couples, Candace and Kris started out as coactivists and moved over several months to being friends and lovers. I asked Candace to describe the blossoming of their romance.

"I first met Kris at the HRC Leadership Conference in D.C., in March of 1995," says Candace. "I was brand-new to the activist scene and found myself with hundreds of gay advocates. A few of the staff kept asking if I had met Kris yet, mentioning that people in the office thought we resembled each other. My curiosity was piqued but I wasn't prepared for her to be as striking as she was. My first impression was feeling tentative. Here I was in a new city with a new job and the first thing I did was fall for a coworker!

". . . I was always thinking *hm* in a romantic sense [about Kris]. But it took Kris a while to see my true inner beauty and come to her senses!" Candace grins mischievously. "We had both been seeing other people and then were both not seeing other people, and next thing we knew our friendly dinners/drinks/baseball games had turned into dates.

"I'm not sure there was an exact point when I had the realization [that it was serious]. I've never really just 'dated' a person without feeling more—and it's usually easy to know one's own feelings. It probably took about eight or nine months before the seriousness became mutual.

"Kris is more of an equal partner than my other lovers [were]. We have more in common—from sarcasm to baseball to being political junkies! I feel much more comfortable and able to open up and communicate my feelings to her, and it's been a change that my partner does the same."

over the years, now acting as a proponent and teacher of women's studies and a feminist author and editor.

It's not surprising, then, that she met her partner, Louise Murray, at a benefit reading for The Feminist Press, a New York–based, women-run publishing house that was founded in 1970. Liza was asked to participate in a bilingual reading in late 1985 to celebrate the publication of an anthology of feminist poems written by Hispanic women since the Middle Ages, and Louise, a poetry maven and a new staffer at The Feminist Press, attended the reading and complimented Liza on her delivery. "I remember Louise's smile and her glasses," says Liza. "She thanked me for having participated. I didn't know who she was or anything."

Months later, at another Feminist Press book party, Liza saw Louise again and got the chance to find out exactly who she was, "and to finally get her name straight," she laughs. Louise had a husband for many years and at that time still used her married name, a Dutch surname that proved a tongue twister for many people.

"She had all of these buttons on that said 'Dump Koch' [then the mayor of New York City] and things like that," Liza smiles. "And we talked about several things. We talked about being bilingual, and we talked about not being American." Liza is originally from Puerto Rico, and Louise is bi-national. Both women grew up traveling—Liza as an "army brat," and Louise as the daughter of an American diplomat and a Dutch mother. In the many locales where they'd lived, they each felt like "the other."

"We had done a lot of thinking about that," Louise points out, "and we were both ready to talk about it."

"We had a real conversation," Liza marvels, "considering it was a social event, and I just felt that we connected very well." She admits to being confused when Louise mentioned her sons, since this was the mid-eighties and a few years before the lesbian baby boom hit in full force. "I had a momentary doubt if she was a lesbian," Liza confesses sheepishly.

But when it became clear that the sons were with their father in Holland, Liza took the plunge and invited Louise out for coffee after the party. Disappointment set in when "she said she had *'other plans'* " Liza sighs.

This is still a bone of contention, over ten years later, though they both laugh when they talk about it. "I really *did* have plans," Louise defends herself. "But it was very enticing. It was one of the first times that somebody I really didn't know well invited me out for coffee." And "coffee," at least among New York dykes, usually means a prelude to something else.

"I remember walking to the subway with two other women," Liza recalls, "and thinking, 'I don't really want to be with anyone—I really want to think about *why* this woman didn't want to have coffee with me!' So I ended up walking home all the way to Fifteenth Street from Sixty-eighth Street, thinking."

Louise seized the initiative next and invited Liza to a fund-raiser in Harlem for the Venceramos Brigade, a Cuban solidarity group with whom she'd been active. But Liza was still miffed by what seemed to her like Louise's rejection of her. "And it took me three weeks to figure out if I should go or not go. I tried to read all sorts of signals into the flyer Louise had sent," she says. Her tortured thought process should be painfully familiar to any lesbian who's felt unsure of herself with another woman. "She had written 'Please come,' or 'I'd love to see you there,' and I was trying to read between the lines. Did she mean that she'd *love* to see me there, or does she just *want* me there? Then, she sent me another flyer, the same flyer, and the stamp was upside down. And I said, 'What does this mean? Does it mean anything?' "

They chuckle at the memory of Liza's obsession with the flyers' hidden meanings. "She must have been on two mailing lists or something like that," Louise reasons. "One I hand wrote because we all know if you handwrite an invitation, it's more personal. The other one, with the upside-down stamp? What can I say?" She shrugs. Obviously, it was just a stamp put on in a hurry by a volunteer pressed for time.

To Liza's disappointment, when she arrived at the event, Louise was with someone else, a woman she'd been seeing for several months. But that relationship was winding down and coming to a natural close. If Louise had any doubts, her own feelings became much clearer to her that night. The connection to Liza felt even stronger than it had when they first spoke months before. "I can remember standing in that space and Liza coming in," she says. "There was a real sense of electricity or whatever, a spark. And that event sort of sticks out as one of those moments when you have a sense of what might be."

Give Me That Old Time Religion

E ven though we've created a vibrant community and culture for ourselves, obstacles still remain that make it difficult for same-sex lovers to connect. The stigma attached to homosexuality has its origins in religion, particularly the Bible, which many homophobic clergy members have trotted out to try to prove that homosexuality is an abomination. Sometimes, these clergy have even stooped to schoolyard name-calling, as when the Moral Majority founder, Jerry Falwell, dubbed Ellen DeGeneres, "Ellen Degenerate."

Ellen DeGeneres and Anne Heche breaking ground in 1997.

Religious fundamentalism is, in fact, the biggest and fastest growing threat to lesbians and gay men. Many religious groups, like the well-funded Promise Keepers and the Christian Coalition, wield political power that threatens to cut away at our civil rights. By gaining the ear of Republican politicians who are afraid to cross them, religious fundamentalists have been able to push forward an antigay agenda. Extremists like hate-monger Fred Phelps may believe that lesbians and gay men should be put to death, but others who want us back in the closet or simply de-sexualized are just as alarming.

In late 1997, for example, the Roman Catholic Church finally softened its stance on homosexuality. The National Conference of Catholic Bishops released an official statement urging parents to love and accept their gay children—a big step forward for this traditional foe of lesbian and gay people. At the same time, however, the bishops advised parents to encourage their lesbian and gay children to seek counseling in order to "lead a chaste life." In other words, nix to lesbian and gay relationships. In other words, lesbians and gay men are still inferior.

Despite the barriers to having full lives placed in front of us by organized religion, many lesbians and gay men have amazingly not lost their faith—they have, in fact, been able to see religion as a positive force, something that enriches their lives rather than simply oppresses them. More and more, lesbians and gay men are reclaiming their right to practice religion and to have an active spiritual life. Not surprisingly, as we affirm that right many of us are able to find partners and lovers within the context of a religious community.

Sunday morning service at the Metropolitan Community Church in New York.

"...Then We'd Go Back to the Bishop"— Carolyn and Genelle

The Church of Jesus Christ of Latter Day Saints—better known as the Mormons—is now one of the most oppressive religions for lesbians and gay men. Recent research, however, indicates that this was not always the case. Scholar D. Michael Quinn suggests that the Mormons of a century ago were much more tolerant of homosexuality than we have thought.[4] One central figure in the church, for example—Evan Stephens, leader of the famous Mormon Tabernacle Choir from 1890 to 1916—was gay and was even able to acknowledge his sexuality in an official church publication in 1919 without repercussion.

Today, the official Mormon line on homosexuality is quite different. Mormons who suspect they are lesbian or gay are encouraged to "repent" and "change." The struggle of Carolyn and Genelle, a lesbian couple in their early thirties who were raised as "good Mormon girls," is a moving one that speaks to the resilience of lesbians and gay men who have made a lasting relationship—one that includes spirituality—despite religious intolerance.

"We met at church," Carolyn explains. "We both graduated from college about the same time, and it's fairly common in the Mormon religion not to marry until you get out of college." Both women lived near San Jose, California, which has a large Mormon population. There they became members of a young adult ward, a group of unmarried Mormons who met every Sunday and who were of approximately the same age. The idea was for young, single Mormon men and women to meet, marry, and settle down. But things worked differently for Carolyn and Genelle.

"We got to be friends pretty quickly," Carolyn remembers, "and you know how you can smell each other out! It didn't take too long to find out that we'd had [lesbian] experiences in college." They both confessed to their bishop, but despite trying to "fight it," Genelle became involved with a married woman in a family ward. Carolyn's lover from college was moving to the area, and she knew they might pick up where they left off. "So Genelle and I started taking walks every single day and became a two-person support group to try to help each other not be gay."

As a result of spending so much time together, Carolyn found herself falling in love with Genelle. On one of their walks, she admitted her feelings for her friend, and Genelle reciprocated. After their relationship became sexual, the two began a difficult six-month period.

"We went through this cycle of going to our bishop, telling him what was going on, repenting, and then being friends again," Carolyn relates. "Then we'd be attracted to each other again and become physical with each other, and then we'd go back to the bishop again to repent."

At the recommendation of their bishop, Carolyn and Genelle started individual therapy with the same Mormon therapist. "Luckily, we had a therapist that was honest with us," Carolyn says. "She didn't say homosexuality wasn't 'curable,' because as a Mormon she couldn't say that. But she did say it was very difficult, a nearly impossible thing to overcome." Without really intending to, the therapist planted a seed of hope in Carolyn's mind—that if they couldn't change their sexual orientation, they might learn to accept it.

After several years of therapy and still trying to be straight, the two women moved in together as friends—a recipe for disaster. Though they had separate bedrooms, Carolyn remembers that they'd sleep apart for two weeks, then together for one. "And then we'd go to the bishop," she says.

Fortuitously, Carolyn and Genelle made friends with a lesbian neighbor who assumed they were a happy couple. But as she got to know them better, the woman realized that they were struggling with their identities. One day the friend asked Carolyn, "Well, maybe you're not going to be gay for the rest of your life, but can you at least say you're gay today?" Carolyn said, "Yes," for the first time in her life admitting she was a lesbian.

"And from that point on, things got better," Carolyn recalls. One thing that especially helped Carolyn's coming out and her ability to be with Genelle without shame or guilt was taking Bible study classes, in which she learned to interpret the Scriptures on her own. God, she came to believe, didn't have to be the cruel God that the Mormons worship. "I'd been afraid of God, because of the horrible sin of being gay," Carolyn observes. "But I came to realize that God was more of a loving and accepting God than the one I was familiar with."

"A Connection That Goes Back Lifetimes"— Barbara and Dalia

Many lesbian and gay people who have been raised with oppressive doctrines have, as adults, sought out the solace of non-Western or nontraditional religions, some of which have proved much more accepting of homosexuality than Judeo-Christian ones. Buddhism, for example, is notable for its tolerance of lesbians and gay men, and the sect both accepts and performs same-sex marriages. For Barbara and Dalia, the spiritual connectedness they found as lesbians within Buddhism has been central to their relationship from their first meeting.

In 1992, Barbara was a recent immigrant from Ireland and Great Britain, who had come to the United States to study at the Art Institute of Chicago. A devout Buddhist who meditated and chanted daily, Barbara was also accustomed to attending events at the local Buddhist Culture Center.

"That summer," Barbara remembers, "I walked in to the center and held the door open to a woman and her son. She asked me in which room the lecture that evening would take place, and we walked up the stairs together."

Barbara usually sat in the front of the room on these occasions, but that night, she had to leave early to go to an African music performance. "So I sat at the back—next to this woman," she says.

Family time for Barbara, Dalia, and son Christopher.

The woman's son was eight years old and not at all as enthused about the lecture as his mom was. He kept poking his mother and nagging her to leave, as kids will do when they're bored.

"I felt bad that the woman couldn't concentrate on what was being said," Barbara recalls. In an act of great kindness, she got up, went to the center's office, and brought back some pens and paper so that the little boy, Chris, could draw outside the meeting room and his mother could enjoy the lecture.

"I must have made some deep, deep impression and connection to him at that moment," Barbara says, "because he started begging his mother to go to the Culture Center every day until we met again two or

"Starting Over:
Young, Gay, Widowed"

BY ROB BANASZAK

. . . A MONTH OR SO BEFORE MARK DIED, we were watching an episode of *Mad About You,* a television show about a young married couple. The character Paul was fantasizing about his death and he was shocked to see that his wife, Jamie, had brought a date—a gorgeous young hunk—to his funeral. "Couldn't you wait for a while to date?" the spirit Paul asks Jamie. Mark turned to me and made an attempt at humor. "Honey, you're going to wait awhile, aren't you?" I started to cry. It hurt too much to think about losing him, and it made me sick to even imagine going back to the dating scene again!

I did wait awhile to date. I moved to Washington, D.C., after Mark died and had a few one-night stands, my need to satisfy my libidinous desires superseding my need for emotional connection. But soon I was doing the "D" word. Dating combined with widowhood is so messy. In addition to the usual insecurity I had with being single and dating (Will he think I'm attractive? Funny? Smart? Interesting?), I found myself strapped with baggage that was impossible to avoid in discussion, even small talk. When asked why I had moved to D.C., I had to talk about losing Mark. He seemed to come up in every conversation, inevitably. So then I worried that my date would feel uncomfortable about the fact that my former lover had died of AIDS. Would he worry that my grief would be too much to handle? Would he be scared off because he would assume I was HIV-positive? Was I sounding too romantic? Morbid? Clichéd? Boring? Talking about one's dead lover makes bad cruising conversation.

The fact is, Mark is part of me now. Whoever is interested in me has to be interested in the spirit of this other being that pulses through my veins. Who I am is defined by our love and our struggle with AIDS and his death. Mark is always going to be in my life, and therefore, for better or worse, he is always on my dates. I once dated a man who told me that being in my apartment made him uncomfortable because he felt that Mark wasn't making room for his presence—he felt crowded! I found this fascinating and amusing because I knew the guy wasn't right for me, and I couldn't help wondering if Mark was, in fact, pushing him out.

. . . As time plows forward I find myself no longer wanting to be defined by my widowhood. I'm tired. Widowhood was a lot of emotional work. I think the time is coming when I will begin to take the pictures down, or at least move them to smaller areas of my apartment, maybe get rid of the shoes of his I kept because they were so tiny and cute. Maybe I'll even take off my wedding ring. I am beginning to think that clearing away some of the external mementos of our life together will allow Mark's presence to move deeper into me instead of just hovering around me. It may make it easier to make emotional room for someone else to come into my life. Maybe some day I'll be blessed beyond what I might deserve and will find another man who, like Mark, makes me feel like more of me, more of who I was supposed to become.

three days later!" It was the first time he'd ever *asked* to go, and so Barbara also made a deep impression on Dalia, the boy's mother.

Barbara and Dalia exchanged phone numbers and made plans to go to the beach with Chris, ostensibly so Barbara and the little boy could be together. "But we soon became very interested in each other," Barbara says, "and in our emotional and mental connection. That kid set us up!" As spiritually in tune as she is, Barbara wonders just how unknowingly Chris did so. Her Buddhist faith includes a belief in reincarnation, and she has little doubt that she was supposed to meet Dalia that night. "Dalia and I feel we have a connection that goes back lifetimes," she explains.

The Next Time Around

It's sometimes hard to talk about "lifetimes" for lesbian and gay couples, because so many of us have lost partners to AIDS, breast and ovarian cancer, and other diseases. AIDS, in particular, has devastated the gay men's community, making many men widowers at a young age, starting over when they thought they'd found their life mates. "I'm in a place now where I'm fifty-one, I'm single again, and what's wrong with this picture," says Robert Woodworth sadly. "Trying to figure out where life goes now is hard. I was supposed to spend the rest of my life with Noli." Like many AIDS widowers, Robert has dated men since Noli's death, but he feels he's not at the place for another relationship. "There's too much comparison of my relationship with Noli going on," he explains. (See also the sidebar, "Starting Over: Young, Gay, Widowed.")

Sharing Grief—Craig and Patrick

For other widowers, moving on has come about more quickly, perhaps from the need to feel intense joy again after intense sadness. Craig Lucas—the renowned playwright and screenwriter, whose works include *Prelude to a Kiss, Blue Window, Longtime Companion,* and *Reckless*—has sustained numerous losses to AIDS, including three lovers, his longtime colleague Norman René, and by his own estimates, close to 100 of his friends. All the loss, he says, has both deepened his appreciation for "the saner joys of being alive"—love, marriage, and family—and skewed his objectivity somewhat.

So when he fell hard and fast for Patrick Barnes, a songwriter, after being a widower for about a year, he was both scared and excited by the quickness of it. The two were introduced by a mutual friend in January

1996. "A friend and I were having dinner at the restaurant where Patrick works," Craig explains. The friend turned out to be a friend of Patrick's, too, and the restaurant was a trendy place called Trattoria Dell'Arte in Manhattan.

"It's a tense place because it's so busy," Patrick says. The owner and staff can get ugly with each other. So when his friend Patrick Merla— "one of the smartest and sweetest men imaginable"—came into the restaurant, Patrick was relieved to see a friendly face and ran up to hug him. He was very excited to find out that Merla was meeting Craig Lucas for dinner. "I have always considered him to be one of the top few good playwrights today," Patrick gushes. "His work deals with the possibilities of life, it's never two people sitting in a restaurant discussing the foibles of dating in the nineties."

So Patrick took the opportunity to be introduced and make a good first impression. "Patrick brought over a large platter of appetizers 'on the house,'" remembers Craig, "and we were introduced." The proverbial sparks flew between the two men.

"He was very cute and puppylike, and I could tell he wanted a date," Patrick recalls. "I immediately found him charming," Craig says. "He exuded an easy comfort, a playfulness, along with a beautiful face and body."

On the pretext of getting one of Patrick's music demo tapes, Craig asked if they could get together the following day. Patrick agreed to meet Craig at the restaurant where he planned to have lunch with Norman René. "I guess I wanted for Patrick and me to visit in someone else's company," Craig muses, "so that I didn't immediately hurl myself at him. But also so that Patrick could see some of what my life was about."

Norman's health was deteriorating fast, and since Tim, Craig's partner of eleven years, had died the previous year, Craig was experiencing what he calls "the deepest grief of my life." As one of his best friends, Norman was the "litmus test" in many things for Craig. "I had this sense that if Patrick didn't take to Norman, he wouldn't be someone I would want to date. And unconsciously, I wanted Norman's take on Patrick, too. I find it too easy to fall in love, or to confuse need and lust for love." Patrick and Norman seemed to like each other, so that was the first hurdle crossed.

After lunch, Patrick remembers that they escorted Norman home and then browsed for furniture and books. Craig bought Patrick a copy of the Maurice Sendak, or illustrated edition of Herman Melville's *Pierre, or the Ambiguities*. When they parted company, Patrick boldly kissed Craig on the lips.

That night, Craig returned to Trattoria Dell'Arte, this time with Tony Kushner in tow. "I think it was to impress me," Patrick says. "And it did.

But I was more caught up in the bright warmth that Craig exuded. Exudes. Being with Craig is a little like being on Ecstasy [the hallucinogenic drug]—he inspires this euphoria about being alive."

Within two weeks, Patrick had separated from the man he had been dating. "He was a really sweet guy, and we were comfortable with each other," Patrick remembers. But it was just casual and his feelings for Craig were different. "I felt," Patrick says of Craig, "that he would be a grand passion."

From the start, Craig's grief and loss have played a role in their relationship that makes them both wax philosophical. "Craig's grief is something he shares with me," says Patrick. "It's beautiful, terrifying, and epic. I try to assuage it when I can. I think my natural inclination is to sniff out happiness."

Which is one thing that drew Craig to him in the first place. "Patrick strikes me as being immensely kind in so many ways," he observes. "If we last I'll be very happy; if we don't, I can't imagine I'll regret having taken the risk."

"Type" Casting

Though love is surely universal, we've seen that lesbians and gay men often experience romance very differently from the way straight people do. Same-sex meeting and dating are complicated by one bottom line fact—that our sexual identity has been rebuked and pathologized, and consequently we've often been invisible to each other. For that matter, we've often been invisible to ourselves.

The stories lesbians and gay men told me all suggest that while there's no magic recipe for same-sex love, there can often be a bit of magic involved. Though many couples I met spoke of instant love and attraction, more often people mentioned coming to feel "easy" with each other or sensing that the other person was "different" from other people. Some people were simply "intrigued at first sight" or felt the desire at first for friendship and nothing more. "I wasn't her type," Dr. Marjorie Hill smiles now, when she recalls how her partner, Christine Edwards, didn't seem interested in her for several years.

Betty Berzon, one of the gurus of same-sex relationships, has observed that lesbian and gay people looking for love often get hung up on the idea of finding someone who is their "type." One's "type" is based on early idols from adolescence, "the-person-you-always-wanted-to-be." The problem with "types," says Berzon, is that, if you focus solely on physical or psychological qualities, "the true objective, to find a *compatible* partner, gets lost in the playing out of the fantasy."[5] And all too often we buy the romantic, storybook notion that love has to happen at first sight, that everything about the other person has to be just so or else it's not the real thing.

My own early role model was my older sister, who was smart, intimidating, and ambivalent about me because I had replaced her as the baby of the family. As an adult lesbian, I kept having my heart broken by women who were (surprise!) smart, intimidating, and deeply ambivalent about me. It got so bad that at one point I was hotly pursuing a woman who would barely give me the time of day. My relationship radar was jammed by my dogged insistence on having a certain "type."

I used to complain to my therapist about this conundrum—the women I thought I had chemistry with were ambivalent; the women who wanted to be with me were seemingly "chem-free." "Is it possible that 'chemistry' can come later on?" she asked me. I was doubtful, but that question did start me thinking about what "chemistry" actually was. What I really wanted, I realized, was not someone like all the others, but a woman who was smart, totally unintimidating, very interested in me, and with whom I had sexual energy. And into my life walked Katie.

When individuals take a second (or third or fourth) look at a potential partner, going beyond mere physical attributes and first impressions, they can often find they have something deeper to share. "It's not going to be perfect," says gay therapist Michael Shernoff. "Nobody is going to be perfect." Shernoff believes that the best relationships grow out of mutual respect. "And genuinely enjoying the company of the other person," he adds thoughtfully. "You've got to have the ability to play together, to really have fun."

In the next chapter, we'll look at how lesbian and gay couples have made the next step past meeting and falling in love, taking their relationships into the more complicated realm of "the serious"—and without any set plan or rules on how to do so.

Notes

1. Michael Shernoff, "Chronically Single: Gay Men in Search of True Love," *In the Family* 1, no. 3 (January 1996), 17.

2. Reverend Michael Piazza, *Rainbow Family Values: Relationship Skills for Lesbian and Gay Couples* (Sources of Hope Publishing, 1995), 56.

3. Sylvia Cole, "The Elusive Lesbian Date," *In the Family* 1, no. 3 (January 1996), 8.

4. D. Michael Quinn, *Same-Sex Dynamics among Nineteenth-Century Americans: A Mormon Example* (University of Illinois Press, 1996).

5. Betty Berzon, *Permanent Partners: Building Gay and Lesbian Relationships That Last* (Plume, 1990), 26.

Seriouser and Seriouser

2

Making It Up

We've all heard the old joke, "What does a lesbian bring on the second date?" Punch line: "A U-Haul." The joke continues, "What does a gay man bring on the second date?" Second punch line: "What second date?" Like all stereotypes, some of us fit them, but many of us do not.

What does it mean for lesbian and gay couples to get serious in a world that doesn't always recognize our right to be together? There seem to be as many meanings as there are grains of sand on the beaches at Provincetown, and they all point to a conundrum. Straight couples have a lot worked out for them by tradition. It's common for them to marry when they get to a turning point in their relationships. But because same-sex couples can't legally marry and, more significantly, because external and internalized homophobia have made us hide our relationships for family, work, or legal reasons, there is no real nomenclature and no established stages for our relationships.

Gay journalist Robert Pela has dubbed the time after dating but before the forever-and-ever of being committed, "the romance hump." With none of the traditional markers of heterosexual relationships—courtship, engagement, marriage—same-sex couples have to make a lot of things up. What steps mark the passing from being casual to being committed? What symbols do we use to validate our relationships? And here's the $64,000 question—what in the world do we call each other?

If you're straight and you get married, chances are pretty good that you'll latch on to the words, "husband," "wife," or "spouse" to identify your beloved. But when I asked lesbian and gay couples how they refer to each other, many people didn't even understand at first what I meant, answering with a shrug, "I call her Honey" or "I call him Punkin."

*Marching as
wife and wife.*

With lesbians and gay men, there's a choice involved in what to call your partner, and it can be a baffling and exhausting one. Some of us have appropriated heterosexual terms, but for lesbians in particular, that choice can be fraught with difficulty. "I always called Susan my wife or spouse," says psychotherapist Dr. April Martin—an unusual move in 1978, the heyday of lesbian-feminist activism, when she and Susan became involved. "You didn't say 'wife,' " April continues. "That was demeaning to women." Many of us still shudder at the idea of being someone's "wife," which for many married women spelled loss of self and identity to a man. But "wife" was the word that felt right to April, the one that conveyed the level of commitment they experienced. Twenty years later, more and more lesbians are reclaiming the word.

Some lesbians and gay men told me that their names for each other changed over the course of their relationships. Whereas a gay male squeeze might start out as a "boyfriend," by the end of year one he might become "lover" or "partner," and after a commitment ceremony, he might transform once again into "spouse" or "husband" (or for a more campy male couple, "wife").

Often, lesbians and gay men say they switch words depending on whom they're addressing. "I tend to use the term 'lover' around lesbian and gay people," says Alicia, who lives in Albany, New York. "To me, 'lover' is more of a passionate term. The term 'partner' comes in when I talk about Nancy to my family or friends. I think people hear the word 'partner,' and they automatically think of two gay or lesbian people."

"Partner" does seem to be the word du jour, but it's not as universally recognized as we might imagine. When Zelle and Lesley refer to each other as partner in public, "We have actually been asked by some very unaware people, 'What business are you in? Is she your law partner?' " laughs Lesley. Joseph Ward and Lamont Williams, a Missouri couple who have been together almost fifteen years, try to solve the problem through a simple addition. "We call each other life partner," Lamont says, and many other couples follow suit.

But Tracey Lind and Fran Goldstein ran into confusion over their use of that term. Tracey, an out Episcopal priest, delivered the eulogy at the

"A Boyfriend by Any Other Name"

BY MUBARAK S. DAHIR

YOU'D THINK WITH ALL THE MEN I've dated (I stopped counting a long time ago) that by now I'd have come up with a half-decent way to introduce one around.

But now that I'm dating someone seriously again, I realize that just isn't the case. When we're together, and we run into a friend or acquaintance he doesn't know, I find myself stumbling for the right word with which to introduce him.

"Hello," I'll say, as my mind races to come up with some credible identifier. "I'd like you to meet Darryl, my . . ."

My *what?*

Friend just isn't intimate enough. After all, you don't sleep with your friends. (At least I don't.)

Special friend is just too, well, *special.*

Boyfriend sounds too junior high school, like we're passing notes in class and holding hands at recess, or maybe carrying each other's trays in the cafeteria.

Partner makes it sound like we run a law firm, or are otherwise intertwined in some sort of business transaction.

Domestic partner is even worse: It makes it sound like he comes over twice a week to scrub the toilet and take out the trash.

Mate makes him sound like we're either breeding dogs or on a sailing trip.

Companion makes me feel like I'm the elderly aunt who gets taken to the obligatory monthly movie and is asked if she needs help with her adult diaper.

Husband? Well, we're not in Hawaii. And besides, he hasn't bought me that ring yet. (Hint, hint.)

Spouse, even more than husband, somehow makes me feel like I'm pathetically trying to mimic a heterosexual couple.

Better half is just too white trash. I might as well say "the little woman."

Significant other always makes me want to ask: significant other *what?*

Lover at least has the word "love" in it, but somehow it's too one-dimensional. After all, we do more than just *that* together.

Then there are terms like *soul mate:* Hey, wow, man! Soul mate, like on the life ride of our "Soul Train" together, like groovy. I don't think so.

Things like *love muffin* or *honey bun* sound like we're in a bakery, not a relationship. They're enough to make anyone's stomach turn.

And the cutesy ones, like *sweetie,* evoke an immediate gag response.

My own list of personal favorites include monikers like "stud-machine" or "man-tamer"— and a lot of others that I can't print here.

This article appeared in the Philadelphia Gay News. © *1996 Mubarak S. Dahir. Reprinted with permission of the author.*

funeral of Fran's mother, introducing herself to the chapel full of mourners as "Fran Goldstein's life partner."

"I did a quick scan and I could see people elbowing each other," Tracey chuckles, "saying, 'Life partner? What's a life partner?' "Then people suddenly got it, hitting each other and mouthing, "Ahh!"

Luckily, we all have a sense of humor about this recurring problem. It's a running joke in lesbian and gay culture that we don't have the convenience of clearly defined titles for our true loves (see Mubarak S. Dahir's sidebar, "A Boyfriend by Any Other Name"). Comedian Sara Cytron's stand-up routine, "Take My Domestic Partner . . . Please!"—a play on the classic Henny Youngman one-liner, "Take my wife . . . please!"—was one of the first to point out just how laughable this really can be. But it's also deadly serious. Without even a word to define our relationships, those relationships too easily become marginalized, both by ourselves and by society around us.

Step to It

It isn't only names, though, that we have to improvise. I don't know about you, but my mom never sat me down and said, "Now, dear, you should wait for at *least* a year before you move in with your lesbian lover!" Without any guidelines and in lieu of marriage as an end, lesbians and gay men have often followed an informal pattern of steps in their relationships that reflect changes in the way the partners feel and think about each other and their level of commitment. My own story gives an idea of what these steps can be like.

Katie and I met five years ago at a conference on lesbian sex, and inspired by all the lusty talk, we spent that very first night together. There are a lot of markers for the subsequent stages our relationship took: our first real date; the first time we spent the whole weekend together; our first shared vacation; the first time we said "I love you"; our monogamy discussion; the day I started telling my friends she was "my girlfriend" instead of "the woman I'm 'seeing' "; meeting each other's families; our first anniversary; exchanging the rings I bought for a dollar at a museum gift shop; the day we officially moved in together (after essentially shacking up for six months); the month we blended our finances; ordering more expensive matching rings; the day we registered as domestic partners; our decision to someday have a . . . dog (I bet you thought I was going to say baby). All of this happened over the course of several years. But if pressed for the exact time when we became "serious," I'm not sure I could do anything but relate this long string of events that led up to the present, when we speak of ourselves as life partners.

Research suggests that the most common step for lesbians and gay men to take to show they've become serious is moving in together. A 1988–89 survey by the Partners Task Force for Gay and Lesbian Couples found that, in fact, 75 percent of the lesbian couples and 82 percent of the gay couples who participated lived together.[1] In his groundbreaking work on male couples a few years back, R. M. Berger discovered that gay men move in together very quickly, usually within a couple of months of meeting. Berger suggested that the act of cohabiting serves as a kind of validation that same-sex couples don't receive from family or the outside world. But it can also become problematic when two people throw in their lot together before they have really gotten to know each other.

Another common marker or step of "seriousness" is exchanging an emblem of commitment, like rings. Rings are an ancient symbol of eternal love; the circle has no beginning or end, like the love of committed couples. Even lesbians and gay men who told me they would never, ever, *ever* have any sort of ceremony, thank you very much, had often slipped rings on their loved ones' fingers. "They're a symbol of our love," couple after couple avowed.

As we become more visible, as legalized same-sex marriage becomes a more likely possibility, and as an increasing number of lesbian and gay couples have public commitment ceremonies and holy unions, some of us are expanding on the markers, taking more formal commitment steps, referring to our "engagements" and our "fiancés." Many even carry out fairy-tale, Hollywood-style proposals.

Does this mean, as some progressive activists worry, that we're becoming too assimilated, that soon no one will be able to distinguish gay from straight? From the way lesbian and gay couples who had engagements talk about them, it seems unlikely. It may be more accurate to say that we're appropriating and transforming the lingo of heterosexual culture, rather than becoming part of it. That makes complete sense, since we've all been influenced by the images delivered by popular culture.

For example, Christine Edwards proposed to Marjorie Hill only six weeks after they started dating, in a classic way, with a ring and a "Honey, will you marry me?" But Marjorie used the engagement as a kind of subtle political statement. "I loved saying, 'This is my fiancée,' " she remembers. "I enjoyed talking [to straight people] about being engaged. It was almost as if being an out, engaged lesbian gave many straight people I knew an opportunity to talk about my life in a way that being a single lesbian did not."

No matter which or how many steps you take, moving through the courtship stage over the hump to commitment can be an arduous process. Popular cultural notions of relationships as breezy and romantic (once you have one) don't make sense for *straight* people, let alone for lesbians and

"I loved saying, 'This is my fiancée.' I enjoyed talking [to straight people] about being engaged. It was almost as if being an out, engaged lesbian gave many straight people I knew an opportunity to talk about my life in a way that being a single lesbian did not."

Several years ago, psychologist Tina Tessina published a self-help book called *Gay Relationships for Men and Women: How to Find Them, How to Improve Them, How to Make Them Last* (Jeremy P. Tarcher, Inc., 1989). Different from other books with similar titles, Tessina's handbook actually includes questions, checklists, and fill-in-the-blanks that can help individuals decide what they want from a relationship and how to work toward it—all while keeping a sense of humor. The section titled "From Dating to Commitment," for example, contains "Waffling Exercise #1" and "#2," to assist a couple when one or both partners feel undecided about the viability of the relationship in the long term.

gay men. If lesbian and gay people are taught that our relationships won't last, will we be willing to do the work required to maintain them?

"There are these Hollywood notions of what relationships are," says Dr. April Martin, who acknowledges that she had those dominant-culture notions implanted in her, too. "I had this fairly self-centered idea that a relationship was about somebody loving me exactly the way I wanted to be loved. I was now going to get my needs met. And sure, I was going to meet hers, too, in ways that were easy for me to do. And I had romantic ideas about, yes, this will be hard work. But I don't think I really understood what the hard work would be."

In this chapter, lesbian and gay couples share how they moved their relationships forward toward commitment, union, "marriage"—without the benefit of a set course, by making things up along the way.

Bringing the U-Haul

One of the most common markers showing that the partners in a same-sex relationship have become "seriouser" is the decision to move in together. Therapists would probably prefer that lesbian and gay couples sit down and think through the decision, basing it on a clear-cut, now's-the-right-time conclusion. In fact, that's how Peter #1 and Peter #2 of upstate New York did it. "After four months of dating," Peter #1 says of their incredibly efficient and rational procedure, "we had spent time with each other's families, had worked through my fear of commitment, were spending most nights together, and both felt that we were working toward a lifetime commitment to each other." Katie and I also took it step-by-step, following a two-year progression in which we spent increasingly more time together until we knew that living together felt right. It doesn't happen that way every time, however, nor does that always have an affect on the relationship's longevity.

"Nothing Formal"

Often, couples simply discover that they're already living together, and the act of renting the moving truck just makes it official. Over and over, I heard comments like those made by Oscar Jones, who began living with his lover, Gregory Cox, in Nebraska a couple of years ago, when Oscar moved from Michigan to go to graduate school. They met at a Mardi Gras party, and though Oscar facetiously admits a certain bias against men from Nebraska, he made concessions for Greg. After several months of dating, their relationship progressed. "It was nothing formal," Oscar said. "Like, 'Oh, you move in here.' He just moved in. It was a natural move because he had been staying with me so often."

When they met in January 1996 at a gay community center workshop, Timothous Mack and Edward Jones spotted each other instantly and had immediate rapport and attraction for each other. "I thought, 'Oh . . . my . . . God. Is he single, married, or *what?*' " laughs Timothous. They began dating right away and knew from long conversations that they both wanted the same things from a relationship.

Then, similar to Oscar and Greg, within a few months of meeting, "We'd spend every day after work together," points out Timothous. "We'd meet up and talk and I'd come to Edward's house. So, it was like we might as well move in together."

Midwesterners Joanne and Elaine[2] got together eight-and-a-half years ago, when a matchmaking friend started to arrange "chance" meetings between the two. Because they lived fifty miles apart, for the first month that they dated their relationship was mostly on the phone. "We actually talked out the boundaries of our relationship before we even kissed!" Joanne recalls. Many issues, like monogamy, were settled very early on.

Their moving in together was casual, something they say happened organically and was never really discussed in a conscious kind of way. "More and more of my stuff started to collect at Elaine's house," Joanne notes. "We found it easier for me to go to her house after work

> "*After four months of dating we had spent time with each other's families, had worked through my fear of commitment, were spending most nights together, and both felt that we were working toward a lifetime commitment to each other.*"

than for her to drive all the way out to the suburbs to my apartment. My apartment became a place to go only to get my mail." Within three months, they were living together.

Playwright Craig Lucas says that he, too, was quickly spending almost every night with his lover, Patrick Barnes. Five months after their first date, they decided to live together, though they were both conscious of the fact that it was quick and that they probably shouldn't.

Living together.
Cooking together.

"I wanted to wait six months," Patrick recalls, "but we were really living together anyway. All I did was rent a small truck and take most of my few possessions to Craig's."

"I missed him when we had to be separated," Craig says. But like other cautious couples, even after they moved in together, they kept Patrick's apartment as a safety net. "We decided he'd use it as a studio for his composing and lyric writing," Craig explains. "So we'd each have our private work space, and if things were being handled too precipitously by one or both of us, he could return to his home without the upheaval of looking for a new apartment, which in New York City has become a nightmare."

Craig worried at first that their cohabiting was too fast, but a year after they've moved in together, he's more philosophical about it. "I might have gone decades before making such a suitable match," he says, so whatever risk they took he feels was worth it.

Julie and Wendy also took a chance by moving in soon after they met almost five years ago. Though they knew intellectually that it might be better to wait, "We moved in together a lot sooner than we planned," Julie admits. When they met, both women were living at their parents' homes in suburban Westchester County, just north of New York City. Because they lived a forty-minute drive from each other, it was hard for them to find any time or place to be alone.

"We spent a lot of time in cars," Julie smiles, adding quickly, "just talking, mind you!" Wendy was in night school, and one evening before class, they parked in her school's parking lot. "Just talking, mind you!" Julie repeats. But then, though they were both long out of high school, they were instantly propelled back to their teenage days.

"Some bright lights appeared behind us," Julie says. "A police car. He asked Wendy to get out of the car and asked me if I was okay." When he ran Wendy's registration number, her car came up as a stolen vehicle. Fortunately, the cop figured out quickly that he was one number off and that the car really did belong to Wendy. But the implicit homophobia of the cop's actions (would he have run the number of an adult heterosexual couple?) was enough to propel Julie and Wendy into a serious consideration of their living arrangements.

"We were both freaked and 'way too old for this'!" says Julie. "We had an apartment within two weeks after that."

Practically Speaking

Faced with the realities of everyday life, lesbian and gay couples often have to make decisions that end up unconsciously acknowledging a serious turn their relationship has already taken. Couples can end up moving in together sooner than they thought they would, for example, when a lease expires or a roommate moves out.

"I had my own little ruler," relates Ruth Carranza. "I told Pam [Walton, her partner of ten years] that after we'd been together three years is when I'd start to feel stable, like we had something together. Pam also did not want to hop in and move in together." But then, as the saying goes, the best laid plans. . . . As it turned out, Pam lost her apartment in the San Francisco Bay area six months after their relationship started, and Ruth broke her own three-year rule and suggested they move in together. To ease Pam's fears about losing her individuality and freedom, they rented a two-bedroom apartment.

© Lulu Geschwitz

Patrick Barnes (top) and Craig Lucas at home.

"I got my own bedroom," Pam says, laughing at the memory of her reluctance. "I was going to sleep in it as much as I wanted, and she was not to think that we would sleep together every night. And in all the years that we've lived together, I think I've slept alone three times—when I had the flu."

Instead of having to search for a place to live, Wanda and Mildred had an apartment literally fall into their laps. "We moved in together because this apartment opened up," Wanda explains. I can understand why she and Mildred jumped at the chance—they have a roomy one-bedroom in Stuyvesant Town, a rent-stabilized apartment complex in New York City where the wait for an apartment can be as long as ten years. Though they'd been together about a year, they were concerned that the move was too quick. Still, the apartment was an offer they couldn't refuse.

"I thought, if Mildred moves in by herself, and then I come, I'm always going to feel like a guest," says Wanda. "This was my own issue. It may not have been real, but at the time, that's what it was. She was going to decorate in her style. I was going to feel like an intruder. So, we really had two days to make a decision." Wanda remembers that there was a lot of "Oh my God, should we do this?" going on between them. But then, they went for it. "And it was the best thing that ever happened. I think it was very difficult. But we talked so much about it without getting too heavy."

An available apartment was also the impetus for Robert Woodworth and Noli Villanueva's decision to begin living together four years after they'd met. "Neither one of us had the space for the other to move in," Robert says of their two tiny apartments, so they maintained their separate residences. But Noli had put his name on a waiting list a few years earlier for subsidized middle-income housing, and his name finally came up for an apartment. He and Robert knew it would be a struggle for them financially to buy the apartment, but because it was too good a deal, they planned on borrowing money and scrimping to afford the new place.

But after the angst of making the decision, "We applied and went through the whole process," Robert remembers, "and it ultimately failed because Noli wasn't a citizen and didn't have his green card [permanent visa]. He didn't qualify for the financing that they had set up for these apartments." (For more on immigration troubles for lesbian and gay couples, see the sidebar, "Green Card Blues.")

Their failed attempt did spur the couple on, though. "We decided we were on the road to moving in together anyway." Robert smiles. "So then we started looking on our own and ultimately found our apartment."

Sometimes the impetus to move in together is the pressing desire to start a family, something lesbian and gay couples have been doing with greater frequency since the late 1980s. Linda Villarosa, former executive editor of *Essence* magazine, and her partner, Vickie, lived two blocks apart for the first three years of their relationship and were happy with that arrangement. But then Linda's biological clock went "way beyond the ticking point," Linda laughs. "We got really serious about having a baby, and we decided, we really can't go on living apart."

Their process of buying a house together in Brooklyn helped cement their relationship, bringing out their complementary sides. "Vickie did all the organizing work—the Realtor, the money, the bank, the contractor. And I was the one who said, 'Oh, that's

> *"More and more of my stuff started to collect at Elaine's house. We found it easier for me to go to her house after work than for her to drive all the way out to the suburbs to my apartment. My apartment became a place to go only to get my mail."*

NOT SINGLE, BUT NOT MARRIED EITHER

Our society is geared toward married couples, and unmarried individuals, whether gay or straight, face a dilemma when they decide to live together. Although the partners aren't technically single, they're not legally married, either. So they need to jump an array of legal hurdles that the institution of marriage takes for granted—things like joint finances and health care proxies.

If you're looking for information on issues that affect couples who live together, a good starting point is *The Unmarried Couple's Legal Survival Guide: Your Rights and Obligations* by Elliot D. Samuelson, J.D. (Citadel Press, 1996). Although it's not primarily targeted to lesbians and gay men, it does have a chapter that focuses attention on the specific concerns of same-sex couples. In addition, various other chapters clearly discuss and analyze how lesbian and gay couples are affected by health care benefits, living wills, and financial agreements.

the house, here it is, this is the one we should get. I see us in this.' Vickie would have been shopping for another year. But then, I didn't want to do any of the work. So I said, 'This is the house, now you get it for us!' I like that we have that kind of complementary relationship."

Expect the Unexpected

Moving in together can sometimes be more complicated than most of these stories suggest. For those coming out of heterosexual marriages, for example, the decision to live with a new lover can have enormous consequences, as in the case of Diane Curtis and Bekki McQuay.

Diane and Bekki, partners for two years, live together in Amarillo, Texas. Three months after Diane and Bekki met and began dating, they decided they wanted to share an apartment, even though "we knew it was going to be a risk," Diane acknowledges. That risk had to do with Diane's ex-husband, to whom she'd been married for twelve years and with whom she had a son.

Diane describes her former husband as "extremely controlling," a prominent and well-respected doctor. After Diane, Bekki, and Diane's son Steven[3] moved in together, the ex-husband began calling Diane and asking a barrage of questions about Bekki. "He asked me if she was a 'homosexual,'" Diane remembers, "and I said yes." That started a year-long nightmare custody battle over Steven. In July 1996, Diane lost custody of her ten-year-old boy—one of many lesbian mothers denied rights simply because of sexual orientation. Conservative judges in southern states like Texas, Florida, and Virginia have been particularly harsh and unfair toward lesbian mothers. (See also chapter 5.)

"I had all the expert testimony on my side," says Diane. "I had the principal of Steven's school on my side. My ex-husband had no one except two mothers who said they wouldn't allow their children to play with Steven anymore because of religious reasons! And my ex-husband won custody."

Julie and Wendy before a lesbian and gay pride run.

Because Diane was not deemed "unfit," she was awarded weekend visitation rights. But her ex-husband was able to get a heinous restriction put on those visits, which bans Bekki from the house from seven P.M. to seven A.M. on the nights Steven sleeps over.

"She isn't allowed to sleep in the house she helps pay for," Diane notes, "and she has to leave so we won't expose Steven to homosexuality. Go figure—do we turn gay after seven P.M.?" The restriction has put stress on their relationship, but Diane gives Bekki credit for being so committed to both her and Steven. "It would be so easy for her to say, 'I'm outta here.' I am very honored to have her as a partner."

Fellow Texans Jackie and Betty also had a rough moving-in story, complicated by Betty's abusive husband. Betty had married a high school boyfriend, even though she'd suspected for a long time that she was a lesbian. Her husband was aware of her feelings and simply figured that she'd "get over it." But after thirteen years and four children with her husband, Betty met Jackie in a mutual friend's beauty salon and instantly fell in love.

At first Jackie didn't want "to go down that road," she says, "to get hurt or break up a family or just be her erotic lesbian experience." But Betty announced that she was leaving her husband because she realized she couldn't live a lie anymore.

One night Betty hung out with Jackie until three in the morning. When she got home, her husband was drunk and beat her up, sending her racing out of the house and back to Jackie's. "She came over to my house and knocked on the window," Jackie recalls. "I opened it up and she crawled in."

Jackie notes that, since that time, the Melissa Etheridge song, "Come to My Window," has held a special, bittersweet meaning for the two of them. "Betty crawled in my window and got into bed with me, and I held her all night. And she's been with me ever since."

Separate but Equal

What about lesbian and gay couples who don't live together? Can people be serious about each other without putting both their names on a lease? I have friends who have been together ten years, with no sign of giving up their separate residences. Yet they're accepted as a steady couple by everyone, including their families of origin. Though cohabiting may seem like the logical step for many of us, some couples suggest that it's not essential.

Though they've been a couple since attending high school together in Sacramento in the mid–1970s, Karin and Maria Kaj have only lived together since 1989. Sophomore year, they sat across from each other in health education class. "She had a piece of cotton in her ear, and I spent our first class together wondering if she knew," Karin recalls. "She had a big Polish nose and Marcia Brady hair—well, ditto for me on the hair."

As high school friends and then lovers, the two girls lived with their parents, following their rules. "It was very scary," Karin says, "and being young, I never felt as if I could say to my parents that I wanted to live with Maria."

GREEN CARD BLUES

When most lesbian and gay couples make the decision to cohabit, they have to consider where they're going to live, who pays how much rent, how many pets they can conceivably keep in one space, who's going to cook and who's going to clean, and a host of other routine things. But imagine that you're a couple that decides to live together, only to have to worry about the very real possibility that someday you'll be forcibly separated from each other.

A futuristic horror story? No, this is what it's like for lesbians and gay men who come to this country on temporary visas to study or visit, fall in love with American citizens, and are unable to obtain green cards—the visas that allows them to stay here permanently. When their visas run out, so do the couples' luck.

The best way for foreigners to obtain a green card is through family connections. That usually means marrying a U.S. citizen, a narrow definition of "family" that excludes same-sex partners. While a heterosexual couple can just get a marriage license to solve their immigration problems, "Lesbian and gay couples don't have that option," says immigration attorney Noemi Masliah. "The way that the same-sex marriage question affects binational couples hasn't really registered with the lesbian and gay community. Yeah, it would be great to file income tax returns together. But if you can't even live in the same *country,* it's pretty unreasonable."

Barbara, an emigrant from Ireland and Great Britain, lives near Chicago with her partner, Dalia. She originally came to the United States on a study visa, fell in love with Dalia, and was able to secure a six-year work visa, because of her valuable skills as a Web page designer and computer whiz. Work visas are mostly issued for technical or scientific jobs, skills that are in demand.

"But those visas eventually run out," notes Lavi Soloway, national coordinator of the Lesbian and Gay Immigration Rights Task Force. "Many couples get stuck in limbo, with the foreign partner being undocumented, unable to travel or work and subject to deportation."

"If we run into problems when my visa expires," Barbara says, "Dalia has offered to support me here. She runs a cleaning service. And we've even talked about moving to another country with gay marriage rights or a more lenient immigration policy and settling there."

Canada, for example, is one of seven countries that have broadened the definition of "family" in their immigration codes, recognizing same-sex rela-

After high school, though they were deeply committed to each other, they postponed living together for twelve years. Karin had a job in Sacramento, and Maria wanted to go to college and then graduate school in Chicago—fifteen hundred miles away. They only spent summers and vacations together at Karin's apartment. "We had a long-distance relationship," Maria explains. "But I think it's good for couples to learn how to balance what they need to do to develop themselves as individuals with what they need to do as a couple. I've always said that the secret to longevity is No Sacrifices."

Yet distance can also strain a relationship, as in the case of Richard Burns and his partner, Tom, who were a couple for three years in Boston before Richard got a job opportunity in New York, almost three hundred

tionships for "humanitarian and compassionate" reasons. One lesbian couple—Beverly, a U.S. citizen originally from Georgia, and Jamie, a Canadian citizen—met in a chat room in cyberspace, fell in love, and are now living in British Columbia. Settling in Canada was the only viable way for them to stay together.

"But it's not as easy as people make it sound," Beverly notes. The process of becoming a legal immigrant in Canada can take two years and costs almost one thousand American dollars. For Beverly and Jamie, that's a formidable sum. Without that status, however, Beverly can't work legally, and she's concerned that an under-the-table job might jeopardize her immigration application. Yet, having to meet all their expenses from Jamie's salary alone makes it impossible for the couple to save for Beverly's application—a classic vicious circle.

Ron Buckmire, the founder of the Queer Resources Directory on the Internet, acknowledges that he has a good chance of obtaining a green card to stay in this country with his lover of over six years, Dean Elzinga, with whom he lives in Los Angeles—a better chance, in fact, than many people. Originally from Grenada, Ron has a father in this country who is a legal immigrant and who can apply for his permanent residency. He also has an advanced degree in mathematics and is a longtime resident as a student in the United States. "I have advantages that other people don't have," Ron says, "but which should really be irrelevant to binational couples being able to start a life together."

Many immigration activists want to see a new classification added to the U.S. immigration code, following the model of Australia and New Zealand. "Those countries look at the viability of the relationship," Noemi Masliah says, "not the gender of the partners." But in the current anti-immigrant climate here, Congress is more interested in deleting immigration classifications than in creating new ones.

The biggest hope for binational couples is a victory for same-sex marriage in Hawaii. Many couples will somehow find the money to go there and legally wed. And when they return, their immigration applications could clog the INS and the court system for years. "For those people who are so set on opposing same-sex marriage rights," Lari Soloway says, "it will be a prime example of how lesbian and gay couples have been treated as unequal."

The Lesbian and Gay Immigration Rights Task Force can be reached at: P.O. Box 7741, New York, NY 10116-7741. Phone: (212) 802-7264; en Español: (212) 802-7267. Their e-mail address is: info@lgirtf.org, and the Task Force Web site features a host of information about the rights and struggles of same-sex binational couples. You can access it at http://www.lgirtf.org.

miles away. For the next nine years, they commuted between the two cities, first every weekend, and then less and less frequently.

"Tom and I were both very focused on our work," Richard says. Neither partner could give up his job to move to the other's city, and the shuttling back and forth became exhausting. "On the one hand, the tension of the distance kept the sexual charge very intense throughout the relationship," Richard notes. "And that was a plus. On the downside, it severely limited our intimacy and slowed down the normal evolution of a relationship. I think that had we lived in the same city or lived together, the relationship would have evolved and succeeded, or it would have ended years sooner."

Partners Diana Shapiro and Lori Berkowitz live in the same city,

Berkeley, but not at the same address. Their homes are about three miles apart, a convenient drive or bike ride. Though they went through a public commitment ceremony, they've decided for themselves that marriage for them doesn't necessitate cohabitation. They had not lived together before the ceremony and figured, "If it ain't broke, don't fix it," Lori says. "Things work out great as they are."

Diana notes that their space and independence are extremely important to them, and those needs influenced their decision not to live together. "We don't want to become a unit," Diana says. "We want to maintain our individuality, and living apart helps us do that." They take turns staying over at each other's homes, mostly because "we both have cats," Diana explains, "and we don't like leaving them alone for too long!"

Still, they haven't closed the door on the possibility of someday living in the same space. Diana guesses that they'd find a place together, or else she would move into the house that Lori owns with several other people. "But I'd have my own room," she notes quickly. They don't feel any pressure to live together just because they've said they're committed. "We'll do it when we want to," Lori says, "not as an automatic result of getting married."

> *"We don't want to become a unit. We want to maintain our individuality, and living apart helps us do that."*

Rings and Things

Probably the second biggest step toward "seriousness" for lesbian and gay couples is wearing some sort of visible symbol of their commitment. In our society, this usually means a ring, a traditional sign of investment in a relationship.

I remember when I was young, exchanging friendship rings with my girlfriends. It was exciting and thrilling, in a prelesbian kind of way. Even though I knew as I grew up that I had no interest in marrying a man, I still held a romantic notion about rings and was jealous of friends who got them from their fiancés. I didn't want the fiancé, just the love and commitment of someone special and the symbol to prove it.

So I was sad when my partner Katie adamantly announced, "No rings." I tried to understand—like many lesbians, she'd been married to a man, and rings and ceremonies held bad connotations for her. I brought up the topic several times, and once she conceded that maybe—just *maybe*—she'd consider wearing a ring on a chain around her neck. A glint of hope.

When we were on a trip to San Diego for a conference, Katie was holed up in our hotel room writing the talk that she was scheduled to give, and I was on my own, sightseeing. I ended up at the San Diego Maritime Museum, which is housed in a boat on the water. But I never made it into the museum proper because I stopped first in the gift shop and found a basket of rings—each one a silver band of alternating pink and white shell triangles—marked ONE DOLLAR. I was sure they'd turn our fingers black or green, but still, I quickly bought two and brought them back to the hotel in a paper bag.

"You don't have to wear it on your finger," I said, sheepishly and apologetically. "You could wear it on a chain. They only cost a dollar." I was positive she wouldn't go for the idea. But when she took the rings out of the bag, she smiled and kissed me and slipped one immediately on her index finger (they were a tad big). Those dollar rings were the first tangible symbol of our commitment as a couple, and we wore them constantly for two years, until we upgraded to sterling bands. (Magically, our first rings never even tarnished.)

For lesbian and gay couples, the meaning of the gesture of exchanging rings or other items is the same as it is for straight couples—the expression or marking of a new level of commitment to each other. Yet because we can't legally marry, the meaning remains a purely metaphoric one. "Our rings are a symbol of our union," explains Tennessean Joy Nelson of the matching rings she and her partner Carlena Calhoun wear. "They show the world our love for each other. They can keep us from being legally married, but they can't change the reality of it."

One couple I spoke to had commitment piercings—but the meaning was essentially the same as if they'd exchanged rings. At a Chicago tattoo shop, "Dalia got a special ring high up in her ear," Barbara describes, "and I got my navel pierced. We wanted to suffer a little for this symbol of commitment."

For Vanessa Marshall and Santa Molina, both deeply spiritual women, exchanging waist beads symbolized their feelings for each other. In the Southwestern desert, they planned to participate in a Native ceremony for women. The week before the ceremony, they sat together in their tent, threading each other's bands with tiny beads, about three hundred for each. "With each bead," explains Vanessa, "we would make a wish or promise or blessing."

"We talked while we did it," Santa says. "Every time we threaded a

"I think it's good for couples to learn how to balance what they need to do to develop themselves as individuals with what they need to do as a couple."

bead, we got to exchange what it was we were wishing." Then, at the opening ceremony, they dressed in white and quietly adorned each other with the waist beads, not telling anyone else the significance of what they were doing. "But people noticed. They said, 'Look at you, you're glowing,'" Vanessa recalls.

Most of the couples I interviewed, though, found rings to be the preferred way to demonstrate that their relationship had taken a turn toward "forever." Several couples told me that, because the gesture symbolized so much to them and was, in fact, the only way to formalize their relationship, they had taken the extra time to design their own rings. Wanda, a chiropractor, and Mildred, a psychologist, are both originally from Puerto Rico. They have been together for ten years, and though they never wanted to spend money on a big wedding ("I'd rather travel!" says Mildred), they did exchange rings about one year into their relationship. The couple had the rings made-to-order by a local lesbian artist.

"We wanted to reflect our commitment and how we saw each other in this relationship," Wanda explains. The rings employ different Native American motifs—a square for equality; an eye for intuition; a circle for everlasting love; a bird for freedom; and a wave of water for clarity. "Then there are arrows pointing in four directions, which is really about being able to feel free to go anywhere we want, like arrows, to change, and then come back," Wanda explains.

> "*Dalia got a special ring high up in her ear, and I got my navel pierced. We wanted to suffer a little for this symbol of commitment.*"

Peggy and Nancy Frantz-Geddes of Oregon had a goldsmith craft their specially designed gold rings with six diamonds in them. "The main diamond is a trillium cut with smaller square diamonds along two sides," Peggy describes. "The triangle is a symbol of the gay community."

Pink triangles were used by the Nazis to label homosexuals in concentration camps, and black triangles denoted women who were prostitutes and social outcasts (in all likelihood, many of them were lesbians). Though a negative reminder of a oppressive past, the triangle has been appropriated and reclaimed by the lesbian and gay community as a symbol of pride and survival, and many people wear jewelry with the triangle motif. (See sidebar "Male [and Female] Order," for some mail order companies that carry gay-themed jewelry.)

For Midwesterners Jim Donovan and Dave Moore, silver rings with gold triangles symbolize both their twenty-year commitment to each other and their pride in being gay. Like other couples I spoke to, Jim and Dave's rings were upgrades from earlier, plainer bands. Christine Mazurkiewicz

MALE (AND FEMALE) ORDER

If the two of you have gotten around to saying, "This is going to last," and you don't want plain bands from the local department store, queer-owned mail order companies stock a variety of lesbian- and gay-specific rings, earrings, and bracelets among their other merchandise, in designs such as pink, black, or gold triangles, rainbow bands, and male/male or female/female symbols. **Poncé**, which donates a portion of its proceeds to AIDS services, carries a wide variety of rings, pendants, bracelets, and earrings; its toll-free number is (800) 969-RING. **Shocking Gray** is a mail-order company out of San Antonio, Texas, which can be reached at (800) 344-4729. **Don't Panic** carries rainbow-themed jewelry and has stores in California, New York, and Provincetown; their toll-free order number is (800) 45-PANIC. They also have an online catalog that can be accessed at http://www.dont-panic.com. **Tzabaco** is a "lesbian and gay general store" that has both a mail-order catalog [(800) 856-1667] and a Web site, accessible at http://www.tzabaco.com. In addition, **GayWebWorld** provides links from its home page to lesbian and gay mail-order companies and catalogs; their URL is http://www.gay-webworld.com. Lesbian and gay bookstores often do mail order and carry jewelry as well as books—the *Gayellow Pages* ($16; order from P.O. Box 533, Village Station, NY, NY 10014; 212-674-0120) will point out the store nearest you, as well as if there are lesbian and gay jewelers in your area.

and Pamela Teal, co-owners of a lesbian mail-order company in New Jersey called Thunder Road Books, even told me how much their ring upgrade cost—an indication of both better finances and an increased commitment over the six years they've been a couple. "We got $19.99 gold bands for our three-year anniversary," Christine says, "and $199.00 gold and diamond bands for our six-year anniversary."

Terri and Belinda, who live in upstate New York, have had three separate sets of rings over their eleven-year relationship, and they wear them all at the same time as a collective symbol of the evolution of their commitment. "The first one we got after we'd been together about a year," Terri recalls. "We wanted to wear matching rings to show our bond to each other." For their commitment ceremony, they had amethyst and peridot (their birthstones) rings made by a lesbian jeweler, and they wear both the first and second bands on their left ring fingers. To mark their tenth anniversary, they ordered diamond rings from the same lesbian jeweler, and those they wear on their right hands.

Though they considered upgrading their rings for their twentieth anniversary, Karin and Maria Kaj opted to spend the money on a fabulous lesbian cruise instead. "Our rings are plain gold bands that we rarely take off," Karin says. "We bought them when we were poor working students. The dent in my ring finger is intense. I'm proud of it." She remembers seeing her father take his wedding ring off once to wash his hands, and admiring the deep, untanned mark it had left on his finger. "I thought it was cool. I pointed it out to him and he laughed and said, 'I'll never pass for single!' I always expected my relationship with Maria to last and maybe that's because my folks have been married for forty years."

Like Karin and Maria, many couples purchase and exchange matching, traditional gold bands that they wear on their left hands. The choosing of them can be a special and significant task, as it was for Chase and Grant,[4] who live in the Southwest and have been together twelve years. The couple made the purchase of their bands into a spontaneous ceremony. "During our second year together," Chase says, "we talked about getting rings but weren't serious about it." Then, while vacationing in Provincetown, they were inspired by the blocks and blocks of gay-owned stores along Commercial Street, the main drag, and embarked on a spur-of-the-moment ring-shopping expedition. "We found traditional wedding bands," Chase relates, "and ended up buying them. We put them on each other's fingers right then and kissed in front of the clerk—to make it official." (For more stories of private ceremonies with rings, see chapter 3.)

Chicagoans Tim and Mario also wear plain matching bands, but on the middle fingers of their left hands, because of a tradition in Europe rather than in this country. Tim, who is Italian, explains, "it's not uncommon to wear them on that finger. It is the heart finger."

Ring placement can a big discussion among lesbian and gay couples. Do we risk looking like heterosexuals if we wear them on our left ring fingers? Or does wearing them on the left hand assert our right to marry? Katie and I recently saw a young man at the supermarket whom, if we'd spotted him in Greenwich Village or Chelsea, we both would have taken for gay. But he had a baby in tow and wore a gold band on his left hand, and we were momentarily perplexed. We decided that he was, in fact, gay and claiming his right to marriage and fatherhood, just like heterosexuals do.

"First I wore mine on my right hand," Fran Goldstein says of the matching bands she and partner Tracey Lind wear. "I figured, 'Well, I'm not heterosexual.' Then I decided at one point that I kind of wanted to claim that symbol of our relationship, so I switched to the left hand." In fact, more and more lesbian and gay couples seem to be following suit, wearing their rings on the traditional "marriage" finger.

Tracey, an Episcopal priest in New Jersey, recalls that she immediately began wearing her ring on her left hand. She wasn't out to the entire parish at that time, but only a ninety-seven-year-old parishioner commented. "He said, 'What did you do? Did you go get married over the weekend?' " she laughs. "It was too complicated to explain it to him. But he was the only one who mentioned it." Now, as they approach their tenth anniversary and Tracey is officially out to her parish, the two are considering buying plain gold bands, which are more traditional.

Tradition, in fact, seems to be as important to lesbian and gay couples as it is to straight ones. Many couples told me wonderful stories about rings that had been passed down through their families, starting out as symbols of heterosexual marriages, but eventually coming to rest on a lesbian or gay man's hand. The ring Timothous Mack gave Edward Jones—a round garnet with a diamond on either side—had been in his family for four generations, "handed down from my great-grandmother to my grandmother to my mother to me," he explains proudly. Without any alterations whatsoever, "it fit him perfectly," Timothous smiles. They purchased a similar ring for Timothous, only his has a pear-cut emerald. Because the couple couldn't really afford it on their own, Timothous's uncle generously picked up the tab for the ring—an amazing show of support for their relationship by an extended family member.

Like Timothous, Paul also had an heirloom ring for his beloved. He and Craig met in Vancouver at a swimming competition at Gay Games III back in 1990. "We used to joke about not getting 'married' until it was legal," remembers Paul. "Then Craig would say, 'I don't see a diamond on my finger!' and wanted to know how I could be asking him to marry me without putting a diamond on his finger."

Paul's great-grandmother had four diamond rings, which were intended for Paul and his three brothers to give to their girlfriends when they got engaged. But in Paul's case, there would be no fiancée. "So a couple of years ago, we were meeting my parents in Hawaii," Paul relates, "and I asked them to bring my ring. I proposed to Craig in Hawaii, and we've been planning a wedding ceremony since then."

Cris Williamson and Tret Fure. Together for more than fifteen years.

© Irene Young

Sometimes, the tradition doesn't go back quite that far. Women's music pioneer Cris Williamson related to me the moving story of how she and partner of sixteen years, musician Tret Fure, came to wear matching bands. After Cris's father died, her mother put his wedding ring away. Her mother eventually remarried, and at that time put away her own ring from her first marriage. "My mother doesn't have much use for the past," Cris observes. "But I have every use for it. Her past is *my* past. And I value it so much. Maybe because I travel a lot, I love those memories."

So Cris negotiated a continued life for her parents' matching wedding rings. "I said, 'Well, Mom, if it's all right, I'd like to have the rings.' She said, 'Oh, of course, honey' and gave them to me. So Tret and I wear my parents' wedding rings. It's very nice. It binds us to our families."

Surprisingly, even lesbians and gay men who swear off heterosexual traditions, saying they hate ceremonies and feel uncomfortable with the whole idea of "marriage," often succumb to exchanging rings. Why? "I wanted something symbolizing our love," says Cheryl of the rings she proposed to her partner, Julie. Though they didn't want any kind of ceremony, the day Cheryl and Julie exchanged their rings has become a sort of anniversary to them, which they call "Ring Day."

"We didn't call them wedding rings," says Richard Burns of the wide gold bands he and his partner, Tom, wore throughout most of their thirteen-year relationship. "Tom was even more fiercely opposed to the concept of marriage than I was at the time."

Tom had inherited a plain gold band from his grandfather, which Richard always admired. One Christmas after they'd been together two years, Tom had a similar band made for Richard and gave it to him as a present. "I was very moved by that," Richard remembers. Though they never formally committed to each other, Richard's ring held a clear emotional meaning for him. When he and Tom broke up and Richard took his band off, it was a devastating experience. "It was part of my emotional process of letting go," he says.

Louise Murray and Liza Fiol-Matta are uncomfortable with vows and claim they will never say "forever" to each other. "Now here comes the great contradiction," Louise grins. "We gave each other rings! And they mean just what you'd think they mean—commitment."

Louise, who is half Dutch, was in Holland taking care of her terminally ill mother, and Liza came from the United States for a long visit. They had already ordered their matching rings, and the day Liza was scheduled to return home, they picked a romantic spot to exchange them. "We went to Amsterdam and sat on a stoop near the canal," Louise recalls. "I can never find it, but Liza knows where it is. We actually took a picture of our hands after we gave each other the rings, and we have it in a frame." She laughs again at the seeming contradiction of exchanging symbols of commitment while not wanting to formally commit. "Go figure," she says.

The universality of lesbians and gay men—of many ages and races, living in all areas of the country—exchanging commitment rings strikes me as very moving. The rituals of heterosexuals, like engagement, don't include us, but we still find ways to pledge our love to each other.

But an obvious question also arises. When heterosexual couples go to jewelers to buy wedding rings, they're greeted with respect and hearty congratulations even from strangers, who immediately want to know if they've set the date. It's part of the excitement of the occasion. Obviously, if lesbians and gay men purchase rings from queer jewelers, they'll get a lot of similar good will and support. But we don't always have access to gay suppliers, and since lesbian and gay relationships don't often elicit happy or celebratory reactions from the straight world, I wondered if the actual process of buying or ordering commitment rings had caused problems for any couples.

"Gay money is still gay money," notes Andrew cynically, when he recalls how he and his partner Mano had no difficulties purchasing matching rings in Bangkok, Thailand. "We were very upfront about the fact that we were buying them for each other, but the merchant seemed unflustered."

In New York City, Paula DiDonato got matching rings a year ago with her partner, Judy Teeven, from a jeweler a friend knew. "A little Italian guy," she explains. "We were both very nervous because I thought, here's this older man in his little jewelry shop. What is he going to think?" But her own fears proved to be unfounded. "There was just no question on his part," she says. "He was wonderful."

"It was fun and exciting, coming out to jewelers," says Dakota, who bought an engagement ring for her partner, Casey, at a Seattle mall. While she was shopping around, the salesclerks asked her who the ring was for. "Well, my girlfriend," Dakota answered honestly. "I'm going to ask her to marry me." Dakota notes that "it was really neat how accepting almost everyone was with that."

> "It was fun and exciting, coming out to jewelers."

But New York City and Seattle are hardly Middle America. Other couples had some difficulties before they were able to purchase their rings. "The first jeweler we went to was kind of shocked," says Lisa, who lives with her partner, Karen, in the Midwest. About a year ago, they went to a suburban mall to purchase their rings. Though the jeweler agreed to size them, Lisa and Karen didn't like the vibes they picked up from her and told her they preferred to look around.

The next store they went into, however, was different. "I don't know if they were gay or not, but these guys were great," Lisa relates. "He was like, 'Oh, okay, cool.' He was really nice about it and happy for us. He said, 'Oh, these are going to be beautiful rings!' "

At about the same time, Mark and Andy, who live in New England, found that the first two jewelers they dealt with were difficult. "One lady was *very* unhelpful," Mark recalls. "The other place was Tiffany's, where the saleslady said in a rather snobby voice, 'We do not sell men's rings with stones in them!' She then added that they did not sell single earrings." Mark rightly took offense at the assumption that every gay man would want a single earring. "So I said, 'That's a good thing, because I don't wear an earring!' "

For Connecticut resident Deb and her partner, Chris, the process of trying on and buying rings was even more complicated. Chris couldn't help feeling scared of what the jewelers would think if two women tried on rings together. "So I browsed through several stores," Deb says, "with Chris hanging out in the background. I'd pull her forward to ask how she felt about different styles, but I couldn't get her to try anything on."

Overcoming Chris's own fears was a challenge for Deb. But when they found a set of matching rings that were perfect for them at a Service Merchandise store, she finally convinced Chris—who is a manual laborer with very large hands—to try on the "man's" ring in the set. It fit perfectly, and the two filled out a joint credit application to purchase the rings on the spot.

Mark and Andy making a life together.

It wasn't until the clerk started dropping things nervously and repeatedly—their credit application, her pen, Chris's driver's license—that they guessed that the clerk had at first mistaken Chris, who is tall with very short hair, for a man. The salesclerk suddenly understood her error when she read the name "Christine" on the ID. Fortunately, she made a quick recovery, congratulated them, but studiously avoided using Chris's name.

"We walked out of the store," Deb remembers, laughing, "wishing we could stay and watch what happened next. We could picture the scene so clearly, the sweet young thing calling over all the other clerks and stammering, 'I can't believe it! I thought he—I mean she—was a guy. But it was two girls!' "

Popping the Question

When I heard the story of Deb and Chris and the salesclerk, I thought defiantly, "Yeah, two girls—she *better* believe it!" More and more, lesbians and gay men are publicly demonstrating their commitment to their relationships, dispelling their anxieties about how the rest of the world responds to their love. As our community matures and we become increasingly more visible, lesbians and gay men are more comfortable thinking of their relationships as permanent and as worthy of respect as straight ones.

We've all been brought up with the same Hollywood and media images—boy meets girl, boy courts girl, boy and girl get married and start a family. It's drummed into us at an early age. And even if we turn out to be lesbian or gay, many of us would still like the whole nine yards and are angry at being left out simply because we're a minority. Because of our cultural traditions, lesbians and gay men have begun to appropriate the language of heterosexual commitment and reclaim it for our own relationships.

No one was more surprised than I was when I found myself, a few years into my relationship with Katie, actually asking her to marry me. Neither of us really remembers when it was, and I definitely didn't go down on one knee. We're hardly what I'd call traditional—the radicals in both our families, we're ardent feminists, with prejudices against and skepticism about heterosexual marriage. We didn't want a wedding, but we both sensed that some other step or statement was called for in our relationship.

But why did I say "marry"? Couldn't I just say, "Hey, what we've got here is nice—wanna keep doing it forever?" When you get right down to it, I'm from a marrying family (my parents have been together for fifty-five years), and I grew up hearing the romantic stories of how my parents met and married. The words literally popped out of my mouth, and the old cliché about popping the question took on new meaning for me. It seemed like the right thing to say. (And by the way, Katie said yes.)

Though some lesbian and gay couples looked at me like I must be kidding when I asked if they'd had an "engagement" or if one of them had "proposed," a surprising number of couples did use that language for their commitment process. And the fact that one of them said "Will you marry me?" almost always signaled that they would take the next step and have a ceremony or union at a future date, an event that they saw as rounding out their relationship.

"Does This Mean We're Engaged?"—Amy and Suzy

In early 1996, Amy Samonds, a Unitarian minister, was living in Maryland and had come back to her hometown of Charlotte, North Carolina, to visit her grandmother, who was very ill and in the hospital. While in

Charlotte, Amy stayed with friends. Little did she know when she arrived what they were planning for her future.

"I was getting out of an icky relationship," Amy relates. "My friends were bound and determined to set me up with someone. I kept insisting that I was not interested in a relationship at that time, that I was rather enjoying not seeing anyone and wanted to keep it that way for a while."

But, despite Amy's protests, her friends set her up a date with Suzy Reno, the lead singer in a local band. The band, Spunky Tingle, did covers of rock, folk, and new country music—a mix of songs that each band member liked. Amy remembered Suzy from having met her briefly several months earlier and hearing her sing with the band. Suzy had also been in an "icky" relationship, but it had ended and both women were available.

The night of their first date, they closed down the restaurant where they went to eat, Suzy remembers. "It was two hours of just being enraptured in conversation. It was one of those experiences where you can't talk fast enough or find out about the person fast enough. I didn't want it to end when the coffee shop closed."

Because neither of them wanted to leave, they sat in the car for a while listening to music. Suzy, who describes herself as shy, overcame her inhibitions. "I sang for her," she recalls, "which is very, very unusual for me, when I've just met someone, to sing for them privately. Yeah, I sing in a band, but a microphone makes a whole lot of difference."

Kris Pratt pops the question to Candace Gingrich on her birthday.

Amy was scheduled to return to Maryland, but having met Suzy made her decide to stay in town. Their connection had been immediate. "It was there physically and emotionally and intellectually and spiritually," Suzy notes. "It just clicked." By the second date, Amy had already confessed that she was falling in love.

"Suzy was playing soccer in the freezing cold," Amy remembers. "I canceled something else so I could watch her play. And Suzy came off the field at one point and I said, 'Okay, I am not even going to try to be coy—I obviously like you a lot to be sitting outside, freezing.' " Amy used the word "smitten" to describe her feelings to Suzy. "She went and looked it up in the dictionary, already knowing full well what it meant," Amy laughs. "She wanted to read it out loud so we could both hear what it meant."

Within a couple of months, Amy had packed up a U-Haul and headed back to Charlotte for good. The two moved in together, "though we would have liked to wait a little longer," Suzy says. "But we were killing ourselves with long distance bills, plane tickets, car mileage, et cetera. We couldn't see Amy getting an apartment and paying rent when we knew we'd be spending all our time together anyway."

In June, Amy and Suzy spent a weekend at the beautiful beach in Huntington State Park in South Carolina. It was there that Suzy got up the nerve to formally propose on June 20, their three-month anniversary.

"We'd been talking about marriage and half-joking about it," Suzy recalls. "But then, we were walking along the beach and I wrote, 'Will you marry me?' in the sand. And she wrote back, 'Yes.' I kind of looked at her and said, 'Does this mean we're engaged?' We squealed. Looks of panic and excitement went across our faces! Suddenly it hit us both that this was very real and it was very intentional and very much a commitment."

Amy and Suzy began planning their ceremony for August 1997. They decided they wanted a public commitment in front of their families and friends to formalize the private one they made that day on the beach. "Couples," explains Amy, "no matter how much they love each other, at some point will need support from people to stay together. Life is hard, and relationships are hard." The homophobia of the outside world adds an extra burden to lesbian and gay unions, one that can be lifted somewhat with the visible support of our loved ones. (See also chapter 4.)

"It's very important to us," says Suzy, "to make a public affirmation that this is not just a relationship, or not just a committed relationship, but that this is a relationship that we're going to go to the mat for."

> "*Couples, no matter how much they love each other, at some point will need support from people to stay together. Life is hard, and relationships are hard.*"

"The Look on His Face" — Shawn and Robert

As romantic as Amy and Suzy's story sounds, Shawn's proposal to Robert took romance to a new level. In the previous chapter, we heard about their meeting as volunteers at the AIDS Dance-a-thon in San Francisco. Though there was an immediate connection and a high comfort level between them, it took Shawn a while (and a few nudges from his friends) to realize that Robert might actually be "the one." Over the course of a year, the two dated, got to know each other better, and spent more time

"No More 'Homophobia'"

BY ZOY KAZAN

. . . WHEN I WAS LIVING a heterosexual lifestyle and reaping the benefits of married status, I was completely unaware of the fact that with my marital status came not only a large party and gifts like toaster ovens and blenders but a complete set of social institutions and services to support me and my heterosexual family. When I was in it, I didn't notice it or consider it particularly remarkable, but when I became involved with a woman years later and found myself on the outside of that exclusive club, I realized that those social supports that had seemed my right as a human being now were not available to me. The way my husband had automatically been included in invitations to social events or family gatherings, or the ease with which I could get a credit card, or the fact that I never once was afraid that my child would be taken away from me because society didn't approve of me, or the fact that I could hide behind my married status to avoid unwanted sexual advances from other men. None of the other mothers worried about leaving the kids with me for the afternoon because I was seen as "normal" and therefore safe and acceptable. And no one ever made rude or intrusive comments about my sexuality—my right to privacy on that score was never challenged. All of these examples come to mind with no trouble at all these days, since I can take none of this for granted as a lesbian.

Changing our words and shifting our thinking can actually expand the possibilities for heterosexuals who want to be supportive allies. Last year, the brother of a friend of mine decided that he and his woman partner would not get married because he didn't see why he should enjoy the social sanction of heterosexual matrimony when his lesbian sister and her long-term partner were barred from this community blessing. Ever since I heard that story, my mind has been playing out scenarios: What would it be like if all my heterosexual friends and

together. Their relationship progressed from there as many couples' relationships do—the nights they spent together became more and more frequent, until it became ridiculous to maintain two apartments.

"He was living in San Francisco," Shawn recalls, "and I lived in Oakland. I was spending more time at his apartment than at my apartment. We would trade off weekends occasionally. It just got to the point where I said, 'We really need to decide if this is going to go forward and if it is, what we're going to do about it.'" And that made Robert announce that what he wanted to do for their one-year anniversary was go apartment hunting.

Like many couples, both Shawn and Robert wanted to live in an entirely new space. "I didn't want to move into his apartment, and he didn't want to move into mine," Shawn relates. "We were adamant about that." Instead of apartment-hunting, what they actually did was shop for a

relatives, clients and neighbors, rejected their privileges and made public statements about why they were doing so?

Imagine this: Heterosexuals boycotting movies that only show heterosexual romance or heterosexual lifestyles, or picketing ones that offer denigrating views of lesbians, gays, and bisexuals. Heterosexual couples refraining from holding hands or kissing in public in order to experience what it is like for lesbian and gay couples every day. Straight allies refusing to buy insurance policies that don't recognize same-sex domestic partners, or writing letters to local newspapers challenging antigay statements and gay/lesbian invisibility in new lands and policies. What if large numbers of heterosexuals protested the way immigration doesn't recognize the right of lesbians and gays to emigrate to the United States to be with a same-sex partner? What if straights refused to send their children to schools that banned discussion about homosexuality as a reasonable lifestyle? What if they spoke out in churches, mosques, and synagogues that teach that homosexuality is a sin or perversion? Imagine what a powerful message it would send if every straight ally in the United States withdrew their sons from Boy Scouts of America in protest of its exclusion of gays?

. . . Recently, I went to the movies with a straight friend and I was touched by the way she brought up the fact that the movie we had just seen insulted lesbians and gays in small, casual ways. I was gratified to realize that she saw it, too. I hope she would have also had that discussion with her straight friends. Not because it's politically correct, not because it's trendy to be "multicultural," but because when something is unfair it should bother everyone. I don't expect all heterosexual couples not to marry, but maybe I want them to do it with some awareness of the benefits they enjoy, and to be relentless in their pursuit of ways to put pressure on the system to include all of us.

house, which they ended up buying together. "That felt like the right thing to do," Shawn says.

Although moving in together was already a big commitment for them, Shawn and Robert both wanted more. "I had always wanted a marriage, a wedding," Shawn admits. "A friend of mine even gave me a wedding planner book. It was like, 'I know you want to get married and here's a little help.' "

When Shawn and Robert went to a friend's wedding in Port Washington, Wisconsin, Shawn made up his mind what he wanted to do. "I had thought long and hard about it," Shawn explains. "I said, this is the person that I could easily spend the rest of my life with. I tried to think what it would be like if he wasn't around anymore. And I really couldn't imagine it. It felt like we'd always been together. And I said, 'Well, that's it.' "

Near their hotel in Port Washington, a city located right on Lake

Michigan, there was a small park. Shawn bought several cards and engaged the help of a few friends to pull off his very elaborate and romantic proposal.

"I left a card in the hotel room that gave very specific instructions," Shawn relates. "It said, 'Listen to this cassette,' and there was a cassette with a beautiful Bette Midler song, which he listened to. Then the tape said, 'Go downstairs and someone will meet you and give you card number two.'"

Downstairs Shawn's friend Karen was waiting to hand Robert a second card, which directed him to go to the park near the hotel with Karen and await further instructions. "I was in the park with my best friend, waiting, with two engagement rings," Shawn says. "Robert and Karen drove up. Robert walked over and I handed him the next card. All it said was, 'Will you marry me?' The look on his face was great. It was priceless. His jaw dropped open."

After a few moments in which Robert was completely stunned and silent, Shawn said, "This usually elicits some kind of response. Can I take that to mean 'Yes'?" And it did mean just that.

One of their friends took a picture of the surprise proposal and framed it. "It was one of our wedding gifts from them," Shawn says. "It shows the look on Robert's face!"

The Six-Year Engagement—Melise and Guillian

Since our engagements and weddings are symbolic and emotional, not ending in a legal state of matrimony, there's no rush to go from the initial question to the assertion of "I dos"—being marginalized means we can take our time. Melise and Guillian, for example, spent a leisurely six years being engaged, something that for a heterosexual couple might indicate hesitancy to finally commit. But for Melise and Guillian, it was simply a question of finding the right day.

Melise Snow had moved to Dallas, Texas, from her hometown in Southern California in 1990. She drove the scenic route, trying to put behind her a ten-year relationship with a straight woman that had ended badly. Soon after relocating, Melise was hanging out at a local lesbian country-western bar called Desert Moon, when an acquaintance introduced her to Guillian Contreras. Coincidentally, Guillian had just ended her eleven-year relationship with a straight woman.

"We didn't really connect or even click," Melise remembers of that first meeting. But the following weekend, Melise returned to the bar, as did Guillian—and this time, they were both alone.

"Guillian just walked up and said, 'Hey, weren't you here last week talking to my friend, Judy?' " Melise smiles. They spent the rest of the night talking to and getting to know each other. "And the rest is history," says Melise.

After several happy months of dating Guillian, Melise decided to celebrate her independence from her prior relationship with a special Christmas present for herself—having a diamond solitaire from her ex remounted as a statement of her freedom. "I told Guillian of my plans," she remembers, "and she wanted to have it done for me. I was touched by her generosity, but I really wanted to do it alone." But Guillian kept asking, and Melise finally agreed to let Guillian give her the ring as a gift, which she notes was "a sign of things to come."

"We upgraded the stone and bought a very unusual setting," Melise says. "What was to be a symbol of my independence became a symbol of our promise and commitment."

They began living together within a few months, moving first into Guillian's house. But after a year, they decided they wanted a new place that would symbolize their life together. "We celebrated our first anniversary having a garage sale in preparation for the move," Melise recalls.

The house they bought together Melise describes as a "storybook cottage, a love nest" on five wooded acres with a pond. Two days after they found it, Guillian proposed.

"Though I'd had long-term relationships, I'd always sworn off taking any kind of vow," Guillian says. "I hadn't met 'the right one' yet."

Then, at a piano bar in Dallas, everything seemed to fall into place. "The pianist was playing Louis Armstrong's 'What a Wonderful World,' " Melise remembers, "and Guillian got all teary-eyed. She leaned over and said, 'Will you marry me?' "

Though Melise said yes right away, they waited to have a commitment ceremony until the anniversary of their first meeting fell on a Saturday, which is what took another six years. "I've often joked," says Melise, "that the only event that's had more advance billing than our wedding is the Second Coming."

When the two women finally got around to having their ceremony, it celebrated not just their future together but also their shared past. And that, as we'll see in the next chapter, is true for many lesbian and gay couples around the country.

"The Most Natural Thing in the World"

Rings, proposals, buying houses together, planning ceremonies—are we more like heterosexuals than we think we are?

Keith Boykin, the executive director of the National Black Lesbian and Gay Leadership Forum, uses a phrase that I love: "We're just like you. Only we're not you." He's specifically talking about black lesbians and gays being just like other black people, only with a difference.

His words, though, can apply to all lesbians and gay men. We're like other people in many ways. We have some of the same cultural assumptions. Many of us want pretty much what everyone else wants—someone to love, a good relationship, a home together. The couples whose stories we've heard in this chapter want all of these things, and they've gone about getting them and keeping them.

But our desires for these basic things are complicated and thwarted just because we're gay. Homophobia has made us into "the other." The fact is, I don't walk around every day thinking, "I'm a lesbian, I'm different." I'm usually too busy working or cooking or hanging out with Katie. Being a lesbian is just a part of me. At the same time, my difference is brought home to me again and again. Sometimes it's overt, and sometimes it's subtle. Katie and I often get harassed on the street if we hold hands, even though we live in New York City. A checkout clerk in the supermarket looks at us funny when we say we're together. Our new gynecologist assumes we care about birth control until we tell her otherwise. Katie mentions her "partner" to one of her students, who grunts "Huh?" in return. (See also the sidebar, "No More 'Homophobia.' ")

Other people's homophobia is exhausting, and it can also exact an emotional toll on a couple. "The isolation lesbians and gay men have experienced in not being visible is profound, and the impact of that on a relationship is profound," says Dr. April Martin. "It's an incredible testimony to the power of loving relationships that so many lesbian and gay couples have survived in isolation." Many young queer kids today, says Martin, still don't know that same-sex relationships last.

It makes perfect sense to me that the biggest civil rights issue for lesbians and gay men in this century has turned out to be the fight for same-sex marriage. Our relationships are a central part of our lives, and like everyone else, we want them to be validated and respected. We've been living together, exchanging symbols of our love, and making commitments to each other for a very long time, all without any help from society or family or the law. That's quite an accomplishment, one we should be proud of and want to affirm.

"This is the most natural and normal thing in the world for me," says Suzy Reno of her desire to marry Amy Samonds. "This is the woman I want to spend the rest of my life with. It's not something I'm going to hide. Our ceremony will be a very public and joyous occasion."

Let's look next at how lesbian and gay couples, without having the option of legal marriage, have created ceremonies, both public and private, to validate their relationships and to profess their love for each other.

Notes

1. The survey of 1,266 couples was limited in its findings to predominantly white, middle-class people.
2. Not their real names.
3. Not his real name.
4. Not their real names.

The Many Meanings of "Marriage"

Marriage as a union of two people has existed throughout the centuries, taking different forms at different times. In ancient China for example, paid matchmakers arranged marriage contracts, consulting horoscopes to determine the compatibility of two individuals who had never met. Throughout medieval and early modern times in Europe, marriage among the aristocracy was a business deal, cementing the wealth and power of the ruling classes; through procreation, married couples ensured the continuance of the noble line. Early Christian marriage was not a sacrament, and only in the twelfth century did the lower classes in Europe begin to be married by the clergy. Right into the modern age, wives and children were considered the property of men, and women swore in their marriage vows to obey their husbands. And courtship and love didn't really figure into most Western marriages until the 1800s. In some Eastern cultures, marriages are still sometimes arranged. So when we speak of "traditional marriage"—a romantic union between one man and one woman—we're talking about something fairly recent and not universally understood.

Over the centuries, many people have been denied access to legal marriage. As early as the fourth century in Rome, same-sex marriage was prohibited. Jews and slaves during the Spanish Inquisition of the 1500s had no marriage rights. In the 1700s in Prussia, blind people couldn't wed. Slaves in antebellum America were likewise forbidden to marry. Under Nazi Germany's Nuremberg Laws, marriages between Jews and Gentiles were *verboten*. And it wasn't until 1967 that the U.S. Supreme

Court finally struck down the miscegenation laws that for centuries had made interracial marriage illegal.

Throughout history, those forbidden to marry have found ingenious ways to get around that prohibition. Many passing women, who assumed the demeanor and dress of men, married other women legally. One such passing woman, Murray Hall, a prominent Tammany Hall politician in nineteenth-century New York, married twice, and his birth gender was not discovered until his death.

More often, those denied legal marriage have created their own rituals, which, though not legal, served a distinct purpose within the oppressed community. Slaves on American plantations, for example, followed their own tradition of jumping the broom, based on African culture, to validate their unions. They were real marriages to the slaves, if not to the masters.

The legal ban on lesbian and gay marriage is a vestige of ancient oppression that continues into our own time. But lesbians and gay men have thumbed their noses at the law and married in their own fashion. Even though the state doesn't recognize our unions, many of us have gone ahead and validated our relationships with private and public ceremonies—testimonies to the power of love in our lives.

"Gee, I Really Love You, and We're Gonna Get Married"

It's an enduring cliché: People cry at weddings. I've done it myself. I've even cried at movie weddings. But why? There's something incredibly compelling about seeing two people stand up in front of their families and friends and make a formal commitment to love each other no matter what—in short, to go through it all together. Weddings are powerful in imagery, and formal marriage vows say that the relationship is way beyond serious, somewhere out there in the realm of the sacred.

Most have us have been brought up with expectations that we'll marry. Our families drop casual and not-so-casual hints about all the wonderful things that will happen at the magic time known as "When you get married . . ." But when lesbians and gay men come out, that door seems to shut forever, because we are legally prohibited from marrying someone of the same gender. Historically, we've had to hide our relationships out of fear and shame; we haven't been given the chance to celebrate them. For many of us, the prospect of never having the powerful ritual of love and devotion that is a wedding can feel like an enormous loss.

For those of us who don't particularly care about having a wedding—

Katie and I, for example, would rather save for a knockout vacation or a house—private ceremonies serve the function of establishing commitment in a very intimate and romantic setting. Only the two parties involved are privy to the vows. Still, the couples who told me they'd had private ceremonies described feeling married just the same.

"Two people couldn't be more married than Wendy and I," says Julie, who worked with me on this book as a researcher and interviewer. She and Wendy have discussed having a commitment ceremony many times over the five years they've been together, but opted for a private one instead. While Julie used to think that public ceremonies and affirmations of vows were important, she's changed her mind over time. "We have said our vows to each other over and over again," she explains. "Our love is so deep and our commitment so strong that I no longer think a public affirmation would change anything."

Elder Zachary Jones performs a commitment ceremony.

© 1993 Donna Binder/Impact Visuals

Fran Goldstein, who has been with her partner, Tracey Lind, for more than nine years, couldn't agree more. A public ceremony isn't necessary for them, she says, simply because "we've done that work. We've made those vows and those promises, and we've exchanged that ring, and I don't need to do it in front of a hundred or two hundred people in order to make it feel real."

Others, though, want the public ceremony they thought they'd never have when they came out as lesbian or gay. In the past half-dozen years especially, we have seen an explosion of public commitment ceremonies celebrating lesbian and gay relationships. There is even a published wedding planner geared to same-sex couples (see the sidebar, " 'Essential' Reading.") The numbers, say the gay and gay-friendly clergy who perform them, are increasing phenomenally. Elder Zachary Jones of Unity Fellowship, a black gay church, relates that when his congregation first started in 1992, he performed about one same-sex wedding a year. "Now, in my calendar starting in February and going on through about September, there's at least two to three weddings per month," Elder Zach observes. "I've connected that to where folks are spiritually and where they feel they sort of fit in to the whole pie of community. People . . . want to create families for themselves, which is so much a part of their value system. It's what we come from."

Rabbi Sharon Kleinbaum of Congregation Beth Simchat Torah, the largest gay synagogue in the world, has to limit the number of ceremonies she performs in a year to just a handful because of her own time constraints, though she refers couples to other sympathetic rabbis. Why are there so many lesbian and gay ceremonies occurring now, at this moment in history? "People are much safer being visible," Rabbi Kleinbaum muses. "Visibility doesn't immediately mean job loss. It doesn't automatically mean family rejection. So people can risk being more visible, and this is as visible as we can get."

For many lesbians and gay men, the reclaiming of both religious and secular wedding ceremonies as a right is an important step toward self-acceptance. "I think at some level, it's the only way that Judy and I were able to proclaim everything we gave up in the past," muses Paula DiDonato of the elaborate wedding at the Rainbow Room in New York City that she and her partner, Judy Teeven, had in June 1996 to celebrate ten years together. "We didn't think we could get married because we were gay. The wedding gave us an opportunity to ask all our friends and family and coworkers to come together and recognize the relationship that we had and how much we loved each other."

Visibility and self-acceptance may explain why, like Paula and Judy, many lesbian and gay couples have commitment ceremonies to pay tribute to their longevity, rather than to signal the beginning of a relationship (as is traditionally the case with heterosexual weddings). "It's typical for me to do a commitment ceremony on somebody's tenth or fifteenth

"The wedding gave us an opportunity to ask all our friends and family and coworkers to come together and recognize the relationship that we had and how much we loved each other"

anniversary," notes Rabbi Kleinbaum. "People have been together, they've been through a lot, have experienced lots of loss and pain and growing up. . . . It's a different place in their lives."

Some clergy have found that more lesbians than gay men are having commitment ceremonies, and my own research seems to bear this out. "More women come to the altar for marriage," states Elder Zachary Jones of his experience performing ceremonies. Why does he think this is true? "I think women are conditioned early in life about commitment. I think also that women tend to be more aware of their own needs much earlier than most men. That's a general statement, but I don't think it's any different from the heterosexual community."

Still, as more and more gay men feel they have "permission" to want commitment and stability in their relationships, more male couples have weddings, too. The AIDS crisis, which has brought home to so many the fragility of life, has been an important factor in the increasing numbers of gay men who are deciding to commit formally to each other. When AIDS threatens to cut short a couple's future, the need for a validation of the union and community recognition of the relationship may be even stronger. "I did one ceremony in a hospital room," says Sharon Kleinbaum, "for a member [of Congregation Beth Simchat Torah] who was just about to die of AIDS. He really couldn't get out of bed. We had a *chuppah* [bridal canopy] over the bed, and his lover stood next to him holding his hands."

Lesbian and gay relationships have been denied the recognition of heterosexual ones, and that has exacted a price for many couples. Without support and validation, it can be harder for same-sex couples to make their relationships work. For many of us, having a ceremony or ritual helps alleviate the isolation of feeling that we're going it alone. "Part of the function of a wedding is to make clear that this union is happening in a community," states Dr. April Martin. "It's to invite the participation of the community to witness the relationship, and to enlist everybody into the responsibility of supporting the union."

Some critics within the lesbian and gay community fear that commitment ceremonies and holy unions simply mean that couples are mimicking heterosexuality. But, on the contrary, there's something inherently transgressive about two women or two men standing up to take vows normally reserved for straight people and asking their families and friends to witness and sanction their union—in effect, *demanding* that people look at the relationship as a committed one. The radical nature of lesbian and gay marriage has made the same-sex marriage debate a hot ticket these last few years, causing religious fundamentalists to foam at the mouth and right-wing legislators to rush to ban it. Lesbian and gay marriage is at heart a subversive act, one that both calls attention to our difference while also outlining our similarities with the rest of the world.

"I didn't get married because I wanted to make a political statement," points out Marjorie Hill, who is, in fact, a very political lesbian. "However, the fact that I am a black lesbian, married in spirit to another black lesbian, is indeed a political act."

Many commitment ceremonies and weddings are primarily political in nature, with lesbian and gay couples taking vows in public spaces, often in front of government buildings, to underline the fact that same-sex couples can't legally marry. These ceremonies happen all over the country, but the largest and showiest was in Washington, D.C., in April 1993, at the third national march for lesbian and gay rights. Three thousand same-sex couples were married in front of the Internal Revenue Service building to demonstrate the inequity with which the U.S. government treats lesbian and gay couples, simply by refusing to acknowledge them. Smaller "wedding actions" take place at different times all across the country. And each day, same-sex couples forthrightly enroll as domestic partners in cities and towns that offer the registry to same-sex couples. (See page 114.)

"Our love is so deep and our commitment so strong that I no longer think a public affirmation would change anything."

We take part in all these ceremonies because they're what is available to us. Our relationships are important, and we want people to know that. Yet though we bind each other together through ceremonies and civil registrations, we still have almost no legal rights as couples. It isn't surprising that same-sex marriage rights have come to the forefront of the lesbian and gay civil rights movement. Since 1970, the year after the Stonewall rebellion, lesbian and gay couples have been trying to marry legally. That year, Jack Baker and Mike McConnell walked up to the counter of the county clerk in Minneapolis and asked for a marriage license; it was denied, and they sued eight different times, unsuccessfully appealing that decision. Various other attempts have been made by same-sex couples over the years, but it was only with a favorable court decision in Hawaii in 1993 that the possibility of same-sex marriage in our lifetimes seemed real. (See "Just Two Guys in Love," page 125.)

In this chapter, we'll talk about the many different varieties of commitment ceremonies and rituals that lesbian and gay male couples have used to celebrate their love over the years. But because the rituals hold mostly emotional and symbolic meaning, we'll also see what couples think about the prospect of legalized same-sex marriage. When lesbians and gay men say "I do," what does it mean now, and what can it mean for our future?

A Private Affair

It's one thing to move in with your partner, blending everything from your silverware to your pets, and it's another to put into words the serious turn a relationship has taken. Again, we're all brought up with heterosexual institutions and traditions, and it's always during the exchange of vows in a wedding ceremony that family and guests start sniffling. Even if we haven't had a wedding, most of us know the traditional vows by heart, or at least the key phrases of them: "to have and to hold," "for better or worse," "till death do us part."

But are words really necessary? Many of the couples I spoke to thought that, in one way or another, speaking your intentions toward your partner was an important part of formalizing a relationship, particularly in lieu of legal marriage. For many, a private exchange of feelings, rings, and vows was vital to cementing the bond between partners.

Though they were ambivalent about public ceremonies, "It was important to both of us to have a private ceremony, just for us," explains Julie of the private vows she took with her partner, Wendy. "It was important to say it out loud . . . together."

Julie and Wendy, who live in suburban Putnam County, New York, have actually had two ceremonies, both of which centered around an exchange of rings. The first occurred the summer after they moved in together. "We exchanged the rings right there in our living room," Julie describes. "We told each other how we felt, how much we loved each other, and how we wanted to stay together forever. Then we put the rings on each other's fingers." Several couples I spoke to mentioned repeating their vows on occasion, but Julie and Wendy make it a daily ceremony.

"At night, our rings sit in a dish of dried flower petals," says Julie. The petals are from flowers they've given each other over the course of their relationship. "We exchange those rings together every morning. It's a way of affirming our love for each other and the lifelong, never-ending commitment that we share."

Four years into their relationship, Julie and Wendy had a separate set of rings made and held a second ceremony. But this one was sort of a private surprise party for Wendy from Julie. When Wendy came home from work one evening, "I had the rings sitting on an Indian wedding vase she had bought me," Julie recalls. "The vase sat in the middle of our living room coffee table, amidst some other mementos. . . . I decorated the room with red heart-shaped balloons and some flowers. We sat at the table, looked through photographs of trips we had taken and holidays we had celebrated." Drinking a toast out of another Indian wedding vase, the couple exchanged the new rings. Then they wrote their vows into a card Julie had bought for the occasion.

Though Julie feels married and can't think of a better term for her relationship with Wendy than "marriage," she still has trouble using the word with people who don't know her and Wendy. When strangers ask if she's married, she still says no—her own homophobia kicking in, unannounced and unwanted. "One day I hope to have the courage to say yes," she says. As it becomes more natural and comfortable for people to come out and admit they're gay, Julie may not have to think twice when someone asks the question.

Like Julie and Wendy, many couples had intimate ceremonies in the privacy of their homes. Marianne and Marie held their ritual in their weekend cabin in the mountains of upstate New York. "We stood in front of a roaring fire," recalls Marianne, "with Anita Baker in the background singing 'You Bring Me Joy.' " Then, they recited the vows they'd written for each other. Even though there was no one else present, Marianne was moved to tears. "I was crying so hard," she says, "when it was my turn to read her the vows I had written, I said, 'Here, read them yourself!' "

For Diane Curtis and Bekki McQuay of Amarillo, Texas, a ceremony at home was not their first choice. After they moved in together, "Bekki and I intended to have a big public ceremony," Diane says. "I had never been so in love and so sure before in my life, and we wanted to marry as soon as possible."

But into their new life together came circumstances beyond their control. In the last chapter (see page 51), we read how Diane's ex-husband sued for custody of their ten-year-old son, Steven[1] and won on the grounds that Diane was a lesbian living with another woman. So, when the messy custody battle hit, the two women tabled their public wedding plans and decided on a private ceremony instead.

"We had our ceremony on December thirty-first in front of our Christmas tree," Diane recalls. "Bekki and I both wrote vows for one another and vows to Steven. We wanted him to feel part of the joining of our family." Because of the turmoil of Diane's divorce and then the custody suit, it was especially important for Steven to play a role in the ceremony.

Despite the fact that the ceremony was informal and at home, Diane and Bekki wanted the celebration to be special. "We struggled over what to wear," she admits. "Something comfortable, but special. We chose silk boxer shorts and cotton T-shirts."

Diane wrote a song for the occasion and played it for Bekki on her guitar. Then they said their vows and a prayer. In addition, they had bought three silver wine goblets—one for Steven, too—with their names etched on them and made champagne toasts after the ceremony.

"Steven was so excited to be part of it," Diane says. "The highlight for me was when I was singing to Bek and she was crying, and I looked at Steven, and he was crying. For the first time in my life, I knew what a wedding really meant."

For Maggie and Kate,[2] their private commitment ceremony fourteen years ago was also dictated by circumstances. Maggie, an ordained minister in a major U.S. religion, could not come out for fear of being stripped of her orders. When Maggie and Kate wanted to have a commitment ceremony, it had to be kept a secret. While the situation is looser in some denominations today, lesbian and gay clergy still have to consider that there may be negative consequences to coming out.

Maggie and Kate had met as teenagers and remained friends through Kate's subsequent marriage to a man. "My husband didn't believe in vacations," Kate says, "so I would take short vacations with Maggie. . . . I would go and visit her. She would come visit two or three times during the course of a year." Their friendship deepened over time into something more.

But it wasn't until Maggie became involved with another woman and started pulling away from Kate that Kate knew she had to put a name to her feelings. "I asked her if I got out of the marriage whether she would marry me," remembers Kate. "And she said yes. I was out of that marriage within a year."

The two women, who were living in different parts of the country, wanted to be together. Maggie decided to give up her parish in Michigan to make a fresh start with Kate in Pennsylvania. As a last move before starting their new life together, they held a private commitment ceremony in Maggie's church.

"Maggie already had her house packed into a twenty-four-foot U-Haul," Kate recalls. Kate flew up to Michigan, and they put a sign on the door of Maggie's church that read, "Your pastor needs some private time to say good-bye." Then they locked the church door.

"We had flowers and candles and communion, which is obviously an important piece of who were are," says Kate. "We said vows and exchanged rings."

The fact that no one witnessed the beautiful ceremony now makes both Maggie and Kate "dreadfully sad, after the fact," Kate allows. "We hope some day to have a recommitment ceremony with all our friends."

Cheryl Lawson and Jennifer Higdon also met as teenagers, in—where else?—the flute section of their Tennessee high school band. They became friends first, then lovers, but were temporarily separated when Jennifer went away to college in Ohio and Cheryl was still in high school. Cheryl's parents made several attempts to break the two girls up, but always unsuccessfully. Instead of giving up, Cheryl and Jennifer focused all their energies on getting Cheryl accepted to Jennifer's college. Two days after graduating from high school, Cheryl moved to Bowling Green, Ohio, to be with Jennifer. They've been together for the fourteen years since then.

After their first seven years together, Jennifer and Cheryl decided that it was important for them to have a ceremony of commitment. "We wanted to make sure the world knew we were planning on being a couple for the rest of our lives," says Jennifer. "As strange as it seems, it was driven by some sort of strong, passionate feeling that this must be done at this time." When I ask why she thinks the feeling was so strong, Jennifer tries to describe it.

"I'm a composer," she says, "and I write music on instinct, and I know that when a strong feeling comes my way that it's the universe saying, 'Hey, pay attention!' " For her, the desire to have a ceremony with Cheryl was that strong a compulsion. "Even though we were already living together and had every intention of being together forever, somehow this felt like we were saying, 'Okay, world, here we are, together as a couple—see the rings?' "

Originally, the women considered a public ceremony, but their families and friends were too spread out across the country, and their own finances as graduate students were too shaky to pull it off. But the two of them did travel back to their home state of Tennessee to exchange their vows, because it was where they met and fell in love, and the location held romantic significance for them.

"It was on a gorgeous August day in the Smoky Mountains National Park," remembers Cheryl. "The ceremony occurred in an area called Cades Cove, which is a beautiful cove nestled in the heart of the park." The spot had been a favorite place for the two of them when they were in school together, and they had enjoyed many special moments there.

Nature seemed to smile on the ceremony. "The fields were full of flowers," Cheryl says, "and there were deer grazing nearby. We said our vows to each other and exchanged rings. It was just me, Jennifer, and God."

> *"The fields were full of flowers, and there were deer grazing nearby. We said our vows to each other and exchanged rings. It was just me, Jennifer, and God."*

Tradition! Tradition!

Cheryl and Jennifer believe that God was present at and smiling on their commitment ceremony. Many of us are brought up experiencing religion as a solace and comfort, and we seek it out in our adult lives, too, only to find that many religious denominations don't practice the love and tolerance they preach. As we have already discussed, many conservative clergy members still point to ancient and misinterpreted quotations from the Bible, which decry homosexuality as an "abomination."

And so, lesbians and gay men have created their own congregations for worshiping, beginning with the founding of the Metropolitan Community Church (MCC) in Los Angeles by Reverend Troy Perry in 1968. Within two years, Perry's MCC congregation had five hundred members. Today, there are MCC churches across the country; the largest one, the Cathedral of Hope in Dallas, has approximately three thousand members.

While working on this book, I met some wonderful lesbian and gay clergy, whose congregations offer warm and supportive environments to lesbian and gay people. "People come to church," says Elder Zachary Jones of his predominantly black gay congregation, Unity Fellowship Church, "and discover that God is not against them for being homosexual." Rabbi Sharon Kleinbaum of Congregation Beth Simchat Torah in New York calls CBST a community that functions as a sort of family of choice. "Holiday celebrations and shabbas are very important to people," she says. "Meals are done together. These connections are very central to the lives of lesbians and gay men."

Still other lesbians and gay men have found nurturing nongay congregations with tolerant and supportive clergy members. And the increased visibility of lesbian and gay churchgoers has allowed many clergy to come out of the closet. Little by little, religion, traditionally an oppressor of lesbian and gay people, is being restored to them, becoming a way to celebrate difference rather than be ashamed of it.

It follows that many lesbian and gay couples who have reclaimed religion have wanted and sought out clergy members to bless their unions. Heterosexual weddings have long been performed by priests, ministers, and rabbis—in fact, in many religious denominations, only those ceremonies performed by clergy are considered valid. For example, I was brought up Roman Catholic, and I knew from a young age that Catholic couples married by a justice of the peace were "living in sin," with all the stigma that carried.

Interestingly, lesbian and gay religious ceremonies have less to do with this idea of stigma—we've long been stigmatized just for being gay—than with the desire for two people to connect spiritually and to have their union blessed. Unlike many heterosexual couples, who have religious ceremonies simply because that's what's expected, many same-sex couples have broadened the meaning of religion in their lives and want their commitment ceremonies to reflect that. "I think people feel a lot of love," says Rabbi Kleinbaum, "and want to share it and do it in a manner that feels like they're spiritually bonded in a deeper way."

One lesbian couple, Paula DiDonato and Judy Teeven, were both raised Roman Catholic, and they were sure at first that they didn't want a traditional, religious wedding. "We started with, we'll have friends do a toast and talk about different things," says Judy. But as they got into the planning of their ceremony, the purpose and meaning of "committing" became clearer to them.

"When you start to define what it is you're going to commit to," says Paula, "there becomes another dimension that is beyond this earth. You're really committing to something much bigger than the two of you. And so it's really hard to identify the language or even the context of what you're doing if you completely leave out spirituality."

Unfortunately, it is sometimes hard for lesbian and gay couples to find clergy willing to officiate at their weddings, and many denominations specifically prohibit their clergy members from blessing same-sex unions. But the list of those who will officially bless lesbian and gay commitment ceremonies is growing. (See the sidebar, "True Tolerance.")

In denominations like the Episcopal Church, in which the church's official position is nebulous and unstated, certain ministers will preside at same-sex weddings because of their own conscience and politics. "Gay and lesbian blessings take place in liberal dioceses," says Reverend Tracey Lind, an out lesbian Episcopal priest. "There is no official rite, but there is a proposal to create such a rite." That proposal was struck down at the Episcopal General Convention in July 1997, but by a margin of only one vote. Its backers remain hopeful that the church will formally sanction same-sex marriage at the next convention in the year 2000.

Reverend Robert Warren Cromey, who is himself heterosexual, performs blessings for same-sex couples at his Episcopal parish in San Francisco. For Cromey, same-sex marriage is the same as heterosexual marriage, because lesbians and gay men enter into it for the purpose of lifelong union, just as straight couples do. Cromey argues that modern church doctrine must adapt to fit the times, instead of rigidly following ancient, outmoded precepts. (See the sidebar, "The Sacrament of Same-Sex Marriage.")

TRUE TOLERANCE

On December 3, 1968, Reverend Troy Perry of the Los Angeles Metropolitan Community Church performed the first same-sex religious ceremony in U.S. history. Neva Joy Heckman and Judith Ann Belew exchanged rings and spoke their vows in their L.A. home. A California statute allowing a common-law union to be formalized by a religious ceremony and a church certificate of marriage made the ceremony possible. The courts, however, ruled the union invalid, citing that the state law specified "man and woman." Since that time, Reverend Perry has personally officiated at about one thousand holy unions for lesbian and gay couples. By his estimation, MCC performs approximately two thousand such unions a year all across the country.

Denominations nationwide are debating whether or not to recognize and perform ceremonies for same-sex marriages. Here are some denominations and houses of worship that have affirmed lesbian and gay unions.

American Baptist
Brethren/Mennonite
Buddhist (all sects)
Episcopal Church
Metropolitan Community Church
Presbyterian Church (U.S.A.)
Quakers (Society of Friends)
Methodist Metropolitan Community Church
Reconstructionist Judaism
Reformed Catholic Church (U.S.A.)
Reform Judaism (Central Conference of American Rabbis)
Unitarian Universalist Church
United Church of Christ
Unity Fellowship Churches

One clear advantage to same-sex couples having religious ceremonies is that many clergy members who perform them also do pre-wedding counseling, just as they do for straight couples. These counseling, or pre-Cana, sessions are the closest thing lesbian and gay couples have to relationship advice—how to make it work—before problems set in. "It got us thinking," says Casey, of the sessions she attended with her partner, Dakota, "about how we viewed the relationship and what our goals were and if we were both coming from the same angle. . . . It helped us clarify a lot of our values and things that maybe, when you're going full speed ahead in a relationship, you really don't touch on."

Because of the nature of same-sex relationships, which take place outside of a defined or legalized structure, Rabbi Sharon Kleinbaum thinks pre-wedding counseling serves an important function for couples. "In the gay and lesbian world," she says, "we tend to lurch from relationship issue to relationship issue. But we don't really sit back and say, 'Is this the person I want to commit to and why do I want to do it?' . . . We tend to typically just start acquiring things together and that starts to be the indication of a commitment. And all of a sudden, you turn around and you have property and financial intermingling but have never really thought about what the

"The Sacrament of Same-Sex Marriage"

BY REVEREND ROBERT WARREN CROMEY

I WAS ASKED if I believed the marriage of same-sex partners was the same as the sacrament of marriage between opposite-sex couples. The question arose after my appearance on ABC's television program *Turning Point,* which aired on Thursday, November 7, 1996. I had allowed the taping of a same-sex marriage in Trinity Church, San Francisco, where I am rector.

Yes, same- and opposite-sex marriage *is* the same.

The articles of faith in the 1978 *Book of Common Prayer,* page 857, says, "The sacraments are the outward and visible signs of inward and spiritual grace, given by Christ as sure and certain means by which we receive that grace." The outward and visible signs in marriage are two people. The inward and spiritual grace is the couple's vows and the assurance of God's blessing on the couple.

Marion Hatchett's book, *Commentary on the American Prayer Book,* page 579, says, "Augustine defined sacrament as a 'sign of a sacred thing,' and medieval theologians stressed the fact that a sacrament not only signified but conveyed what it signified." Marriage conveys what it signifies. Marriage conveys vows of fidelity, lifelong union, and love. One doesn't have to be of the opposite sex to convey the significance of marriage.

We also know that the ministers in the marriage are not the clergy, but the couple. This means that the sacrament of marriage happens with or without the clergy and the church. It happens when the couple chooses to enter into the covenant of marriage. They may go to the church and ask the assistance of the clergy for counsel, prayer, and, in the American church, sign some legal documents. These have nothing to do with the sacramental nature of the marriage. The church is ready to assist straight people but not gays and lesbians.

The Book of Common Prayer continues on page 861 with, "Holy Matrimony is Christian marriage, in which woman and man enter into a lifelong union, make their vows before God and the Church, and receive the grace and blessing of God to help them fulfill their vows."

I believe that same-sex couples enter marriage and holy matrimony when they "enter into a lifelong union, make their vows before God and the Church, and receive the grace and blessing of God to help them fulfill their vows."

It has been my experience that some same-sex couples clearly desire to "enter into a lifelong union." That is their wish, desire, and intent. They "make their vows before God and the church."

I believe they "receive grace and blessing of God to help them fulfill their vows." As celebrant and witness to such blessings, I ask God to give grace and bless the couple. I assume God does that. I am not willing to limit God's grace and blessing in any matter. I assume God graces and blesses same-sex couples as He does opposite-sex couples, just because they ask for God's blessing and grace. We have no proof that God provides those gifts, we accept on faith that He does—for opposite-sex as well as same-sex couples.

Paul's words are that marriage is the sign of the mystical union between Christ and His church. The personal and sexual intimacy between the couples speaks of a deep connection, unity, and bonding. That intimacy is a sign of our oneness with God and all creatures. The exhilaration of sexual and orgasmic union reflects the creative, intimate, and explosive character of divine energy available to all human beings. That intimacy happens to same-sex couples as well as opposite-sex couples. It is not dependent on procreation. It is dependent on robust sexual connection, trust, love, and joy.

Some say the purpose of marriage is procreation. *The Book of Common Prayer* indicates three purposes of marriage. "The union of husband and wife in heart, body, and mind is intended by God for their mutual joy: for the help and comfort given one another in prosperity and adversity; and, when it is God's will, for the procreation of children."

While same-sex couples cannot have children biologically, they are quite capable of having children by adoption, in vitro fertilization, and foster care. The church allows straight couples to be married who are too old to have children, who are not physically able to have children, or just plain don't want children. Procreation is not a necessary requirement for marriage. Same-sex couples can pledge each other mutual joy, help, and comfort in prosperity and adversity without the expectation of procreation.

I also believe that God enters human history and brings about change in the social order. Saul and David were permitted many wives. Jesus said a man should not divorce his wife. We know now that men could divorce wives, but women could not divorce husbands. Jesus's proscription of divorce was to protect women and not marriage. Even the idea of faithful, lifelong monogamy was a development within the Jewish people of God from a society that permitted polygamy.

We know that slavery in many varied forms was permitted in Jewish and Christian societies. Heroes like Wilberforce in England and the abolitionists in the United States felt called by God to abolish the institution of slavery. I believe God acted in and through these prophets to change existing religious notions, bring freedom to people in bondage and offer them full humanity.

The church once held that the ordination to the priesthood was reserved for men. God acted in and through the church to bring about change and justice so that women are ordained priest and bishop. We know that all Christians do not agree with this change. But the church, her rules, theology, and liturgies are always changing and developing.

Cuthbert Simpson's old book, *Revelation and Response,* indicated God reveals himself in human history and we, God's people, respond, change, and develop, as did the ancient prophets and people of Israel.

Jesus indicated the law was made for man, not man for the law. The sacraments are made for man, not man for the sacraments. The laws and sacraments of the church now say marriage is only for heterosexuals. I believe God reveals to us today a new creation, a new being, a new phenomenon. We live in a time when some same-sex couples want to enter lifelong faithful relationships.

Some homosexuals, not all by any means, want to vow to be with each other "to have and to hold from this day forward, for better for worse, for richer for poorer, in sickness and in health, to love and to cherish, until we are parted by death." They want to make a solemn vow.

The writers of Leviticus didn't face this. Paul never heard of such a thing. The ancient fathers, the theologians, the reformers, the writers of prayer books and liturgies never faced a situation where same-sex couples came to the church asking for a blessing, a marriage, a wedding ceremony, or a nuptial mass. Homosexuality in the past was seen only as fun for the initiated, and perversity and abomination and immorality by the church at large. We are in a new world now. God is revealing new things through our homosexual brothers and sisters. They are not going away. They will always be with us no matter how badly we treat them.

God's law on social custom is not immutable. It has always changed and will continue to do so. The sacrament of marriage is nowhere near the doctrine of the Incarnation, the Trinity, and Eucharist in power and strength. Even in those we know there is a wide variety of interpretation about those great statements of belief. The doctrine of Christian marriage must be expanded to include the marriage of same-sex persons if it is their desire to seek the blessing of God through the church. Neither the church nor the sacrament of marriage needs protection. They are large enough in heart and compassion to expand even further to include the new being of homosexual love and marriage.

This article first appeared online. Reprinted with permission of the author.

relationship is about and how the soul is being fed." Sometimes the sessions help couples realize that they are not on the same track and don't want the same things out of the relationship.

Elder Zachary Jones believes that the lack of role models for lesbian and gay couples can have a negative effect on relationships, even those that are celebrated with a commitment ceremony. For many, the only model is that of their parents, who may or may not have had a positive relationship. "The idea [for counseling sessions] was to ensure . . . that we at least begin some dialogue about what this thing called marriage is. And what does it mean to same-sex couples," says Elder Zach. Over a period of six months, couples discuss everything pertaining to a relationship—romance, sexuality, roles, finances, family, and communication. Of the dozens of couples Elder Zach has married over the past five years, only one has broken up so far.

The number and variety of religious same-sex weddings is a stunning testimony to the power of faith in people's lives, particularly people who have repeatedly been told they are "sinners" because of the way they love. That faith is as much in themselves and their commitment to each other as in a higher being, as the stories of lesbian and gay weddings attest.

"So Traditional"—Deacon and Jim

Lesbian and gay commitment ceremonies have been getting a lot of attention recently, and we've even seen them depicted on prime-time sitcoms like *Friends* and *Roseanne*. But in fact, couples have been having religious ceremonies to celebrate and bless their unions for years. Deacon Mac-Cubbin and Jim Bennett, co-owners of Lambda Rising Bookstore in Washington, D.C., held their ceremony back in 1982, before it was common to do so.

Deacon describes himself, laughingly, as "so traditional." After he and Jim had been together two years, Deacon took Jim aside and said, "I have something very important to ask you. This is no joke, and there are only two acceptable answers—'Yes' or 'Not today.' Will you marry me?"

Jim laughed at first, even though Deacon had warned him it wasn't a joke. Proposing marriage was not a part of gay male culture in 1980, but marriage was what Deacon wanted for their relationship. Finally, Jim realized Deacon was serious and so responded simply, "Not today." And almost every day for the next two years, Deacon asked the same question, always getting a "Not today" response. One day, Jim's answer changed to "Maybe someday, but not today."

Deacon was so used to his partner's waffling that two years later, when Deacon asked the question again, he got a surprise. Jim finally said yes, informing Deacon, "You know, I said yes almost two weeks ago, but you didn't hear me! I figured you'd ask again!"

Because they assumed they'd marry only once and for life, Deacon and Jim wanted to do the event up right. They took a full six months to plan their wedding, "and we needed every day of it," Deacon grins. Reflecting his and Jim's tastes, the ceremony was traditional, but they personalized it in distinct ways. Their wedding theme, for example, was quintessentially gay. "We had vacationed in Key West several times," Deacon points out, "so we decided on a tropical theme and filled the church with bird-of-paradise and other tropical flowers." For their rings, they chose gold bands that they designed with a lambda (the Greek letter that has become an international symbol of lesbian and gay rights) on them.

For their officiant, they settled for nothing but the best. "We wanted 'the Gay Pope,'" Deacon laughs of their choice of Reverend Troy Perry, founder of Metropolitan Community Church. It's no wonder they went all out, so to speak: Three hundred and fifty of their "closest friends," including members of the City Council and representatives from the mayor's office, witnessed their commitment.

The two extemporized their vows but didn't fumble for words. "We thought about what we intended to say to each other, but we didn't write our comments in advance," Deacon says. "We preferred to speak from the heart." Though it was an emotional and spontaneous moment, no one tape-recorded or filmed the vows, so Deacon isn't quite sure what they said. "The gist of it was that we promised honesty, compassion, and commitment to each other," he recalls. "And that promise continues to be fulfilled daily."

> "We promised honesty, compassion, and commitment to each other. And that promise continues to be fulfilled daily."

"We've Come This Far by Faith"—Marjorie and Christine

When Marjorie Hill and Christine Edwards said "I do" in June 1996, a year and a half after falling in love, the church was packed with almost as many people as had witnessed Deacon and Jim's wedding. Because of Marjorie's standing in the lesbian and gay community—she was former New York Mayor David Dinkins's liaison to the community and is a nationally known activist—the church was overflowing with politicians, activists, family, and friends. And three hundred people—including Marjorie—had to wait forty-five minutes for the wedding to start.

"I was stuck in traffic," says Christine. "She hasn't forgiven me yet." Christine and her mother were in a limo trying to get from Manhattan to the Brooklyn church, but rush-hour traffic was impossible. "My mother said, 'Well, dear, they certainly can't do this without you, can they?' " remembers Christine. "She was right. We have a great photo of me running into the rectory."

Who can blame Marjorie for being miffed? She and Christine had spent more than a year getting ready for their special day, booking the restaurant for their reception as early as March 1995. The restaurant was, as Christine describes it, "old-line Italian, with the best white-glove service and the most superb Italian food," and she had known for a long time that if she ever married, she wanted to have her reception there. But it was located in Howard Beach, the Queens, New York, neighborhood that was the scene of racial conflict in the 1980s when two African American men were attacked and killed by a gang of whites. Its name quickly became synonymous with racial tension. Christine and Marjorie weren't sure what to expect when they, two African American lesbians, tried to book their wedding reception there.

"I called [the restaurant] and said, 'I'd like to talk to you about the possibility of having my wedding reception there,' " Christine recalls. "I said, 'It's a nontraditional wedding. It's two women.' " But the woman in charge of booking weddings never missed a beat. She simply asked Christine, "Oh, would you like to use our chapel to get married?" (See also the sidebar, "Coming Out to Vendors.")

As is true for many African Americans, religion plays a major role in the lives of Christine and Marjorie. They decided early on to have their ceremony in Unity Fellowship Church, a black gay congregation in Brooklyn, where they regularly attend services. Their ceremony, like Deacon and Jim's, was "very traditionally structured." Once Christine finally arrived, the attendants walked down the aisle to the black hymn, "We've Come This Far by Faith," a song that aptly sums up the relationship of two spiritual lesbians like Marjorie and Christine. Then Marjorie came in to "Here Comes the Bride."

"Of *course,*" she smiles. "I came in and everyone said, 'Ooh, ah.' " Marjorie was arrayed in an elaborate white gown with a billowing train. When she first started looking for gowns, Marjorie intended to buy an evening dress that she could wear again. But then she found herself in a bridal salon, trying on traditional gowns that "just felt right for me," she says. To some, this may have seemed incongruous with Marjorie's strong feminist beliefs, but she has another take on it. "The whole notion of fem-

COMING OUT TO VENDORS

Planning a wedding is hard work for any couple, but when you're lesbian or gay, there's an additional step involved. If you're not using lesbian or gay vendors for your cake, your invitations, your wedding wear, and so on, getting married can require coming out over and over again.

Years back, same-sex couples may have found it easier to fudge the facts with nongay wedding vendors. Brendan Hadash and Alan Hultquist, for example, who had their ceremony back in 1985 in a small town in Vermont, did some quick thinking when they went to rent their tuxes. "We had a difficult time convincing them that we wanted identical tuxes," recalls Alan. "They automatically assumed we were a groom and best man, and there is a slight difference in groom and best man tuxes." Brendan and Alan decided to pretend they were both getting married to women, so that they could get the same tuxedo. "The salesman asked me who the bride was," says Alan, "and I offered the name of one of my sister's old friends."

But times have changed. In 1996, when Marjorie Hill and Christine Edwards hired all nongay vendors for their wedding, they chose to be upfront with everyone. When Marjorie was trying on wedding gowns at a small bridal salon in western New York state, the saleswoman who was assisting her asked how tall the groom was. Marjorie took a deep breath and informed the woman that there were, in fact, two brides, and then told her Christine's height. The woman didn't miss a beat. "Oh, then you'll want to wear something full . . ." she began, showing Marjorie specific styles.

None of Marjorie and Christine's suppliers had ever serviced a lesbian or gay wedding before; in fact, they probably hadn't thought much about same-sex couples getting married. Still, Marjorie and Christine had no problems or uncomfortable experiences while making their wedding arrangements. Christine attributes the acceptance and respect they encountered to the fact that she and Marjorie projected "an energy that says 'I'm worthy.' . . . I believe the only thing people cared about was that we were two people who were going to make the ultimate commitment, and they were delighted to be involved in helping that take place."

Their experience suggests that being totally out with vendors is a good policy. "Everyone picked up on our humanity," Marjorie adds, "and we were very respectful of their humanity. And I think there were some folks who probably went home and said, 'You know, honey, those two women are no different than us except they're two women.' "

inism as I interpret and live it is basically doing the things that make you happy and that you are comfortable with," Marjorie notes, "not adhering to any notions that are restrictive or not reflective of who you are." And the dress was definitely "her."

Christine's preferred formal wear is a tux, but for her wedding, she wanted something different because her mother was coming. "She didn't know she was coming," she laughs, "but my mother *was* coming." Christine's mother at first expressed ambivalence about attending her daughter's wedding, because of her religious beliefs. But when Christine made it clear how important the event was to her and how much she wanted her there, her mother agreed to come. "This was going to be the first event ever where her daughter was openly acknowledging her lesbianism," says Christine. "So I didn't want to be in a tuxedo and have my mother think I was trying to be a man." Instead, Christine wore a flowing white tunic and pants that she had specially made, and she marched down the aisle to one of her favorite hymns, "Your Grace and Mercy." The couple said their vows early in the service. "I don't know who started crying first," says Marjorie. "It sounded like it was my mother, and then it sounded like Christine's mother, but then there was not a dry eye in the house. I was crying, too."

> "*People don't give you Tiffany crystal if you're going to be together for five minutes. It's an assumption that this is a gift for a lifetime.*"

They remember the wedding as a deeply spiritual event that changed them both and deepened their relationship. "It's impossible *not* to be changed by that kind of intense experience, with your family, my aunts, my cousins, Christine's sisters, coworkers, straight people, gay people, black people, white people, rabbis, atheists—all celebrating our finding each other in a world where that's a wonderful thing," says Marjorie. "And to sort of collectively pray for our success."

After the wedding, the reception in Howard Beach was "the best party any of those one hundred and ten people had been to in their entire existence," Christine smiles. "At one point, everybody in the room was on the dance floor. Black people, white people, my mother, her mother." Eventually, guests from other wedding receptions in other parts of the restaurant came in to join the dancing at Christine and Marjorie's, drawn by the music and good times.

For Marjorie, a public wedding with Christine stated to all their family and friends that their relationship meant "forever." "There is a quality of uncertainty and almost presumed instability to gay and lesbian relationships," says Marjorie. But she and Christine are now considered married in the eyes of their loved ones, and Marjorie feels that people are collectively pulling for them and their relationship.

"Look, people don't give you Tiffany crystal if you're going to be together for five minutes," Marjorie quips. "It's an assumption that this is a gift for a lifetime. To have that kind of shared presumption, that shared witness and support, feeds your relationship."

"A Little Flamboyant, but Normal"—Paul and Mark

Marjorie and Christine decided to marry early on in their relationship, as has been the tradition for straight couples. But, as we've noted before, lesbian and gay couples often have ceremonies to celebrate their longevity rather than the start of their lives together. This was the case for Paul and Mark Schibley Schreiber, who had a Jewish wedding to commemorate their twentieth anniversary of being a couple. What they didn't realize when they began planning it was that it would turn into a media event.

Paul and Mark met in 1975, when they were both in their twenties and living at the Vanderbilt YMCA on East Forty-seventh Street in New York City. Paul was from a Jewish family, and as a youngster, his life had centered around the local synagogue. Mark was raised as a Methodist but had rebelled against Christianity at a young age. As an adult couple in New York, Paul and Mark found solace in worshiping at Congregation Beth Simchat Torah, the largest gay synagogue in the world.

"Mark was the one who felt that for our twentieth anniversary we should have some type of commitment ceremony to bind our relationship in the eyes of God," Paul explains. They both found CBST's rabbi, Sharon Kleinbaum, "so inspirational and spiritual and together" that they wanted her to perform their ceremony for them.

The wedding they planned was, by their own account, a traditional Jewish ceremony, witnessed by 140 people. Paul's parents are no longer alive, so he was escorted down the aisle by several good friends; Mark's mother walked him down the aisle. Then they were married under a *chuppah*, walked around each other seven times, and had seven blessings recited by seven people. They also had a handmade *ketubah* (wedding document).

Though their ceremony was designed to bless their relationship, Paul and Mark took the opportunity to make a political statement. Their wedding was taking place in the summer of 1996, at the same time that the Defense of Marriage Act (DOMA) was being voted on in Congress to establish marriage in federal law as "the union of one man and one woman." Paul approached *The New York Times* about having their wedding covered on the society page and was told that was impossible. But he was put in touch with a writer who wanted to do a feature article to coincide with the passage of DOMA, and the reporter interviewed Paul and Mark.

When the *Times* article appeared in print, two television networks, ABC and NBC, immediately came calling, asking to film Paul and Mark's ceremony. "We wanted to keep it a private, solemn thing," Paul says, "but we felt that as good gay men, we had an obligation to the community to share this and to show we're normal people. A little flamboyant, but normal." The rabbi reluctantly agreed, and "we had all these people in the synagogue, videotaping the whole thing." What started out as a private, solemn affair became a media event. But the news stories that subsequently aired, Paul feels, "presented gay marriage in a very positive light."

Despite the spectacle that their ceremony became, Paul and Mark still felt changed by the event. "We felt more bonded," Paul explains. "The clarity of the love we express for each other was heightened and made more clear. I understand the power of marriage, of this binding together, and it is powerful. Even when we're apart, we're one."

The wedding also helped their families to view them as a married couple. "Even the religious conservatives in Mark's family," Paul notes, "are questioning why the state isn't recognizing our union."

"Revitalizing Ancient Texts"—Jim and Dave

Like Paul and Mark, Jim Donovan and Dave Moore have been together a little more than two decades. They live together on a farm in western Illinois that they have gaily named Rainbow Ridge. For their twentieth anniversary, they wanted to celebrate and bless their union and chose to do so in a religious ceremony.

"We're both strongly religious people," says Dave, even though he speaks openly about "the harm organized religion has done and is now doing to the lesbian and gay community." He and Jim are lifelong church-goers who have often felt excluded by organized religion, particularly in their conservative region of the country. So when they were visiting friends and discovered a liberal and welcoming Episcopal parish in Provincetown, Massachusetts, they knew immediately that they wanted to have the rector there perform their ceremony.

But they didn't want a standard religious ceremony, one that was also used for straight couples. They chose instead one of the ancient same-sex liturgies that the late historian John Boswell uncovered in his research for his book, *Same-Sex Unions in Pre-Modern Europe.* Boswell traced a Slavic same-sex liturgy, the Belgrade Liturgy, back to the eleventh century, but Jim and Dave chose the fourteenth-century version for their wedding. "I viewed our act of revitalizing these ancient texts," says Dave, "as an expression of hope that the process of healing is possible: for the Christian community, for the nations of eastern Europe, for gay people."

They did make several variations in the ancient ritual, omitting the choir—"that wasn't practical for us!" says Dave—and adding their own hymns. They also included an exchange of rings, which Boswell said did not occur in same-sex unions because the partners were equal and there was no call for a property exchange. But Jim and Dave wanted rings—"They've become a widely recognized and powerful symbol of mutual commitment," Dave explains. Their rings were sterling silver with gold triangles, a symbol of the gay community's oppression and survival.

On October 31, 1995, Dave wore his best suit and Jim, who is retired from the Navy, wore his dress blues. "I really did want to make a statement!" Jim notes. In front of the priest and eleven other people, Jim and Dave exchanged their vows and rings at St. Mary of the Harbor in Provincetown. Jim professed his continuing love for Dave, and Dave spoke of both the joy and the trials of their twenty year together, ending with these words:

> With gratitude for your constant love, for lending your courage when I have been afraid, for sustaining me through weakness by the strength of your embrace, for sharing your life with me these past twenty years, both the laughter and the tears, I come today, bringing only that which is already yours: my life, my hopes, our dreams.

One of the highlights of the day for Jim occurred right after the ceremony was over. "Father Welles reminded us that we had to sign the official church registry," Jim recalls. "Just like straight couples. This really brought home to me the inclusiveness of that church."

That afternoon, Jim and Dave's friends had a reception for them and their guests. They also surprised Jim and Dave by decorating their room at the inn like a bridal suite. The following day, Jim and Dave went back to St. Mary's for All Saints' Day services, referring to it proudly as "the parish where we were married."

"For a heterosexual couple," Dave says, "that's a common expression, but for us to be able to use that phrase is a profoundly moving recollection of one holy place where we not only exchanged our mutual pledge and tokens of love, but found charity, genuine acceptance, and wholeness."

"What Really Mattered"—Nancy and Alicia

Unlike many of the other couples mentioned here, Alicia and Nancy were only twenty-one and twenty-four when they had their ceremony six years ago, and they necessarily had to cut corners. But their wedding was a moving ritual that demonstrated their commitment to each other.

After they had been lovers for about a year, Alicia and Nancy decided that they wanted to express their love publicly. "I always wanted to be a bride," Alicia notes. "I wanted to wear the white dress and celebrate my love for the person I would spend the rest of my life with. I guess it all boils down to tradition." She saw marriage as the next logical step after courtship, even if they were a lesbian and not a straight couple. "I never see my relationship with Nancy as anything other than a couple-ship like everyone else has," she points out. "Marriage was the next step of sequence."

HONEYMOON SWEET

Lesbian and gay couples sometimes follow up traditional commitment ceremonies with traditional honeymoons, though the location and length of the vacation depend a lot on financial resources. "After paying for the ceremony, Terri and I couldn't afford a honeymoon!" laughs Belinda of upstate New York. "We still plan on a belated honeymoon to Hawaii someday."

The following were some honeymoons that couples I interviewed found memorable and "gay":

Melise and Guillian Zoë of Amarillo, Texas: "We had heard that P-town [Provincetown, Massachusetts] is a lesbigay mecca of sorts. We were ready to go to a place where we could be ourselves and tell the whole city that we were newlyweds! Unfortunately, the city was closing for the winter [when they arrived], and we left early and spent some time in New York City. . . . We loved the accepting vibe we felt in Greenwich Village the most."

Paul and Kurt Jacobowitz-Cain of Phoenix, Arizona: "We went to Hawaii for a week's vacation in October 1990 [seven months *before* their wedding]. When you're gay you can do 'traditional' things in any order you choose: we bought rings, then did the honeymoon, then had the ceremony!"

Shawn and Robert Walker-Smith of San Francisco: "We went on a honeymoon to Villa Messina in Healdsburg [California], a bed-and-breakfast inn that caters to a mixed but largely gay/lesbian clientele. . . . The fact that we could walk in, meet the hosts, and have them say, 'Oh, yes, you're the couple on their honeymoon!' meant a lot to us."

Diana Shapiro and Lori Berkowitz of Berkeley, California: "We rented all the rooms of an inn in Guerneville [a Russian River resort town north of San Francisco] and invited thirty-five of our closest relatives and friends to spend the weekend with us. We partied all weekend, barbecued, went boating, played Frisbee and hacky sack. The best part was that Diana's parents came and got to know our friends and really liked them."

Marjorie Hill and Christine Edwards of New York City: "We went to St. Bart's [St. Bartholomew, a Caribbean island], which was an interesting experience because it's a very French island. It was really like being in France. French food, French language. We saw very few people of color. But the thing was, they were very accepting of us as a couple or just didn't really notice."

Lamont Williams and Joseph Ward of Kansas City, Missouri, whose first trip together as a couple was a drive along the California coast in 1982: "We flew to San Francisco, rented a car, and retraced our original path down Highway 1. We stopped at several of the same places. We visited a few friends who couldn't come to the ceremony and celebrated the event with them."

Beverly and Jamie of British Columbia: "We couldn't afford a honeymoon of our own, so Jamie's friends at work got together and pooled their money to pay for a night in an expensive hotel in LaConner, Washington. . . . We had the honeymoon suite with the largest bed and a Jacuzzi."

Alicia had been raised Jewish, and the two women approached a female rabbi in Albany, New York, about performing the ceremony for them. The rabbi, however, wanted Nancy to convert to Judaism. Because Nancy wasn't interested in converting, their second choice was the local Unitarian Universalist Church.

But marrying in a Christian church went against Alicia's upbringing. "When my sister, who is very religious, found this out," Alicia recalls, "she helped me talk to my parents, and it was decided that their house would be an okay place to hold the ceremony. Regardless of how my family felt about my sexual orientation, they did not want to see me get married in a different religious setting than the one I was brought up in." In lieu of a rabbi to officiate, Alicia's sister agreed to serve as the lay celebrant. Though Alicia's parents did make their backyard available, "they were not as involved with my wedding as they were with my heterosexual sister's," Alicia says, sadly.

Unfortunately, Nancy did not feel comfortable inviting her family. "Nancy didn't invite her dad and stepmom because she felt they wouldn't understand what she was doing," Alicia explains. What hurt most, though, was that "a lot of our heterosexual friends did not show up or even respond to our invitations," Alicia notes. "But we knew we had the important people around us and that's what really mattered."

In keeping with a color scheme that represented Israel, Alicia wore a white wedding gown that she bought on sale at a bridal shop, and Nancy wore a simple blue silk dress. Some of their friends volunteered to make their blue-and-white bouquets.

The ceremony consisted of Alicia's sister reading first, and then Alicia and Nancy making the commitment statements they had written for each other. "We wrote about what commitment meant to us," says Alicia. "We also read a social justice poem and had Jewish music playing."

After a deli-style lunch and a cake that Alicia's sister had bought for them, the couple was bombarded with confetti as they drove off to a short honeymoon in Seneca Falls, New York, an apt location—it was the site of the 1848 convention for women's rights. (See the sidebar "Honeymoon Sweet" for some other vacation ideas.) "The highlight of the day was just having my whole family, grandparents, too, around me at such a special time," notes Alicia.

> "*I always wanted to be a bride. I wanted to wear the white dress and celebrate my love for the person I would spend the rest of my life with.*"

Right in Your Own Backyard

Because so many of us have felt excluded from organized religion and Judeo-Christian traditions, lesbians and gay men have often sought out alternative forms of spirituality, incorporating Native rituals, Eastern beliefs, or pagan rites into their lives. "What constitutes God or the divine is up for grabs," writes gay journalist, Edward M. Gomez. So, in backyards across the country, lesbian and gay couples are creating new wedding rituals for themselves from spiritual traditions that seem to embrace difference. By blending social customs with aspects of different faiths, lesbians and gay men are proving that, as gay Episcopal priest Malcolm Boyd avers, "Nobody *owns* God."

"Something Like a 'Normal' Wedding"—Melise and Guillian

For Melise-Claire Snow and Guillian Contreras, the wooded land around the home they bought together in Texas in 1991 proved the perfect setting for the commitment ceremony they held there five years later. They even have their own pond, complete with fish, ducks, and geese. "We knew our choice to have the wedding on the pier that overlooks the pond would be very meaningful," says Melise. "Every time the fish splashed during the ceremony, it was like they were applauding us. There were even butterflies landing on my veil throughout the ceremony."

A father's toast on wedding day.

It was precisely because they're a "nontraditional" couple that Melise and Guillian wanted "something like a 'normal' wedding," but one that was still distinct from other weddings. Certain traditions were important to them and were used and transformed. "We were a very established couple before the wedding," says Melise, "yet I knew I wanted someone to walk me down the aisle. I chose a good friend of the family, a woman who has been a sort of 'father figure' to me throughout my life."

For the ceremony, Melise wore an ivory lace dress with a train, while Guillian donned a black tux with tails. The attendants, at the suggestion of Melise's mother, wore dresses in the pastel colors of the rainbow. Both of their families pitched in to decorate their house and the grounds with flowers, vines, white Christmas lights, and torches to ward off bugs.

They selected two officiants, a close friend who is not a clergy person and a lay minister of the Cathedral of Hope/MCC in Dallas. The ceremony was filled with poems and songs from many sources, all of which held meaning for them and blended different parts of their lives, celebrating their past and their future. Instead of a Christian blessing, they chose the gender-free Apache Wedding Blessing instead:

> *Now for you there is no rain,*
> *for one is shelter to the other.*
> *Now for you there is no darkness,*
> *for one is counsel to the other.*

Now for you there is no pain,
*   for one is comfort to the other.*
Now for you there is no night,
*   for one is light to the other.*
Now for you there is no cold,
*   for one is warmth to the other.*
Now for you the snow has ended always;
*   your fears, your wants, your needs are at rest.*
For you are two persons,
*   but there is one life before you.*
Go now into your dwelling place
To enter into the days of your togetherness,
And may your days be good and long upon the earth.

Melise and Guillian wanted some concrete changes to take place in their lives as a result of their ceremony, since they couldn't legally marry. So they elected to change their names officially during their wedding, because they wanted to be bound together as a family. Since neither wanted to be subsumed under the other's last name, they settled on the new last name "Zoë," which means "life." The two women are each a mix of ethnicities—Guillian is Mexican American, French, and Portuguese, and Melise is Choctaw, Irish, and German—so they wanted an ethnically neutral last name. (See the sidebar, "The Name Game.") A notary was on hand during their wedding to stamp their official name-change declarations and pronounce, "You are now Zoës." Melise admits, "We both got goose bumps."

Melise and Guillian become "the Zoës."

A highlight of the ceremony was when the sixty-five people present (primarily straight) were asked to repeat a community vow to support Melise and Guillian as a couple. Everyone gave a resounding "We do!" followed by whoops, whistles, and clapping. Then, instead of rice or birdseed, Melise and Guillian had their guests blow bubbles at the end of the ceremony.

At the reception that followed, there were both a bouquet and a garter toss—heterosexual traditions—but the same guests who came forward to catch the bouquet also tried to catch the garter. "In many ways," says Melise, "it was a gender-bending affair. . . . It was amusing and heartwarming to see the whirl of dresses dancing with dresses, tuxes with tuxes, and everything in between, on the dance floor."

What Melise and Guillian remember most was how their families came together to share the day and to make it special. From mundane things like cleaning and cooking, to offering their emotional support, both families came through. The toast that Melise's mother offered at the reception speaks worlds to the tolerance and love their families offered:

May you live in a castle of your own invention,
  well fortified against the dragon of convention.
And may your world be canopied with rainbow hue,
  so that your vision will reflect many points of view.
May your love be a benediction to all you know,
  So that in it and through it we will be challenged to grow.
Utmost, my dear children—on this day—your touchstone,
  May you have found in each other for your hearts a home!

"A Lease on the Next Two Lifetimes"—Joeline and Sandy

As do Melise and Guillian, Joeline and Sandy come from vastly different ethnic backgrounds. Joeline is Native American, and Sandy is Caucasian, of English descent. But in their spiritual beliefs, they are united—they both practice Wicca, or witchcraft.

Wicca is increasingly a religion of choice for lesbians and gay men, since witches have traditionally been outcasts from society. Says Starhawk, a writer on paganism and witchcraft: "To be a Witch is to identify with . . . victims of bigotry and hatred and to take responsibility for shaping a world in which prejudice claims no more victims." Rich Wandel, a high priest of a Wiccan coven, has noted that "the whole idea of Wicca in general . . . is that we are empowering people to do for themselves, to have their own personal contact with the divine, especially the Goddess."

Joeline and Sandy, who live in California, met thirteen years ago through a mutual friend, and they've been together ever since. When they decided to marry, they wanted a religious ceremony and chose to have a Wiccan hand-fasting.

Hand-fastings can be done in two ways, Joeline points out: They can be specified for a limited period of time, the minimum being a year and a day, or they can involve a karmic tie, which is what Joeline and Sandy chose. In a karmic tie, the two people involved agree to take on karmic (meaning fate or destiny) responsibility for each other.

"For those of us who believe in reincarnation," Joeline says, "this particular commitment takes on an intensely important meaning, since the behavior of one affects the other for lifetimes to come. The karmic tie continues even if the relationship fails." So much for Wiccan divorce! Joeline laughs, "Sandy says she has a lease on the next two lifetimes. I'm not going to argue with her."

THE NAME GAME

By tradition, heterosexual women have taken their husbands' last names when they marry, though more and more, they opt to keep their own names or to hyphenate. Now, when same-sex couples join together in a commitment ceremony or holy union, they are also deciding whether to change or combine their names, especially when children are involved.

Hyphenation remains the most common way to link family members, but it can be cumbersome. "Our hyphenated name has taken some getting used to," notes Teresa, who combined her last name with her partner's, creating a new name with seventeen letters in it. "When we first talked to our son about changing our last names, he burst into tears. His six-year-old concern was that his name would be too long for him to write." And Teresa admits, "It doesn't fit on most forms. But we do believe it has helped in validating us as a family. Our last name helped when we petitioned for and were granted guardianship of each other's birth sons."

If you're concerned about creating an unwieldy name through hyphenation, there are other ways to blend together as a family. Aaron and Eric Happel, a young gay couple in Minneapolis, chose Aaron's last name for their common name. "Eric seemed not to care for his name," Aaron explains, "and asked if he could take my name. I felt it an honor and a privilege to have him ask me this, and I said yes immediately."

After much research and consideration, Melise and Guillian Zoë, who live in Texas, picked a completely new and ethnically neutral last name that means "life." Renee and Jackie of Illinois also chose a common last name for themselves—Griffin, a mythical beast that is half eagle, half lion.

Perry and Hoa of California created a unique one-word name from a combination of their two family names, one of which is European and the other Asian. Karin and Maria Kaj also blended their names to make a shorter new one. "We both had hard-to-pronounce names," Karin explains. "Mine was quite long." They found that the legal procedure of changing names cost them about a thousand dollars, whereas, if they'd been a heterosexual couple, the switch would have been free. Yet they feel the change was worth it. "Sharing last names has had a profound effect on the way the world treats us," Karin observes. "Even the secretary of state sent us our voter's pamphlet addressed to 'The Kaj Family.' "

You don't need a court to change your name. (You do need a court order to change the name of a child, though.) But if you change your name just by using the new name, you should be consistent. You could run into problems with airlines and customs officials, for example, if the name on the plane ticket doesn't match the name on your passport. If the name on your tax return doesn't jive with the one the IRS knows, you could have trouble getting your refund, or worse, be targeted for an audit. To avoid these hassles, be sure to request name-change forms from credit card companies, the motor vehicle department, the Social Security Administration, the passport office, your bank, and any organizations to which you belong.

If you decide to change your name by court order, you need to complete a petition, file it at the local courthouse, attend a court hearing at which you state why you want to change your name, and publish a legal notice in a newspaper. Name-change laws vary from state to state, so check with a lawyer in your area or at the local courthouse for specific instructions.

Wiccan rituals are normally held outdoors, and Joeline and Sandy's hand-fasting aptly took place in their backyard. "We have this lovely backyard," Joeline says, "with a tree right in the center. Our backyard gets borrowed for weddings quite often."

Witches generally wear robes for their rituals, which need to be loose-fitting. "It's difficult to do magic with something that's binding you," Joeline notes. For their hand-fasting, Joeline made matching robes for her and Sandy—one was black with teal trim, the other teal with black trim. The other witches in attendance also wore robes.

Joeline and Sandy are both licensed Wiccan clergy, but they chose to have friends who are high priests and priestesses officiate at their ceremony. The text of the ceremony was not that different from traditional weddings except that "some of the promises are more spiritual," Joeline notes. During the wedding, they exchanged gold rings, which they had had custom-made—two hands clasping each other, which symbolized the hand-fasting part of the ceremony. The actual binding together of their two hands with a ribbon—literally "tying the knot"—was the centerpiece of the ritual.

> *"When we first talked to our son about changing our last names, he burst into tears. His six-year-old concern was that his name would be too long for him to write."*

For Joeline and Sandy, the hand-fasting was an opportunity to bring their two worlds together—the Wiccan community with the lesbian and gay community. "We have a high percentage of straight friends," Joeline says. "Our guest list was about half straight and half gay. We had a lot of gay couples who came to the wedding who'd never been to a Wiccan ceremony and were really blown away. And then, we had a lot of Wiccans who had never been around a lot of gay people. Believe me, it was fun!"

The ceremony brought them both respect for their relationship and a certain amount of subtle pressure to stay together. "It's seen as a marriage among our Wiccan friends," Joeline says. "As far as they're concerned, a commitment is a commitment. It wouldn't force us to stay together, but yeah, there is real support for our relationship. Not everybody gets that."

"A Deeper Symbolism"— Barbara and Dalia

Barbara and Dalia met in the context of their Buddhist faith (see page 34), and it seemed fitting that a Buddhist ritual would be a part of their commitment ceremony. Both were raised in other religions and came to Buddhism as adults.

"One thing we like so much about this religion," says Barbara, who was raised Catholic in Ireland, "is that it is such a diverse community. If you go to a meeting [in Chicago, where they live], you'll see people of all races, ages, economic backgrounds, and sexual orientations. This is a wonderful feeling and it gives us hope for the future of humanity."

Part of their practice of Buddhism involves daily chanting while focusing on a mandala, or scroll, inscribed with Sanskrit characters, each of which holds a wealth of meaning. "You generally receive only one mandala in your life, so it is a very special object," Barbara explains.

Barbara and Dalia decided that they wanted to declare their love for each other and have their friends witness it. But instead of a traditional wedding, Barbara and Dalia chose to devise their own ritual.

They attended a new members ceremony at the Soka Gakai International Culture Center in Chicago, where new Buddhists can receive a mandala. There they handed in their two individual scrolls and applied for one new mandala—a symbol of their union. "This was unusual, and we had asked a senior Buddhist about it," Barbara says. "He supported our wish. A few of our Buddhist friends were there to witness the exchange."

After exchanging the mandala, Barbara and Dalia invited friends to their house to witness the enshrinement of their new scroll on their altar. "People brought us gifts, which surprised us," Barbara says. Barbara's family lives overseas and couldn't attend. But Dalia's family, which lives nearby, simply chose not to. "The significance was somewhat lost on them," Barbara says. Because it was a very personal commitment for Barbara and Dalia, they didn't mind that Dalia's family avoided the ceremony.

For the enshrinement, the altar was set up with candles (symbolizing wisdom and truth), incense (for purification of the senses), a vase of evergreen leaves (for eternity of life), and a cup of water (meaning the offering of life). A lesbian friend who has also been a Buddhist for many years performed the ritual, with Dalia, Barbara, and their young son Chris sitting behind her. The ceremony involved an elaborate unrolling of the scroll, which all three took part in. Following the enshrinement, the entire group chanted and said evening prayers, then had a party on Barbara and Dalia's back porch.

The exchange of the mandala and its enshrinement on their altar "had a deeper symbolism for us than a conventional wedding," Barbara notes. "Having given up our individual scrolls kind of ties us together. The gesture brought us closer than a marriage certificate ever could."

"Commitment Doesn't Take a Piece of Paper"— Santa and Vanessa

Santa Molina and Vanessa Marshall are deeply spiritual women whose faith incorporates many of their cultural traditions, from Christian to

BINDING LOVE

Several lesbian and gay couples offered to share the solemn vows they took at their religious services. The following are a few samples of vows that couples wrote themselves for their special ceremonies.

Paula DiDonato and Judy Teeven

> With this ring, I give you my promise
>   that from this day forward
>   you shall not walk alone.
> May my heart be your shelter
>   and my arms be your home.
> May God bless you always.
> May we walk together through all things.
> May you feel deeply loved, for indeed you are.
> May you always see the innocence in my eyes.
> With this ring, I give you my heart.
> I have no greater gift to give.
> I promise I shall do my best. I shall always try.
> I feel so honored to call you my life.
> May we feel this joy forever.
> I thank God.
> I thank you.
> Amen.

(Paula and Judy had an Episcopal priest and a Catholic nun officiate at their ceremony, which was held in the Rainbow Room at Rockefeller Center in New York City.)

Timothous Mack-Jones and Edward Jones-Mack. "One mind, one heart, one thought."

Timothous Mack-Jones and Edward Jones-Mack

> One mind, one heart, one thought . . . together alike.
> Yet always the self, the self rules . . . two minds, two hearts, two thoughts . . . the self . . . two selves . . . in tandem, linked, merged . . . understanding alike, different, together, apart.
> We are individuals with separate feelings and separate personalities, whose unqualified love for each other makes us join as one.
> As we work to make each other become a stronger individual, we can only become

African to Native American. Their public commitment ceremony, held on their first anniversary as a couple in the community hall of their apartment building in New York City, was a blending of all those traditions. It was a spiritual experience, without being tied to any one religion.

Vanessa and Santa wanted their guests to participate in their union, so as guests walked in, they were each handed a candle and a cowrie shell—a traditional African symbol of wealth and success—which they were instructed to hold during the ceremony. As Vanessa and Santa entered the room, walking to the front together, they lit the candles on each side of them while a friend sang "Divine Mother." By the time they reached the

stronger together. Our lives are enriched as we watch each other grow in God.

We come together to share our strengths, our weakness, our hopes, and our knowledge.

We come together to share our love, our lives, and our future.

We are always two, but we will always be one.

I love and respect all that you are.

I embrace all that is yours with all that I am.

(Timothous and Edward had a wedding ceremony at Unity Fellowship Church in Brooklyn, New York.)

Beverly and Jamie

I promise to love and care for you,
through times of joy and times of sorrow,
to rejoice when you are happy,
and grieve when you suffer,
to share your interests,
and hopes for the future,
to try to understand you
even when I do not agree,
to do all in my power
to help you be your true self,
the person God calls you to be.
In all this, I ask for God's help,
now and in the days to come.

(Beverly and Jamie were married at their apartment in Vancouver, British Columbia, by a lesbian Unitarian minister.)

Lori Berkowitz and Diana Shapiro

I promise to be your partner in times of joy and in times of trouble, to provide for and support you in friendship, trust, and love. I promise to work with you to build our lives together. May we grow, our lives intertwined, our love bringing us closer. Let us create a home based on love. May it be a home filled with peace, with happiness, and with love.

(Lori and Diana had a ceremony at home in Berkeley, California, "loosely based on Jewish traditions," with a chuppah *made out of a sheet and a* ketubah *in Hebrew and English.)*

Diana Shapiro (left) and Lori Berkowitz marry under a homemade chuppah.

© Miriam Stahl

front of the room, all 120 candles were lit, a beautiful sight on a wintry December evening.

The ceremony itself consisted of different songs, which Santa and Vanessa sang to each other while they washed each other's feet in sandalwood and sage. Rather than being about submission, "That was a sign of being humble in the relationship," Vanessa points out. In addition, they exchanged rings and vows, "which we wrote and didn't get to hear until that day," Vanessa recalls. "They were about what we wanted for each other and how we were going to be in our relationship."

At the close of the ceremony, Vanessa and Santa asked their guests to

"Tom and Walter Got Married"

BY RICHARD COHEN

TOM STODDARD AND WALTER RIEMAN went shopping at Tiffany's last month. The salesman was polite but distant. After asking him dozens of questions, after trying on this one and then that, they decided to buy what Tom had wanted from the start: two plain gold bands. Tom and Walter took the rings home to their apartment on the West Side, put them in a drawer, and did not take them out until December 4, which is the day Tom and Walter got married.

One morning a week or so before the ceremony, we rang the bell of Tom and Walter's apartment. When the door opened, both Tom and Walter were there, looking flushed and concerned. "Walter's lost the seating chart," Tom said. "He's going off to work to search his desk." "All right," Walter said, grabbing his coat. "I'm going." Walter, a thirty-eight-year-old trial lawyer, was recently elected to partnership at Paul, Weiss, Rifkind, Wharton & Garrison, the first openly gay person to achieve this. His manner is solemn and intense, and he has a prodigious memory: he can retrieve childhood anecdotes, slights suffered long ago, the minutiae of legal decisions concerning people generations dead.

Losing the seating chart for his wedding was not something that Walter took lightly. After Walter left, Tom dropped onto an overstuffed couch and sighed. Tom met Walter at a fund-raiser on Fire Island five years ago, and they moved in together six months later, but the last few days, Tom told us, had been a whole new relationship. "A gay man getting married has so many things to worry about," he said, folding his arms. "Even the small

things assume hidden meanings and are riddled with symbolism." Tom, who is forty-five years old, is a lawyer, too, but may be better known as an activist in behalf of gay rights. Last spring, before the big gay march on Washington, he met Bill Clinton at the White House to discuss, among other things, the administration's position on gays in the military. For six years, Tom was the executive director of the Lambda Legal Defense and Education Fund, but he resigned the post in January 1992, in part because he had recently been found to have AIDS.

"Now I reserve strength for choice battles," he said. The next big battle, Tom said, is gay marriage. "It's just so emotion-laden, so tangled with convention, that it is bound to test straight people more profoundly than any other gay issue," he said. So far, no state government has legally recognized same-sex marriages—Tom and Walter will be classified as domestic partners by New York City—but around the country a growing number of gay couples are demanding legal recognition. The fight for such recognition has progressed furthest in Hawaii, where the state supreme court recently found the law barring same-sex marriage to be a form of gender discrimination and in violation of the state's constitution. Along with the issue of fairness—if a man can marry a woman, why can't a woman marry a woman or a man marry a man?—activists stress various rights and privileges that are denied to gays because they cannot obtain a marriage license: the ability to extend American citizenship to a spouse; the opportunity to file a joint

make a wish or blessing for them on the cowrie shells they were holding. Then the two women handed each guest a small medicine bag in which to place his or her cowrie shell. "We asked them to carry that prayer for us with them," says Santa, "and keep the medicine bag as a place of honor for the shell. So we've got all these little medicine bags all over the world—

tax return; the chance to qualify for a partner's health plan.

"If Walter and I were legal, I could go on his firm's medical," Tom said. "And considering my illness, that's no small thing." Though the Hawaiian case has been returned to trial court, a number of legal scholars have predicted that the state will soon recognize gay marriage. If it happens, Tom thinks, Honolulu may well become a kind of Reno for gays—a city of all-night altars and neon chapels. And if *that* happens—if thousands of gay men and lesbians flock to Hawaii and get married—other states may well be forced to recognize the marriages, nationwide recognition being the general rule with regard to straight marriages, regardless of where the license was obtained.

The phone rang. "Can that be Walter?" Tom said. He let the machine pick up, and soon the voice of Walter said, "The chart's not here. Call before I start turning over the desks."

"I'll show you what really got me thinking about marriage," Tom said, and stood up. He took us to the bedroom, and there we saw an elegant photograph of Tom and Walter locked in a mild embrace. "Several months ago, Annie Leibovitz, as a present for our fifth anniversary, shot me and Walter," Tom said. "The picture got me thinking about appearances—the importance of declaring our commitment before people we love." Then he remarked that whereas the subtext of so many straight weddings is about expanding possibility, for gay men with AIDS it has more to do with closure. "The relationship has that precious quality of something that's going away," he said. We left not long afterward, with the seating chart still missing. When we next spoke with Tom and Walter, a couple of days before the wedding, Walter had come down with a traditional case of the

screaming meemies. He had found the seating chart by then, but he had begun to wonder if some hidden voice wasn't saying, "Don't commit." "For lesbians and gay men, marriage is scary," Tom told us. (Walter wasn't talking.) "After all, gay rights is about challenging tradition, and what's more traditional than a wedding?"

The wedding was held on a rainy Saturday afternoon at Chanterelle, in TriBeCa. Walter's jitters were gone. He wore a gray suit and a red tie. Tom, too, was dressed in gray. During the cocktail hour, more than seventy people, including Walter's brother and two sisters, Tom's brother, and a New York Supreme Court justice, drank champagne and filled the room with stories about Tom and Walter. The two men then appeared in a clearing between tables. Facing each other, they exchanged vows ("I commit to you my life and my love for the rest of our days"), put on their gold rings, and were married. When Tom and Walter kissed, the crowd cheered and guests began toasting everything in sight: Tom toasted Walter's family; Walter toasted Tom's brother; Tom and Walter toasted Karen and David Waltuck, who own Chanterelle; Karen thanked them and ran from the room teary-eyed. Then, after rapping on a glass (half empty, half full), which quieted the room, Tom's brother John said, "Tom and Walter have done something that gay people have dreamed of for thousands of years. Let's raise our glasses to Tom and Walter: May you continue your life together in a more perfect union, in good health, and always with adventure and purpose and love."

NOTE: Tom Stoddard died of AIDS-related complications in February, 1997. Reprinted by permission; © 1993 The New Yorker magazine, Inc. All rights reserved.

people holding onto our prayers, holding our relationship in a sacred way." Though the cowrie-shell ritual took more time than they figured, it gave Vanessa and Santa the chance to talk to each of their guests "and really have them share what they felt, what they wanted for us," Santa explains.

Sadly, as often happens at lesbian and gay weddings, the event was marred by the fact that Vanessa's mother chose not to attend for religious reasons. "It was something she couldn't do," says Santa. "Go before God to honor our relationship."

"I was extremely hurt to the point where I wouldn't even speak to her for a while," Vanessa remembers. "I was shocked, because my mother has always been very supportive of my relationships. She's always had good relationships with my partners." Vanessa eventually let go of the pain. "It took a lot of strength for her to say she wasn't going to attend my ceremony," she reasons. "On some levels, she would have rather died than say that to me. But she was able to." Their relationship was strong enough to endure the hurt and go on from there.

The rest of their families were present, including Santa's mother, whose support and love helped make up for the fact that Vanessa's mother didn't attend. "In the middle of the ceremony, Santa's mom yelled out, 'I love you, Vanessa!' " remembers Vanessa fondly. "That made me feel great. I felt supported by her being there."

Though both women were dedicated and devoted to each other before the ceremony took place, they feel that the ritual had an impact on the way other people looked at their relationship. "Commitment doesn't take a piece of paper saying you have a commitment," notes Vanessa. "For me, the ceremony was about saying to the world that this is the woman I love and I'm presenting her to all the people who mean anything to me."

"For me, the ceremony was about saying to the world that this is the woman I love and I'm presenting her to all the people who mean anything to me."

In the Public Eye

Vanessa's desire to speak her love for Santa is the common thread running throughout all public commitment ceremonies, large and small, religious and secular. Many lesbians and gay men express the need to have their relationships acknowledged and validated by those whom they hold dear. Secular ceremonies accomplish this as much as religious ones, bringing the couple's community forward to witness the promises they make to each other.

A couple's financial resources often determine the kind of wedding they have. While some have expensive affairs—like lawyers Tom Stoddard and Walter Rieman, who could afford a trendy restaurant in Manhattan (see the sidebar, "Tom and Walter Got Married")—many couples have ceremonies that are considerably less "chic" but just as meaningful. Whatever the venue, lesbian and gay ceremonies break taboos by requesting that family, friends, and coworkers come together to wish the couple well. For many couples, the acceptance and support they garner from those who witness their ceremonies can be the most significant aspect of their unions.

"The Most Ordinary Thing to Do"—Steve and Ric

Steve and Ric, who met and began living together in Southern California in 1976 (see page 21), saw the need early on to have others recognize and support their relationship. "Setting up a household is one thing. Creating a life that will last is another," says Steve. They realized that they needed a support system to get them through, just the way straight couples have people urging them on. "We needed people to call us to task, to make it more difficult to just walk away when the going was rough."

Ric got the idea of having a ceremony from reading Patricia Nell Warren's novel, *The Front Runner* (1974), which may have been the first American novel to portray a same-sex wedding. Because their ceremony took place more than twenty years ago, when fewer lesbians and gay men were visibly out, Ric and Steve weren't ready to include their families in the guest list. Instead, they invited all their friends—even some from high school and college who didn't yet know they were gay.

They had no idea where to get their invitations, so they picked a printer in Pasadena, near where they lived, and just walked in. "To this day I admire the way the man behind the counter didn't skip a beat," says Steve. "He looked over the layout, checked the text, and took the order. Remember, this was 1976! I tried to take a lesson from that experience. Whenever possible we just approach something potentially hazardous as if it were the most ordinary thing to do."

They opted to have the ceremony in the new apartment they had just begun to share, mostly because they were young and an at-home ceremony was inexpensive but intimate. Friends gathered, and Steve and Ric sat in front of a pair of candles, which they still have. The ceremony began with a reading from the Antoine de Saint-Exupéry story, *The Little Prince*. "We both suggested this to each other almost simultaneously," Steve notes. "The chapter about his meeting with the fox."

> *It is only with the heart that one can see rightly;*
> *what is essential is invisible to the eye.*

Then Steve and Ric were silent while Jim Croce's song, "Time in a Bottle," played in the background. (Remember, this was 1976!) They made promises to each other and embraced, and followed up the ceremony with champagne and food.

"It was very informal," Steve recalls, "but comfortable—almost a sixties sort of thing." The response of their friends—most of whom were straight—was encouraging and supportive. The following year, Steve and Ric exchanged rings in front of the same group of people. "And each year thereafter we have celebrated with our friends, hosting a potluck as a way of saying thank you for loving us and caring about us."

"A Commitment to Ourselves and the Community"— Ellen and Nancy

Unlike Steve and Ric, who met when they were in their early twenties, Nancy Spannbauer and Ellen Ensig-Brodsky were both middle-aged women with ex-husbands and grown children when they met in 1987. "It was at a sixties dance sponsored by the Lesbian Herstory Archives," Nancy recalls. "I was standing with my hands in my pockets looking out at the dance floor, and this woman came up and said, 'Do you do this stuff?' And I said yeah. So we started to dance." Actually, Nancy corrects herself, it wasn't so much dancing as "standing there and moving a little bit. But that's what everybody else was doing, too!"

Thus began Ellen and Nancy's relationship, which was cemented a year later when they moved in together and had a commitment ceremony for their friends and family (including all their children and grandchildren) at the location where they first met—New York's lesbian and gay community center. The celebration was both for their own relationship and for the community center that had made it possible. They invited more than fifty people, and though they exchanged rings and made speeches, there was no real ceremony. "Nancy was dead set against the idea of marriage," Ellen points out. "It was too heterosexual." So, basically, Ellen says, "We had this party."

When their guests arrived, Ellen and Nancy went to the front of the room. They were both just wearing slacks and shirts "like good dykes," smiles Ellen. Nancy thanked everyone for coming and stated how happy they were to be spending their lives together. "I said something like, I knew Ellen was really committed because she went out and bought the food for the feast without regard for coupons," Nancy quips. A friend of theirs shouted out, "Wow, it must be true love!"

Then Ellen read a prepared statement:

A little over a year ago, Nancy and I met in this building. From that moment began a mutual pairing that has now grown into a defined life partnership of love and commitment. This very building . . . is in itself a statement of caring. Caring and loving. Woman to woman. Man to man. Between men and women. It is not only a great work, but a basis for true community. So, as we begin to embrace each other in our lives, we clearly recognize that each of you have enabled this moment through your nurturing of us as individuals. As a couple, we can now double our caring for each of you. Thank you for joining us tonight in this, joyously celebrating such community.

After the simple nonceremony, which they have photos and a videotape of, guests were treated to a buffet, with "more macaroni salad than you've ever seen," Ellen laughs. Because they were on a tight budget, the food was all homemade. "We bought delicious rolls and made tons of macaroni salad," says Ellen. "We had so much left over, we ate it and ate it. Ever since then, I don't care if I ever see macaroni salad!"

Though the party wasn't formal or traditional, "it was a commitment to ourselves and to the community," explains Ellen. Now, each year on their anniversary, they give an extra donation to the center where they met, in appreciation for the fact that it exists as a way for lesbians and gay men to meet friends and partners.

Both Ellen and Nancy felt changed by the celebration of their relationship; the public expression of their commitment made it seem even more binding. "Once you get up and say something publicly in front of people who know you and it starts coming out of your mouth, well, something does happen," Ellen remarks. "You have made a commitment and other people have borne witness to that. You don't back out of it."

"A Giant Coming-Out Party"—Mark and Andy

Musicians Mark and Andy met while they were both graduate students at the New England Conservatory of Music in 1985. But it wasn't until their tenth anniversary that they decided to formally commit to each other with a public ceremony.

For them, as for so many other lesbian and gay couples, having a public ceremony was a bold step, because it meant officially acknowledging their sexual orientation to family. Mark and Andy started preparing people a year ahead of time. "It was sort of a giant coming-out party," says Andy, who is Asian American and had only told his family he was gay when he and Mark began planning their ceremony. "They suspected, of course. . . . They all came to the ceremony, and I think they were quite surprised. I had such a fear of having family and friends ridicule us for something that was so meaningful. I underestimated their open-mindedness." For Andy, reading Bob and Rod Jackson-Paris's book, *Straight from the Heart: A Love Story*—which tells the story of the bodybuilders' relationship and commitment ceremony—helped. "It gave me a lot of hope and courage," Andy notes. "It helped ease my fears about coming out to my family."

Mark's mother had a difficult time with the idea of her son marrying another man. "She said that she could not call it a wedding," Mark recalls. "I eventually wrote her a letter that explained how important the ceremony was to me. I wrote, 'Because I intend to be with Andy for the rest of my life, this is as close to a wedding as I will ever have.' " To her credit, she attended despite her reservations. But it wasn't until a couple of years after the ceremony that Mark's mother was able to look back and refer to it as "the wedding."

Though they originally planned to have the ceremony at their home, the guest list quickly outgrew the space, and they rented a room in a restaurant with windows overlooking a small waterfall. Because Mark and Andy both consider themselves spiritual but not religious, they elected to have a lay celebrant, a woman who had been referred to them by a justice of the peace. The theme they chose for the day was "Ten Years into Forever."

"We researched several books to find readings that seemed to capture our sense of love and devotion," says Andy. "One funny way that we found some materials was to go to a craft fair. Usually at these fairs they have calligraphers . . . who have examples of flowery poems about love and life, so we took time to look through all of those. Actually, we found most of our readings that way."

"We had no set tradition to follow," Mark notes, "so we made up what we wanted." The ceremony began with the celebrant doing a blessing of the four directions, with each of the people taking part in the ceremony coming up and putting a rose on a table. Because music is such an integral part of their lives, they incorporated music by a cello quartet into the event. There were readings, some words from the celebrant, and then a taped song, "The Moose and the Cow." "It's a fun song about how society deals with alternative relationships," Andy says, explaining the unusual musical selection.

Mark and Andy then spoke their vows, which they had each written in advance. They tied their rings together and passed them through the room, so that each of the seventy guests could say a few words or just hold the rings and make a wish for the couple on them. "The things people said were so touching," Andy recalls. "The amount of love and support that was there was incredible."

"Many people said that of all the weddings they had attended, this was the most emotional they had seen," Mark recalls fondly. "One older friend said that she had not cried at any of her three sons' weddings but cried at ours!" What made it so emotional? "The highlight of the ceremony was the vows that Andy and I read to each other," Mark says. "For the people gathered, the raw emotion that we showed was almost overwhelming." As part of his vows, Mark said, "You are my life, you are my hero, you are everything I wish I could be. You are the best thing that ever happened to me, and you are still my knight in shining armor." Equally emotional, Andy told Mark, "You are my first and only love . . . my best friend and the love of my life."

Like most other lesbian and gay couples who have gone through a ceremony of some kind, Mark and Andy felt differently about their relationship after the event. "There are now seventy people who view us as a married couple," Mark observes. "Our families treat us that way." He didn't imagine that after ten years together, one celebration would make a big difference, but it did. "It just feels so good to be out," Mark says.

"One older friend said that she had not cried at any of her three sons' weddings but cried at ours!"

"Sleepy Town Awakes to Fulfill Dreams of Eager Couples"

BY DEB PRICE

THE SLEEPY-EYED JUSTICE of the peace clearly wants to tell the couple at his front door to come back at a more reasonable hour. But their eagerness to be legally joined is so touching that he beckons them in from the night.

Within moments, the justice of the peace and his wife have pulled together the sweet, makeshift wedding ceremony that's a staple of old Hollywood movies.

Because Joyce is a stubborn romantic, I've watched more than my share of big-screen elopements. Yet I never expected we'd star in what felt like a Gay Nineties remake of those classic scenes:

The alarm clock rang so early that our canine companions, Jazz and Eddie, doggedly refused to get up. But we jumped into nice clothes and quickly drove to the town hall. We were intent on being first, on making a tiny bit of history. Four equally eager couples lined up behind us.

The ten of us were greeted by Takoma Park, Maryland, officials as if we were guests at a party they had forgotten they were throwing. Yes, this was the first day unmarried couples could legally register their domestic partnerships, but town officials clearly hadn't expected anyone to show up—at least not so soon.

Quite a bit of good-natured bustling ensued as the officials found the application forms, double-checked the $25 fee, and determined that permanent certificates had not yet been printed. What about a notary? A frantic call went out.

If you don't want to wait for the notary, an apologetic official told us, just come back later. We'd all already waited years for legal recognition. No one budged.

Soon, Joyce and I signed a declaration "that we are in a familial relationship characterized by mutual caring and the sharing of a mutual domicile."

So "Domestic"

Many lesbian and gay couples who aren't interested in having a commitment ceremony, either religious or secular, opt to register as domestic partners. If the option isn't available in their area, they sometimes register in another place if that jurisdiction will allow it. For example, singer-musician Janis Ian and her partner of eight years, Pat Snyder, live in Nashville, Tennessee, but registered as domestic partners in Provincetown, Massachusetts, in 1993. "We were there on vacation," Janis explains, "and we were the second couple to register."

What's the point of registering? Domestic partnership carries no real legal weight and is not a substitute for marriage. But in some jurisdictions and in many companies and organizations across the country, domestic partners can at least receive joint health insurance benefits, like heterosex-

As the notary's seal bit into the document, my government-approved domestic partner and I felt an unexpected surge of pride and, yes, validation.

Unlike a marriage license, our domestic partnership certificate really will be just a piece of paper: no tangible benefits, no legal responsibilities. Yet all ten of us felt we'd taken a major step.

"Politically, it's a really important step for the culture to be forced to reckon with us," says Marilee Lindemann, who registered with her partner of nine years. "Psychologically, it's extremely important for us to have certificates and rituals. The older I get, the more important that becomes to me."

After Berkeley, California, voted in 1984 to recognize domestic partners, a dozen cities followed suit. I wasn't surprised when Takoma Park, the most progressive suburb of Washington, D.C., joined the list. But Joyce's proposal that we sign up floored me.

Joyce had always been far more stubborn than romantic about domestic partnership registration. "No second-class citizenship for gay couples!" she'd declare. "Marriage or nothing. Our own commitment is what matters."

Her attitude abruptly changed, she now tells me, after we began using a joint checking account. If having our creditors see us as a couple felt good, she reasoned, wouldn't having the recognition of our little town feel terrific? Takoma Park, after all, was offering everything it could. It cannot change the state marriage law.

Many Americans believe a sexually active couple must be legally married to be "honest." Even the attorney trying to help lesbian Sharon Bottoms regain custody of her son is ensnared by that myth. "She can't make herself an honest woman and marry April Wade," he told a Virginia court this fall.

But isn't it our lawmakers and judges who aren't honest? They see gay couples wedded to a lifetime together yet refuse to recognize our right to marry. By slamming the door in our faces, they tell us this isn't a reasonable time.

As the hour changes, we'll knock again on justice's door. Domestic partnership is not enough for a first-class relationship. Honest.

ual married couples. (See the sidebar, "I Take You to Be My Domestic Partner.") "We wanted to have proof in the event our jobs got domestic partner benefits," Esther says of the reason she and Lynne registered in San Francisco.

Louise Murray and Liza Fiol-Matta registered in New York City, to take advantage of the health care benefits offered by the city to its employees' domestic partners. At first, the two of them were ambivalent about registering because they didn't want any official stamp on their relationship. But Louise's two grown sons urged them to do it, and the cut-and-dried bureaucratic process became a celebration of sorts.

"It was very important to the boys," Liza points out, "that we formalize our relationship. So we all trooped down to city hall." They were six in all—Liza, Louise, Louise's sons, and both of the sons' girlfriends. "We walked around as a little group and got the affidavit and went to the notary and then went back and got the certificate. And then we all went out and had a Chinese dinner. That was a really sweet and beautiful thing, going there together and registering."

Even when no tangible benefits are attached to domestic partnership, couples still take advantage of the option. For Andrew and Mano, their

Registering as domestic partners in San Francisco, 1991.

registration as domestic partners was their wedding. San Francisco City Hall was "a gorgeous setting," says Andrew. Though the "ceremony" was only a matter of paying the fee and signing the document, it meant a lot to them. "We were surrounded by other couples, straight and gay," says Mano, "and the clerk made a point of describing the commitments we were about to make to one another." After, Andrew and Mano kissed and descended the grand staircase of city hall hand in hand. They sent their families and friends a "traditional, lacy" announcement after the fact. "We didn't want them to think they had to *do* something, like in a hetero wedding," Mano says.

Terry Boggis, the director of Center Kids, one of the largest gay family organizations in the country, registered with her late partner Rosemary three years ago in New York City. Like Andrew and Mano, the two of them made their domestic partnership registration into a ceremony, mostly for the benefit of their five-year-old son, Ned. "It's enormously beneficial to our children to have our unions validated," Terry points out. "We feed them a lot of information from the cradle: Gay is good, we're together, we're married, we're just as married as your friends' parents. But at some point, they start to realize that it's not quite the same. And it's just another way for them to feel like less."

Terry recalls that they dressed Ned in a suit that morning, then picked him up at his school at lunchtime to go to city hall for what they described as their marriage. Two of their friends joined them to witness the event. "We were schlepping across Chambers Street," Terry remembers, "and Ned said, 'I thought you were already married.' He was only five, and we'd been telling him all along that we were married. He didn't really get it." Terry had to think fast and come up with a good reason for the city hall ceremony. "I said, 'God knows we're married, but the government doesn't. So this is for the government.' " The confusion that children of gay people experience over their parents not being able to legally marry is enough to make Terry think that equal marriage rights would be beneficial. "Children from straight marriages don't have that uncertainty of 'What are we?' and 'How are we different?' " she notes.

In lieu of marriage rights, Aaron and Eric Happel felt that registering as domestic partners "was as close to full commitment as current law would allow," says Aaron of their decision to register in Minneapolis last year. "But we hated the process." In Minneapolis, couples mail in the form with a twenty-dollar check, and their application can either be rejected or accepted. "If approved, they complete a certificate on whatever day they wish," says Aaron. But because they wanted to express their love for each other, Aaron and Eric went ahead with it anyway. In addition, Eric changed his last name to Aaron's.

For Susan Stratton of Seattle, who plans to register with Jo Ellen Elliott, the bureaucratic process is not the point; it's the symbolism behind it that is important. "There's nothing that you get with domestic partnership," she notes. "It's symbolic only. But you got to do what you got to do."

Shaking It Up

Couples, gay or straight, want to marry primarily because they're in love. But for same-sex couples, whose marriages are not legally recognized, personal commitments are also inherently political, in a way that heterosexual weddings are not.

Even thirty years ago, many lesbians and gay men would not have dreamed of standing up in front of family and straight friends and publicly proclaiming love for a same-sex partner. Instead, homosexuality was something to be ashamed of and hide away in the closet, not celebrate. We've come a long way since Stonewall, but it's still earth-shaking to say "I do" with someone of the same gender. First and foremost, it means coming out, which is one of the strongest political statements lesbians and gay men can make.

While many lesbian and gay couples don't intend for their personal commitments to make headlines, others take the opportunity to make a statement by joining together as wife and wife or husband and husband. At both the 1987 and the 1993 marches on Washington for lesbian and gay rights, mass weddings were held in front of the Internal Revenue Service to demonstrate against our second-class citizenship. In all, the Government Accounting Office (GAO) estimates that heterosexual married couples enjoy exactly 1,049 benefits that same-sex couples cannot partake of, because the government doesn't recognize our unions. (See the sidebar, "For the Record" for a sampling of the benefits lesbian and gay couples miss out on in one state, and for an overview of federal income tax law, which seems to be the only area in which same-sex couples are at an economic advantage.)

Carmen Vázquez, a well-known lesbian activist and director of public

FOR THE RECORD

The issue of whether or not to legalize marriage for same-sex couples has been hotly debated during the last several years. In April 1997, the Association of the Bar of the City of New York issued the following statement in *The Record* (volume 52, number 3): "There is currently a national debate over the right of same-sex couples to state-sanctioned marriage. This *Report* considers the current state of New York law and concludes that New York should permit same-sex couples to marry and should recognize same-sex marriages entered into in sister states."

Accompanying this statement was a list of the legal rights and responsibilities of individuals recognized as legally married. With special thanks to Martha Harris at the Bar Association of New York, the list of legal rights is reprinted in part below:

1. When a married individual becomes incompetent the decision-making process is usually transferred to a relative, frequently the spouse. If a person is not married, then his or her parents, children, or other relatives will be appointed as the decision maker.

2. A married person is obligated to support the spouse if the spouse is receiving, or is likely to receive and depend on public assistance.

3. Under New York and federal law married couples are exempt from paying taxes on employer-provided health insurance extended to either spouse. Lesbian and gay employees must pay taxes on the value of the benefits going to their same-sex partners.

4. Transfers of property from one spouse to the other during the marriage or at death are exempt from gift tax and estate tax.

5. Federal Income Tax Law

   a) Standard Deduction
   The standard deduction in 1996 for a single person was $650 greater than it is for a married person.

   (b) Income Tax Rates
   A married couple who both earn income are at a disadvantage because the amount of combined income that can be taxed at a lower rate for two single people is greater than it is for a married couple.

   (c) Earned Income Credit
   To use the earned income credit, a couple must have a child and earn less than a specified amount each year. An unmarried couple need not combine their income to determine whether they can use this credit.

   (d) Personal Exemptions and Itemized Deductions
   Personal exemptions and itemized deductions phase out with higher incomes. The combined exemptions for two single people (who need not combine their incomes) is therefore greater than a married couple's exemption.

   (e) IRA
   Until 1998, if one spouse participates in a qualified pension plan and earns income over a specified amount, the other spouse cannot invest $2,000 into his or her own IRA for the tax advantage. These rules have been amended, effective in 1998.

   f) Capital Losses
   Unmarried couples may take double the tax deduction each year than married couples may take for capital losses.

   (g) Passive Trades
   Unmarried couples may take double the tax deduction each year for passive trades, such as real estate, than married couples may take.

6. A person can tax deduct alimony or "spousal maintenance" payments only if he or she was once married to the person to whom he or she makes the payments.

7. Federal law requires that certain benefits of a retirement plan participant extend to a surviving spouse. If the employee elects out of such benefits, a formalized consent form must be obtained from his or her spouse.

8. Rights Upon Death

   (a) Right to Claim Decedent's Remains

When a spouse dies, the other spouse has rights as next of kin to claim the deceased person's remains, and if the deceased person has not made any legal provisions of their own, the spouse has the right to make organ donor contributions with respect to the decedent's body. If a person is not legally married to his or her significant other, then other relatives have these rights.

(b) Intestate Rights

When a spouse dies without a will, New York law entitles a surviving spouse to receive a share of the deceased spouse's probate estate and certain property transferred during the deceased spouse's lifetime. And even if a spouse dies with a will the surviving spouse is entitled to a minimum amount. These rights are not available to surviving partners of same-sex relationships.

9. If a third party causes the death of a spouse through the third party's negligence or deliberate act then the decedent's spouse (but not an unmarried long-term partner) may recover for economic losses in a wrongful death suit.

10. If a third person negligently injures a married person, and the spouse is deprived of care and companionship, the spouse may sue the third party for loss of companionship.

11. Pursuant to New York Executive Law, a surviving spouse is eligible to receive a financial award if his or her spouse dies as a result of being a crime victim.

12. When an individual is criminally prosecuted, the government may not force the spouse of the accused person to testify against the accused, nor does the spouse need to reveal confidential marital communications during a civil trial. The accused may share otherwise privileged information with his or her spouse without waiving the underlying privilege.

13. Pursuant to New York Civil Procedure Law and Rules, a spouse has the power to waive the physician-patient privilege of a deceased spouse and gain access to medical records, for the purposes of litigation or otherwise.

14. Under New York law, a spouse is exempt from any wrongful act claims. However, in some instances when pertaining to claims for tortious interference with a contract, a spouse's immunity is limited based on the argument that he or she convinced the spouse to back out of a contract. There is no spousal immunity, however, if the allegations pertain to wrongful conduct, such as physical threats or fraud. In addition, in New York, any communication between spouses is not legal cause for slander.

15. Only a married couple may hold real property by the entireties. Such ownership of property will effectively protect a non-bankruptcy-filing spouse's title of the property from the attack of the creditors of the filer. Moreover, if the filer dies before the other spouse, the other spouse has complete title and the creditors of the filer get nothing. Spouses may also file jointly for bankruptcy.

16. The federal government has extremely restrictive immigration laws. However, a foreign-born national who marries an American citizen may immediately enter the United States as a long-term resident.

17. The Family and Medical Leave Act of 1993 requires all employers with fifty or more employees to allow employees up to twelve weeks per year in unpaid leave to care for a spouse with a "serious health" condition. It makes no similar provision for unmarried significant others.

18. Matrimonial court files containing information about cases involving married couples are not usually available to the public. Files concerning court cases between unmarried couples, such as breach of contract, are usually available to the general public.

19. Since July 19, 1980, New York law has viewed marriage as both a social and economic partnership. Therefore, when a marriage dissolves, New York courts consider equitable distribution of all marital assets. Even if one spouse earns less than the other, that spouse will still receive an "equitable" portion of all

marital property. In fact, New York courts may even take into account the imbalances in earning capacity by considering the differences in each spouse's position in the distribution of property. Large assets including pension contributions earned or made during the marriage may be divided between the parties.

Spouses may also be compensated for helping each other obtain a professional license or advanced degree during the marriage, which ultimately enhances the other spouse's earning capacity. In addition, upon divorce, spouses may be entitled to receive spousal maintenance to assist them in becoming self-supporting. Neither the equitable distribution of assets nor spousal maintenance are available to couples who are not legally married, thus same-sex couples will not be subject to the rights and responsibilities included in New York's divorce laws unless they are able to marry legally.

policy at New York's Lesbian and Gay Community Services Center, participated in what she dubs "the big old demonstration" in front of the IRS building in 1987. At "The Wedding," approximately two thousand couples said "I do."

"Marcie [her partner at that time] called it the Moonie Wedding," Carmen laughs. Though it was both a campy event and a political demonstration, the moving part for Carmen and Marcie was that they had family support for being part of a dramatic statement about civil rights. "Marcie's brothers actually came to Washington for it," Carmen recalls. "Then they met us back at the hotel and had a bottle of Cold Duck or something for us. I was like, 'Oh please, do I have to drink it?' But they were very supportive and celebratory."

Gary Ivanish and Tom Scarpitta from Baltimore have been part of two political weddings. The first was the 1993 wedding in front of the IRS. "We always considered ourselves married," says Gary, who has been with Tom for six years, "but we wanted to make it more official." By most estimates, Gary and Tom were one of three thousand couples who were married in that demonstration in the nation's capital.

"It was pretty neat," remembers Gary. "It was intense and very crowded. Some people were dressed up, and others weren't. It was a big mixture of people."

Their second wedding, though, was the most meaningful for them. It happened two years later, as part of the National Organization for Women's (NOW) Valentine's Day of Action. From February 14 to 16, 1996, 100 NOW chapters across the country staged same-sex wedding ceremonies, rallies at state capitol buildings, and postcard campaigns to legislators in support of lesbian and gay couples. As Patricia Ireland,

NOW's president, put it, "What better day than Valentine's Day, the day we celebrate love and long-term commitments, for activists of all sexual orientations to speak up for the rights of lesbian and gay couples?"

Gary and Tom wore tuxes for the action they took part in—a double marriage ceremony in front of the Legislative Services Building in Annapolis, in the shadow of the Maryland state house. Joining them was a lesbian couple, Elva Miller and Connie Albus. In Maryland, state legislators have been unable to pass either a pro–gay marriage or anti–gay marriage bill. "Emmett Burns, one of the council members, had an anti–gay marriage bill in for the second year in a row," explains Gary, "and we were protesting against that."

While more than a hundred people looked on as witnesses and the television cameras rolled, a Unitarian husband-and-wife pastor team officiated at the ceremony, refusing to call it a "mock" wedding. "This is a real wedding sanctioned by a real church," Reverend Phyllis Hubbel stated. "Maybe one day, if God and the legislature see fit, these weddings will also be legally recognized."[3]

While Gary and Tom's wedding had deep personal meaning to them, it also affected the political situation in Maryland. "We changed some people's minds [about the anti–gay marriage bill]," he explains. "The bill didn't get into a committee, so it was killed for another year. We ended up beating the bill back two years in a row. Unfortunately, the pro-marriage bill was also killed. That was kind of crummy, but then next year there will be a whole new council."

For them, their Annapolis wedding was definitely "a real wedding." Family members showed up for the event, and after, Tom's mother took the wedding party out to dinner as her present to the couple. She even rented a Cadillac limousine for them.

"We got a real marriage certificate," Gary says. Did it change them as a couple in any way, the way nonpolitical ceremonies can? "It really made us closer," Gary muses. "We feel we're a little bit invincible now, because of that."

Halfway across the country in Indiana, Harriet Clare and Becky Thacker also took part in a NOW Valentine's Day action. The couple, who have been together nine years, celebrated their commitment with a medieval hand-fasting at the National Women's Music Festival in Bloomington, which Harriet's grown children attended. But Harriet and Becky also decided to make a political statement about their union. They advised the local press that on Valentine's Day 1996, they planned to walk into the City-County Building in downtown Indianapolis and request a marriage license. The news made the front page of the local paper and caused a flurry of media excitement.

"The NOW folks drove us to the [marriage license] bureau in a van," Becky recalls. "When we arrived there were banks of TV cameras pointed at us, which we really didn't expect. What made it especially cool was that we couldn't get the van door open! We envisioned hetero America giggling and saying, 'They're no threat, they can't even find their way out of an unlocked van.' "

With TV cameras rolling, Harriet and Becky made their way to the marriage license counter. The cameras raced behind the marriage clerks to get the whole event on film. A group of supporters, many dressed in tuxes and bridal gowns, joined them in protest against the Indiana law that states, "A marriage between persons of the same gender is void in Indiana even if the marriage is lawful in the state where it is solemnized."

The heterosexual couple in front of them in line found themselves in the limelight, too. When interviewed by reporters, the woman in the couple said, "I think people who are in love should be allowed to get married."

When it was Harriet and Becky's turn, the clerk declined to let them file an application, saying she was prohibited by law from doing so. But the clerk encouraged them to lobby to get the law changed. "That's the great thing about this country," the clerk noted. "Laws can always be changed."

After, while they were waiting to be picked up by the NOW van, Harriet and Becky encountered a woman on the street who seemed to be a city employee. "Did they give you that license?" she asked. When they told her no, the woman muttered, "Those dickheads!" and then proceeded toward the City–County Building.

> *"We never knew it was going to become a national issue, let alone a highly controversial one with lots of anger, death threats, fights, picketing. We never thought that just wanting to get married would cause such a problem."*

Not everyone was so thrilled by Harriet and Becky's attempt to marry. Typically, the TV crews sought out and found negative responses from people on the street. " 'I think it's terrible' was one comment," Becky remembers. "But they didn't pursue that with the obvious question, 'What's so terrible about it?' " The TV reporters also took the time to get the opinion of Woody Burton, a vehemently antigay state legislator who, Becky says, "always mentions bestiality in the same sentence with same-sex marriage, and the TV stations always air it. Often that's the last thing viewers hear."

All over the country, same-sex couples have staged similar protests against the oppressive, anti–gay marriage laws that numerous state legislatures, fearing the possibility that Hawaii may legalize same-sex marriage, have rushed to enact. Even the U.S. Congress has gotten into the act, overwhelmingly passing the Defense of Marriage Act (DOMA) in September 1996, a bill that narrowly defines marriage as being "a legal union between one man and one woman." President Clinton signed the bill shortly after, but quietly, in the wee hours of the morning, instead of in a traditional, public Rose Garden ceremony.

In June 1996, North Carolina passed a bill banning gay marriages and the recognition of gay marriages throughout the state. Of 138 legislators, only 15 voted against the bill. One month later, local lesbian and gay activists staged a political protest in Raleigh across from the North Carolina state capitol building. With several dozen guests as witnesses, lesbian writer and activist Mab Segrest officiated at the dual wedding of two lesbians, Ana and Joy, and two gay men, John-Mark and Glen, followed by a brief reception where punch and wedding cake were served. Segrest stated, "The legislature may have the legal authority, but it has no moral or spiritual authority over us. I join these two women and these two men through the power invested in me, not by the General Assembly, not by the Christian church, but by the gay and lesbian community."

Later, the guests paired off into hand-holding, same-sex couples and marched defiantly through the state capitol building before being ushered out by the police.

"Just Two Guys in Love"

What sparked all of these actions on the part of state legislatures, Congress, and lesbian and gay activists was an event that took place at the end of 1990, when three same-sex couples—one gay couple and two lesbian ones—applied for marriage licenses in Honolulu, Hawaii. The story is now legend, though Patrick Lagon and Joseph Kealapua Melillo, who have been a couple for twenty years and say they're "just two guys in love," had no idea what they were starting.

"We never knew it was going to become a national issue," says Joe, "let alone a highly controversial one with lots of anger, death threats, fights, picketing. We never thought that just wanting to get married would cause such a problem."

On their tenth anniversary in 1987, Joe and Pat decided they wanted to have a commitment ceremony to celebrate their union. "We'd have a bunch of friends over and have a party," Joe says. But their plans quickly changed when a gay activist friend heard of their intentions.

Joe and Pat were involved in planning and fund-raising for Hawaii's first-ever gay pride parade that year. They mentioned to their friend that they were going to have a commitment ceremony to publicly acknowledge their union, and he suggested that they try to get thirty or forty couples together to do a mass wedding right after the parade, to make a political statement.

However, they couldn't get a group of couples together, so the mass wedding idea fell through. But their friend came up with the idea of trying to marry legally. "Hawaii's state law doesn't specifically say that two guys can't get married," Joe explains. "They gender-neutralized the laws at one of the constitutional conventions. They took out 'man and woman' and put 'one spouse and another spouse.' "

Patrick Lagon and Joseph Melillo, plaintiffs in the landmark Hawaii same-sex marriage case.

Instead of rushing into it, though, Joe, Pat, and other activists carefully investigated the idea for the next three years, waiting for the right political climate. Finally, after an historic state law was passed eliminating discrimination from the workplace, they decided the time was right to tackle same-sex marriage rights.

Their first step was to go to the Sunday newspaper, the *Honolulu Advertiser,* and tell them their intentions: "We said, 'We're in love with each other, and we want to get married,' " says Joe. The feature story appeared on the front page of the paper in November 1990. When the story was publicized, two other same-sex couples contacted Joe and Pat and asked if they could apply for licenses with them. On December 17, 1990, Joe and Pat, Genora Dancel and Ninia Baehr, and Tammi Rodgrigues and Antoinette Pregil—backed by other activists and also by media coverage—marched up to the marriage license counter at the State Department of Health in Honolulu and filled out applications for licenses. The three applications were not expressly denied, but instead were put into a "holding file."

"We walked over to the ACLU [American Civil Liberties Union] offices," recalls Joe, "and told them we'd been denied our equal rights and would they help us with this discrimination case." But the ACLU took four months to decide that it couldn't handle the case. The three couples then hired a lawyer, Dan Foley, at their own personal expense. "We had to go and hustle the money," Joe says. "We begged for money." After a long process, on May 5, 1993, the Supreme Court of Hawaii held that the couples had the legal right to marry, and that they had been discriminated against on the basis of sex, not sexual orientation. The state was ordered to prove there were "compelling reasons" not to allow the marriage, or else to issue the marriage licenses. "And that was the beginning of the national publicity," Joe says.

MARRIAGE RIGHTS ONLINE

The campaign for equal marriage rights is ongoing and constantly changing. Most recently, suits were filed in New York and Vermont, though both were thrown out on technicalities. State legislatures continue to debate both anti– and pro–gay marriage bills, and same-sex marriage activists struggle against the right-wing backlash. The best place to go for updates is online, and the following are a few of the most helpful Internet resources.

The Equal Marriage Rights Home Page–
www.ucc.gu.uwa.edu.au/~rod/gay/marriage.html
This is a huge online source, with links to maps of the United States that show state-by-state status of legislation, national news, state news pages that detail pro and con legislative efforts, links to marriage rights groups throughout the country, a reference guide with links to recent articles that have appeared in various newspapers and magazines, as well as links to other same-sex marriage sites.

The National Freedom to Marry Coalition (FTM)—
www.ftm.org
This organization is dedicated to winning the fight to legalize and recognize same-sex marriages in every state. Through committees that meet regularly across the country, FTM advocates via public relations and education campaigns, speakers bureaus, and lobbying efforts to give lesbians and gay men the right to take advantage of civil marriage wherever they live in the United States. FTM's Web site includes a listing of the benefits that come with legal marriage, and the texts of documents on same-sex marriage from organizations like the American Civil Liberties Union and Lambda Legal Defense and Education Fund.

The Forum on the Right to Marry (FORM)—
www.calico-company.com/formboston
FORM is a grassroots organization that engages in education and outreach on same-sex marriage rights, providing resources and training to other groups around the country. Some of the resources they offer at their Web site include: a primer on the Hawaii marriage case; the legal history of same-sex marriage; a press kit; a same-sex marriage timeline; and a list of newspapers that publish same-sex wedding announcements. FORM can also be accessed through the "onQ Gay and Lesbian Community Forum" (keyword: on Q) on America Online, under the link "Home and Families."

The Marriage Mailing List
If you're a same-sex marriage junkie, you can get a big fix through this mailing list. The list was designed to facilitate activism and the exchange of ideas and resources on the struggle for same-sex marriage rights, not just in Hawaii but around the country. The recommended version is the digest form, which lands in your in box every few days and to which you can subscribe by sending an e-mail message to majordomo@abacus.oxy.edu. In the body of the message, type "subscribe marriage-digest [Your e-mail address]."

At that point, Lambda Legal Defense and Education Fund came into the fight, setting up its Marriage Project, directed by attorney Evan Wolfson, who says he has been an advocate for equal marriage rights since he was a third-year law student at Harvard in the early 1980s. Wolfson became co-counsel with Foley for the plaintiffs.

The biggest breakthrough was still to come. The state of Hawaii tried to find some "compelling reason" not to issue marriage licenses to same-sex couples but failed miserably. The state based its weak case on the idea that lesbian and gay couples can't biologically have children together (neither can a lot of heterosexual couples) and that children raised by same-sex couples are at a disadvantage (proved false by numerous studies). The reasoning on both counts was shown to be faulty, and on December 3, 1996, Judge Kevin Chang ruled that the state had been unable to prove its case and that it should begin to issue marriage licenses to lesbian and gay couples immediately. The state, however, was able to get a stay, and the case is currently waiting for a final ruling by the state supreme court, where same-sex marriage rights are expected to prevail.

Still, right-wing players in Hawaii were able to push for a popular vote on a constitutional amendment that would nullify the high court's decision by making same-sex marriage illegal. In a state where 70 percent of the populace opposes same-sex marriage, this vote, scheduled for November 1998, could spell doom for equal marriage rights there.

Fortunately, the struggle for marriage rights is now a national movement. "This is not just about Hawaii," Evan Wolfson points out. "We have a national strategy." According to Wolfson, there are three core tasks for lesbians and gay men to achieve equal marriage rights. "The first is to win in Hawaii and other states," he says. "Second, we've got to beat back the backlash in as many states as possible." This means defeating the proposed anti–gay marriage bills in many state legislatures. The third piece of the work, says Wolfson, "is the affirmative engagement of nongay people and nongay groups . . . to create a climate of receptivity in the public's mind. It's in that climate that judges and legislatures will ultimately make their decisions." Much of this work is being done by individuals and by grassroots organizations like the Forum on the Right to Marry. (See the sidebar, "Marriage Rights Online").

Wolfson is confident that lesbian and gay marriage rights will be won in Hawaii. And how will Joe Melillo and Pat Lagon go about tying the knot, once it's legal?

"Pat and I are ministers and are both legal marriage performers in the state of Hawaii," Joe says. "The day we get our license, we're just going to pronounce each other husband and husband, fill out the certificate, and send it right back in to the state health department, so they can't take it away from us again."

After it's official, Joe and Pat expect to affirm their vows at a *paina*, or party. "And we'll probably have a very large reception," Joe smiles, "because everybody's asked for one!"

"In a Heartbeat"

When I began the research for this book, I wasn't sure what I would learn about people's views on same-sex marriage. I knew it was a hot topic, and one that had been furiously debated within the lesbian and gay community. On the one hand, many progressive queer activists have viewed marriage as a conservative goal that lesbian and gay men should not aspire to. In their view, we should instead be focusing on changing the social order so that marriage is not, as Patricia Nell Warren tells us "The Ultimate Perk." (See sidebar.) "It's not the issue *I* would have chosen for the community to focus on," is the message I got from more than one progressive lesbian or gay man.

When I asked if she and Cris Williamson, her partner of sixteen years, would legally marry if they could, musician Tret Fure was adamant that they would not. She finds the whole focus on marriage troubling. "There are more important things to be discussing in politics," she noted. Cris agreed with her, chiming in, "Yeah, like pollution."

Linda Villarosa, the former executive editor of *Essence* magazine, says the focus on same-sex marriage rights makes her mad. "I would really like to focus on some of the schisms we have within the community," she notes, "like around race and health care, rather than spending all our energy trying to get what heterosexuals have and what doesn't work for them given the fifty percent divorce rate." On a personal note, she explains that her parents' marriage didn't last, and that her heterosexual sister is also not interested in marriage. "There's just no energy toward marriage in my life," Linda says.

Many lesbians view same-sex marriage suspiciously, because of the negative connotations they have with heterosexual marriage as an oppressive institution for women. Cartoonist Alison Bechdel, creator of the popular comic strip, "Dykes to Watch Out For," avows she would never legally marry, "for all kinds of feminist reasons."

"I also think a relationship should be optional, not perfunctory," says Alison. "Being with my partner just because we feel like it gives me a smug feeling of moral superiority over all the legally bound drones in the world."

Other lesbians and gay men simply cut me off when I asked about the political debate in Hawaii and elsewhere. "I'm not into marriage," one lesbian activist told me curtly. Many still believe that marriage is just an attempt to mimic heterosexuals, to somehow become less "gay."

Yet since the start of this project, I suspected that marriage was an issue that hit home for many lesbians and gay men. Why else were we hearing about an increase in same-sex commitment ceremonies across the country? Why were we seeing commitment ceremonies on television sitcoms? And why had such a large grassroots network formed to work for equal marriage rights?

As the possibility of a win in Hawaii became ever more likely, many lesbians and gay men began stating in no uncertain terms that they did indeed view marriage as an important issue for them. In a *Newsweek* poll in June 1994, 91 percent of the lesbians polled and 79 percent of the gay men said they considered marriage rights either "very important" or "somewhat important" to the lesbian and gay movement. Why is marriage so vital? Because it directly impacts people's lives in a way other civil rights issues—like gays in the military, for example—might not. "I've done a fair amount of political organizing," says Dr. Marjorie Hill, "but this is the first time I feel like I'm living something that I want to happen as opposed to fighting for something that may happen. It really is in the truest sense making the personal political."

Over and over, I asked lesbians and gay men across the country, "If you could legally marry, would you, and why or why not?" and the response I heard most often was "In a heartbeat." The reasons they gave varied, but the most common were for the legal benefits and validation that marriage brings with it.

"Civil marriage affords protections and responsibilities and obligations and rewards that are very hard to come by otherwise," says Richard Jasper of Atlanta, who was once married to a woman and would marry his partner, Jeremy Corry, if he could.

"Recently one of us had outpatient surgery," says Belinda, who lives in upstate New York with her partner, Terri. "And we couldn't find our health care proxies! Marriage would eliminate the need for those documents."

Dan and Matt,[4] who live in Washington State, say they have a network of documents, as well as supportive families. "If something were to happen to one of us," says Dan, "I don't think there would be any problems, but you hear all sorts of horror stories." Marriage, he says, would make things a lot simpler and more clear-cut.

Oscar Jones of Nebraska would also like the convenience a simple, twenty- or thirty-dollar marriage license brings. "When you get married legally," he says, "it's just all said and done. You have that one license that says, okay, if one of us takes ill, you are married to him. You are the one who takes care of him. You don't have to worry about a parent saying, 'No, you have no say-so.' You don't have to worry about the courts or anyone else saying, 'You weren't that important in his life.' "

Joy Nelson, who lives in Tennessee with Carlena Calhoun, also notes the enormous amount of paperwork necessary for same-sex couples to try to simulate marriage rights. "I'd like the legal protection and the health insurance benefits," she says. "It would make it easier to plan for the future without having to cover your backside with all of the legal papers that we have to use now." (See page 148.)

"We're tired of scrambling with the lawyers, trying to keep everything straight," sighs Joeline, who lives with Sandy in California. "Medical benefits are a big item with us. Sandy's employer will not allow her to add me to her insurance, even if we pay for it! That is positively stupid." Sandy has four more years to go before she retires, and then "she's going to take her retirement fund out in a lump sum and invest it," says Joeline, "because they won't pay me anything if something happens to her."

Being able to have health insurance for her partner, Harriet Clare, would be a big plus for Becky Thacker of Indiana, too. "Recently Harriet has closed her business," Becky relates, "and she's been out of work for three months now. We're down to one income and have to also pay for her health insurance, not a cheap thing when you're over fifty." But when Becky petitioned the trustees of the university where she works for domestic partner benefits, only one person bothered to respond—and did so by turning her down.

Paul Jacobowitz-Cain of Phoenix says that he and his partner Kurt have put all their legal paperwork in order. But the blatant inequity of the marriage laws grates on him. "We're a couple of eight years standing," Paul notes. "What sense does it make for the law to protect a man and a woman who choose to marry after knowing each other for five minutes, yet treats gay and lesbian couples of many years standing as total strangers?"

The issue of equality is important to Shawn Walker-Smith of San Francisco, too. "Here I am paying into a system and able to vote within a system that I can't necessarily participate in," he explains. "There's a whole fairness issue that bothers me. I think it bothers a lot of people."

Karin Kaj finds a big discrepancy in the way she's treated by the government and by everyone else. "Living in the San Francisco Bay area," she explains, "means that almost every entity we deal with treats us as a couple. Maria's employer does, our bank and creditors do, our families do, the diaper company does. In fact, the only aspect of our lives where we are *not* treated as a family is in dealing with the government."

"We are as married or more married than the average couple," Karin's partner, Maria Kaj, agrees. "I don't check 'single' on surveys or on the cen-

> *"If the Hawaiian courts make same-sex marriage legal, we will be on a boat or plane faster than one of Martina's tennis serves!"*

"Marriage: The Ultimate Perk"

BY PATRICIA NELL WARREN

FOR MONTHS NOW, the news has echoed with angry sound bytes from enemies of same-sex marriage. Homosexual nuptials, it's being said, will tarnish the "sanctity" of heterosexual marriage.

Gosh, do these folks ever read the newspaper? Or a history book? Marriage has already been deeply desanctified by centuries of festering heterosexual pragmatism.

Admittedly my views are colored by experience. For sixteen years I tried to be the perfect straight wife . . . gave it the old college try. But I never felt sacred—just more and more stifled and dishonest. When my homophobic spouse finally found out about me, he told me I was "sick." My first and only visit to a shrink revealed that he shared my spouse's opinion. So I ran for my life—divorce and coming out. Apologists for "traditional values" seem to forget the real history of marriage. Christian civilization was built by royalty and nobility who saw marriage as dynastic. People wedded for titles, wealth, feudal estates, vassals, heirs—to link empires and win wars. Lifelong monogamy and chastity belts were invented to ensure that a husband passed his inheritance only to his genetic offspring. While these marriages were sprinkled in holy water by ministers of "heaven," many of them were made in hell—as the tortured histories of blueblood families can tell us.

The American Revolution, and separation of church and state, separated marriage from legal church control. Marriage became basically a civil arrangement. Today, many American marriages still start with church bells. But the "sanctity" of civil marriage rights is arguable, since it boils down to a list of legal privileges that judges can rule on. These include inheritance rights, tax breaks, hospital visitation, pensions, joint custody. These are the things that homosexuals want, too, and are told they can't have, in the name of "sanctity." Since when do arbiters of "sanctity" include probate courts, hospital receptionists, company pension plans, and the IRS?

Americans also rely on marriage for certain perks and conveniences. For minors, getting married is a way of evading parental custody. For embarrassed parents of a pregnant teen, a shotgun marriage hopefully preserves the family honor. Marriage can get you free airline travel, a dental plan, diplomatic privileges, free housing on military bases, U.S. citizenship, the boss's daughter, a Mafia dynasty, and slave labor in the form of lots of kids. Marriage enhances a celebrity career, even serves as cover for some CIA intelligence work. Repeated marriage and divorce allows some folks to cloak sexual adventure in legality. Years of living together in "common law" can equal marital status, or at least get you a nasty "palimony" lawsuit. To the man or woman who marries for nice things, marriage may equal prostitution.

Are these profane perks protected by state and federal law? Yes. Are they sacred? Hardly. It is amusing to think how many heterosexual Americans would scream bloody murder if they lost their "right" to this array of conveniences. Yet they would deny those same perks to gay people.

Closet marriages go beyond perks, into prevarication. "Closet" is how homosexuals historically conformed to the old feudal mandate. Nobody tries harder to make marriage work than a fag or dyke or bi who is hell-bent on passing! We have even pumped out children to be cannon fodder for feudalism. Indeed, the gay community's love of drag and theater may be instilled in us by those long centuries of performing with sword held to our throat. But an Oscar-winning act is still an act, no matter how brilliantly sequined in "sanctity" it might be.

Interestingly enough, homosexuals don't monopolize the closet. Marriage is a good place for certain straights to hide too. Like the prostitute with heart of gold who hides her past by marrying Mr. Respectable with heart of gold. Or the "missing person" who hides in a marriage to start a new life and cover the trail. Or the straight military man who grudgingly marries to advance his career because the brass don't like to promote bachelors to admiral.

Marriage has no global agreement about what makes it "sacred." It's social silly-putty, squished into a thousand shapes by bias and blind belief. To the Israelites of the Ten Commandments, "sanctity" of marriage included polygamy and a man's right to kill his wife and children if they got out of line. To feudal lords, the "sacredness" of a serf wedding required the bride to give her virginity to the lord. To the American colonists, a woman could work her way into marriage through contract labor or being an indentured servant.

To Southern slaveowners, marriage was out of bounds for black people. To my Irish Catholic forebears, the marriage knot required a priest's "authority." To my Protestant forebears, Catholic sacraments were "evil popery," so only a preacher's words could authorize the knot. But to bride and groom on the high seas, a ship captain's authority is "sacred" enough.

Some of my Native American forebears had more sensible views. A couple stood before Creation and married each other on their own authority as human beings. They had no concept of being married by the power of some other person's religion or authority. "Nobody tells a Cheyenne what to do," my cousins used to say. If things went bad, all the aggrieved person had to do was put the partner's moccasins outside the teepee door . . . with the toes pointing away.

Can today's American marriage overcome its sorry history as a list of perks? Can a person make it sacred and wonderful?

Yes, I believe so. Real sacredness is infused into any relationship only by the two people themselves, be they straight or gay. They build a balance between their own self-respect and their respect for each other—and for their children, if they have them. If this sacredness is not deeply felt on the personal level, no law or sermon or tax break can put it there! Not even God and Goddess!

Not every heterosexual wants this kind of relationship. Not every homosexual does either. But those who do deserve the best that marriage can offer.

So yes . . . marriage in the nineties is darkly tarnished. But denying marriage to gay men, lesbians, bisexuals, and transgendered people will not untarnish it!

Heterosexuals have to take responsibility for the mess they've made of marriage. They were the ones who wanted to have marriage. They have spent three thousand years making it a juggernaut of Judeo-Christian empire, politics, patriarchy, property, including their "right" to control of wife, children, and genetic heritage. Now, in the ultimate paradox, heterosexuals may actually need the help of us homosexuals, if they want to put some sacredness back in marriage.

sus anymore. I don't care what the legal definition is. I haven't been 'single' since I was sixteen." Maria and Karin would make the trip to Hawaii if marriage is legalized there, even though they might run into complications when they return home to California. "I plan to get married as many times as I can until it counts for good," Maria says.

"The fact that we can't legally marry is a continuing source of frustration," says Deborah, who lives with her partner Chris in Connecticut. "It hurts to be reminded that, in the eyes of the law and the public at large, we are not 'really' married, despite our having registered as domestic partners in Hartford." Her tone changes to a lighter one: "If the Hawaiian courts make same-sex marriage legal, we will be on a boat or plane faster than one of Martina's tennis serves!"

For some couples, marriage would bring with it validation for their families. "We'll do whatever we can to protect our children," says Teresa, who lives with her partner Lori and two sons in Wisconsin. Carole and Jackie, a California couple who have been together fifteen years and have a thirteen-year-old daughter, couldn't agree more. "As a couple, we don't require anyone's approval of our relationship," Carole says. "But we will definitely make our relationship legal for our daughter's sake."

"As a couple, we don't require anyone's approval of our relationship, but we will definitely make our relationship legal for our daughter's sake."

Lori Berkowitz of Berkeley, California, thinks that she and her partner Diana Shapiro might marry simply for the political impact and to make a statement about the nature of "family." "To be a number—for visibility," Lori notes. "It might help change the way people think about what and who makes up a family if different kinds of families were legal." Diana, however, says that the legal aspects of marriage don't interest her.

John, who has been with his partner Martin for thirty-six years, observes that the two of them don't really need the economic benefits of marriage at this point in their lives. "But I want the respect," he says solemnly.

Martin agrees with him. The two of them lived in the closet for years, afraid of losing their teaching jobs and the love of their families. "Psychologically," Martin says, "I think being able to marry would be wonderful. To stand up and make a public statement like that, which is what marriage is, a public statement—well, that would be absolutely wonderful."

A Very Old Desire

For those of us who can't afford the plane fare to Hawaii, the legalization of marriage in one state isn't going to make an immediate difference to our relationships. But no matter what happens in Hawaii or in any other states where litigation has been brought, one thing seems clear: Lesbian and gay couples will still fall in love and marry, even if the government continues to refuse to recognize their unions. Lesbian and gay

YOUR WEDDING OR YOUR JOB?

The decision to have a wedding or commitment ceremony is a very personal and private one, made by the two people involved. But when Robin Shahar and her female partner chose to celebrate their relationship with a ceremony, Shahar suddenly found herself without a job.

After graduating sixth in her class from Emory Law School, Shahar was offered a job as a staff attorney in the office of Atlanta District Attorney, Michael Bowers—the same D.A. who had successfully prosecuted Michael Hardwick for having consensual sex with another man in his own bedroom. *Bowers vs. Hardwick* was upheld in an infamous Supreme Court decision in 1986, which backed up Georgia's sodomy law.

But when Bowers discovered Shahar's plans for a private Jewish commitment ceremony, he withdrew the offer of employment. "As chief legal officer of this state," wrote Bowers, "inaction on my part would constitute tacit approval of this purported marriage and jeopardize the proper functioning of this office." Shahar sued, but in June 1997, a federal appeals court ruled 8 to 4 that Bowers had not violated the constitution. The American Civil Liberties Union attempted to appeal to the U.S. Supreme Court, but the high court declined to hear the case. "Lesbians and gay men ought to have the right to a job and a relationship," says Matt Coles, director of the ACLU's Lesbian and Gay Rights Project, "without having to choose between the two—just like everybody else."

Shortly after the federal appeals court decision, it was revealed that Michael Bowers had had a ten-year adulterous affair during his tenure as Atlanta's D.A.

couples have been committing to each other for a long time, and as more and more people become visible, the desire to do so will become even stronger.

What, after all, does "marriage" mean? Is it a legal document, or is it the consensual joining of two individuals who decide to throw their lot in together? Should the state be able to determine who has the right to do so? Many religious denominations hold that it is two people who in the company of witnesses *marry each other,* and furthermore, that the ultimate sanction of their union lies with God (or some higher power), not the state. Lamont Williams of Missouri concurred with this when he told me that he and his longtime partner, Joseph Ward, didn't really need the state to approve their marriage. "We had our union blessed by God and witnessed by our friends," Lamont observed, matter-of-factly. "But what we want are all the benefits of marriage."

What strikes me is how firmly lesbians and gay men—like their heterosexual counterparts—are rooted in the culture and traditions in which they grew up. Most of us are brought up to think that commitment follows courtship, and commitment means marriage. While same-sex commitment ceremonies cannot legally bind two women or two men, they do serve an important emotional function for lesbians and gay men. They create a strong sense of union and validation, in the same way that heterosexual weddings do.

"There's a desire that people have that I think is very old in our psyches," comments lesbian activist Carmen Vázquez, "and that's to have our relationships celebrated. To walk down the aisle and then have a party and have people raise a toast to wish us well. To give strength to the relationship in a communal way. And that's a good thing. All human beings should have a right to do that. And I think, on an emotional level, that's what people want."

Virtually all the couples who spoke to me about their commitment ceremonies thought they had gained something emotionally through the event. For some, like Jackie, who married Renee in a backyard ceremony three years ago, the emotional gain was the support they got from those people closest to them, both gay and straight. "Our friends will forever see us as a couple," Jackie says, "and just as with any married couple, they'll work to keep us together." Heterosexuals get this wholehearted support when they marry—everyone is pulling for them—and same-sex couples need it, too, in order to make their unions work.

For Shawn Walker-Smith, who married his partner Robert at their San Francisco home, a change occurred within his own thinking about their relationship. "Being married offers solidity to a relationship," Shawn points out. "It makes it a little bit harder to say, 'Well, I'm not happy anymore, this isn't working out, see ya.' If we hadn't done the commitment ceremony, it would seem to me like we were still dating, and I would feel like we hadn't gone to that next phase."

Still, the fact remains that lesbian and gay marriages have no legal weight, are often viewed as a "sham" by society at large, and consequently have to endure stresses and injustices that heterosexual unions don't have to deal with. (See, for example, the sidebar, "Your Wedding or Your Job?")

The option to have a legally sanctioned union would be a big psychological plus for many lesbians and gay men. "The biggest problem for same-sex couples is our inability to look at our relationships as permanent," concludes therapist Michael Shernoff. "If marriage were legal, I think that would have a big, big advantage emotionally."

It is a real statement about the power of same-sex love and commitment that lesbians and gay men have made their "extra-legal" relationships work over the long haul. In the next chapter, we'll explore just how same-sex couples make their unions last through both the "better" and the "worse." It's a fairly simple recipe, though one that requires work and care. "We live together, share our lives, hopes and dreams," says Liz of her ten-year relationship with Judi. "We are there for each other throughout the good times and bad, in sickness and health, till death do us part."

Notes

1. Not his real name.
2. Not their real names.
3. Quoted in Tom Scarpitta, "Valentines and Vows Exchanged in Maryland," *The GLOBE Spin: The GLOBE of Bell Atlantic Newsletter,* vol. 5, no. 1 (March 1997), 9.
4. Not their real names.

"For Better or Worse, For Richer or Poorer . . ."

4

Our Own Kind of Marriage

We all know these words. An important phrase in traditional wedding vows, "for better or worse . . ." indicates everything that comes after the bliss of the marriage ceremony and honeymoon. When a straight couple gets married, social custom ordains what happens next. Traditionally, after the honeymoon the couple settles down into domestic life—setting up housekeeping, blending their assets, getting used to each other's quirks and habits, choosing which in-laws to visit on which holiday, deciding whether and when to have children. Unfortunately, though the feminist movement has made major inroads toward questioning traditional roles for husband and wife, women still bear most of the responsibility for domestic labor, child rearing, and the process of actually making a home.

Because lesbian and gay couples can't legally marry, and because even being gay still carries a stigma, there's no socially determined plan for two people of the same gender who decide to join their lives and futures. This lack of preset models can be both an advantage and a hindrance to same-sex couples trying to create a life together.

Having to make things up along the way—particularly having no set or expected gender roles—seems to allow same-sex couples to create relationships that are more egalitarian than many traditional heterosexual ones. For example, lesbian and gay couples who live together told me that they divide up household chores according to who likes to do a certain task or who is better at it. There is no expectation that one person will be better at cooking than another. "We do what we do best," Mark told me when I asked how he and his partner Andy split up the housework. Same-sex couples also have fewer preconceived notions about one person being "the breadwinner," since both partners are used to working for a living and expect to go on doing so after they commit to each other. When both partners are the same gender, gender roles are decidedly less significant in the relationship.

This lack of defined roles is not only a plus for same-sex couples, but it also offers a model to the dominant culture. "I think we're going to see a much broader social change if [same-sex] marriage is legalized," therapist Michael Shernoff hypothesizes. That potential for change is precisely what scares the right-wing opponents of same-sex marriage. Shernoff adds, "I think [legal lesbian and gay marriage] will let all people know that relationships are based on love and not about possessiveness and acquisition of another human being."

Another advantage for same-sex relationships is that the lesbians and gay men are an extremely diverse minority group—the lesbian and gay community is, in fact, a lot of different communities at the same time, consisting of various races, religions, ethnicities, ages, classes, and genders. Consequently, many lesbians and gay men have created marriages across differences like race and cultural background, in ways that heterosexual couples have less often done. "I have a lot of people from different cultures in my life," remarks Linda Villarosa, a black woman who has been partnered with a white woman for more than six years, "unlike a lot of the straight black and white people that I know. In the gay community, I think there is a lot more cross-race socialization." Many of us are therefore learning firsthand about both the stresses and rewards of dealing with our differences.

At the same time that there are definite pluses to same-sex relationships having no set plan, there seem to be more fuzzy gray areas for same-sex couples than there are for their heterosexual counterparts. Though it's usually assumed that straight married couples will combine their finances, for example, the question of money remains a difficult one for many lesbian and gay couples. Should we mingle all our assets, and if so, when? Should we have a joint bank account, but also keep our separate ones, just in case? The difficulty is, of course, that lesbian and gay couples aren't bound to each other legally but purely by choice, and most of us are instilled early on with the idea that such relationships can't last. So should we really tie up all our money together if somewhere down the road our relationship may come to an end? As Michael Shernoff points out, lesbian and gay couples have "an inability to look at our relationships as permanent." It's hard to imagine any but the most negative-thinking and masochistic straight couples taking divorce for granted when they first decide to commit. If anything, straight couples probably more often assume they'll be the ones to beat the 50 percent divorce odds.

Sexual fidelity is another area in which lesbian and gay couples have no real guidance. Legal marriage in this country prescribes monogamy, though some heterosexual spouses go against custom and set up open marriages. But lesbian and gay relationships, long stereotyped as fleeting and purely sexual, don't experience the same pressure to be sexually exclusive. Should lesbian and gay relationships strive for monogamy? Or should lesbians and gay men instead take the initiative to set up more experimental couplings (or groupings) with looser rules and fewer expectations? And how do we determine what "unfaithful" means when there are no set rules?

But by far the biggest challenge for lesbian and gay couples has to be their relationships with each other's families of origin, particularly parents. Granted, heterosexual couples have some of these same difficulties, and all the jokes straight male comedians have told over the years at the expense of their mothers-in-law attest to the tension of the in-law relationship. But lesbians and gay men are at a unique disadvantage in this area: Our marriages aren't sanctioned by law. My partner Katie's family members aren't really my "in-laws," though I refer to them that way; they are instead, as one lesbian writer has quipped, my "if-there-were-a-laws."[1] Sometimes same-sex committed relationships aren't even tolerated or acknowledged by the individuals' parents; occasionally lesbians and gay men face the open hostility of their partner's family members. In general, straight couples don't face such intense opposition except in some instances of racial or religious difference.

> "It was an occasion for cheering when we didn't get terrible opposition from our families. And the best we felt we could have was to have people not opposing us."

This kind of resistance from families can take its toll on a lesbian or gay couple. Heterosexual couples look to their families, first and foremost, to support their relationships. For lesbian and gay couples, families aren't always a reliable source of support, and many of us learn to expect very little from them. "It was an occasion for cheering when we didn't get terrible opposition from our families," psychologist April Martin notes of the announcement of her relationship with her partner, Susan, twenty years ago. "And the best we felt we could have was to have people not opposing us."

"How our families behave toward our gay or lesbian lover," psychologist Betty Berzon writes in her book, *Permanent Partners,* "can make the difference between a partnership enriched by family ties . . . and one that suffers tension and strain when anything concerning family comes up."[2]

Even when our families behave themselves, homophobia can rear its head when our relationships end through break ups or death. When my second serious relationship ended, my mother was visibly relieved and started dropping broad hints about my meeting up again with my high school boyfriend. (As long as I wasn't with a woman, there was hope that I could really be straight after all.) Even the lesbian therapist that my ex-lover and I went to for help in easing our break up told me simply, "You'll find someone else," as if one's partners were easily replaced and I shouldn't expect more from a lover than a couple of fun years. That was eleven years ago, but unfortunately, there are still very few services for same-sex couples who need help in resolving conflicts or ending unsalvageable relationships in a constructive and supportive way.

For lesbian and gay widows and widowers, lack of support for their grieving process can prove particularly devastating. The trauma of a partner's death is exacerbated by the fact that there is no legal, and often no social, recognition that the relationship ever existed. Michael Shernoff says that he published his book, *Gay Widowers: Surviving the Death of a Partner* (Harrington Park Press, 1997), because when he himself was widowed through AIDS, he couldn't find many written sources that addressed gay male grief specifically. There are also few resources to train counselors about lesbian and gay bereavement. "The vast majority of professional literature about the experience of bereavement by adults after the loss of a spouse," says Shernoff, "fails to consider that perhaps not all grieving spouses are heterosexual."

> *"Learning to love ourselves as lesbians and gay men doesn't always come that easily and it is something we have all had to work at."*

It's amazing that despite the pervasiveness of homophobia, despite the lack of support and recognition for our relationships, lesbians and gay men can both make their unions last over the long term—often growing old together—and also keep moving forward after a break up or the death of a partner. The odds would seem to be against it, but the resiliency of our commitments is, to me, awe-inspiring. Just how do we do it?

Most of the couples I spoke to stressed "The Big C"—Communication—which seems necessary and basic to any lasting relationship, gay or straight. Yet when a relationship is weighted down by homophobia, both external and internal, even basic things can be hard to achieve. "The psychic wounds of homophobia are intense," Michael Shernoff notes. "They're so pervasive and so often subtle that people don't even recognize them."

Self-love and self-reflection, therapist Vanessa Marshall remarks, are also critical to the success of our relationships. "I don't think I could have been who I am today," Marshall adds on a personal note, "had I not taken the time [between relationships] to really look at what I wanted and what

I needed to do about me to get it." Yet learning to love ourselves as lesbians and gay men doesn't always come that easily and is something we have all had to work at.

In this chapter, we'll look at the "for better or worse" of same-sex relationships: how we construct our marriages, how we get over the rough patches, how we make our unions last, and what we do when "forever" is shorter than we hoped it would be.

Settling Down

Whether or not lesbian and gay couples have a private or public ceremony, there comes a time in a relationship when things begin to move into a different, more serious phase. As we saw in chapter 2, this might take the form of beginning to cohabit or exchanging rings or another symbol of commitment. The couple might take the relationship even one step further—get engaged, hold a commitment ceremony or wedding, or register as domestic partners. Whatever outward step the new level of commitment involves, it also entails thinking about the relationship in new terms and imposing some structure on it. Straight married couples call this "settling down"—establishing a household, then following the social guidelines, routines, and customs of married life.

But lesbian and gay couples don't have the same expectations placed on their relationships by society. In fact, society in general expects our unions to fail. So any steps we take to settle down we make up on our own, borrowing old patterns and creating new ones as the need arises.

Many of us don't think about what it means to create a household together until we're faced with certain mundane decisions. Who cooks? Who cleans? Who buys the groceries? Who walks the dog? Are we financially independent or interdependent? How do we compensate for the fact that, as a couple, we have no legal standing or rights? Again, straight couples have traditionally been bound by social custom, though many have broken free of it. But all you have to do is watch a few television sitcoms and their accompanying commercials to see how deeply ingrained gender roles still are in our society, even thirty years into the second wave of feminist activism. It's Heterosexual Wife and Mother who is in charge of cooking, cleaning, laundry, and child care, even if she also works outside the home. If Heterosexual Husband and Father performs any of this "women's work," he's usually laughably and endearingly bad at it, or his efforts are seen as something just short of heroic. Even in a savvy sitcom like *Mad About You,* in which both partners have careers that are important to them, Paul the husband is virtually helpless around the house when Jamie the wife goes away on a business trip.

Breakfast together before work.

Take away prescribed gender roles, and what's left? Lesbian and gay couples have been living together all along without the gender-role expectations that face straight couples. If there are two women spouses, who's the "homemaker"? And if there are two men, who's the "breadwinner"? The answer is both, and neither.

This lack of gender roles is eternally confounding to many straight people. Same-sex couples repeatedly talk about how heterosexuals want to know who's the "man" and who's the "woman" in the relationship. The assumption is that without gender roles, no one would know how to act. But clearly, lesbian and gay couples have worked it out, and in ways that make much more sense than predetermined gender roles ever have.

Switch-hitting

Over and over, lesbian and gay couples described to me an amazingly egalitarian, democratic approach to household maintenance. "The roles are very fluid," says Dan of the way he and his partner Matt[3] have set up their day-to-day home life in Washington State. "Matt does most of the cooking, and I do most of the financial stuff, but we spend time switching off."

Mark, who lives with Andy in New England, outlines a similar situation in their relationship. "I have had some problems with health that really made me assess my priorities in life," Mark notes. "So at this time, I don't mind doing more of the work around the house. I know that this could change and we would switch places. It's happened in the past."

Doug, who lives in Denver with Jerry,[4] says that, in their household, "Whatever needs to get done, gets done. . . . Who cares who does it?" The only sticking point for them seems to be the laundry, which Doug says they "both struggle over. . . . We can put it in the wash, but who folds it?"

Like Doug and Jerry, Ric and Steve of Los Angeles "just do what needs doing." Who performs which task around the house seems exceedingly trivial to them. "Should we have a thermonuclear conflict over who will put the clothes in the dryer this time?" Steve laughs. "I don't think so." Ric, however, draws the line at cooking. "Steve cooks," he says, "because we dread the alternative!"

"The roles are very fluid. Matt does most of the cooking, and I do most of the financial stuff, but we spend time switching off."

Mano and Andrew say that they have also switched roles back and forth over the six years they've been together. "To be honest, I was sort of afraid at first of being labeled 'the wife' if I did household chores," Andrew admits. "So I really tried not to do them. I'd fix stuff and balance the checkbook, because those were 'manly' things." But that has changed over the years. "We try to keep mindful of the workload and stress level we both have," Mano says, "and then kick in whatever things need to be done."

Instead of interchangeable roles, Jill and Randi, who live in the Northeast, have chosen household tasks that they're good at—a sensible solution for an egalitarian household. "Randi does ninety-nine percent of the cooking because she likes to cook," says Jill, "and I get home from work late a lot. I do ninety-nine percent of the cleaning. She's more outgoing than I am, so she is usually the one who will do most of the calling if we're making plans with friends." Jill describes their daily relationship as "a good balance."

Jamie and her partner Beverly live in British Columbia and find that their division of chores usually surprises people. Because of their gender presentation, people expect them to follow prescribed male/female roles. "Jamie is much more butch than I am," says Beverly, "but she does most of the cooking and cleaning. And I haven't done dishes since we moved in together." Other tasks, Beverly notes, come down to a very practical "who doesn't mind doing it."

Who "Wears the Pants"?

In money matters, the situation gets more complicated, particularly when same-sex partners make differing amounts of money at their jobs. Who decides how money gets spent and thus wields more financial power—or, in traditional heterosexual terms, who "wears the pants"? And how financially interdependent are lesbian and gay couples compared with their heterosexual counterparts?

Recently I got a call from a telephone salesperson who asked if he could speak to "the decision maker." Clearly, the guy had offended more than one woman by asking for "the man of the house." But the idea of one partner making financial decisions for the family was foreign to me. (Unfortunately, I was at a loss for a snappy comeback to the solicitor's query. Later, Katie suggested that I might have replied, "Call the White House.")

> *"Steve cooks, because we dread the alternative!"*

For me, it was a relief when Katie and I decided late last year to merge our finances. We were both self-employed at the time, neither of us earning very much money, and pooling our limited resources seemed to make the most sense for our situation. It was a more complicated decision for Katie, since she had been married to a man who had subtly used the fact that he made more money as a way to wield power in the relationship. Being conscious of this helped both of us. As a result of our "merger," we now make decisions about spending money jointly, which isn't without its trials and tribulations. I'm much more of a tightwad than she is; I tend to catastrophize and worry about the future. But we've found, in most cases, that our differing styles of approaching money have balanced each other out.

It took us several years to get to the point of financial blending, though, and that has been the case for other couples as well. Like Katie, many lesbians have in the back of their minds the power imbalances in heterosexual marriages based on money. "I remember for a long time being the 'holdout' on merging our bank accounts," recalls Maria Kaj. "I knew that heterosexual couples had constant difficulties about finances, usually because the man had a monetary advantage. . . . I didn't want us to make the hetero mistake of mingling finances only to find one person disenfranchised." For a while, Maria and her partner Karin, who were both trained as accountants, went through a complicated reconciling process to keep their records straight and their expenditures fair and equal. Many of their friends, Maria says, thought their elaborate personal accounting system was laughable.

"Looking back on it now, it does seem stupid," Maria admits. "What a lot of work to go through when you're positive you're married forever! We finally commingled everything and that actually helped me think of us more as a family and helped me plan better when Karin decided to leave a salaried job to take care of our child, whom I gave birth to. Because that's what's fair: the family makes decisions together for what's best for the family."

Julie and Wendy make comparable salaries now but didn't always, and they believe that is all the more reason for couples to blend their finances. "That way you don't know what comes from where," Julie reasons. "Wendy came to the relationship with a lot of debt. . . . We worked hard to get rid of all the debt. It's just what marriage is all about—you take each other completely. And now we're buying a house together."

Lynne and Esther agree wholeheartedly with the idea of "for richer or poorer." "I think that if people make different salaries, that shouldn't count," Lynne says. "You're a family. Our salaries are really different, but it should just all go together."

Esther recalls a monthly lesbian and gay discussion group that she and Lynne set up in San Francisco called "Coffee Talk." One evening, the group discussed finances, and Esther was confused by the way the gay male couples approached the topic. "Everything is separate [for them], even down to the grocery bills," she says, amazed. "They each give half." Even if one partner earns less and is struggling to pay his share, she notes, they still maintain separate finances. "I just don't think that's fair," Esther concludes.

Dan and Matt[5] handled the gap between their incomes by merging everything. "I made five times as much money as he did in the beginning," Dan says, "and he was scrambling. We couldn't have functioned [as a couple] if we didn't intertwine."

For some couples, a big discrepancy in salaries brings up deeply ingrained issues about money and power that are hard to shake and that put stress on the relationship. Ben Munisteri and his late partner, Steven Powsner, never joined finances and assets, and it caused angst for Ben at the beginning of their seven-year relationship. "Steven had a lot of money," Ben notes. "I had very little income. He ended up paying for a lot of things. The expensive stuff, like dinners out, theater, cabs."

Ben voiced his concern that he would look like "a kept man" and didn't want to rely on Steven financially. Steven—though glad that Ben had those values—tried to brush aside the concern because he wanted them to live in the comfort that his money could buy them. Still, Ben per-

> *"Wendy came to the relationship with a lot of debt. . . . We worked hard to get rid of all the debt. It's just what marriage is all about—you take each other completely."*

A PLETHORA OF PAPERWORK: ESSENTIAL LEGAL DOCUMENTS FOR LESBIAN AND GAY COUPLES

Lacking the option of marriage in a society built around marriage, lesbian and gay couples have encountered arbitrary and often cruel legalities that create obstacles to family relationships and threaten personal security. But there are documents that can help protect these bonds and try to make laws work to the advantage of lesbian and gay families. If you can afford it, it's a good idea to enlist the help of a lawyer in drawing up the following documents, which vary from state to state. This paperwork will act as a safety net, helping to ensure that the intentions of those involved are carried out. With special thanks to Judith Turkel, Esq., of Turkel and Forman, the following documents are among those often suggested to lesbian and gay couples.

- General Power of Attorney
  (may be durable or not)

  This designates a person (or people) to act on your behalf. The designee is called an attorney-in-fact. You can limit the powers of the attorney-in-fact by excluding certain areas (like taxes, stock and bond transactions, and so on) or grant the attorney-in-fact broad powers with no exclusions. Matters to consider include: real estate, personal property, securities, banking, business, insurance, estates, litigation, government benefits, retirement plans, and taxes. A durable power of attorney will remain in effect even if you become incapacitated or incompetent.

- Health Care Proxy / Durable Power of Attorney for Health Care

  This document designates an agent to make health care decisions on your behalf when you are unable to do so yourself. It grants the person the power to advise your doctor to administer medical procedures and to make decisions about treatment. In addition to this legal document, it's a good idea for gays and lesbians to carry a card that identifies the person's partner and advises medical personnel to contact this individual in the event of an emergency. Without these protections, partners are sometimes denied the right to make important medical decisions and can even be prevented from visiting loved ones in the hospital.

- Living Will

  A living will is a legal document that provides for a person (or the person's legal agent in the case of incapacitation) to reject medical procedures or refrain from taking "heroic" measures. Living wills are used to authorize medical personnel to terminate or refuse treatment such as intravenous feeding and respirators when they're the only measures keeping the patient alive.

- Will

  If a person dies without a will, the person's property goes to the next of kin, the order of which is determined by individual state laws and may include children, parents, siblings, and so on. If the

sisted, and they agreed on an arrangement whereby they shared the monthly maintenance fee on their co-op apartment and each paid into the household expenses a set percentage of his income. "So I'd contribute five dollars to something, and he'd contribute twenty," Ben explains. "It was the same percentage." But it helped Ben feel like he was actively contributing to the household.

person has no relatives, the property goes to the state. This is why it's essential for gays and lesbians to draw up wills—to ensure that assets pass to intended survivors and that the intentions of the individual are carried out after his or her death. In addition to property, matters to be considered are who will be the legal guardians for children and who will be the executor of the estate. The person who makes the will must sign it in the presence of at least two witnesses who are also required to sign the document. It is very important to be sure that the will meets the strict legal requirements of the state of residence.

- Cohabitation Agreements

Cohabitation agreements are documents designed to protect the interests of couples who live together but are not married. There are two general types: one in which the parties agree to maintain separate property and incomes, and one in which the parties agree to share property and income, but variations of the two can be incorporated into each type. Written properly, cohabitation agreements can go a long way to prevent conflicts on a day-to-day basis or in the event the relationship breaks up. Many of these agreements also include provisions for alternative conflict resolution, such as mediation and arbitration.

- Legal Forms of Ownership and Property

Joint Tenancy: Ownership as joint tenants with right of survivorship provides for the equal ownership of property and the right for each party to have the use of all of it. An important aspect of joint tenancy is the "right of survivorship," which means that in the event of the death of

one of the parties named in the agreement, the surviving co-owner gets the share of the deceased person.

Tenants in Common: Another legal form of property ownership is tenancy in common. Tenants in common, however, are not protected by right of survivorship, although a major advantage to tenancy in common agreements is that the parties can be equal owners of the property.

- Child Custody or Guardianship

If children are a part of your family, your documents should also include provisions concerning guardianship and enabling the nonlegal parent to make medical and other legal decisions regarding the child, and a coparenting agreement which spells out each parent's support obligations in the event of a break up. If your child has been conceived through donor insemination, you will also need a donor/recipient agreement outlining the specifications of your arrangement.

For those without the resources to hire an attorney, Hayden Curry, Denis Clifford, and Robin Leonard's do-it-yourself book, *The Legal Guide for Lesbian and Gay Couples* (Nolo Press, 1996), contains samples of all of these forms in the appendix.

Still, it's a good idea to have a lawyer look over your paperwork. Some cities have lesbian and gay bar associations that offer referrals. In addition, many lesbian and gay community centers sponsor free or low-cost legal clinics. (Visit the directory of centers at http://www.gaycenter.org/ or call New York's Lesbian and Gay Community Services Center at 212-620-7310 for the center nearest you.)

The emotional impact of widely diverging incomes can be felt by both partners. Karen is still in school, while her partner Lisa is "the primary breadwinner," and Karen notes that this has caused stress in their relationship. "There are some control issues we have to work on," she acknowledges. "But then I'm only in school for another year. Then I won't feel so incomplete because I'll have a paycheck and she can get off my butt about the bills." Communication in cases like this can be the key, and Karen and Lisa see a couples' counselor to work on some of their power issues.

Jill recalls that when she was in school, "Randi pretty much supported us. She paid the rent, she paid the bills. . . . There was this huge difference in our incomes. And that was difficult." But the problems began to ease up when Jill graduated. "Once I started working, things changed a little bit. I think she felt she wasn't supporting me as much and it was more of an equal partnership even though our salaries were still not equal. But it was more the fact that we were both contributing to the household that made a difference in how we both perceived the relationship. It really started to feel like a marriage."

The "Illusion" of Legality

Another big issue for same-sex couples is the paperwork necessary to afford their extra-legal relationships some legal protections. When lesbian and gay couples commit or marry, they do not enjoy the protections and benefits that come with legal marriage. If they can afford a trip to the attorney, however, they can amass an array of documents designed to help validate their relationship in case of illness, emergency, or death. (See the sidebar, "A Plethora of Paperwork.")

I have to admit that Katie and I only recently set up our paperwork, mostly because of financial constraints—we didn't have an extra thousand dollars to pay an attorney. If Katie and I were able to marry legally, protections for our relationship would come automatically with the thirty-dollar license. Other couples have postponed their legal documents for the same financial reason. "We really don't have the money right now," says Karen.

The fact that lesbian and gay couples have to jump through hoops just to attain some semblance of legality is a point that makes many of us understandably angry. "We have our powers of attorney and all the legal aspects," Oscar Jones says of his relationship with Gregory Cox. "They create the *illusion* of partnership that would be said and done with a marriage license."

For Jill and Randi, as for many other couples, the trip to the lawyer took a long time to schedule. "It's just one of those things you don't want to do," Jill notes. "We haven't done it because we're lazy, not because we're not committed." What has spurred them to do it now is that they have begun to think about having a child together. One of the purposes of legal marriage, after all, is to validate and protect family relationships—to ensure that children have legal guardians and financial support. But without the right to marry, lesbian and gay couples have to set up elaborate documentation as protection for their families.

Even though they have had their legal documents for a long time, Martin and John, who are in their sixties and have been together thirty-six years, note that same-sex couples always have to think about whether or not the paperwork can be contested. "Let's say you made out your will in 1970," Martin explains. "Twenty years later, someone could say that in that time you lost your mental capacity."

Many couples expressed the fear that without legal paperwork, their relationship might very likely be ignored or invalidated in a medical emergency. The infamous case of Karen Thompson and Sharon Kowalski brought this fear home to many lesbian and gay couples.

In 1983, Sharon Kowalski suffered brain damage in a car accident, and her lover of four years, Karen Thompson, stayed by her side throughout her early hospitalization. Sharon's family of origin at first believed Karen to be only a concerned friend. When Sharon's parents discovered the true nature of the women's relationship, they banned Karen from visiting Sharon, calling her "sick." It wasn't until 1989 that Karen won visitation rights, and it was only in 1991, after a grueling legal battle, that she finally obtained guardianship over her lover. Karen and Sharon's nightmare was well covered in the lesbian and gay press and demonstrated that, without legal documents, same-sex couples have to rely on the "good will" of health care practitioners and families of origin.

> *"We live in a state that supports us, but there could come a time that Andy would not be let into my hospital room because he is not considered next of kin."*

Two years ago, for example, Carolyn's partner Genelle was injured while riding a horse. She was with her father, who managed to get Genelle to the hospital. "I half expected him to call his wife first," Carolyn says now, but she was pleasantly surprised when he called Carolyn instead. "When I thanked him for calling me, he told me he just did what Genelle would want him to do. So he respected our relationship in doing that." At the San Jose, California, hospital where Genelle was treated, the medical team also allowed Carolyn to be with Genelle at every step of the way. "We felt a huge pressure go away," Carolyn says.

But even when couples have family or institutional support, there can be nagging doubts and cause for worry. "We live in a state that supports us," says Mark, "but there could come a time that Andy would not be let into my hospital room because he is not considered next of kin."

All too often, as many AIDS widowers have found out, a medical cri-

"Wedded to an Illusion"

BY FENTON JOHNSON

IN THE MOST PROFOUND RELATIONSHIP I have known, my partner and I followed a pattern typical of an enduring gay male relationship. We wrangled over monogamy, ultimately deciding to permit safe sex outside the relationship. In fact, he never acted on that permission; I acted on it exactly once, in an incident we discussed the next day. We were bound not by sexual exclusivity but by trust, mutual support, and fidelity—in a word, love, only one manifestation of which is monogamy.

[Nancy] Polikoff tells of another model, unconventional by the standards of the larger culture but common among gay and lesbian communities: A friend died of breast cancer; her blood family arrived for the funeral. "They were astounded to discover that their daughter had a group of people who were a family—somebody had organized a schedule, somebody brought food every night," she says. "In some ways it was the absence of marriage as a dominant institution that created space for the development of a family defined in much broader ways." I find it difficult to imagine either of these relationships—mine or that described by Polikoff—developing in the presence of marriage as practiced by most of our forebears; easier to imagine our experiences influencing the evolution of marriage to a more encompassing, compassionate place.

Earlier I called myself an "AIDS widower," but I was playing fast and loose with words; I can't be a widower since my partner and I were never married. He was the only child of Holocaust survivors, and he taught me, an HIV-negative man preoccupied with the future, the lessons his parents had taught him: the value of living fully in the present and the power of love.

He fell ill while we were traveling in France, during what we knew would be our last vacation. After checking him into a Paris hospital, I had to sneak past the staff to be at his side; each time they ordered me out, until finally they told me they would call the police. Faced with the threat of violence, I left the room. He died alone as I paced the hall outside his door, frantic to be at his side but with no recourse—I was, after all, only his friend.

sis can show that even expensive and carefully drawn-up paperwork falls short of legal marriage. Ben Munisteri, for example, had power of attorney for his terminally ill partner, Steven Powsner, but it was still not quite sufficient when he needed it most. "When Steven had brain damage [from toxoplasmosis], I was his power of attorney," Ben relates. "I was his guardian. I made the decisions. That was on a piece of paper. But it was frequently questioned by people at the bank. Even though I had power of attorney, they'd say, 'Well, Mr. Munisteri, we don't know if we can have you sign on Mr. Powsner's accounts.' "

With Steven in and out of the hospital, Ben found his position as Steven's partner very vulnerable. "Fortunately, Steven's family didn't want much to do with his health care," he notes. "So I did make all the decisions, but I was always wary about alienating the family. . . . I knew he was going to die and I'd be left to face them alone and maybe I could lose everything—our apartment, our money. I could lose everything if they decided to challenge me."

As a final insult, even though Steven had written down his wish to be cremated and had the affidavit notarized, the Jewish funeral home they chose for his service would not respect his and Ben's wishes, because cremation goes against the Jewish faith. Though Ben had been Steven's primary caretaker and husband for over seven years, Steven's parents, who had virtually nothing to do with their son while he was ill, had to give permission for the cremation. Ben recalls the funeral director's position with much bitterness: "He said [the decision] had to be from 'the family' and I was not 'the family.' " (See also the sidebar, "Wedded to an Illusion.")

Out in the World

As Ben's story shows, the perception of lesbian and gay couples by the world outside can play a significant role in our relationships. Health care practitioners, employers, bank officials, insurance companies, landlords and Realtors, and the like all have the power to accept our marriages or to treat us as "outlaws."

Coming out over and over can be exhausting. Does *everyone* really need to know? "You can't just come out once and have it be done with," Maria Kaj observes. "You have to have 'the' conversation over and over again with people who didn't hear it or didn't hear the whole story or the grocery clerk or the insurance salesman or somebody new to the company. You've have to steel yourself to doing it until it becomes second nature and you don't have to react to their reaction anymore."

Obviously, coming out is a political act, and some lesbians and gay men feel they don't want to be activists. But social change happens slowly, and only when stereotypes are broken down and civil rights are demanded. No one's going to hand lesbians and gay men equal rights, protections, and respect. So we've got to show our faces, lift our voices, and make our presence felt. We've got to let the rest of the world know that there's nothing wrong with being gay. Being out as individuals and as couples is an assertive step that shows the world that we're here, we're queer, and—hey, what do you know?—we're in lasting relationships, too.

Our relationships, in fact, provide a good way of bringing the issue of sexual orientation home. It's far easier to mention casually "my partner Dave" than to come right out with, "Oh, by the way, I'm gay." "Marriage is such a familiar issue," comments Quirk, the lesbian founder of the Gay and Lesbian Community Forum (now called "on Q") of America Online. "To talk about sexual orientation within that context makes it a lot less threatening. It's something people can relate to."

Outing Ourselves

It sounds easy on paper, but how do lesbian and gay couples actually negotiate the repeated act of coming out? For Karin Kaj, as for many others, the formula is simple. "I've found that people tend to treat you the way you make it plain you expect to be treated," Karin observes. "If you act secretive, people interpret it as shame."

"I'm still basically a private person," Karin's partner, Maria, states, "but I want people treating us as a couple, not as 'Are you sisters?' " Karin and Maria are out to all the important service providers in their lives, and most importantly, to their doctors. "Here is someone you have to trust with your life," Maria says. "You can't lie to them. If you're lying to your gynecologist, for example, about your sex life, you're going to have a meaningless conversation. They need to know that you're not as susceptible to yeast infections or pelvic diseases and that you don't need birth control."

But what about the less important people, the ones who don't necessarily "need" to know? Karin and Maria recently wanted to sign up with their young son Kelson for a family discount card at the zoo. They found to their surprise that they didn't have to fight to do it, just ask, and that in asking, they were opening one man's eyes. "There was an old fella at the booth," Maria recalls, "and I asked what was the definition of 'family.' He said, 'A husband, a wife, and up to four kids.' I bristled for a fight and told him we were a family, we were partners, this was our child, you wanna make something out of it."

But Maria suddenly realized that it wasn't bigotry on the man's part, but the fact that he didn't realize there was an alternative to his set concept of family. "He said fine and showed us where to put our names," Maria says. "He smiled at our son and took our credit card. To me that's it: Most people these days are not trying to pick a fight. They're just ignorant and they need to be shown how to fill out the forms and apply the rules."

Karin and Maria, though, live in the San Francisco Bay area. What about couples in less gay-friendly parts of the country—do they feel they can be as out as Karin and Maria? "You can't be a closeted gay couple in a town of eight hundred people," Alan Hultquist points out. He and his partner of fourteen years, Brendan Hadash, have been out in their tiny Vermont community since they moved into a new house together. "News spreads incredibly fast," Alan notes. "We've had joint bank accounts for at least ten years, and my physicians have always known, although I haven't officially told the dentist."

When they fell in love, Bekki McQuay and Diane Curtis told their families, neighbors, and service providers about their relationship. But then they found themselves outed in their community in Amarillo, Texas, by a messy and publicized court case, in which Diane and her ex-husband battled for custody of their ten-year-old son. (See also page 51.) "That pretty well took care of all those we didn't personally tell," Diane says wryly. Still, their rule has been to be as honest as possible about their relationship. "We are two women in love, and I think that is reflected wherever we go," Diane comments. Their openness extends even to minor creditors. "Bekki just acquired a Discover card, and she told them I was her spouse and requested a card in my name on her credit," Diane relates. "They honored that. So I'm going to get her cards on my credit, too, just so we can let other companies know we exist."

"We are out to absolutely everyone," says Jackie Griffin, who lives with her partner Renee in Washington State. "It's one of the most freeing things. Nothing to hide, nothing to protect, everything to celebrate." But some lesbian and gay couples would challenge Jackie's "out and proud" assertion. It's fine to be out with doctors and bank officials, but as Peggy Frantz-Geddes of Oregon puts it, "We don't go out of our way to be out with strangers, unless they ask." For many who don't live in progressive or liberal areas, being openly lesbian or gay to the neighbors, for example, can be risky.

"We live in a hick town," says Michelle of Texas, adding simply, "We'd get shot." But when the information seems relevant, Michelle and her partner (also named Michelle) tell service providers and doctors. "Hairdressers, dentists, sure," she adds.

Melise and Guillian Zoë, who also live in Texas (near Dallas, though, not in a small town), are able to be out to most service providers in their lives—their mechanic, hairstylist, doctors, insurance agent, Realtor, and many more. "Everyone we do business with on a regular basis knows," says Melise. But they don't feel free enough to be out on the street. "We don't hold hands or even hug in public," she notes. "Living in the South, this is just smart. We do have rainbow flags on one of the cars, but opted not to put them on our new truck, just in case."

Like Melise and Guillian, Beverly says that she and partner Jamie can be out in most aspects of their lives in British Columbia. But like many lesbians and gay men, they draw the line "when our safety needs to be

"You can't be a closeted gay couple in a town of eight hundred people. News spreads incredibly fast."

considered." They are often not able to walk hand in hand on the street, for example, the way straight couples do, for fear of verbal harassment or physical assault.

Carlena Calhoun and Joy Nelson live in Tennessee and also have reason to be circumspect at times when safety is an issue. "We live at the buckle of the Bible Belt," Joy says, "and they are twenty years behind the rest of the world. Sodomy is still on the books as being illegal." Then she adds, laughing, "Actually, it is still on the books in Tennessee that if a woman is driving, a man has to walk ten to twenty feet in front of the car to warn other drivers!"

Lesbians and gay men who are parents find they have to come out as couples and as families even more than they did before they had children. "Since our son was born," says Teresa, who lives in Wisconsin, "Lori and I find we are coming out constantly. We feel very strongly about being open and honest about our family so that our children can be proud. Over the years, it has become much easier to be out in whatever situation presents itself."

Siobhan Hinckley, who lives with her partner Anita in Albany, New York, has found that, when people see her as a mother, they always assume she's straight. She has to make snap decisions about whether or not to be up front with strangers all the time. Unless she's really tired, she says, she almost always comes out, mostly because she wants to send her young son and daughter the right message about having lesbian parents. "If you're going to raise your children without shame, you need to be proud of who you are and out about who you are," she notes. (For more on lesbian and gay parents coming out in their communities, see chapter 5, pages 247–250.)

> "If you're going to raise your children without shame, you need to be proud of who you are and out about who you are."

Out on the Job

Being out to the doctor or your mechanic is one thing, but being out at work—in a country that has yet to pass the Employment Non-Discrimination Act (ENDA)—can get you fired. Alicia, a bank manager in Albany, New York, found that being open about her lesbianism at work got her slapped with a charge of sexual harassment from a disgruntled subordinate. An investigation followed, in which Alicia was interrogated without legal counsel for over three hours by the bank's human resources officials. "Their questions involved many facets of my personal life with Nancy [her partner]," Alicia recalls. She was threatened with firing and with a civil suit if the allegations proved to be true. "Additionally, I was told that I talked about my personal life at work too often and was advised not to talk about it at all," Alicia says. The underlying assumption was that even *mentioning* her relationship with Nancy at work was a kind of sexual harassment of straight women. (Wouldn't it be something if this worked the other way, too—if lesbians and gay men could claim sexual harassment at work for having to listen to endless stories of heterosexual romance and procreation?)

Though the bank could find no hard evidence against Alicia and she got to keep her job, the incident raised suspicions about her in the eyes of her coworkers. "I heard one employee say, 'I'd never want to go into the bathroom when *she* was in there.' " Alicia remembers. Soon after, Alicia left that position for a new job where the fact that she is a lesbian is not an issue.

Sometimes, though, changing jobs can cause greater problems. Dan and Matt[6] found that when they switched jobs they could no longer be open. In their former jobs, they were both very out to their colleagues. But now Dan, who is a pediatrician, finds that in his new position at a small clinic "in the boondocks" of Washington State, things are more difficult and he is much more circumspect about his personal life. "There are some fundamentalist Christian people I work with," he notes, "who would get upset with me and take it to their church." Matt also has a new job, as a college swimming coach, and there has been a recent backlash against openly lesbian and gay coaches. "I used to go to university functions with him," Dan says, "but now I don't, because parents might find out and pull their kids off the team." The situation is hard on both of them, Dan says—"It's really difficult because it feels like a step backward." For Dan and Matt, the frustratingly common stereotype of gay men as pedophiles holds them as hostages in the closet.

The discrimination and fear of reprisal that lesbian and gay employees face and the threats that are used to manipulate them point to a real need for legislation to protect gay employees' civil liberties. Some lesbians and gay men have found that, even though they could be out at work, when they asked about the possibility of domestic partner benefits for their spouses, they faced possible recrimination. Laura, who works in Oklahoma City as an airline reservation agent, found a fair amount of tolerance for her sexual orientation at her job. But when she began trying to start a committee to investigate domestic partner benefits, management told her basically to "knock it off, or else."

Andrew, who lives in San Francisco with his partner Mano, recently

"COMING OUT" FOR GAY RIGHTS

Almost every day another company "comes out" in support of their lesbian and gay employees. There are hundreds of private employers across the country that now offer benefits to the domestic partners of their employees, and a partial list follows. Contact Lambda Legal Defense and Education Fund at (212) 809-8585 for a complete listing of companies, organizations, and government agencies that offer such benefits.

Adobe Systems	Dow Chemical	Novell Corporation
American Express	Eastman Kodak	Paramount Pictures
Apple Computer	Fannie Mae	PBS
Atlantic Records	The Ford Foundation	Showtime
Barnes & Noble Booksellers	Glaxo Wellcome	Sierra Club
Bell Atlantic	Hewlett-Packard Corporation	Sony Music
Ben & Jerry's	Home Box Office	Starbucks Coffee
Boston Globe	IBM	Sun Microsystems
Capital Cities/ABC, Inc.	Intel	TicketMaster
Consumers Union	Levi Strauss & Co.	Viacom International
Coors Brewing Company	MCA/Universal, Inc.	Warner Brothers
Creative Artists Agency	Microsoft Corp.	Xerox Corporation
Discovery Channel	NEXT Computer	
Disney Corporation	Northern Telecom	

A helpful resource for lobbying for domestic partner benefits at your job is *Try This at Home: A Do-It-Yourself Guide to Winning Lesbian and Gay Civil Rights Policy* (W. W. Norton & Company, 1996), written by Matt Coles, director of the American Civil Liberties Union's Lesbian and Gay Rights project. This step-by-step guide for individuals and groups suggests the most effective strategies for changing company policies regarding employment and benefits. Coles includes tips on what works and what doesn't and gives samples of domestic partnership clauses from actual employee manuals. Follow Coles's advice, and learn how to add your company's name to the list above.*

*There may be financial drawbacks to acquiring domestic partner benefits. Unless your partner can be claimed as your dependent, you will pay income tax on the value of the domestic partner benefits.

found out about the "or else"—he was fired for inquiring about domestic partner benefits with his employer. He has brought a lawsuit against the company, which maintains that Andrew was fired for other reasons.

Though many lesbians and gay men have horror stories to tell about their jobs, other lesbians and gay men have found ways not only to be open at work, but also to acquire some benefits for their spouses in the bargain. Changing times and increased visibility for lesbians and gay men have improved many work environments. (See the sidebar, " 'Coming Out' for Gay Rights.")

Judi, who works at a big electronics firm in Oregon, displays photos of her partner Liz and their son Ben proudly in her work cubicle. "Liz and I go to work social events together," Judi says. "I get real annoyed if I suspect that folks don't see Liz and Ben as my family."

Judi has been active in the gay/lesbian/bisexual employees' group at work. It took the group about a year of lobbying to become an officially sanctioned employee group with a small budget from the company. And just within the past year, the firm began offering health care benefits to same-sex domestic partners. Judi thinks that the employee group's pressure on the company helped, but that the need to recruit good workers finally "broke the logjam." "Several other [electronics] companies began offering these benefits," she notes. "It's tough to find qualified folks for a growing company, and it was important that [my company's] benefit package be competitive with other potential employers."

Belinda and Terri live in upstate New York and are both out at their jobs, Terri as a nurse and Belinda as a research scientist for the state Department of Health. They find they are treated as a couple and invited together to parties, employee weddings, and other work-related functions. Though the state, Belinda's employer, offered them domestic partner benefits, the couple had to "jump through hoops," Terri says, to actually get them. "We had to fill out several forms, have them notarized, and provide proof of financial interdependence and commitment. No kidding! Married people don't have to do that crap."

Many other lesbian and gay employees have not been able to obtain health care benefits for their spouses, even though they feel free to be out at work. Illinois state policewoman Joanne[7] is protected by her union's antidiscrimination clause, which includes sexual orientation. Though the police force is homophobic, Joanne says that "with the union backing, I have the confidence to be open." She talks about her partner and their baby at work, just as her coworkers talk about their families. "We even got a present when our son was born," she adds. The union, however, drew the line at same-sex domestic partner benefits. "I brought it up once," Joanne recalls, "and the response was just to be happy with the no discrimination policy."

At Pat Catlett's place of employment in Albuquerque—where one of the owners is gay, and about six of sixty employees are out—Pat was unable to get health care benefits for her partner when she needed them. "Karen was without insurance for about a year," Pat says, "and I tried to get her on my policy. The human resources person looked into it and then came back and said the board of directors just wasn't ready to do that yet." They did, however, support Pat in other ways, by agreeing to give her maternity leave when she and Karen adopt a child.

Other lesbians and gay men have come out at work quietly, in a way that felt natural and less threatening to them. While they were never exactly in the closet, they wanted to assess the situation and not make any pronouncements about their sexual orientation. For Julie, when she started her new job with a publishing company in Westchester County, New York, it was a question of never saying anything openly but not hiding her relationship with Wendy either. "I always spoke about what 'we' had done over the weekend," Julie explains, "or what 'we' were doing for the holidays. I always spoke about Wendy but never used the words 'gay' or 'partner' in those conversations." When she and Wendy took a vacation, Julie discovered that her boss had definitely figured things out. "He handed me a hundred-dollar bill," she recalls, "and said, 'Take Wendy out for a fantastic dinner while you're in Orlando.' That was his way of saying, 'I know and it's great and I hope the two of you have fun on your vacation.'"

Oscar Jones, who is in graduate school in Nebraska, has done several internships as part of his training in education administration. At his first internship, he was very out, and many of his coworkers came to the commitment ceremony he had with his partner, Greg Cox. But the second internship was in a much larger office where it was harder to get to know people, and not many of his colleagues knew about his relationship with Greg.

"I remember at Valentine's Day," Oscar says, "Greg sent me a rose. And people said, 'Oh, your wife sent you that.' And it was just in passing, and I didn't feel it was necessary to clarify that. But when people ask, 'Are you married?' I say yes. And if they follow up with 'What's her name?' I say Greg. . . . And then, for a second, people will pause, and then it's okay. I've not really had a negative backlash. People are just like, whatever."

"When people ask, 'Are you married?' I say yes. And if they follow up with 'What's her name?' I say Greg. . . . And then, for a second, people will pause, and then it's okay."

Some people discover that, even though they haven't felt free to be openly gay at their jobs, their coworkers know and accept them anyway. "I never knew until the day I left," says Doug,[8] who worked for a national restaurant chain in Denver, "that people knew throughout the company and had no problem with it at all. *I* had more of a problem because I thought, 'Oh my God, what are they going to think about me?'" What he realized was that his coworkers had liked him for who he was, regardless of his sexual orientation, and his own internalized homophobia had prevented him from giving them the chance to show their tolerance.

HURRAY FOR PFLAG!

Maybe because my own parents had a hard time accepting my sexual orientation, I always get weepy when the PFLAG delegation marches through during the annual New York City gay pride march. Founded in 1981 in New York City by Jeanne Manford, the mother of a gay son, Parents, Families, and Friends of Lesbians and Gays (PFLAG) is a support group with chapters in four hundred communities across the country. PFLAG has grown over the years from its initial twenty members to more than 69,000, with the mission of promoting the health and well-being of lesbian, gay, bisexual, and transgendered people through support, education, and advocacy.

Project Open Mind, PFLAG's public education campaign to counteract gay and lesbian hate speech, included four thirty-second television commercials, speakers, public exhibits, and media interviews. Other PFLAG programs have included a conference for educators; local and national lobbying efforts against antigay and -lesbian legislation; a campaign to reach out to Asian and Pacific Islander families; quarterly publications *PFLAGpole* and *Tips and Tactics;* Straight Spouse Support Network (cosponsored with the Gay and Lesbian Parents Coalition International); and a comprehensive Web site.

PFLAG is a tremendous resource for the people who love lesbians and gay men to gain insight, understanding, and support and to meet, mingle, and feel connected.

For more information, contact :

Parents, Families and Friends of Lesbians and Gay Men
1101 14th Street NW, Suite 1030
Washington, DC 20005
(202) 638-4200
e-mail: info@pflag.org
Web site: http://www.pflag.org

"Outlaws" and In-Laws

Perhaps more than anyone in the outside world, our families wield a significant amount of influence on our relationships. Unlike any other minority group, lesbians and gay men often have to deal with family members who disapprove of them or openly reject them. Even families that are tolerant or have learned to live with a child or sibling's sexual orientation may react with something less than enthusiasm when Jill or John decides to bring the spouse home to meet the folks. And that can affect a relationship, putting undue stress on a same-sex couple every time the question of family comes up.

In Jamie and Beverly's extreme case, Jamie's parents are openly hostile toward their relationship and have essentially forced Jamie to choose—"us" or "her." Beverly says her in-laws think of her as "the bitch that 'turned' their daughter into a sinner." They refuse to meet Beverly or even see a picture of her. At Christmas, they expected Jamie to come for a "family dinner," but without Beverly. Jamie chose to stay with Beverly. "She told them she would not leave me at home alone on Christmas," Beverly recalls, "and that I am an important part of the family, even if they can't accept that."

Some parents are less harsh but still unaccepting, conveniently forgetting our partner's name or labeling a son's or daughter's same-sex spouse a "friend." My mother used to call my partner Katie "the other girl," but her memory in this regard has improved over the years. (In fact, on our recent visit, she called us "whatchamacallit and Katie.") Christine Mazurkiewicz had a similar experience with her partner Pam Teal's mother. "Up until recently," Christine says, "Pam's mom referred to me as 'what's-her-name.' "

Parents welcome a third generation.

Judi describes another common example of a lukewarm family response to a same-sex relationship. "Frankly, Liz and I aren't approved of," she says of her Jewish family of origin, "but we are accepted." Judi describes her parents' approach to her relationship with Liz as "realistic." "My family knows that if Liz and Ben [their son] aren't welcome, then I won't be there either." So they have spent many of the Jewish holidays and other family get-togethers with her parents and siblings.

Karin and Maria Kaj have also experienced acceptance from their families of origin. But as Karin points out, "Acceptance is not exactly what a heterosexual couple expects. 'It's okay' is not the resounding joy and support most other couples hear as they begin their lives together. I know it's more than many gay couples ever get, but that doesn't make it enough."

"No matter how 'accepting' our parents are," Maria adds, "they still don't really treat us as a couple. My mother tried for many years to get me to go on vacations with her without my wife, as if a heterosexual couple would do that. And she accused us of 'being in our own world.' Now, would you say that to hetero newlyweds?"

Peter #1 relates a situation that is all too familiar to many lesbians and gay men. Though his partner Peter #2's siblings and their spouses are very welcoming of the couple, they are closeted about the relationship with their friends and colleagues. "They're worried about what people will think," Peter #1 states. "So when we go to visit and 'town folk' are around, I feel pretty invisible—people are afraid to introduce me to anyone for fear they would have to explain the connection."

Just like lesbians and gay men, relatives have to go through a coming out process, and fortunately, there is a support network to help them do so. (See the sidebar, "Hurray for PFLAG.") It's not, after all, enough just to accept us—we need our families to have pride in us, our accomplishments, and our lasting relationships.

For some lesbian and gay couples, a family's initially chilly response to a son's or daughter's partner may turn around in time. My own father—who six years ago angrily demanded why I couldn't be "normal"—just recently embraced Katie and me as a couple, ending our visit to my hometown by urging us to "take care of each other."

Sometimes a committed relationship will urge a lesbian or gay man to vocalize what her or his family never really acknowledged. When Mildred became involved with Wanda, she wanted to be more open with her parents than she had been in the past. "There was always a sense that I was gay," she says, "but I never put it into words." After Mildred and Wanda had been together a couple of years, had moved in together, and exchanged rings, Mildred called her mother in Puerto Rico and told her she was married to a woman. Mildred recalls her mother's reaction: "She said, 'Oh no, it's a joke.'" Her mother and father agreed that Mildred was welcome to visit, but not Wanda. Mildred, however, stood her ground and said she would not visit without Wanda, her life partner.

"I usually call home every week," Mildred says, "but after that, I didn't call. I said, okay, I'll divorce them." When they didn't hear from her, Mildred's parents called to make amends. "Then they met Wanda," Mildred recalls. "My mother loved her . . . and my father came to terms." After a rocky start with both families, Mildred and Wanda feel their relationships with their in-laws are now "respectful."

Dan tells a moving story of his partner Matt's[9] father working through his homophobia to gain acceptance of his son and his relationship. When Matt was a teenager, his father—whom Dan describes as "a big old redneck"—had taken Matt out to the garage for a serious talk, telling him that he couldn't stand that Matt was gay and never wanted to see him again. After that, they had only sporadic contact with each other, until many years later, when Matt's family had a surprise birthday party for Matt's grandmother.

A supportive mother on Gay Pride Day.

"Matt's uncle, who was dying of AIDS, lived with the grandmother and thought we should come," Dan recalls, "but he warned me that it would probably be uncomfortable with Matt's father and stepmother there." Before the party, Matt's father took him out to the garage a second time—but on this occasion, it was to tell Matt he realized he'd been a horrible father and wanted Matt's forgiveness.

"And they started crying," Dan says. "His stepmother came out, too, and started crying, and then his older brother came out and said this was the day he'd been waiting for. Then they all came into dinner, and I didn't have a clue that any of this had happened!" In front of thirty people at the dinner table, Matt's father and stepmother made toasts, welcoming both Dan and a new grandchild into the family.

Though her partner Fran's family was always accepting of her, Tracey Lind recalls the specific moment when she really became part of the Goldstein family. The sad occasion was Fran's mother's funeral in New York City two years ago, when Tracey, an Episcopal priest, was honored when the family asked her to deliver the eulogy and officiate at the Jewish ceremony.

Tracey asked for the family's input on what they wanted her to say, and Fran's father assured her that it didn't matter—he just wanted her to state clearly that she was part of the family. "And no Jesus stuff," he added quickly.

So Tracey did as he requested, introducing herself as Fran's life partner and explaining that she had been asked to officiate because Fran's parents—who had moved to Florida from New York years earlier—no longer had a synagogue in the area. That was how the 350 friends and extended family present found out that Mrs. Goldstein's youngest daughter was a lesbian. Tracey delivered a moving and personal eulogy, telling stories about her mother-in-law and the rest of Fran's family, whom she describes as "the people whom I love more dearly than anybody in the world."

After the ceremony, when the family was sitting shiva at Fran's sister's home, Tracey recalls that family friends and many extended family members came up to her and thanked her for her words, telling her that Mrs. Goldstein would have been proud. "One of them, I can't remember who," Tracey says, "said, 'Well, you're really a Goldstein now.'" Various people even asked if Tracey would "do" their funerals.

"To me," Tracey muses, "that was the moment in time when I think Fran and I were affirmed in the eyes of her family. . . . Fran's father really gave us a gift, but he had no idea he was giving it." Fran adds, "He gave the whole family a gift."

Several lesbians and gay men told me that their partner's family members had inquired about their "intentions," just as they might of a heterosexual boyfriend or girlfriend. When Joanne met Elaine's[10] parents for the

> "Acceptance is not exactly what a heterosexual couple expects. 'It's okay' is not the resounding joy and support most other couples hear as they begin their lives together. I know it's more than many gay couples ever get, but that doesn't make it enough."

first time, Elaine's father "gave me the fifth degree," Joanne says, asking questions like, "How much money do you make?" and "Do you drink?" Later, Joanne discovered that Elaine's ex-lover had had a drinking problem, and Elaine's parents were worried that she would get hurt again. "Now we just laugh about it," Joanne says, "but at the time I felt like I was going through the Inquisition!"

Santa Molina found that her partner Vanessa Marshall's grown niece wanted to know if Santa was serious about Vanessa or just trying out lesbianism. Santa had been married to a man for thirteen years, and her relationship with Vanessa was her first with a woman. Vanessa's niece "said something like, 'You better know what you're doing with my aunt because she's like my mother and I hope you're not going to hurt her,' " Santa recalls. "She gave me this whole lecture about how heterosexual women don't know what they want sometimes. And then a month later, before our commitment ceremony, she actually gave me a card that said, 'Welcome to the family.' It wasn't just a card. It really signified that she was saying, all right, you're cool, we welcome you and accept you. I still have that card. It's very meaningful to me."

It was encouraging to learn that the families of many lesbians and gay men had wholeheartedly accepted their spouses from the start. "My mom and dad refer to Guillian as their daughter-in-law, even though my step-dad is two years younger than Guillian," says Melise Zoë. "One day we were doing some pretty heavy lifting and hauling, helping my parents around the house, when my Dad said, 'Guillian, you're the son I never had.' " Because her stepfather cooks and cross-stitches and doesn't follow traditional male gender roles, Guillian quipped, "Yep, and you're the daughter I never had!" Melise says that Guillian's Mexican parents refer to her as *hija,* which is "daughter" in Spanish. What is wonderful, Melise points out, is that "our family members see us in relation to themselves, within the entire family context."

Jo Ellen Elliott says that her partner, Susan Stratton's, mother is even open about her daughter's relationship at work. "Susan's mother changed careers and had only been in her job about a month," Jo Ellen recalls. "We had gone to visit and she took us into her work and hadn't really thought about [how to introduce me]. In her previous job, I was her daughter-in-law. So she kind of stopped for a minute, And as soon as she looked at me, it was like the hell with this—this is my daughter-in-law."

Sometimes parents and siblings form a deep attachment to a lesbian or gay partner. Joeline quips that her mother "swears if I ever leave Sandy, she's keeping Sandy and getting rid of me!" Cheryl Lawson's mother has occasionally gotten angry at Cheryl if her partner, Jennifer Higdon, hasn't come with her to visit.

"Wounded Attachments"

BY CARMEN VÁZQUEZ

CULTURALLY, MARRIAGE IS ABOUT FAMILY, about belonging. Who among us can honestly say that we wouldn't give anything for that moment when our brothers and sisters, our parents, our friends and ex-lovers, our coworkers and our community gather together to raise a toast in celebration of our love? For that walk down the aisle and all those presents, as my friend Emery once said? The denial of this very, very fundamental human ritual is a terrible and very old wound to our soul. It is an attachment too ancient to be dismissed, to be severed completely from our collective conscious even when we understand perfectly how it has wounded us all these many centuries.

I understand it. I really understand it. Marcie and I have lived in "for better or for worse" unshakable commitment to each other and shared a life together for twelve years. Until very recently, we were the principal celebrants of the anniversary of our union. Last July, we got a call from Marcie's mom and dad, and in addition to our usual banter about sports and family gossip, Ed, Marcie's father, announced that he and Marcie's mom, Betty, had arrived at a decision.

You have to understand Ed. He is seventy-four years old and a loquacious, charming, tough Italian working-class guy. He had many jobs, mostly in sales, but no career. He is a World War II vet who didn't get beyond a high school education, but follows CNN passionately. He waited up for Marcie when she was still dating guys. He really believed that Marcie's future was best served by learning to be a good secretary with DuPont. He grunts, and the instant coffee with artificial creamer and fake sugar appear, delivered by the women in his life. He is priceless, and the quintessential working-class European immigrant version of the patriarch.

Ed and Betty had been watching and listening to all this fuss about live-in couples on television and the newspapers, and it occurred to them that all the time Marcie and I had been together, they had never recognized our anniversary. "Recognize" in mom- and dad-speak means a card and a check. They had been doing this for Shelly and Michael, and Rose and Eddie, but not for Marce and Carms. That wasn't right, Ed said. "I mean, am I going to be like the state or am I going to be like Disney World?" Disney World, of course, had just adopted a domestic partner policy that incurred the wrath of the Christian Radical Right. "I'll do like Disney World!" Dad said.

They told us that beginning in July, they'd be recognizing our "live-in marriage" just like they did Eddie's and Michael's. He seemed not impressed when we told him our anniversary was in

Richard Burns relates that his family of origin was "very sad" when he and Tom, his partner of thirteen years, broke up. Richard and Tom had spent most Thanksgivings with Richard's family and visited them at other times during the year, too. "Christmas dinner this past year," Richard recalls, "I'm sitting at my mother's table in Hendersonville, North Carolina, and my stepfather suddenly announces during dinner, 'I miss Tom.' And then, they all pipe up with 'Yeah, I miss Tom.' I was very moved by that . . . that in the course of thirteen years Tom had been very well integrated into my family of origin. They still ask me about him."

October, not July, nor did he fall for a question about retroactive recognition.

The note they later sent had an ACLU Post-it that read: Defenders of the Bill of Rights. It was dated effective July 4, 1995. Underneath it, Ed wrote in his own handwriting:

"Issued to Marcia Gallo and Carmen Vázquez for meritorious and unselfish dedicated service."

. . . Then:

"Hi Guys, a little late in establishing this momentous occasion, but as they say, better late than never. Happy Anniversary.

We love and miss you very much.
See you soon.

Love, Mom and Dad."

Marcie and I cried like two kids. We felt proud and recognized and *so prodigal.* I really do understand how much we need to heal this wound, how much we need to overcome the power that belonging and being just like any old regular family has over us.

What will heal this wound for Marcie and me and for all of us, however, is not the elevation of marriage to the single most critical civil rights issue facing our movement, as Andrew Sullivan suggests, but the development and implementation—with the help of our straight but not narrow allies—of a progressive American Families Agenda.

That agenda needs to include the legal recognition of our committed relationships to people of our own gender, but it can't end there. It must also speak clearly to the need for the protection of our rights as parents, and the protection of our children and all children and their right to an education, to health care, and to freedom from abuse of any kind. It must speak to the demand for the repeal of all sodomy laws, because you don't have autonomy in human sexuality while sodomy laws still exist. It must speak to the right of all children born in this nation—citizen children and immigrant children, documented and undocumented—to a guarantee that they will be clothed and sheltered and fed and educated and receive adequate health care.

I didn't say a progressive lesbian and gay, bisexual and transgender Families Agenda. I said a progressive *American Families Agenda.* This is not my resurgent patriotism slipping out. This is a very deliberate choice of language, for I believe that we must accept the responsibility of being not just lesbian/gay/bisexual/transgender progressive activists but of being progressive activists with the right and responsibility to work in, give voice to, and help lead an American Progressive Movement for Social Justice.

This is not theory. This is my life.

Excerpted from "Wounded Attachments," a keynote address delivered at the 1996 Creating Change Conference. Reprinted with permission of the author.

Carmen Vázquez says that her breakup with her longtime partner was made even more difficult by the thought of losing each other's families. "Over the course of twelve years," Carmen says, "we had developed these incredibly strong family ties. So when we broke up, it wasn't just us, it was all of these people. . . . There were nieces and nephews that had to be talked to, just like any old divorce in America." (See also the sidebar, "Wounded Attachments.")

To get to the point of integration into each other's families of origin that Carmen Vázquez describes can be challenging for many lesbian and

"Out to the In-Laws"

BY E. J. GRAFF

. . . THE TRADITIONAL ASSUMPTION about lesbians and gay men—that, lacking the maturity of marriage, we're stuck in adolescent puppy love, not quite grown—refers also to progeny. For many, the fact of heterosexual marriage implies children, while lesbian and gay couples imply "barrenness," that harsher terrain. As a result, newly married heterosexuals are often treated as if they are stepping up to adulthood; "the girls" or "the boys" are treated as if trying to stay kids ourselves.

When we do have children, the response is complex enough for its own essay, often disorienting all four or six (or more) new grandparents. Appearing at family events becomes mandatory, even for the most willful queer escapee, lest new grandparents and aunties begin shrieking or sulking about being kept away from the blessed infants. For those who do aim at conventional family citizenship—Jerry and Myron, for example, who've triumphed by delivering the first grandchild—that shift can be quite satisfying.

But my intention is not just that we insinuate ourselves into the bosoms of our families; my main point is political. Given that lesbians and gay men are related to everyone in the country, when we give them reasons—and teach them how—to speak about us in public, we buttress the country against the right wing. My friend Marcie tells how when her accomplished brother died of AIDS, a Los Angeles Jewish newspaper wanted to print his obituary—but called for permission to delete mention of his surviving partner. Marcie's father refused. The paper buckled.

Back in Ohio, I've had a similar experience with my politician mom. At my stepfather's seventy-fifth, my mother introduced me to colleagues—while ignoring [my partner] Marilyn, whose eyebrows shot up high. I took my mother aside and suggested this sentence: "And this is Marilyn, E. J's friend-partner-spouse." My mother chose "friend," admittedly the baby word but nevertheless risky in the Bible Belt, where her reelection is hardly guaranteed. Would such parents have had the determination to stand up for us without

gay couples. But as writer E. J. Graff points out, lesbians and gay men (even in the Bible Belt where Graff grew up) can take control of how their families view their relationships, often successfully easing their way into the clan by expressing their humanity. Graff's essay, "Out to the In-Laws" (see sidebar), points out the ways in which lesbians and gay men can, simply by winning their in-laws' hearts, effect real social change.

Making It Last

On the face of things, the odds against lesbian and gay relationships lasting longer than a few months or years should be pretty great. After all, partners in same-sex couples—more than those in heterosexual cou-

years spent squeezing our couples into the family's wide-angled photos, thanking our spouses for helping clean up after dinner, getting to know the human beings inside?

Hardly. Lesbians and gay men find the strength to stand up to a still-nasty social climate because of all we gain from living by our own gyroscopes, and because we can turn to the communities we've created. But—do urban queers forget this?—most of our families are still isolated out in Peoria, where things have not gotten any less scary since we've moved away. Our families spend day after day with their coworkers' faggot jokes, talk TV's freak shows, and the apocalyptic pronouncements of the marriage defenders. Of course all that sinks in.

Since our families never forget we're queer, they know—consciously or not—that by putting us in the wedding party or obituary page, they're publicly endorsing the still-subversive philosophy that sex is acceptable even if no babies can result. People like my mother's Ohio colleagues, Jerry's Detroit clan, and Marcie's bicoastal Jewish community must now think of someone they know before slinging slurs. That's one way hate language becomes socially outré, making prejudice less available for widespread infection. Since so many lesbians and gay men flee to where it's more comfortable—giving up the mindshare to bigots—don't we have a responsibility to infiltrate our in-laws' hearts, turning them (however mildly) into agents of social change?

Yes, our attempts can be complicated by personality clashes, racial or cultural gaps, different tastes in house decor, and the whole groaning tradition of in-law strain. But our infiltrations can bring a bonus result. Before I met Marilyn's family, I decided to win over these people I expected to know the rest of my life. That took the form of being a good girl, an act I found entertaining: washing the dishes, getting her mom to talk about her favorite subjects (books, food, family), encouraging her dad to tease me about my taste in movies. A funny thing resulted: love. Should my father-in-law's threatening heart finally fail, taking away a man who has treated me with more kindness than has my own father, I will—like so many straight in-laws—gain the mixed privilege of real grief.

Excerpted from "Out to the In-Laws," The Village Voice, October 15, 1996. Reprinted with permission of the author.

ples can even begin to imagine—face resistance from their families of origin, from the outside world, and from their employers. They can't legally marry and have no real protections for their relationships. Homophobia is widespread and can lead to verbal or physical assault if they are openly affectionate on the street. They may even experience internalized homophobia, not expecting same-sex relationships to survive beyond a brief, romantic/sexual period.

But amazingly, lesbian and gay couples have bucked the odds and created lasting unions despite all the strikes against them. What's the magic formula? Most of the couples in this book, as well as the therapists who deal with lesbian and gay couple and family issues, agreed that communication and respect are key to the survival of any relationship. "You have to be able to state what you feel," says Vanessa Marshall, a therapist in private practice. "When you have self-love, you're going to [communicate] in a way where you're not going to attack your partner. You're going to honor and respect your partner in a way that's healthy." Vanessa and her life and business partner, Santa Molina, work with lesbian and gay couples on issues of trust—"getting them to trust enough to not feel like [their partner] is going to run out the door because they spoke their truth."

"That's a hard thing," Santa observes, "because so many of us have been wounded, and we don't know whether or not we can come out with the truth and then be received and [have] it be okay."

Vanessa suggests that couples "be real from the beginning." Partners, she believes, should talk about everything openly and honestly right from the start, "so there won't be any surprises down the road."

Michael Shernoff, also a therapist in private practice, agrees with these ideas. "To me," Shernoff notes, "the biggest emotional glue is that each partner cares what the other is feeling." He also recommends that partners in a couple be willing to work hard on the relationship. Shernoff finds that gay men in particular have a problem figuring out when to "prioritize someone's needs as more important than your own in a non-codependent way. . . . Each partner has to be able to take care of the other when he or she needs it."

In addition, Shernoff thinks that some couples run into difficulties because they enter a relationship expecting it to be perfect and always be the same. "But things change," he says, "especially sex. . . . [The partners] will not always be at that level of initial sexual excitement, but there can be an evolving richness and texture which is compensation for perhaps a diminished intensity or a diminished frequency." None of these observations, he adds, are specific to lesbian or gay relationships. But same-sex couples are less likely to work on their problems if internalized homophobia kicks in, telling them their relationships aren't that important. (See also the sidebar, "Howdy, Partner.")

Despite the homophobia that they have faced, both in the outside world and in themselves, Martin and John are two gay men who have definitely made their relationship work—for thirty-six years and counting. "A great deal of it is luck," Martin smiles, when I ask him their secret to longevity. "You meet the right person. A lot of it is love. An *awful* lot of it is respect. And selfishness. I mean selfishness in this way—'Where would I be without him? What would I do without him? This is good for *me*.' . . . So it's sort of a combination of all that."

Mark and Andy, who have been together eleven years, think their relationship has survived because they've been willing to work on it. Twice, they have lived in isolated places with "no friends to go stay with if we had a fight," Mark says. This forced them to work out their issues on their own.

"There were also times," notes Mark, "when we had to put our relationship before other things." Mark recalls that seven years back he interviewed and was chosen for a plum university teaching job in the Midwest. "It was what I had always wanted to do," he says, "but the town was such that Andy would have had nothing to do. There was no airport in town, so commuting back and forth would have been difficult." Mark turned the job down and remained with Andy in New England.

Andy says that "Never go to bed angry"—a popular dictum for straight couples, too—has been an important motto in their relationship. "We never let anger and frustrations stay with us," he says. Being each other's best friend, he says, is also key. "We have both helped each other get through some difficult times in our lives."

Mark would advise new couples that, "You can have everything you want—relationship, home, family, and respect. Don't lower your standards for anyone. Nothing is easy. If you love your partner, then work for it. Work hard! Have the strength to say 'I'm sorry.' Do set boundaries of what you will and will not accept. But remember that compromise is everything."

Karen Schmiege and Pat Catlett of Albuquerque, a couple for eight years, agree that "working for it" is vital. "We've been through each one of us not having jobs," Karen observes. "We've been through my mother's death. . . . The most important part is that we're always together and we always talk about it. It doesn't mean that we always come to the same conclusions, but we keep learning from each other. That helps us grow and gives us the strength and courage to go out and do whatever we need to do."

Knowing how to argue, Pat adds, can add to the success of a relationship. Pat tells the story of how she and Karen were having a disagreement in front of one of their friends, who later asked who "won." "I looked at her, because I didn't quite get the question," Pat says. "I didn't even see it as a fight. It was just a disagreement about who was walking too fast or something—I don't know—a discussion. But to her [the friend], she thought when you had a quarrel, somebody had to win and therefore somebody lost. I said, 'Oh no, I think we both win.' It's not about winning or losing. It's a dialogue because you can't always agree about everything you do." Karen and Pat have ongoing discussions about the issues that are vital to their relationship, like whether or not to adopt children.

Beverly and Jamie also spend a lot of time together, "talking and getting to know each other better," Beverly says. "We tell each other we love

HOWDY, PARTNER

It's hard work making any relationship last, but same-sex relationships face particular difficulties. The Partners Task Force for Gay and Lesbian Couples is a Seattle-based organization, which provides information, support, and advocacy for same-sex couples. Through publications, surveys, videos, and a comprehensive Web site (featuring links to other Web sites of interest to same-sex couples), Partners Task Force is committed to ensuring that lesbians and gay men involved in long-term relationships get social and legal recognition, as well as emotional support.

The founders and directors of the task force, Stevie Bryant and Demian—themselves a committed couple of fifteen years—are activists who have appeared on radio and television and have written articles for the gay and mainstream press on same-sex partner issues. Stevie and Demian started the task force as a newsletter in 1986, wanting to provide an educational tool for the community. "Unless the gay community has a clearer understanding of what same-sex marriage means socially, spiritually, and economically," says Demian, "it won't happen, because no one's going to ask for this besides our community." *

Some of the materials available from the task force are:

BOOKLETS

"An Indispensable Guide for Couples"—a sixty-four page primer containing facts, tips, and insights on finances, legal planning, job benefits, sex, and children.

Domestic Partnership List—features articles on

Quoted in Suzanne Sherman, ed., Lesbian and Gay Marriage: Private Commitments, Public Ceremonies (Temple University Press, 1992), 77.

the other one every day without fail." Beverly and Jamie also make special time for each other, including a regular Friday night at-home "date." "When we start to drift away from each other," Beverly says, "we start romancing each other again. We work hard at it."

Jill and Randi have likewise stayed together by talking a lot. "It's really important to talk," says Jill, "but also to have a sense of humor. You don't need to process everything to death—sometimes a cigar is a cigar. The most important thing is to be honest with each other." Jill recalls the time when she wanted to have a commitment ceremony, but Randi didn't. Randi's hesitance hurt Jill, but when they talked through their feelings, Jill realized "it really wasn't about me," she says. "It wasn't personal."

Jill says she sees friends struggling in their relationships "because they're talking to us, not each other. Each one is telling us what's going on, but they're not talking to each other, and the relationships are unraveling."

Musicians Cris Williamson and Tret Fure, partners for sixteen years, maintain that a sense of humor is key. "Tret makes me laugh so hard every day," Cris says, "and we never go to bed mad. Never, never, never."

"When we do fight, which is rare," adds Tret, "we just end up laughing at each other and laughing about it. Nothing is that serious but the love that we share." Their fights and misunderstandings, notes Cris, "are nothing that divert us from our intention, our true intention. I truly love this person at all times, every inch of her, however she is. She's just fine with me. People have to grow—if you grow in a parallel fashion, then you should be all right."

Maria and Karin Kaj have been growing together for twenty years, since they were teenagers. The two of them lived in different cities fifteen hundred miles apart for the first twelve years of their relationship (see page 53), but their commitment was to someday be together. "I've always said the secret to longevity is No Sacrifices," Maria comments. "You don't sacrifice what you really want for the relationship, nor do you sacrifice the relationship for your career or individual needs. Both of them are first priority."

For Karin, a self-described romantic, love is the key. "I believe in love, the power of love, and every drippy, sentimental thing that has ever been said about love," she rhapsodizes. "I read a Harlequin romance every day for about two years in my teens.[11] I guess that's why I write lesbian romances now. I have a happily-ever-after life. I want other lesbians to believe it can happen for them, too. And that they *deserve* happiness."

Steve and Ric also felt they deserved to have a good, strong, and lasting relationship. "We've been through some tough times," says Steve of their twenty-year relationship. "But we just wanted it so badly." Steve believes that wanting the relationship to work is key—"You must really want it, and you must go into it with your eyes as open as possible."

Which Way Works?

Two different kinds of lesbian and gay couples emerged while I was talking to people, pointing to two distinct theories about love and relationships—is it important to have a great deal in common, or do opposites, as the saying goes, attract?

My partner Katie and I happen to have a lot in common—not just our interests, but our values and our modes of being in the world. Katie says that one of the things that first drew her to me was the realization that I was essentially a homebody. Some of our friends are amazed that we have lived in a teeny, tiny one-bedroom apartment for over two years without any real tension. Also, because of our work schedules, we have been fortunate to spend a lot of time with each other, including eating most meals together. While some couples might find that closeness stifling, others say it works for them, too.

"I enjoy spending so much time with Ellen," Pat remarks. "I could spend all day with Ellen and that would be an ideal day. No matter what we did. We could sit around the house."

"You hear a lot of couples go out and do things separately," Ellen adds. "But there's nothing I would really want to do without Pat."

That's also true for Joe Melillo and Pat Lagon, plaintiffs in the Hawaii same-sex marriage case (see pages 125–128). "We like to do all the same things," says Joe of their twenty-year relationship. "We've been able to work together. We built a [silk-screening] business together. I think that's probably what's held us together—just how well we work together and live together." Joe says that their relationship always feels new, that each day he wakes up, "it feels like I just met Pat the day before."

Singer Janis Ian says that she and her partner of eight years Pat Snyder are not exactly alike, but are still "compatible in a lot of areas where I had

> *"I have a happy-ever-after life. I want other lesbians to believe it can happen for them, too."*

never been compatible with somebody before." They enjoy many of the same things and agree on most political issues. Yet, she notes, their ways of "dealing with everything" are very different. "Pat thinks before she speaks," Janis says. "I can't think without thinking out loud. Pat will mull over something for a long time. I just go in jumps."

For many couples, being opposites has actually helped them stay together. Brendan Hadash and Alan Hultquist, who have been a couple for fourteen years, "are two different people with very little in common," says Alan. "We go our own ways and let the other person be who he is."

"During the first year we were together," Brendan recalls, "we spent a lot of time trying to change each other. We fought a lot that year. But then we realized that it just didn't matter. We love each other, and that's what's important." Alan adds that Brendan has given him more unconditional love than he had ever experienced before.

When I ask Fran Goldstein and Tracey Lind how they have stayed together for nine years, Fran quips, "We don't see each other that often." On a more serious note, she says that, though their values are similar, their differences have sometimes been hard to work through. "We are different in practically every single imaginable way," she remarks. "Personalities, interests."

"We don't like the same music, we don't like the same food, we don't do the same things in our pastimes," Tracey says, enumerating their differences. "We don't read the same kind of books. We don't like the same kind of movies. We don't like the same kind of television [programs]. But we do love each other."

Fran thinks that what is important is that there's a willingness between them to try new things. "I feel like I've grown a lot and expanded my interests and activities because of Tracey," she says. "I think I've really grown in terms of who I am because she's so different."

"Fran keeps me sane," Tracey muses. "I think that's where our opposites work. Fran is my anchor. Without Fran, I'm bouncing off ceilings and walls. And I'm a hot-air balloon for her."

Shawn and Robert Walker-Smith express a similar idea about their relationship. "Shawn speeds me up," says Robert. "I slow him down. I want to sit and watch the clouds roll by; he wants to be up and race the wind. When we're out in the world, he's gregarious and talkative, while I smile and nod. But at home, I can talk from daybreak to bedtime, while he can go hours without a word. We know that we are both exceptional people," he says, "not at all what we would have expected to find, much less fall in love with." But what's important, he remarks, is that "heart speaks to heart." Very soon after they met, they couldn't imagine not seeing each other if they had the chance. "That's when I knew," Robert says.

Marjorie Hill spends five or six nights a month away from her partner, Christine Edwards, traveling in her official capacity as commissioner of workers' compensation for the state of New York. In addition, Marjorie is busy with professional and political responsibilities several nights of the week. Christine thinks their independent existences have helped their relationship, because the time they spend together is so precious. "Whenever we're together," she notes, "it really feels special."

Marjorie says they reserve weekends for each other, and that during these special times, they have fun together. Christine's great sense of humor and spirit of playfulness have taught Marjorie "to be very silly," she says, "which is something I don't generally do in my life. I have not historically done that in my relationships. Once I did a Tina Turner review just for Christine, 'Rollin' on the River' and all that, and we were both in stitches. We have a lot of fun. And we still try to have dates. That's important."

Cultural Gaps, Cultural Bridges

Many lesbian and gay couples have come together and stayed together across more considerable differences than just diverging tastes in movies or books. Racial and cultural differences, in particular, can significantly affect a relationship, but many same-sex couples have shown a propensity to deal with and work on these issues in a healthy and direct way. (See also the sidebar, "Across the Glittering Sea.")

Loving our differences.

Shawn Walker-Smith's marriage to Robert is not the first interracial relationship for either of them. "But it's the first relationship where I've been really aware of the fact," says Shawn, who is African American, while his partner is white. "Primarily because Robert is so aware of it. But it's not like it's a preoccupation for him. He's very open and supportive and always very interested in other ethnicities, as I am." But, Shawn notes, Robert's curiosity about other cultures as a white man "isn't about apologizing for past transgressions or wanting to become part of that race that is 'exotic' or different. He very much knows who he is. And I approach things from the same kind of perspective. . . . We sort of teach each other back and forth."

Andrew, who is white, and Mano, who is Asian American, say that race has been the topic of a number of spirited "debates" between the two of them over the course of their six-year relationship. "Even here in San Francisco," Andrew notes, "there is a stereotype of Asian-Caucasian relationships—the older, sugar daddy white guy, and the young, 'smooth,' submissive Asian boy toy. I felt compelled early on to show Mano that I loved him for many reasons beyond the color of his skin."

But Mano points out Andrew's naïveté about racism. "Andrew kind of likes to believe that everyone is equal," Mano says thoughtfully, "that no one gets treated differently because of race. It's a great concept, but it just isn't true." Mano recalls times when they've gone out to dinner, and the waiter speaks first to Andrew, then turns to Mano with the question, "Do you speak English?" "It really affects you," Mano remarks. And it is a feeling that Andrew, as a white man, will never know.

Linda Villarosa notes that there are things from her upbringing as an African American that her partner, Vickie, who is white, had to get used to. "I hate to be barefoot," Linda gives as an example. "I hate to run around naked. I had to tell her black people, because we've been accused of being hypersexual, are sometimes very conservative [in this way]."

Linda discovered that Vickie, though she's extremely racially and culturally aware, has a sense of privilege that was foreign to Linda. "In the subway, she'd put her legs up on the pole," Linda explains. "I'm like, 'Put your legs down.' . . . In my mind, you don't get into trouble. Because if you're black and you get into trouble, you're going to get arrested, you'll be thrown into jail, you won't be able to get out." These "subtle cultural differences," as Linda calls them, have caused the couple some difficulties in their six years together, but they worked on those and other issues in couples' therapy. Now Vickie understands Linda's cultural background better. "She doesn't just think I'm some conservative square, she realizes this is America's fault," Linda says.

Liza Fiol-Matta and Louise Murray, who are Puerto Rican and Dutch respectively, have found they have enormous similarities, even though they are from different cultures. Liza was raised on various military bases as an "army brat," while Louise's family traveled around the world for her father's diplomatic job. They were both raised Catholic and middle class. But their first languages are Spanish and Dutch, neither of which the other speaks.

Liza says that, because they are both very strong in their identities, "talking about difference or confronting difference or living difference doesn't become a defensive thing. If Louise is on the phone talking to somebody in Dutch, I'm not sitting somewhere thinking, 'What are they saying? Are they talking about me?' And if I'm speaking Spanish, she's not thinking that either. We're not going around saying, 'I'm excluded, I'm

"Across the Glittering Sea"

BY JEWELLE GOMEZ

I'M JUST SETTLING DOWN in my first monogamous, committed relationship, with a woman who is not Black, so I have more questions than answers. If I begin with simply the term "committed relationship," the genesis of many issues that will be raised is obvious. If Diane and I were heterosexual I'd be able to say "marriage." There would be a set of (sometimes tedious) social engagements which would have marked our rite of passage from single to couple.

These rites, like all such activities, help to ease the participants into their new status and help to cement the relationship. They provide a background of supportive voices, a net of experiences, a validation. In an interracial, heterosexual relationship they might be a difficult gauntlet that must be run before the couple gets on with life. But even in those trials, the relationship can be made stronger. When Sidney Poitier nobly endured the parental barbs of Katherine Hepburn and Spencer Tracy in *Guess Who's Coming to Dinner?* in 1967, the audience knew in the end the family unit would ultimately expand to include him. The simple fact that there's a title for him—husband—means he has a role in the family, whatever his ethnicity.

For us there've been no similar social activities or titles to provide us with the security of acknowledgment, so we must explore these unknown waters on our own. Some interracial lesbian couples try to avoid family contact altogether, fearing that the fact of a partner's being a woman and the "wrong" color might send the family over the edge. Diane and I have not chosen that type of distance because we're both too committed to our families even when the gauntlets are unpredictable. When I attended Diane's sister's wedding this year it didn't occur to us until we were almost at the ceremony that I might be the only Black person there. In fact I wasn't the only one. I spotted an elegantly dressed Black woman about my age during the reception. We greeted each other with easy recognition, but she moved away quickly. She was the new in-laws' housekeeper. It's not the first social situation I've been in where the only other person of color was service staff, and it won't be the last. But I felt badly that she didn't feel comfortable talking to me, and that I couldn't be sure if it was

excluded.' I think that happens in relationships that haven't resolved their differences."

Louise has taken Spanish lessons but hasn't progressed very far. "Let's say I'm an expert in beginning Spanish," she smiles. Liza confesses that she once bought a book called *Dutch in Three Months* but barely opened it. "Our relationship is in English," Louise comments, "but there is a real caring about the other languages in this relationship."

For Mario, who is Latino, his seven-year relationship with Tim, who is Italian, has grown because they learn from each other's cultural differences. Latino men, Mario notes, are not very emotionally talkative. "We are not taught to express our emotions, to talk about them," he explains. "You have to be real macho about it. I detest that!" In order to help his re-

because of our differing "status" (which is rarely acknowledged in this country) or because I was the lesbian in-law. I will probably never know.

From past experience I've developed one approach to overcome the negative impact of family influences. Long ago, I decided not to hold anything the "in-laws" do to me against my partner; after all, they raised her, she didn't raise them. Several years ago I journeyed with another white girlfriend to meet her parents and they served (from their favorite take-out place) a spread of fried chicken, collard greens, potato salad, and cornbread. My girlfriend kept reassuring me that they always ate this way, that they weren't feeding me "soul food" as a way of condescending to me. I let her know that, conscious or not, her parents were making a statement about me which she should not remain naive about. But I also let her know I didn't care. Her parents had their own set of issues, which did not have to be mine or hers if she didn't let them be. As long as my lover recognized the complexity of the situation enough to want to address it, I was satisfied. I think it was easier for me to do that because we're lesbians; we are outsiders together.

Heterosexism regularly forces us to see our lives as independent of and unlike that of our parents. I accepted my girlfriend as a separate entity, capable of making better choices than her parents. She needed to be able to see their racism and to see herself apart from them. I needed to not make everything "all right" for her.

Once the family is put in a proper perspective, it is more a question of how I place myself and my ego in relationship to my partner. Diane says that, given the nature of U.S. culture, it's not *if* she'll do or say something racist or at least insensitive, but *when*. That she's smart enough to understand this and still not be too afraid to engage with a woman of color means a lot to me. I don't worry so much about when she'll do something, as that I will be looking so hard for her to do it I'll be a nervous wreck. I don't think I could live a life in which I'm on my guard constantly, and a full, long-term relationship can't be built on anxiety. Yet I have to be realistic and acknowledge that we both grew up in a racist society and be prepared to deal with the question if/when it comes up. Diane might do or say something racist, just as a Black male relative sooner or later might say something sexist.

This essay originally appeared in Skin Deep: Black Women and White Women Write About Race, *ed. by Marita Golden and Susan Richards Shreve (Anchor Books, 1995). Reprinted with permission from Doubleday, a division of Bantam Doubleday Dell Publishing Group, Inc.*

lationship with Tim, Mario says he's learned to be more "gringo" about expressing himself. "I don't mean to use the word 'gringo' in a negative manner, but the opposite," Mario adds quickly. "I see that [white] people here tend to talk more about their emotional needs, and I admire that."

Robert Woodworth observes that racial differences for him and his late partner, Noli Villanueva, were less significant than class ones. Noli was from an upper-middle-class Filipino family with servants and a great deal of privilege, while Robert came from white, working-class Connecticut. "When you lived in the economic class Noli lived in," Robert points out, "stateside was good, Filipino second-rate. You had GE appliances, you bought canned Dole pineapple instead of fresh. The post–World War II Philippines were very American-friendly." Noli started saving his money early on to immigrate to the United States. When he and Robert became a couple in 1984, their experience as an interracial couple was more of sharing rather than of clashing cultures. "It was an enriching part of the relationship."

One issue that gave them some difficulty, though, was Robert's Yankee work ethic. Robert was working (and still works) for a gay organization that demands a lot of his time. "The biggest struggles were around the amount of hours I worked," he recalls. "In Filipino culture, familial ties and responsibilities and time requirements are looked at as more important than work. So that was always a tug of war [between us]."

Maria Iannozzi and Naomi Barbee are an interracial couple who have been together for five years. Maria is Italian American, and Naomi is black and transgendered. (She doesn't use the term "African American," because she doesn't identify as American.) "Most of the impact that we've experienced as a result of racial and cultural differences," Naomi observes, "has been thrust on us from the outside—racism on the part of Maria's family and ignorant people in general." Once, at a large family Christmas gathering, Maria's great-aunt served pig's feet, even though it wasn't common for their holiday meal, because she made the racist assumption that it was what all black people ate. "And I absolutely hate pig's feet," Naomi says.

Like Robert and Noli, Maria finds that class has been a bigger issue in her relationship with Naomi than race or culture. "Naomi's poor," Maria explains, "and has very few prospects for improving that situation. . . . Being black and trans puts her at a disadvantage, to say the least." Maria, on the other hand, was raised in what she calls "an upwardly mobile working-class family" and attended an Ivy League school. "I've never had any difficulty finding employment," she says, "and have managed to create a business from a major in English. Before I met Naomi, I was a victim of middle-class myths: work hard, and you'll attain what you want to attain." Maria notes that she found out about the "real world" by living with Naomi—"someone with obvious talent who nonetheless was denied a great deal of opportunity. . . . [Naomi] can't make the assumption that a bachelor's or even a master's degree will guarantee [her] success." And so, Maria says, she has learned some important life lessons about class, race, and social and economic achievement.

Open communication and a willingness to learn seem to be significant factors in surviving racial and cultural differences. "Love is the key," adds Lamont Williams, an African American who has been partnered with Joseph Williams, a white man, for fifteen years. "It transcends cultural and ethnic boundaries." But sometimes lesbian and gay couples can have a hard time if they haven't really learned to respect each other's divergent cultures.

Ruth Carranza, who is Mexican American, finds that cultural differences with her Caucasian partner of ten years, Pam Walton, have been hard. Ruth has had a difficult time, for example, getting Pam—who has created a family of choice from her lesbian friends but isn't close to her own family of origin—to recognize the importance in Ruth's life of extended family, a vital part of Latin culture.

"I have to plead guilty to this," Pam acknowledges, "since I'm a member of the dominant culture. I see a big difference between Ruth's family and what I consider my family. Ruth's family is very traditional and very heterosexual. She has a lot of very macho brothers. . . . For the most part, it's like we live on separate planets."

Ruth feels sad because "I become more assimilated living with Pam. . . . The Hispanic culture is less and less in my active life. You start to lose your connections and your hold on your own culture if you don't take care of it."

"True to You in My Fashion"

One of the hottest potatoes in any relationship is the issue of monogamy. Most of us are raised by heterosexuals, and one of the prevailing traditions in heterosexual love relationships in this country is fidelity. (Or at the very least, the *appearance* of fidelity.) Those who wed in the Christian church vow to "forsake all others," and adultery is right up there in the Ten Commandments. But even secular marriages have the requirement of monogamy built into them, and unless a straight couple agrees on an open marriage, infidelity is a surefire grounds for divorce. To top it off, monogamy is also reinforced by popular culture. Let's face it—if the concepts of fidelity and infidelity ceased to exist, the pop and country music industries would collapse.

When you have a culture that isn't part of the mainstream, one in which couples can't legally marry and thereby pledge their troth, do the same rules apply? When they become "serious," do lesbians and gay men hold their relationships to the fidelity test, even though they don't have to?

I remember very clearly when "monogamy" was a dirty word among both lesbians and gay men. In the late 1970s and early 1980s, my friends and I scoffed at people who demanded fidelity from their lovers. In those days, "So Many Women, So Little Time" was a popular button for lesbians to wear at the Gay Pride March, and women's music pioneer Alix Dobkin trilled in one of her catchier tunes, "I'm not mo-no-ga-mous anymore. . . ." Gay men engaged in even greater sexual experimentation, and "It's Raining Men" was the disco anthem. For both lesbians and gay men, our sexuality had been controlled and repressed for so long, we all wanted to feel as free to express it as we possibly could.

Have things changed or stayed the same for lesbian and gay couples? For many lesbians, dissing monogamy no longer seems to be a favorite pastime. A 1988 survey by the Partners Task Force for Gay and Lesbian Couples found that 91 percent of lesbian couples practiced sexual exclusivity.

Seeming to prove that survey accurate, the women I interviewed, of many ages and races, were overwhelmingly monogamous, though they didn't have a lot to say about what it meant to them. My experience in the lesbian community in general suggests that many lesbians are reticent to discuss sexuality openly—another by-product, I'm sure, of our socialization as women. It doesn't mean we don't have sex, just that we're trained from an early age to act as if we don't.

This may be changing among younger lesbians who frequent places like the Clit Club in New York. In fact, the few women I spoke to who admitted struggling with monogamy were young. "I flirt a lot," Michelle, twenty-two, who has been with her partner for two years, told me. "It's hard."

Beverly, who is twenty-one, and Jamie, thirty, chose monogamy from the start of their relationship two years ago. "Neither of us felt comfortable with it being any other way," Beverly points out. "We view sex as an extension, an act of love. If we weren't monogamous, we wouldn't have the trust that we have now."

Do they ever get tempted to stray? "If we get bored, we seduce each other all over again," Beverly says. "We pretend to meet for the first time in a bar or restaurant or something."

With gay men, the same Partners Task Force survey found that 63 percent were sexually exclusive, while an additional quarter of the couples were "monogamous with exceptions." Gay therapist Michael Shernoff has found a lot of variety in types of gay male sexual relationships, everything from sexual exclusivity to open relationships to nonsexual liaisons. But according to Shernoff, it's the establishing of a set of rules that is important in any sexual relationship. The couple defines just what "infidelity" means, and it isn't the same for everyone. " 'Infidelities' occur when one member of the couple breaks one of the rules the couple has set up regarding how they will conduct themselves sexually," Shernoff says.[12]

For many gay couples, the issue of monogamy has been complicated by the AIDS crisis. (See also the sidebar, "A Controversial View of Gay Marriage.") Steve and his partner of twenty years, Ric, think that their early choice of monogamy saved their lives. "That is a sobering thought we have considered more than once," Steve says. "But who could have

A CONTROVERSIAL VIEW OF GAY MARRIAGE

Writer-activist Gabriel Rotello's recent book, *Sexual Ecology: AIDS and the Destiny of Gay Men*, posits what has become a highly controversial, much-debated, yet original theory in the gay community. Gay men, he says, continue to become HIV-infected, even after years of AIDS education work, because safer sex and the condom code alone aren't enough; it's the high number of sexual partners that many gay men have that threatens to keep the epidemic in business. The legalization of same-sex marriage, Rotello states, would give validation to gay relationships and encourage serial monogamy, thus reducing the risk for HIV infection.

I asked Rotello when he first theorized the importance of same-sex marriage to both gay liberation and to the containment of AIDS, and he replied:

"I've always felt that gay people should have all of the same rights as straight people, whether we want to avail ourselves of those rights or not. And I felt that way about same-sex marriage twenty years ago. . . . If the ultimate validation of heterosexuality is marriage—and I think that the ultimate social sanction of heterosexuality is marriage—then gay liberation will not be able to be said to have succeeded until we get that ultimate validation as well. . . .

"As far as AIDS is concerned, . . . I don't think that my idea about the importance of marriage as AIDS prevention . . . really began to solidify until the studies began coming in the early nineties showing the failure of safe sex to contain the epidemic and showing . . . that a major portion of the reason for that failure is the fact that the [sexual] contact rate is still too high, that we need to bring it down. So, that is really what connected in my mind the idea of marriage as the way that every society has attempted to lower its contact rate, usually not for epidemiological reasons but for cultural or religious or social or material reasons, but nonetheless, that's how they've done it. . . . Wouldn't it make sense that we would apply the same mechanism that every other society in all of history has applied?"

Since nonmonogamy is a sacred cow to many gay men, Rotello's points have raised a lot of ire in the gay community. Joining with him in the critique of gay male sexual culture have been writers and activists Michaelangelo Signorile and Larry Kramer. As therapist and early gay liberation activist Michael Shernoff says, the discussion of gay sexual behavior is "long overdue."

"I'm happy that all these discussions are happening," says Shernoff. "What I'd like to see is that the gay men's community is strong enough and mature enough that we can say, yes, not everyone chooses to be monogamously coupled. Yet, let's look at what the ramifications of nonmonogamy are."

known?" Steve and Ric were simply not comfortable in the sexually experimental gay male world of the mid-1970s, when they met, so they retreated from it. In addition to keeping them healthy, "I think our choice to separate ourselves from the vocal gay male culture has contributed to our success as a couple, as well as our social isolation," Steve observes.

Andrew and Mano practice sexual exclusivity, but they say they are open to changing that, should the desire arise. "If we ever get the 'urge' to have sex with someone else," says Andrew, "we've agreed that we will first talk to each other about the desire. If we follow through, it would most likely be in a three-way or something."

For Andrew and Mano, sexual attraction to others isn't a sign of a relationship's weakness. "Hiding those feelings or acting on them behind the partner's back," says Andrew, "is where troubles begin."

That's what happened when, last year, Oscar "cheated" on his partner, Greg. "We were in a very difficult situation," Oscar says. "It was all downhill. We were talking *at* each other, not *to* each other." In lieu of breaking up, the two decided to see a couples' counselor. "We saw him several times and he helped us find ways to talk through our problems," Oscar says. "We worked through the anger."

Richard Jasper and Jeremy Corry agreed from the start of their relationship to be nonmonogamous. "We don't like to call them 'rules,' " says Richard, "but I think it's safe to say we have some fairly well-established 'understandings' at this point. The basic rule is that we always go home together, even if we sometimes bring someone home with us. If we're apart because one of us is out of town at a conference or something, we play apart." Most importantly, Richard says, "we don't keep secrets—we tell each other *all* the details."

"We never let each other feel excluded," Jeremy adds. "We're not monogamous, but we're firmly committed to each other sexually, as we are in every other way."

"... or Worse"

Infidelity, however we define that, is just one issue that can cause problems between partners in any couple, gay or straight. Same-sex partners are even more susceptible to tensions in their relationship if one or both of the partners isn't out or if they experience homophobia from family and the outside world.

"People kind of discount or disbelieve our love," says Karen, who has been coupled with Lisa for a little over a year. Like many couples after the honeymoon stage, they have started to encounter problems in the relationship, some of which stem from the strain of not being accepted by the world around them as a couple. "It's like a constant daily battle," says Karen, "that I think sometimes just gets me right to the bone."

In my first two serious lesbian relationships, when we hit the "or worse" part that Karen and Lisa have faced, we simply split up. There was no sense of commitment over the long haul. My second partner, in particular, had a pattern of seeking out a new lover soon after the intensely romantic part of a relationship had metamorphosed into familiarity. We didn't seek guidance from a counselor until the end, when we had already made the decision to break up and there was too much water under the bridge. There was no support from anyone, not even our friends, to stay together; even the therapist we spoke to told me to take heart because I'd "find somebody else."

But acknowledging that lesbians and gay men have caring, committed relationships means that we must also acknowledge that we hit snags and impasses in those relationships. We may have irreconcilable problems, but we may also be able to work through our difficulties with some outside help. A number of individuals and couples I spoke to had used a couples' counselor to get over the rough patches of their relationship.

Singer Janis Ian recalls that, "One of the things [Pat and I] both agreed on when we first got together was that if either of us ever asked the other to go into therapy, the other would agree." A year ago, after being together seven years, they reached that point.

In the case of Janis and Pat, distance and spending too much time apart was their pitfall. Janis was busily promoting her album, *Revenge,* while Pat was immersed in her law school studies. "I got home from five months on tour," Janis says, "and suddenly realized that Pat was in law school and not home. And even though I'd known that intellectually, it was a whole other reality. Then she came home and talked like a lawyer, and that was even weirder!" They found a couples' counselor in their hometown of Nashville who specialized in "sorting out" problems and were able to work through their fears and anxieties about the changes in their relationship. "And it was real good for both of us," Janis points out.

Dan and Matt[13] made a similar promise when they first committed to each other. "If either one of us ever felt like we were really getting lost," Dan says, "before we would even think about breaking up, we would go to counseling." Two years into their relationship, they did just that. "We went to a marriage counselor," Dan recalls, "and we've never needed to do it again. It was just having someone there to help us communicate better."

When problems escalate and remained unchecked and not discussed, domestic violence or the threat of it can happen even in same-sex relationships. (See the sidebar, "Same-Sex Domestic Violence.") Four years ago, Sandy was undergoing a lot of pressure at her job and was taking her frustrations out on her longtime partner, Joeline. "It got to the point where she was coming home and exploding on me," Joeline recalls. "She

"*It's the establishing of a set of rules that is important in any sexual relationship. The couple defines just what 'infidelity' means, and it isn't the same for everyone.*"

SAME-SEX DOMESTIC VIOLENCE

"They're at it again," I say to my partner, Katie. It's Saturday night, and a couple in our building is fighting so loudly, people can probably hear them down the block. One partner is screeching and throwing breakable objects. "I pay for this apartment, and you have the nerve to . . ." Katie and I, as well as other people in our building, automatically call the cops. Just a routine incident of domestic violence? Hardly. Our battling neighbors are gay. I'd never thought much about same-sex domestic violence until my neighbors literally brought the issue home.

A couple of years ago, the New York City Gay and Lesbian Anti-Violence Project (AVP) began a subway ad campaign that pictured an outstretched hand and the statement, "If your same-sex partner is using one of these to hurt you, we have one to help you." During the first year the ad ran, AVP saw a 42 percent increase in the number of same-sex domestic violence reports filed in their office. AVP's outreach program finally gave lesbians and gay men permission to speak out and do something about the dangers they face in their own homes, from their own "loving" partners—something our community has been hesitant to face.

"It's hard for us to acknowledge that danger exists within our communities and our relationships," said Judy Yu, a counselor to battered women, at a recent panel in New York on lesbian and gay domestic violence. With antigay hate crimes on the rise, we'd like to think that in our homes, at least, we're safe.

Our society has traditionally defined domestic violence as a private matter between a man and a woman that is no one else's business, something the couple should work out on its own. Funding for shelters has always been limited, and this has made it hard for many battered women to find the help they need.

When abuse occurs in same-sex relationships, the situation is complicated by homophobia, both internalized and external. Lesbians and gay men who are subconsciously ashamed of being gay and who are without a positive picture of same-sex relationships may think that battering comes with the territory or that their partners are driven to violence by the pressures of being gay. "She just came out, and it's been hard on her," is one excuse for a partner's behavior. Domestic violence within same-sex couples can take many forms beyond physical battering, including the economic intimidation my neighbor uses, emotional and verbal abuse, isolation, and in the case of closeted individuals, threats of outing.

Same-sex couples also face institutionalized homophobia when incidents of domestic violence are reported. Katie and I were sorry that we'd called the police on our neighbors when officers showed up and started laughing at them, asking offensive questions like, "Do you have AIDS?" In addition, cops often don't know how to distinguish the batterer from the battered because they're trained to assume that men hit women, period. So all too often, a lesbian or gay male couple may be treated like roommates, brought into the police station together, and held in the same cell for up to seventy-two hours, increasing the chances of further abuse.

Shelter workers can be equally ignorant about same-sex domestic violence. Though a shelter worker wouldn't dream of accusing a straight woman of egging on her male batterer, she might not think twice about asking a lesbian why she "let" another woman hit her. Homophobia in the court system, too, can level the blame against the battered instead of the batterer. In 1996, a judge in Delaware threatened to put a lesbian in jail if she bothered the court again by bringing charges against her lover; the plaintiff was told to deal with her "funny" situation on her own. Sixteen states currently don't give access to family court—which handles domestic violence cases and issues orders of protection—to same-sex couples, because legislators don't want to appear to validate lesbian and gay relationships.

"Legal interventions are way too late and problematic," Widney Brown, a lawyer with AVP, notes. Once again, our community has to hold itself accountable, to regard same-sex relationships as real and worthy of respect.

In cases of same-sex domestic violence, there are a number of lesbian and gay antiviolence projects around the country that can help both the abused partner and the abuser. If one isn't listed for your area, the following projects may also assist you with finding help in your region:

Anti-Violence Project/Valley of
the Sun Gay and Lesbian
Community Center
3136 N. Third Avenue
Phoenix, AZ 85013
(602) 265-7283

Gay and Lesbian Community
Services Center/Anti-Violence
Project
1625 N. Schrader Boulevard
Los Angeles, CA 90028
(213) 993-7400

Community United Against
Violence
973 Market Street, Suite 500
San Francisco, CA 94103
(415) 777-5500

Anti-Violence Project, c/o
Equality Colorado
P.O. Box 300476
Denver, CO 80203
(303) 839-5540

Gay Men and Lesbians
Opposing Violence
P.O. Box 34622
Washington, DC 20005
(202) 737-4568/4569

Horizons Anti-Violence Project
961 W. Montana
Chicago, IL 60614
(773) 871-CARE

Fenway Community
Health Center,
Victim Recovery Program
7 Haviland Street
Boston, MA 02115
(617) 267-0900 ext. 311

Lesbian and Gay Network
of Western Michigan—
Stop the Violence Project
909 Cherry Street SE
Grand Rapids, MI 49506
(616) 458-3511

St. Louis Lesbian and Gay
Anti-Violence Project
Dept. of Psychology, University
of Missouri/St. Louis
St. Louis, MO 63121
(314) 826-7067

New York Gay and Lesbian
Anti-Violence Project
647 Hudson Street
New York, NY 10014
(212) 807-0197

Gay/Lesbian Helpline of
Wake County
P.O. Box 36207
Raleigh, NC 27603
(919) 781-7574

Lesbian and Gay Victim's
Assistance Program
11 Doric Avenue
Cranston, RI 02901
(401) 781-3990

Anti-Violence Project
200 E. Crescent Parkway, #179
Sandy, UT 84070
(801) 297-4004

was so angry, and this [their home] was the only safe place to vent." It wouldn't take much to set Sandy off—"She'd walk in and trip over something or stumble on a rug," Joeline says, and then, "she'd go off."

Joeline knew the relationship was headed for disaster. "I was actually becoming slightly physically afraid," she acknowledges. "Not that she would have ever taken a swing at me, but I wasn't sure." When Joeline admitted her fears to Sandy, Sandy stopped cold and started calling around for a good couples' counselor they could both agree on.

It took several months, but one evening in therapy, Sandy began to recognize the source of her tension. "Sandy started ranting and raving at the therapist about stuff that had gone on at work," Joeline remembers. "After about twenty minutes, she and the therapist looked at each other and Sandy said, 'I cannot believe what I have put Joeline through because of this job.' " Sandy realized she was in an abusive work environment, and she hired an attorney and made an official grievance that got positive results. The company, in fact, had to pick up the tab for the therapy Sandy and Joeline had received. Though their relationship went back to normal, Joeline says, "It was close."

There are other ways, outside of expensive couples' counseling, that same-sex couples can find support when they feel isolated or pressured. "The community should do more workshops for couples," Dr. April Martin says, "with long-term couples mentoring young couples and others going through conflicts. As hard as it is to make a good relationship work, it's that much harder in isolation." Martin points out that same-sex parenting groups sponsor meetings where partners can talk through the obstacles relationships encounter. Many lesbian and gay community centers have groups and workshops for couples.

Some lesbians and gay men have created their own ways to deal with the stresses that are unique to same-sex relationships, among them isolation and feeling "abnormal." One evening at a benefit for a local gay organization, Jill and Randi met up with another lesbian couple and two gay male couples that they knew slightly. "One of the men said, 'We know lots of straight couples, and we know lots of single gay people, but we really don't know any gay couples,' " Jill recalls. "He suggested we could all go out to dinner once a month. So for the past three years, [some of us] have been going out to dinner every month, and we created a little support network." Though sometimes they only talk about "who hogs the covers and those types of things," Jill views it as important validation for their relationship. "I hate the word 'normal,' " Jill says, "but it just makes everything so normal."

D-I-V-O-R-C-E

In these days when everyone from Rolonda to Newt Gingrich has a take on same-sex marriage, it strikes me how little we hear about same-sex divorce. There are, of course, scattered stories about celebrity breakups in the gay press, like Bob and Rod Jackson-Paris dehyphenating their names. (See also the sidebar, "Breaking Up Under Glass.") But in general, divorce is a largely unexamined topic in our communities, a subject we seem to "divorce" ourselves from.

MEDIATING OUR DIFFERENCES

When I was younger, lesbians and gay men slipped in and out of each other's lives like they were parking spaces, banking that there might be a "better" one right up the block. It was fairly uncomplicated, at least in a practical sense, to leave a lover—you packed up the extra underwear and T-shirts you kept at her house and hit the road.

But today, same-sex relationships in which partners have kids together, share a home, are financially interdependent, and play a part in each other's families of origin are not so easy to pry apart. Lesbians and gay men with financial means may turn to couples' counselors or sympathetic lawyers. But what about when couples can't afford those costs?

Mediation is one way for lesbian and gay couples to settle their differences and divide up their belongings. It's a viable option to a court system that has never been very queer-friendly. The key element of mediation—and maybe the hardest aspect of it—is that couples must sit down *together* to come up with a solution that suits both people. Even heterosexual couples, who are able to legally divorce, have been increasingly praising the merits of mediation in solving disputes between separating partners relatively painlessly.

The New York Lesbian and Gay Community Services Center's mediation service (212-620-7310) is run by a trained group of volunteer lawyers and mental health professionals. The Massachusetts-based Academy of Family Mediators (1-800-292-4236), though geared toward heterosexuals, can also make recommendations of mediators in your area.

Yet same-sex couples, like their heterosexual counterparts, experience unreconcilable problems in their relationships. What happens? Simply what happens to many couples, gay or straight. Differences arise that can't be worked through. The rules are broken, and trust unravels. One partner becomes involved with someone else. Distance creates a barrier. Talking about divorce in our community is important if we're going to take our relationships seriously.

For Richard Burns and his ex-lover Tom, several of these problems occurred. Richard and Tom lived in New York and Boston, respectively, for nine of the thirteen years they were a couple. Neither was willing or able to give up his work to relocate for the other, and the distance between them created a lot of stress. "We were both exhausted by commuting," says Richard, who explains that they traveled to see each other every weekend for about five years. Eventually, the visits tapered off, until near the end they were seeing each other only about once a month. "The relationship . . . became less satisfying for both of us."

The other factor in their breakup was that Richard became involved with Donald, who lived in New York. "Now it's shocking to me," Richard says, "but at the time, I thought it was possible to carry on a relationship

"Breaking Up Under Glass"

BY JUDY NELSON

. . . I HAVE EXPERIENCED both a private heterosexual breakup (with a husband of seventeen years) and a public breakup (with a partner of almost eight years). The recovery time, the emotions involved, and the stages one must go through in order to heal and grow are the same. In my rather private divorce from my husband, we settled quietly, following the laws of the land—those laws that are available to every person in the United States except gays and lesbians—which helped us settle our differences without judgment from others. In my very public breakup with my lover [tennis star Martina Navratilova], we found ourselves being judged not only by a harshly scrutinizing press and court system and a homophobic wider community but also by our own homosexual community.

Lacking the guidelines and structures provided to legally married couples, we gays and lesbians have conflicted emotions even among ourselves about what responsibility one partner bears to the other in same-sex relationships. That confusion is even more evident in a public breakup, where one is judged—or misjudged—by people who have never even met you. As in most things available to the public eye, the case is defined in terms of black and white: The public wants a winner, and therefore they must have a loser.

In both public and private breakups, the two people most involved lose something. In the private one, however, the losses are reflected on by the intimate few. In a public breakup the losses are examined by many, and thus the parents, the children, the relatives, and the friends of the couple find themselves helplessly involved and often hurt beyond the pain that normally accompanies any separation or divorce. The wounds inflicted by public bullets that could not be dodged take a long, long time to heal. Sometimes the scars remain a lifetime. At best we can use those scars to remind us that we are still alive and perhaps just a little wiser, a little more resilient.

It's ironic, but what we need, of course, is for more gay and lesbian relationships to go public—not just celebrities and not just when they break up. Only then will we have faces—faces that the heterosexual community already knows but does not know they know. We must come forward. Only then will the public begin to validate our contracts. Stand up and be counted! We do count. We do matter. If anyone has any serious doubts on that point, then perhaps we should do as Rita Mae Brown once suggested to me that we do: If everyone who is homosexual would take one day and go on strike, then we would see the world stop. Theater, cinema, churches, hospitals, industry, sports—work of all kinds would have to close. A point would be made.

We are here. We are everywhere. We always have been. Now it is time to come forward and be public about our relationships. It's not about getting "in your face"; it's about saying, "This is my face." In the end celebrity status is irrelevant. What matters is that all of our relationships become visible, not just those of the celebrated few.

This essay originally appeared in The Advocate, *December 10, 1996. Reprinted with permission of the author.*

with two people at the same time." What actually happened, he recognizes, was an emotionally damaging situation for the three members of the triangle. "We were all miserable," Richard notes.

Though he entered couples' counseling at different times with Tom and then with Donald, both relationships ultimately ended. "My inability to end my relationship with Tom," he reflects, "really doomed my relationship with Donald, and the relationship with Donald exacerbated the problems with Tom."

Richard retains a close friendship with Donald, but things with Tom are on shakier ground. After the breakup, they didn't see each other for over a year. "I never expected it to be a year," he says. "I thought we wouldn't see each other for a few months, and then we would just evolve into friends." But healing from a relationship can take a long time, especially when one person feels aggrieved.

When Carmen Vázquez and her partner, Marcie, broke up after twelve years together, there was a lot of pain. "It tore both of us up," says Carmen. Carmen and Marcie had met and lived together in San Francisco, but then Carmen took a new job in New York. "That was the beginning of the end," Carmen observes. Only Carmen had good reason to move, and Marcie didn't want to—she had to uproot herself from her friends and her job in California. "It's very hard on a couple to make a move like that," says Carmen. The two were separated for ten months while Marcie prepared to move to the East Coast.

The separation, Carmen says, "took its toll." Even after Marcie relocated, their relationship was strained. In the meantime, Carmen had met someone else. "That always becomes the straw that breaks the camel's back," says Carmen. "But the process of coming to terms with the fact that we shouldn't be together probably went on for three years before we broke up."

Carmen suggested couples' counseling to ease the pain of their breakup, but Marcie was only willing to invest that time if Carmen would agree to try to preserve the relationship. Carmen, however, was unwilling to give up her new love interest. Tensions mounted, and Carmen and Marcie finally split.

But it was a messy divorce in terms of splitting up property. Fortunately, they were able to work some of their immediate problems out through the use of the New York Lesbian and Gay Community Services Center's low-cost mediation service, which functions as a sort of alternative divorce court for same-sex couples. The mediation service is run by a trained group of volunteer lawyers and mental health professionals. Mediation sessions can help couples establish child visitation rights or decide more mundane matters like who gets the computer or the VCR. (See the sidebar, "Mediating Our Differences.")

"Mediation is an idea we should export as much as possible," notes Carmen. "[Marcie and I] came in miles apart and actually walked out feeling like fairness had happened here. [Without mediation] I would have been in a state of anger and rancor for a long time."

"Till Death Do Us Part"

The number of funerals my friends and I have attended in the last decade astounds me. Who among us ever imagined that we would see so many members of the lesbian and gay community die prematurely? I'm not just speaking about AIDS, which has ravaged the gay male community. Cancer—particularly breast cancer and ovarian cancer—has made too many lesbians widows at a young age.

Grief, a natural part of life, is made even more difficult for lesbians and gay men when the larger society doesn't acknowledge that mourning as real or legitimate. Because same-sex relationships aren't viewed as valid much of the time, neither is our grief at losing those relationships. For example, "There are very few companies, even if they have domestic partnership, that will give a [gay] man bereavement leave," notes therapist Michael Shernoff, editor of a book called *Gay Widowers: Surviving the Death of a Partner.* "He may often have to use personal leave or vacation . . . and may not be given the latitude that a [heterosexual] husband or wife would be."

If lesbians and gay men were allowed to legally marry, Shernoff speculates that they would not have to experience what he calls "disenfranchised grief." Shernoff says he has actually seen gay widowers denied access to their lovers' funerals. "There are all kinds of indignities that happen during the final dying and after that could be avoided by marriage."

These "indignities" include outright discrimination and deep, institutionalized homophobia. When Marie's partner of three years became sick, "even with power of attorney, I faced problems from doctors who wouldn't acknowledge my position," Marie recalls. "They insisted on speaking to the 'real' next of kin. I refused to provide any names."

Ben Munisteri (left) and his partner, Steven Powsner, who died of AIDS in 1995.

Often our relationships are wiped off the slate by homophobic newspapers. Fashion mogul Gianni Versace's *New York Times* obituary, for example, mentioned only his family of origin and not his partner of eleven years, Antonio D'Amico. When Robert Woodworth's partner Noli died in 1995, the *New York Times* excised the word "lover" from his paid death notice, substituting the more "acceptable" phrase "longtime companion" instead. Robert's friend and boss, Richard Burns, who had placed the ad, wrote an angry letter to the *Times* demanding that the obituary be rerun

"Grieving in Silence"

BY MURRAY DUBIN

A HUSBAND OR WIFE DIES, and a present and future shatters. Grief is enveloping. It may be worse when you're young because no one is supposed to die young. Friends aren't bereaved, few understand your continued mourning. You're alone because people prefer avoiding painful situations, and suddenly, that's what you are—a painful situation.

If gay or lesbian, that painful situation may be more complicated, and you may be even more alone. First, people may not know of your loss. And if they do, they often assume that you don't hurt that much.

"People feel badly for you, but many minimize the amount of love and commitment that can exist in a same-sex relationship," says Carole Smith, who lost her partner in 1989.

You don't have the same support systems, and your family often does not support you in the same way," says Jay Segal, a psychologist who runs a substance-abuse program in Bucks County [Pennsylvania] for gays and lesbians.

"People have to confront their own homophobia because it doesn't allow them to be more open and get support from their family and from work. Then you have our society, which creates the fear of a gay man coming into the workplace and saying, 'My lover is dying.' They don't feel safe, and they're not protected."

The result, Segal says, is often a reluctance to acknowledge relationships—no picture of a partner on a desk at work, not changing insurance beneficiaries because someone at the office might find out, introducing a loved one as "my roommate."

Sister Kathleen Schneider has coordinated the St. Luke's Hospitality Center for People with HIV/AIDS in Center City [Philadelphia] since 1989. She sees bereavement constantly, including family reaction to homosexuality and AIDS.

"People don't ask what your husband did to get cancer. But when it's AIDS, they ask if he was gay. Did he use drugs? Was he promiscuous? They look at the way people got the disease, and then withhold sympathy to the person who is ill and to the caregiver.

"It's hard on the caregiver. They're dealing with diarrhea, dementia, constant care. Partners work all day and care for someone all night. . . . I've never seen such fidelity.

"The family is often not involved. . . . At the end, they come in and take over. It's cruel, it's not unusual. Sometimes, the caregivers are put out of their homes because the will says the family gets the home."

In her experience, "supportive families are the exception."

Reprinted with permission from The Philadelphia Inquirer, *October 22, 1995.*

as originally written. When, after several phone calls, the *Times* agreed, it was the first time the paper had ever allowed the term "lover" to designate a gay widower.

Ben Munisteri found himself "frozen out of the family room" at the funeral home prior to the service for his lover, Steven Powsner. Even though Steven's family of origin had been conspicuously absent during his illness and Ben had been the one to nurse Steven through his last year,

"I had to stand in the hall," Ben recalls bitterly. "I wasn't afforded any respect [from the family]. At least the rabbi [Sharon Kleinbaum, of the gay synagogue, Congregation Beth Simchat Torah] stood with me and the gay activists who paid their respects." The uncle who spoke for the family at the service neglected to even mention Ben's part in caring for Steven, and Ben was not invited to sit shiva with Steven's family. The disrespect Ben and other widows and widowers like him face only complicates the actual grieving process, which is common to all people who lose their partners. "I'll learn to live with [Steven's death]," Ben says, "like a person lives with a disability. You learn to take your insulin shots. You learn to manage your cane or your crutches pretty well. Almost as if they weren't there. But it's always there." (See also the sidebar, "Grieving in Silence.")

Unexpected Transitions

So far, this book has focused on same-sex couples and how their relationships work and sometimes don't. But our community is actually much broader and much more complex than just being "lesbian and gay." Some of the people I interviewed identify as bisexual, but have chosen same-sex partners for their life mates. And more and more people are coming out as transgendered and making their voices heard, much as lesbians and gay men first did in large numbers after the Stonewall Rebellion.

Psychologists don't really know why some people have a gender identity that doesn't match their birth gender. Gary Sanders, director of the Human Sexuality Program at the University of Calgary in Canada, says, however, that "it occurs at a very early age and is unchangeable."[14]

In couples in which one partner discovers that he or she is transgendered, the relationship can experience added and unexpected stresses. For Loree and Marcelle Cook-Daniels, who met in 1983, that was exactly what happened.

Loree and Marcelle were both lesbians—Loree a white woman, and Marcelle a black butch—who met through a lesbian pen pal service. In 1985, they married at what Loree calls "a quickie marriage mill" in South Carolina, where blood tests were not required. "Marcelle wore typical butch clothing designed to minimize breasts," recalls Loree, "and strategically scuffed the place on his driver's license that said 'F.' " The following year, they had what they call their "real marriage"—a commitment ceremony in front of friends and family in which they made promises to each other about their relationship. That year, they also hyphenated their names to formalize their commitment.

But one thing kept them from being like "any other lesbian couple."

"Marcelle told me within the first month we were together," Loree says, "that he was taking testosterone and wanted to have surgery and begin living as a man." Marcelle had felt transgendered from childhood and had first discussed surgery at age seventeen with a psychologist.

Loree, however, totally identified as lesbian and could not see herself being involved with a man. She wanted Marcelle as a woman. So she gave Marcelle an ultimatum—their relationship or the surgery. Marcelle chose the relationship. "It's hard enough to find love," Marcelle explains.

Though Marcelle brought up the issue occasionally after that, "basically we didn't talk about it much at all," Loree remembers. "It was the proverbial elephant in the living room that everyone stepped around and no one talked about." They moved in together, held their commitment ceremony, had a son. Yet Marcelle thought about having surgery practically every day.

It took Loree nine years to recognize that she was blocking her partner's true identity. If Marcelle transitioned to a male body, Loree's biggest fear was of losing her own lesbian identity and the community that she had been an active part of for so many years. But the silence around Marcelle's gender identity caused a strain on their relationship.

For a long time, "I had very low self-esteem," Marcelle notes, "but as I became more self-confident and sure of what I needed to do, Loree stayed fast in her belief that my motivations were neurotic and unhealthy. She didn't trust me to know what was right for me, and she put her own biases in the way of my need to feel whole."

Eventually, Loree supported Marcelle's desire to undergo sexual reassignment surgery, which he did two years ago. Marcelle also changed all his legal documents, and even his birth certificate now reads "male," as he believes it should have from the start. For many couples, one partner's desire to transition can break the relationship in half, but Loree and Marcelle have remained together through a lot of hard work and self-reflection. They also had to deal with the fact that Marcelle's transitioning was a major topic of discussion in the Washington, D.C., lesbian community, with which Loree and Marcelle were actively involved.

"We ended up leaving one mixed lesbian/gay male group we had belonged to for years," says Loree, "because they were unable to provide me support when I needed it, bombarding me with incredulous questions and talking endlessly about how shocked they were." Within their interracial lesbian couples' group, though, they found three other couples who were also dealing with gender issues. Though they lost support from some members of the lesbian community, they gained it from others.

Since Marcelle's surgery, the couple has moved to California, where their story isn't immediately known, and they find they are assumed to be

TRANS POWER

Like the nascent lesbian and gay movement of thirty years ago, the transgender movement has exploded nationwide. Until very recently, there were few places to go for support, but there are now a variety of groups and online resources for the transgendered community and the families and significant others of transsexuals. The largest national organizations are:

American Educational Gender Information Service, P.O. Box 33724, Decatur, GA 30033-0724; (770) 939-2128; e-mail: AEGIS@gender.org.—publishes *Chrysalis, AEGISNews,* and several pamphlets on transgender issues; also book sales and extensive referral network for all transgender issues.

International Foundation for Gender Education, 14 Felton Street, Waltham, MA 02154; (617) 899-2212; e-mail: ifge@world.std.com—founded in 1978, IFGE publishes *TV/TS Tapestry,* reprints, and books on TV/TS subjects.

Renaissance Education Assoc., Inc., 987 Old Eagle School Road, Suite 719, Wayne, PA 19087; (610) 975-9119 (twenty-four-hour answering service); e-mail: bensalem@bbs.cpcn.com—

membership organization; fee of $36 includes a twenty-four-page monthly newsletter, *Renaissance News & Views;* also publishes Background Papers and Community Outreach Bulletins on transgender issues for personal and professional use; speakers available for classroom, corporate, or media discussions of transgender issues.

Also, many transgendered people have found their first support and encouragement online. The following are a couple of the growing online resources for the TG/TS community:

Above and Beyond (http://www.abmall.com)—extensive links to the personal Web pages of many transgendered folks, newsletters from TG/TS organizations, lists of newsgroups and chat rooms, articles on TG/TS issues, and fiction and nonfiction by transgendered writers.

Transgender Community Forum on America Online—accessible through keyword "TCF" (or through the Gay and Lesbian Community Forum—keyword "on Q"); has links to national and local TG/TS organization Web sites, and chat rooms and message boards for the TG/TS community on a variety of relevant topics.

a heterosexual couple by straight and gay people alike. "I feel invisible to the lesbian community," says Marcelle, who identifies as queer. Loree has had to adjust to being the only woman in a house full of men and to being perceived by outsiders as a straight wife and mother.

But "we no longer have that elephant in the living room," Loree says. "Overall, emotionally we're doing better because Marcelle's more comfortable with himself."

For Jan and Mary Lou, who live in a small town in western Pennsylvania and have been together for twenty-two years, the elephant in their living room has also disappeared. Until three years ago, Jan was John. "I knew from five years old that I wanted to be a girl," Jan says of her former self. "In puberty, I knew that something was desperately wrong. But we're talking a time period where you didn't do this thing [have sexual reassignment surgery]." So John tried to live a "normal" life, falling in love and marrying Mary Lou in a big church wedding, and being, for all intents and purposes, heterosexual.

But a year and a half into their marriage, John began to cross-dress. Mary Lou says she at first felt "repulsed" by this aspect of her husband but gradually began to see that it was simply who John was. They both started to get support—John from online transsexual bulletin boards and chat rooms, and Mary Lou from a group in the Pittsburgh area. (See the sidebar, "Trans Power.") John eventually took hormones and underwent surgery, becoming reborn as Jan. If John hadn't transitioned, they both believe he would have eventually committed suicide.

Though the heterosexual marriages of many male-to-female transsexuals dissolve under the pressure, Jan and Mary Lou's has endured. They know other long-term couples who have weathered the same storm—two of their friends, Mary Lou says, have been together for thirty-seven years. "I thought, if they can do it, I can do it," Mary Lou asserts. In what is the reverse of Loree and Marcelle's case, Jan and Mary Lou had to become accustomed to being perceived as lesbians, whereas before they had been a heterosexual couple. It was a long education process, but now, Mary Lou says, "I don't really give a damn what anyone else says."

Jan sees their relationship now as "stronger." "We both feel free to be ourselves," Jan points out. "And I think our love is deeper. We've gone through so much together." And she adds, "John and Mary Lou were dying in this little town." Jan and Mary Lou, on the other hand, have broadened their circle of friends and become activists, lecturing at universities on transsexual issues and attending transgender conferences. "The truth is," Jan says, "Jan and Mary Lou are much more interesting than John and Mary Lou ever were." (See also the sidebar, "Deconstructing DOMA.")

When I'm Sixty-Four

Straight people who don't understand lesbians and gay men often still believe that homosexuality means living and dying alone. "It's a hard life," one friend from high school told me, shaking her head sadly, when I came out to her. In fact, the only things I have found "hard" about being a lesbian are the homophobia I face, the stereotypes that still persist about lesbians and gay men, and the general ignorance of straight people about what it means to be gay.

Contrary to homophobic beliefs, several recent studies have shown

DECONSTRUCTING DOMA

It's something Congress didn't face when it passed the Defense of Marriage Act (DOMA), and the lesbian and gay community as a whole is not really aware of. But there are an estimated two hundred to four hundred already legally married same-sex couples in the United States, as the result of one of the spouses having undergone sexual reassignment surgery.

Jan and Mary Lou, for example, were married twenty-two years ago as John and Mary Lou (see page 196). But nineteen years later, John transitioned and became Jan, changing all her legal documents, including her birth certificate, to reflect her female gender. Then Jan and Mary Lou filed a joint federal tax return, as they were accustomed to doing, but this time they crossed "John" off their self-adhesive address label and substituted "Janet." With their return, they sent documentation about John's official name and gender change. But the following year, the IRS sent their return once again to "John and Mary Lou," totally ignoring their new reality.

Though many of these same-sex couples are out about their circumstances, most dread what could happen if the government wanted to challenge the legality of their marriages. This is a time bomb waiting to explode, a preview of the legal snarl that will occur if same-sex marriage becomes legalized in Hawaii but is not recognized by other states. If there is a judgment for same-sex marriage in Hawaii, Evan Wolfson of Lambda Legal Defense's Marriage Project has hypothesized that the many state antigay marriage laws that have been passed will severely jeopardize people's right to travel between states and settle where they choose. Bearing this out, Janet and Mary Lou already travel at their own risk. "When we travel, we take all our papers with us, including our marriage license," says Mary Lou, "in case something happens to one of us. We know that we're on very shaky legal ground."

If you are transsexual or have a transsexual spouse and need information or help about your legal status, contact Lambda Legal Defense and Education Fund's Marriage Project at (212) 809-8585; fax (212) 809-0055.

that older lesbians and gay men who have been open about their sexual orientation are neither isolated nor lonely. In fact, many lesbian and gay male couples have been fortunate enough to grow older together.

Martin and John, for example, have been together thirty-six years. They came of age in the pre-Stonewall era, when society was much more narrow-minded about homosexuality than today, and they sheltered themselves in a suburban community, having little contact with other gay people and being too frightened to come out. Though they lived just an hour from New York City, with one of the largest gay populations in the country, they almost never left their suburban enclave. "We would rarely go into the city except to see a show," recalls John, "and then we'd run right back to suburbia where we felt very safe." It was seventeen years into their relationship, John says, before they "came out to the world." As more and more gay people started becoming visible in the suburbs, Martin and John were able to feel comfortable being openly gay.

Now, Martin says, he comes out to everyone, even telephone solicitors. "I got so tired of changing pronouns," Martin sighs, speaking of the years in the closet when he would refer to John as "she" to people who didn't know the two of them. "I thought, what am I doing that I have to lie?" They have become politically active with their local chapter of Parents, Families, and Friends of Lesbians and Gays (PFLAG) and have taken over the coordination of the organization's speakers' bureau.

Martin and John, like many gay seniors, comment that contemporary gay culture is ageist, but they believe this is a reflection of American society in general. "As soon as you pass thirty," John remarks, "you're over the hill. Just look at the ads [in magazines]. . . . When we do go to gay bars, I feel more than a generation or two removed."

Both in their sixties and retired, Martin and John say their relationship has changed a lot from the early days they were together, and not just in their ability to be more open and honest about it. Their commitment to each other, says Martin, has "matured and deepened. Of course, now we're together twenty-four hours a day, and sometimes we get into each other's hair." Martin recalls that they've had their share of relationship "battles," but he confides their secret for getting past even the worst argument.

© 1992 Alain McLaughlin/Impact Visuals

"Never once did either one of us think of leaving," he says. "Before it got to that, we would laugh. We'd be screaming, and then both of us would stop to laugh."

Unlike Martin and John, who have been together since both they and the lesbian and gay liberation movement were young, life partners Nancy Spannbauer and Ellen Ensig-Brodsky met in the mid-1980s as middle-aged women who had both had heterosexual marriages and raised children. They have now been together ten years and have every intention of growing older together. Because they are both over fifty-five and have worked professionally with senior citizens, they have become activists in senior gay issues and have founded an organization in New York City called Pride Senior Network.[15]

Lasting love after more than twenty-five years.

"I run a senior center," says Nancy, explaining how the senior network got started, "and [before she retired] Ellen was a surveyor for the Health Care Financing Administration. Our suppertime conversation was always around senior issues, and what would happen if I were in a nursing home. Would I be able to be out? Have Ellen's picture there as my significant other? The answer is no, for the most part. I'd feel too vulnerable."

"People around us were in the same boat," Ellen notes, "because our friends are roughly about the same age as us." So Pride Senior Network was born, a network of lesbian- and gay-friendly services and businesses (such as financial planners, lawyers, Realtors, and travel agents) of interest to the gay senior community. Members of the network know that they can comfortably turn to these service providers with questions and needs. Pride Senior Network also publishes a newsletter that focuses on senior issues, and it operates a telephone events and information hot line. A Web page is also in the works.

In addition, Nancy and Ellen undertake public education with senior agencies and nursing homes around the metropolitan area to try to get them to understand the specific needs of lesbian and gay seniors. Like Martin and John, Nancy and Ellen also think that "within the gay community, the consciousness about getting old requires a lot of work." They've called on the Empire State Pride Agenda (the New York State lesbian and gay lobbying group), trying to make sure senior concerns are part of the group's advocacy work in the state capital.

Though several gay senior groups are working to develop lesbian and gay retirement homes (see the sidebar, "Retiring . . . But Not Shy"), both Nancy and Ellen favor a more intergenerational gay community. "I've been in this field over twenty years," says Nancy, "and the people that are happiest, most enjoying their later years, are the ones that have friends that are younger, as well as friends their own age."

Ellen thinks the lesbian and gay community has been too isolated along age lines, and that it hurts everyone along the spectrum. "Young gay people need role models," says Ellen, "and they need to teach us [older people] computers! In exchange, we have a lot of life experience to give back. [Young people] need to know you can be gay and have a very productive life and close relationships."

Partners in Life and Love

Lesbian and gay couples have a lot to learn from each other, both our successes and our mistakes. Because we're still essentially "outlaws," we have, in fact, no real choice but to share what we know. If we don't, we're bound to continue feeling isolated and like we're going it alone, the first same-sex couple ever to face relationship pitfalls. "What's amazing to me," says psychotherapist Dr. April Martin, "is that I'm still seeing, time after time, lots of young queers who don't know that our relationships last, because we're still age segregated. And those of us who've had partners for twenty years aren't going out to bars."

RETIRING . . . BUT NOT SHY

Two senior organizations are currently advocating for lesbian and gay retirement communities and nursing homes. With no gay alternatives, many lesbian and gay seniors have had to find housing in heterosexual institutions, where it may not be comfortable or safe for them to be out. With the large baby boom generation hitting its fifties, the question of a safe and happy retirement for lesbians and gay men is going to become an even more important issue in the next few decades.

Senior Action in a Gay Community (SAGE) was founded in New York in 1977, and its programs include support groups, counseling services, a drop-in center, women's events, AIDS programs and education, and public outreach on senior issues. I went to a SAGE panel that was totally inspiring on the topic of lesbian and gay relationships—one male couple had been together for almost fifty years! SAGE has also conducted a survey among its members and found that 87 percent of the respondents would be interested in living in a gay retirement facility; thus, the SAGE retirement project was born. For more information, contact: Senior Action in a Gay Environment, SAGE, 305 Seventh Avenue, 6th Floor, New York, NY 10001; (212) 741-2247.

The Gay and Lesbian Association of Retiring Persons (GLARP)—the gay version of the American Association of Retired Persons (AARP)—was founded twenty years after SAGE but is also actively pursuing the issue of lesbian and gay retirement homes and nursing facilities. Says one of its founders, Mary Thorndal, "It would be horrible if we had to go back into the closet when we got vulnerable and old." For more information, contact GLARP, 10940 Wilshire Boulevard, Suite 1600, Los Angeles, CA 90024; (310) 966-1500.

Martin would like to see older lesbian and gay couples mentoring younger ones, giving them guidance in the way that parents do with heterosexual married children. After all, it's a rare straight parent who counsels his or her gay offspring about same-sex relationships. Maybe you were luckier than I was, but my mother's advice to me when I was growing up was all about what to look for in a husband; the idea that I might, in fact, want a wife didn't even enter her consciousness. With virtually no help from our families or society as a whole, lesbians and gay men need to take on the responsibility ourselves and break down the barriers that senior couples like Martin and John and Nancy and Ellen talk about. "Segregation by age," writes Michaelangelo Signorile, "has each new generation [of gay people] going through the same laborious learning process and often repeating the same mistakes—socially, culturally, and politically."[16]

It's important for gay and straight people alike to confront the stereotype of "the lonely homosexual" and to realize that lesbian and gay couples have, in fact, beaten the odds against their relationships lasting. Many long-term couples have endured despite societal prejudices and their own internalized homophobia, despite the lack of role models and any set guidelines for or advice on how same-sex relationships should work. Our marriages are exactly that—marriages in everything but legal standing. And we have the squabbles over the laundry, the money issues, and the communication problems to prove it.

Yet it's precisely because our relationships are extra-legal that they present a model for what marriage, at its best, should be—a sharing partnership, without the baggage of fixed gender roles, one in which fidelity is defined from the inside rather than by society. I think this is why I've come to use the term "partner" for Katie, after years of trying on a lot of others that didn't feel quite right. It's what we are, really—partners in life and in love.

Lesbians and gay men, sometimes shunned or simply misunderstood by their families of origin, have created another kind of model, too—families of choice. "Heterosexual married couples," observes Richard Burns, executive director of New York City's Lesbian and Gay Community Services Center, "can provide for us a very strict and repressive model on the appropriate place for love, the appropriate place for sex, the appropriate places for blending of finances. I think where gay people have the opportunity to lead this culture in a more loving and positive way is toward families of affiliation and love that are families of choice—that we'll take care of one another in sickness and in health and richer and poorer, for better or for worse, by *choice*."

In the next chapter, we'll look at how lesbians and gay men bring their lives full-circle and create unique families—occasionally with ex-lovers, often with good friends, sometimes with children from heterosexual marriages, and more and more, with adopted or biological children they choose to parent as out gay people.

Notes

1. Judy MacLean, "An Afternoon with My If-There-Were-a-Laws," in *Dyke Life: From Growing Up to Growing Old,* edited by Karla Jay (BasicBooks, 1995), 23.

2. Betty Berzon, *Permanent Partners: Building Gay and Lesbian Relationships That Last* (Plume, 1990), 286.

3. Not their real names.

4. Not their real names.

5. Not their real names.

6. Not their real names.

7. Not her real name.

8. Not his real name.

9. Not their real names.

10. Not their real names.

11. Karin writes under the pseudonym Karin Kallmaker and publishes with Naiad Press.

12. Michael Shernoff, "Male Couples and Their Relationship Styles," *Journal of Gay and Lesbian Social Services* 2, no. 2 (1995), 45.

13. Not their real names.

14. Quoted in Laura Markowitz, "When the Mirror Is Wrong: An Interview with Gary Sanders," *In the Family* 1, no. 2 (October 1995), 8.

15. Pride Senior Network can be reached at 1756 Broadway, Suite 11H, New York, NY 10019, (212) 757-3203.

16. Michaelangelo Signorile, "Closing the Gay Generation Gap," *Out* (August 1997), 38.

The Family Way

5

Toward a Broader Concept of Family

Many of us still remember the balmy August night in 1992, when right-wing pundit Pat Buchanan stood up in front of the Republican National Convention, damning lesbians and gay men and pontificating on the need for a return to real "family values." For Buchanan and his conservative cohorts, the phrase "family values" signified the traditional family—breadwinner father married to homemaker mother, raising a couple of biological kids. This, the right-wingers tell us, should be the real meaning of family—the sacred heterosexual family, which, they contend, lesbians and gay men have tried to subvert and corrupt and that society must do everything in its power to protect.

Well, there are quite a few holes in this vision of family, and they're big enough to walk an elephant through. To begin with, "family" is a loaded word, and there are a lot of myths associated with it. The family *is* the basic unit of our society, but a minority of children live in the kind of family configuration that the radical right depicts as the "norm." Many more children live in other types of families—with a single parent, with lesbian and gay parents, with grandparents or other relatives, or in blended stepfamilies. Furthermore, a shocking number of children, particularly girls, have suffered physical or sexual abuse within their families of origin, especially from fathers and other male relatives. Many have emotional scarring from unsupportive or uncaring parents. And about half of all heterosexual marriages end in divorce.

In fact, a quick history lesson shows that American families have hardly ever been the ideal that the right wing would like us to believe. What is commonly called the traditional family (the dad-mom-kids configuration) prevailed mostly during the immediate post–World War II era—the time, of course, when many of us were raised. "The 1950s was the most atypical decade in the entire history of American marriage and family life," historian Stephanie Coontz points out. Problems within families, she notes, like alcoholism, domestic violence, and child abuse, were routinely hushed up in those "good old days."

> *"Families can be defined as two or more people who share responsibility, care, and love; teachers encounter many kinds of families beyond 'traditional' groupings."*

The conservative, Ozzie and Harriet view of family leaves a lot of people out in the cold, particularly lesbians and gay men. Many heterosexuals seem to think that lesbians and gay men spring out of nowhere—that we have no families, no caring circles of people who love and nurture us. In addition, the ignorant fear that lesbians and gay men prey on children and teenagers, trying to recruit them to homosexuality, sadly still persists, stemming from a lack of firsthand knowledge of gay people.

One particularly ugly battle over "family values" occurred in the New York City public schools in 1989. That year, a group of city public school teachers and administrators began writing a curriculum for first-graders that would teach tolerance of the city's many ethnic and racial groups. Called "Children of the Rainbow," the curriculum guide also encouraged the teaching of respect for lesbians and gay men and their families.

When a school board in the borough of Queens refused to adopt the curriculum in 1992, misunderstanding, ignorance, and a near-revolution in the city's public education system broke out. Conservative school board members frightened parents, wrongly charging that, by sanctioning "Children of the Rainbow," schools chancellor Joseph A. Fernandez was giving teachers the green light to "promote" homosexuality and to discuss specific sexual behaviors with six-year-olds. But what the chancellor's guide actually said was simple and basic and very much about family values.

> *Families can be defined as two or more people who share responsibility, care, and love; teachers encounter many kinds of families beyond "traditional" groupings. Families may have a single parent or dual-career parents; some are blended groups, with children from two or more families. Any of these combinations might include grandparents, teenagers, foster parents, lesbian/gay parents, or adoptive parents. By treating all families with attention, courtesy, and respect, the teacher models accepting behaviors for the children and helps develop an expanded vision of the human experience.*

Chancellor Fernandez ultimately lost his battle and was forced to step down from his post. But the discussion over what constitutes a family has continued to rage in communities and school districts throughout the country, a battle between conservative and progressive views. "There are so many definitions of family," Joy Nelson of Tennessee told me, "that you can't put it into a neat little box anymore. It's not that simple anymore, and society is having a hard time understanding."

The results have been more encouraging in other areas of the country than they were in New York. In Oregon, for example, the state Parent-Teacher Association (PTA) adopted a groundbreaking resolution in 1994, opposing prejudice against parents, students, or teachers based on sexual orientation. The PTA went a step further, denouncing "all legislative attempts to suppress discussion of family diversity and sexual orientation." And this in the state where the ugly, antigay Ballot Measure 9 was narrowly defeated in 1992.

Slowly but surely, inroads are made when lesbian and gay men and their families become more visible, but there are still a lot of misperceptions out there. "Every time some conservative commentator calls gay families 'pretend' I want to smack them," says lesbian mom Karin Kaj bitterly. "There is nothing 'pretend' about changing diapers, planning meals, cleaning the house, and pulling weeds in the backyard. There is nothing 'pretend' about the depth of our love for each other." In fact, too few heterosexuals understand that, just as lesbians and gay men have always created relationships without the benefit of legal marriage, they have also always created loving and supportive family configurations.

A queer family.

And why wouldn't we? "Family" is a powerful and enduring concept, which is supposed to be based on love, acceptance, and nurturing. Many of us, expelled from or simply misunderstood by our own families of origin, have fashioned large, extended chosen families out of our friends and ex-lovers. Some of us, either on our own or with a lesbian or gay partner, have raised children from previous heterosexual relationships. And a growing number in our community are having or adopting children as openly lesbian and gay individuals and couples. There are an estimated six to fourteen million children living in families with a lesbian or gay parent, so it's clear that the word "family" needs a wider definition than many conservatives would like to give it.

How can we as a community help broaden the definition of "family" so it is more inclusive, not just of lesbians and gay men, but of all families that don't fit the conservative standard? In this chapter, we'll look at some of the trends in lesbian and gay families and see how queer concepts can expand on and advance the meaning of "family" in this society. Just as marriages should be defined by love, not gender, so should families. "A family is a bunch of people, or not so many, who love each other," says Lisa, a seven-year-old who is featured with her lesbian moms in the homophobia-busting exhibit "Love Makes a Family." (See the sidebar.) No one could have said it any better.

Chosen People

Eight years ago, I edited an anthology of short stories by women writers about sisters. In my acknowledgments, I thanked not only my two biological sisters, but also five women whom I designated as my "metaphoric" sisters, my sisterhood of choice. I had worked with all of them, either at a paying job or at a volunteer activity, and several of them had been my roommates. They were women I had shared both joys and sadnesses with, who had seen me through break ups, given me a couch to sleep on when I lost my apartment, greeted my first book like it was a brand-new baby in the family, and swapped everything from confidences to political observations to clothes with me. In short, they were family, though I was related by blood to none of them. Two of them—in true lesbian fashion—were ex-lovers of mine.

© 1997 JEB (Joan E. Biren)

Loving our life together.

My chosen family today is a slightly different configuration; it has changed and shifted over the years. Now it consists primarily of Katie, my partner of five years, and a few good friends. I've picked up a few gay "brothers" and one gay male friend I tease about being "the son I never wanted." We sometimes squabble like members of any family do, but we share a kinship that goes beyond blood ties. I couldn't survive without them—but then, who *can* survive for long without family?

The phenomenon I've just described certainly isn't unique to me. Lesbians and gay men have always formed families of choice to share the good times and help them get through the bad ones. We've done this partly because many of us have been ostracized or misunderstood by our own families of origin. But we've also created families of choice as a protective measure, a way of survival in a world that has been hostile to our very existence. In essence, we've taken a very bad situation—widespread fear and ignorance about gay people—and made something very good out of it.

"Our friends are our major support system," says Joy Nelson of Tennessee. "Carlena and I have a family of choice, a few couples that we've been friends with for years. They are closer than our relatives."

"One of the things I encourage people to do is create their own families," says therapist Vanessa Marshall. "Most of my close friends are like family. When things go down, I think extended family is sometimes more 'family' than blood family is."

"I don't have a large blood family that I interact with on a daily basis," says Santa Molina, Vanessa's partner in life and business. "But it's been nice because Vanessa came with all these friends and all these people that really loved her. . . . Now they love me, too. My concept of what family and friendship means has just really taken on a whole other dimension."

Santa recalls a time when her ex-husband was phoning and harassing her, making her very frightened. One of Vanessa's best friends, a "sister" who had also grown to love Santa, said, "We'll go out there and we'll fix him," a sentiment that touched Santa deeply, even though she knew physical threats weren't the way to handle the situation. Still, "I felt that protected and that much a part of something," Santa says. "My definition of what a family is has definitely extended quite a bit."

"Blood and biology alone do not make a family," agrees Tim, who, with his partner Mario, has a small group of friends who are "dependable, reliable, loving, supportive, and nonjudgmental." The group is also "eclectic"—Tim and Mario shared a combination Easter and Passover with one Christian friend and one Jewish, eating both ham and noodle kugel.

What's the difference between friends and friends who are family?

"Friends become family when you can be totally yourself with them," comments Diana Shapiro. "You know you'll always be there for them, and vice versa. I'm friends with some coworkers and an ex-lover, but they're just friends. It takes years for a friend to become like family."

Diana's partner, Lori Berkowitz, concurs. She says of her chosen family, "We've been through a lot together, good and bad, and we're still there for each other. That's what a family is, blood or no blood." Like many other lesbians and gay men I spoke to, Lori includes a pet, her cat Shiksa, in her family constellation.

"Friends become family when you can be totally yourself with them."

For Mildred and Wanda, their best friends are even closer to them than their families of origin. "We share things and talk about things that I will never even discuss with my brother or my family," notes Mildred. "I have cousins I never see, but Liza and Louise [their friends] I see every week."

As far as her blood family is concerned, Wanda says, "I'm stuck with these people. But friends are people that I choose or they choose me unconditionally. . . . I can come to their home, and I'm coming home. I can open their refrigerator and serve myself ice cream if I want to. I can fall asleep in their face when they're talking to me because I'm dead tired, and they won't feel offended." Mildred and Wanda have even discussed buying a retirement house with their best friends. "I would never consider living with anyone else," says Wanda, "except my partner."

Many lesbians and gay men find their chosen families within the context of a community, either religious or social or political. All of Timothous Mack-Jones and Edward Jones-Mack's gay family are members of their church, Unity Fellowship. They count four lesbian couples and two gay male couples in their immediate circle. "We're pretty much there for each other," says Timothous, "ups, downs, crying spells, elated spells, everything." Though Timothous is also close to his family of origin, he says, "It's good to have a core family that *chose* each other."

For young lesbians and gay men in particular, having a community-based family of choice in addition to a family of origin is extremely important. "My family—the people I live with—are my mother and my two brothers," one teenaged lesbian of color said, speaking at a panel in New York City on the meaning of family. But what she calls her "real" family is a group of about thirty queer teenagers who meet every Saturday at the lesbian and gay community center. "Basically, we've become a family because some of our real families, our nuclear families, our biological families, . . . haven't completely accepted us. . . . [Here at the community center] I don't have to worry about making someone feel awkward, because we all accept each other and we all love each other. And I think that's what families should be."

Richard Burns, executive director of New York's Lesbian and Gay Community Services Center, also has a large chosen family of friends whom he has known for almost twenty years. Richard met most of them while working for the Boston-based newspaper, *Gay Community News,* in the late 1970s and early 1980s, and others went to law school with him. Though many live in different cities now, they have remained close, vacationing together in Provincetown, celebrating birthdays, and gathering for a member's commitment ceremony. "It's a pretty tight family," he says, one from which he has received a great deal of support.

Richard's lover of thirteen years, Tom, was also a member of this extended clan, and a break up within a gay family can throw the group off balance. "Our relationship existed and ended within the context of a larger gay and lesbian family," Richard explains. Last summer, when the gay family vacationed in P-town, "Tom didn't come. . . . I think he thought it would be awkward." Richard still has hopes that his relationship with Tom will evolve into a friendship; they're on their way, but they're not there yet. "It's both sad and fine," says Richard, when I ask about the status of his relationship with Tom today.

"We've been through a lot together, good and bad, and we're still there for each other. That's what a family is, blood or no blood."

Why do our chosen families so often include ex-lovers? Or more importantly, why do we *want* them to? I know I remained friends with several exes because we'd been friends first, before we'd taken our relationship to a different level. Despite the difficulties of what has been called "ex-lover shit," we thought the friendship was worth preserving in some form.

"Sexual intimacy is how lesbians make family, how we make kinship bonds," observes writer Stephanie Grant in a recent issue of *Out* magazine. "Like the familial bonds of sister, father, or mother, *ex-girlfriend* is irreducible."[1]

Though Grant writes that gay men don't as often keep ex-lovers in their lives, many of the gay men I interviewed had done just that. "I don't want to see something that was loving turned into something destructive," Richard Burns remarks. He speaks to his ex-lover Donald on a daily basis and considers him family. "Many heterosexual couples that split . . . turn it into a hostile estrangement." Like Richard, many in our community believe that our ability to remain connected to ex-lovers is something the straight world should pay attention to and learn from.

Not all lesbians and gay men weigh their chosen families more heavily than their biological ones, and for those who maintain close ties to their families of origin, the meaning of "family" can be two-pronged. "I feel I have two families," remarks Alicia, "but both are equally important."

In addition to her biological family, Alicia has an extended family that includes her partner, Nancy, their friends, some coworkers, a lot of children, and quite a few animals. The two families rarely intersect, though they did at Alicia and Nancy's commitment ceremony.

Alan Hultquist has experienced a similar phenomenon. "My family has two very separate parts to it," he notes. "One part consists of Brendan [his partner of thirteen years], a group of friends, an ex, and to a lesser extent, Brendan's mother. The other part is my biological family. They are two separate entities that don't interact. I wish they did, but the latter have no interest in the former."

"Maybe a person has various family circles," muses Kurt Jacobowitz, who lives with his partner Paul Cain in Phoenix. "One's family of origin composes one circle, and the people you share [most of] your life with compose another." In addition to biological family, Kurt and Paul have "a large network of friends that grows and shrinks based on frequency, quality, and intensity of interactions." Kurt says he hasn't seen two of his lesbian friends in ten years, "but if we met again tomorrow, I believe we'd pick up the relationship without pause."

Some lesbians and gay men are lucky enough to have families of origin that are completely accepting, and for them, creating chosen families has seemed unimportant. Singer Janis Ian finds that, though she and her partner Pat have close friends, they haven't needed an extended family because "our families are pretty good. I wouldn't have a problem turning to my dad or Pat to her sister. . . . My brother and my nephews call Pat 'Aunt Pat.' I guess we haven't felt the need to create an alternative family because our families have been there for us."

Gigi, who lives in Buffalo, New York, with her partner Sandy, is equally fortunate. She hesitates to call her friends "family," because her own biological family has been so close. On her father's side, "No matter how long it's been since we last saw each other," she comments, "even the cousins and second cousins and great-aunts always blend together with absolutely no 'getting-to-know-you-again' hesitation. . . . Everyone is tolerant of the differences and idiosyncrasies. I think this is the best example of 'family' that I know. Any group of people willing to give this kind of acceptance and support and love to each other."

"I guess we haven't felt the need to create an alternative family because our families have been there for us."

Out of Our (Straight) Past

With the rise of the lesbian and gay parenting movement in the past decade and all the media attention on issues such as same-sex marriage and lesbian and gay adoption rights, our families have come to the attention of the larger society. To hear the radical right tell it, lesbian and gay parenting is a brand-new phenomenon that must be nipped in the bud. But lesbians and gay men have been raising children for centuries.

Did you know, for example, that Louise Bryant, the early twentieth-century writer and wife of John Reed (remember the movie *Reds*?), lost custody of her daughter in 1930 to her third husband, largely because he found out Bryant had had a lesbian relationship with sculptor Gwen Le Gallienne? I'm willing to bet you didn't know that Louise Bryant even *had* a lesbian relationship.

Why? Sexual orientation as a way of identifying oneself is a fairly recent thing. Many people hid their sexuality because it was viewed as deviant or criminal, something to be ashamed and not proud of. Unfortunately, many continue to think this way. And it's no wonder, when lesbians and gay men still have virtually no civil rights in this country. Twenty states have anti-sodomy laws on their books, criminalizing our sexuality. And horror stories like that of Louise Bryant from way back in 1930 abound even today—children being taken away from lesbian mothers by a homophobic court system. In one horrific example in 1995, Mary Ward, a mother in Pensacola, Florida, temporarily lost custody of her daughter to her former husband, a convicted felon who had served eight years for murdering his first wife. Ward lost simply because she was a lesbian, which

Activist Maxine Wolfe with her two daughters.

was seen as more heinous than being a murderer. Fortunately, the ruling was overturned on appeal by a more liberal and compassionate judge. But in 1997, the beleaguered Ward died at forty-one of a heart attack.

The fact is, many of us have identified as heterosexual or bisexual, and our pasts produced children. While we left our heterosexual partners behind, the kids have remained a part of our lives. I interviewed many lesbians and gay men for whom parenting and stepparenting children from heterosexual relationships was a major part of their lives, full of both joys and difficulties.

After eleven years in a heterosexual marriage and two kids, Richard Jasper found the courage to come out to himself and his wife, Janet, in the summer of 1993. A few days later, because "they knew something was up," he also came out to his son and daughter, then aged six and four. That summer was a traumatic time, filled with therapy and support groups, but Richard feels he and his wife dealt with their subsequent separation in a mature way. He and Janet have remained friends, and Richard now sees the kids every weekend. "For the most part, they've been *very okay* with it," says Richard. "They continue to ask questions, which is as it should be, and we answer them as they come up. They're smart, well-adjusted kids, and in some ways, I think they have an advantage over their peers."

Since the breakup with Janet, Richard has become seriously involved with Jeremy Corry, and the two now live together in Atlanta and spend a lot of time with Richard's children. They also celebrate holidays and the children's birthdays with Janet and the kids, and they can envision including Janet's partner in their family circle, if and when she is again in a couple.

Very open about their relationship, both Richard and Jeremy say they make "few adjustments" in their behavior when the kids are around. Richard says it is simply a matter of degree. "We try not to exhibit overt sexual behavior toward each other in their presence," says Jeremy, "but we do express affection—we kiss, hug, and so forth."

Jeremy's role is "stepdad," but the kids simply call him by his first name. Fortunately, Jeremy is good with kids, and they all get along well. "Their understanding of the situation has evolved over time," Jeremy notes. "At first Emily was very insistent that one of us had to be the wife. Now when we play [the board game] 'Life,' they feel free to choose a husband or wife regardless of the gender of their playing piece."

Two years ago, Richard started a Web site filled with information to help dads like himself, who have come out while married to women.[2] He had found his first support online and wanted to give some back. "I've probably heard from a couple of dads a week, on average," says Richard, "who say they've stumbled across my [Web] page. Some went through [coming out] long before I did, others are going through it now, others are thinking about it. I point out that it's different for everyone."

His advice to other gay dads who are leaving or have left heterosexual marriages is simple. "Be honest with yourself, and be realistic," he offers. "And don't get hung up on not wanting to 'hurt' your wife and children by coming out. There is always some hurt associated with change, but life-affirming changes wind up producing enough good things to help salve the hurt. The way I looked at it, I was either going to come out or kill my-self; either way, people were going to feel hurt. The only difference is with the second, there's *no* chance for reconciliation, no opportunity to help them work through the hurt."

Louise Murray came out as a lesbian when her two sons were young teens. "I left my husband, and I had a period when I hardly saw [the boys]," she recalls, because they lived in Holland with their father while Louise lived in New York City. Without any guidelines on how to approach telling them, "I came out to them in a terrible way," she says sheepishly, "which they now love to tease me about. I was dropping them off at the train in Holland—they were going from me to their dad—and I said, 'Oh, by the way . . .' A really bad case, classically bad."

Both sons said they had already guessed and that it was okay with them. "But of course it wasn't," Louise says. The hardest part for the boys was having their parents go through a divorce. "That was much tougher, and they were in the middle of adolescence—ugh."

The explosion came several years later, when Louise's younger son, Peter,[3] decided he wanted to attend college in the United States. Louise had become seriously involved with Liza Fiol-Matta, with whom she has now been partnered for nine years. "He was one profoundly angry young man when he turned up here in the States," Louise remembers. "We had one evening that none of us will forget. . . . His anger had to be let out, and thank God he did it. I had a sense of what you need to do to gain a sense of power within yourself, and you need to speak to your offender. The issue was not to deny anything he said, but in fact to validate what he was saying and see if we could get beyond that."

After Peter expressed his anger about Louise's coming out and leaving him and his brother, they were, in fact, able to move on. Peter is now in his mid-twenties, and "Liza and I have a very, very real relationship with him," Louise notes. "We've been extraordinarily lucky, and we've worked at it consciously."

Liza is stepmother, the one who counseled Peter in writing his college application essays and ended up taking him shopping for clothes for school because Louise was out of the country. Liza has had to work through her own issues about acquiring instant sons. "Learning the language of saying, 'These are my sons,' has been a little weird," she admits. "Sometimes it feels like I'm appropriating the word 'son' or the relationship 'mother.' But I'm getting better with it." (See also the sidebar, "A Peach of a Georgian Mom.")

The clearer Louise and Liza have been about the strength of their relationship, "the better it's been for everybody," Louise remarks. As a result, when Peter was recently in a crisis with his girlfriend and thinking about ending the relationship, he went to Louise and Liza for advice, not to his father and his wife.

> "We care about our kids, we maintain our civic responsibilities, we try to present good role models for our kids, and we make mistakes sometimes, just like everyone else."

"We are the relationship that's stable," Louise says. "He actually said that."

Dave and Skip, who live in Florida and have been a couple for twenty-four years, also have a close and loving relationship with Skip's grown children from his heterosexual marriage. Both of them receive Father's Day cards from Skip's children. "Always!" says Skip. "My son Eric refers to both of us as his dads." And now they are also grandfathers. Skip feels his kids are "more tolerant, less judgmental, and far more accepting than most folks of their generation."

How have they managed to maintain such a good relationship? "My ex-wife and Dave deserve much credit," Skip notes thoughtfully. "She for her influence in keeping the kids close to their dads, and Dave for being a wonderful father to three kids that were not even his."

For some lesbians and gay men who have come out of heterosexual relationships, however, the children's transition hasn't been so smooth or complete. The age of the children, according to psychologists, can make a big difference in how they respond, with younger and older children the most accepting. Those in adolescence may have a particularly hard time dealing with both the divorce of their parents and a mother or father's homosexuality. After all, they themselves are going through a sexual identity crisis.

"Our most accepting child is the youngest, Nell. She is happy to have two moms who are lesbians; it makes her feel different and special."

"Our most accepting child is the youngest, Nell," says Coleen, who lives with her partner Ava in the Midwest and the four children they had from straight marriages. "She is happy to have two moms who are lesbians; it makes her feel different and special." But Nell is only nine, and the couple also has three teenagers—a different situation all together. "They're into their own sexual identity searches, peer pressures, and growing up," Coleen notes. "They'd rather not deal with their moms' relationship. If only we would go away . . . until they need a lift to their friends' houses or to a movie."

Terri, who lives in Maryland, was divorced from a man when she met her partner Debbie seven years ago. She and her two daughters had been on their own for a long time, and the two girls, who are now teenagers, have never really accepted Debbie as a second mom. The older girl "seems to be okay with our relationship," Terri notes, "but my youngest daughter is totally against it, has nothing to do with Debbie, and treats me with no respect whatsoever." On a good day, she says, they called them Mom and Debbie. "The rest of the time," Terri quips, "you can't print what they call us!"

Consequently, Terri presents herself at her daughters' school as a single mother. Neither of her daughters is out about having a lesbian mom and stepmom. "They really don't want anyone to know," Terri says, "and we have to respect their feelings."

The decision to be closeted "for the kids' sake" or open for their own peace of mind seems to haunt a number of lesbian and gay parents who have left heterosexual marriages. "We walk a careful line," comments Jackie Griffin. She and her partner Renee, who have been together six years, each had two children from their marriages to men. They came out to the kids by "simply telling them that we love each other," Jackie recalls.

In terms of the outside world, "We don't lie, but we try to respect the kids' wishes," Jackie notes. "We have found them to be very open while younger, then hidden in the middle grades, when conformity is oh-so-important, then open again in high school." Jackie and Renee do go to parent-teacher meetings together, however, and leave their wedding photos out when the kids' friends stay over. And two years ago, they had a son together through alternative insemination. They expect to be as open with him about their relationship as they can be. "We will tell Casey that his family is one of many kinds of families," Jackie says, a prescription followed by many lesbian and gay parents who have had children together. (See the following section, "Boom Time.")

Jackie and Renee leave their wedding photos on display in their home when the kids have friends over.

Early on, Jackie and Renee agreed that one of them should be a stay-at-home parent, and Renee assumed the role. "We are firmly the center of our children's lives," Jackie says, explaining how they have worked out family issues. "We both believe that family is everything."

Barbara and Dalia, who live in Chicago, are planning on having children together, and Barbara is now pregnant. But their family also includes Dalia's biological son Chris, now twelve, who actually brought them together four years ago at a Buddhist meeting (see page 34).

"Chris sees me as stepmom," Barbara relates, "and accepts me in a parental role." They explained their relationship to him early on, telling Chris that they loved each other and that there are many kinds of families. In the years since then, Chris has done a great deal of thinking about his lesbian mothers and what the addition of a new baby will mean to him. He agreed to share his own thoughts on his blended family.

At first I asked about two or three questions like, what is the difference between being gay or being a lesbian? And does this mean I will not have a brother or sister? I don't care at all because there is nothing wrong with it. I do not tell my friends because I think it is none of their business. Whenever my friends come over I do not panic that they might find out about my moms. I also go to a lot of moms' groups, and I practice being a good brother with all the little babies, because I know that some day I will be a brother.

I call my mother mom, but I call Barbara by her first name. If I become a brother then I might have to start calling Barbara mom too so the baby won't call her Barbara. I hope that we can move to California. That would be great because San Francisco has a lot of gay people, and I won't have to be secret, and there will not be a lot of prejudiced people because most of the people are gay.

Boom Time

Though lesbians and gay men have been raising children for years, many of those families have been gay by default—that is, because lesbians and gay men came out during or after a straight relationship in which children were involved. Since the late 1980s, however, there has been an enormous increase in the number of openly lesbian and gay couples or individuals who are *deciding* to have children. What was at first jokingly called "the gayby boom" is now a fixture of our community. Even lesbian celebrities like Melissa Etheridge and Amanda Bearse have gotten into the act.

Two moms and a baby.

Why the sudden surge of kids? It used to be that coming out as a lesbian or gay man meant forgoing parenthood, unless you already had children from a straight relationship. Many lesbians in particular, and later gay men, resented the fact that they had to choose between living happily as a gay person and having a family that included children.

But during the 1970s and 1980s, with the rise of a lesbian and gay movement replete with community centers, civil rights organizations, health care groups, and pride marches, a visible community began to make its presence felt. Still, there were few resources for lesbian and gay couples who wanted to take on parenthood. Dr. April Martin, author of the groundbreaking *Lesbian and Gay Parenting Handbook,* recalls finding one self-published pamphlet at the Lesbian Herstory Archives in 1979, written anonymously by two lesbians. Through it, April and her partner Susan learned about alternative insemination with a turkey baster. "The impact of knowing that other lesbians were, in fact, making babies was profound," writes April.[4] She and Susan didn't have to feel alone or freakish because they wanted to live as lesbians *and* experience parenthood, too.

By the late 1980s, more lesbians and gay men were ready to claim "family" openly as something they had a right to. They started small and built a strong and vibrant lesbian and gay parenting movement. Terry Boggis, director of Center Kids, one of the largest gay family projects in the country, recalls that the program got started back in 1988, "when a handful of families found each other. I don't even remember how. I think it was a word-of-mouth thing. We had a picnic, and there were half a dozen of us with children and babies."

The picnic helped Terry, her partner Rosemary, and the other couples feel less isolated. They could now share needed information and compare notes on the joys and stresses of bringing children into lesbian and gay families. "People were so excited to find one another," Terry remembers, "and just so enthusiastic about all these new babies and all these plans to have families."

After that first picnic, the group grew rapidly as friends told friends. Pretty soon the families were too numerous to congregate in the apartments of the members. When they realized they needed more space for meetings, the group approached the Lesbian and Gay Community Services Center of New York for support, and that's how Center Kids was born. What started as a small social network developed quickly into a large and active information exchange and advocacy group for lesbian and gay family needs and rights.

"There are about 2300 on the database now," Terry says, who has become the program's full-time paid staff member. "About half of those people are considering [parenthood]." What happened with Center Kids in New York—an exponential growth in the numbers of lesbians and gay men seeking parenthood or already raising children—has likewise happened all over the country. Not only are support groups and parenting organizations sprouting up everywhere (see the sidebar, "Gay and Lesbian Parents Coalition International"), but printed and online resources for people without direct access to groups have grown to meet the needs of lesbian and gay parents and parent wannabes. (See the sidebars, "For Your Bookshelf" and "Families Online.") "It doesn't take a huge network," Terry observes. "If people just find two or three families, . . . they feel shored up enough."

"*Society says, 'Why don't you want to be a mom? That's not normal. You're a woman, you're supposed to be a mother,' Well, no. I'm a woman. I'm supposed to be a woman. That's enough.*"

"A Peach of a Georgian Mom"

BY LINDA F. HARRISON

I UNDERSTAND WHY the goddesses give a woman nine months between conception and birth. You need that kind of lead time to mentally prepare for the change that will affect the rest of your life. For me, the process of becoming a mother was much more rapid than that, as I suspect it is for a lot of women in my situation. I met a woman who had a child and was pregnant with her second child. She and I fell in love while she was still married to her husband, and we moved in together immediately after the birth of her second child, whom I had the indescribable pleasure of photographing during her birth. One day I was a typical carefree dyke in her first month of law school, and then I had a family consisting of a partner and two wonderful babies. What an adjustment!

The kids rounded out my existence like entering the eye of a hurricane can do. My partner was beginning a new job and divorcing her husband. I was trying desperately to complete my first year of law school, and we were both trying to figure out how we were going to relate to each other—all with no training on my part. It felt like the right thing to do, but what an overload.

After things calmed down a bit, we adopted another daughter and now there are three kids, ages sixteen, fourteen, and seven. "The girls," as we call them, are nothing short of miracles to me. I have always loved kids and love being around them more than anything. They are growing so fast and maturing so slowly that I wonder how any of us made it through that treacherous period known as adolescence without killing ourselves. I see the same mistakes I made being made by them and hear the same admonitions of doom my mother warned me about coming from my lips aimed at my errant teenagers. Right now, I'm wondering exactly what to pack in my survival kit—and more so, what to pack in theirs.

Being a lesbian and a mother hasn't complicated my life in any unpredictable way. I speak often to women's groups and women's studies classes about being a lesbian and a mother. Usually the curiosity is about how to function in

Maybe Baby

My first lesbian relationship, which started almost twenty years ago, collapsed in part because my lover had always wanted children and didn't think it was possible to be a parent *and* a lesbian. She sincerely believed that in order to have her greatest desire—a house and kids—she would have to marry a man. At that time, there were few gay parenting role models. Lesbians and gay men who wanted to be parents had to suppress either one desire (to be openly gay) or the other (to be parents).

Luckily, my ex-lover didn't repress her lesbianism. The "gayby boom"

this society as a nontraditional family, and how we present ourselves to our families, friends, neighbors, and community. In my life, there hasn't been much of a problem with any of those groups. Our families have accepted us as a family and the kids as our kids. That's not to say that some members of our families don't have problems accepting our relationship, but whatever problems they have are not reflected in their treatment of the kids.

School and other institutions have not been a problem either. For the two teenagers, my partner is listed as their mother, and I am listed as their guardian. For the youngest, I am the mother and my partner is the guardian. For neighbors and anyone at school or church, we are their parents and talking to one of us is like talking to the other in terms of anything that needs a parent's attention. There has been very little in the way of us being accepted as a regular family, and I don't expect that to change.

There's a saying that prejudice rarely survives experience. Either that's true, or we've run into the most accepting people around. I tend to think it's the former, because we have always lived in the South, where people tend to be more uptight about things like nontraditional families (although they certainly don't have the market cornered on that attitude). It helps that we are both pretty "square" as people go, although we're not conservative. We care about our kids, we maintain our civic responsibilities, we try to present good role models for our kids, and we make mistakes sometimes, just like everyone else.

Every woman who is a mother comes with her own additional labels. Jewish mother, Latino mother, Muslim mother, feminist mother, disabled mother, etc. One thing that remains constant for all of us is the process of being a mother, and I suspect that isn't significantly different regardless of what other descriptions apply to you. How is it being a lesbian mother? Ask my mother. It's fraught with happiness, thrills, bills, worries, heartache, cuts and bruises, ballet lessons, gymnastics, art classes, schools, chauffeuring the kids, McDonald's, car sickness, eyeglasses, proms, dating, driver's licenses, rap music—in other words, it's just like being a mom.

This essay originally appeared in Girlfriends, *November/December 1994. Reprinted with permission of the author.*

came along just in time and helped many lesbians and gay men see that they could have both their true sexual identities in addition to the identity of "parent." Now she and her longtime partner are the happy, out lesbian parents of a six-year-old girl.

Today, many of us who never considered parenting when we were younger now see it as a viable option. In our heterosexual pasts, neither Katie nor I wanted children with men. But together, we have talked about it a lot, finally deciding once and for all that children don't fit our life plan. Both writers and teachers, we can't even find the time to have a dog, let alone a child.

Though it's the right decision for us, it is also a hard one. Are we missing something? Will we regret our choice? And how can we have kids—

GAY AND LESBIAN PARENTS COALITION INTERNATIONAL (GLPCI)

GLPCI is an invaluable source of support for the estimated four million lesbian and gay parents who face the challenges and joys of raising children. This premier gay parenting organization transmits a message of love, integrity, and responsibility and works to gain acceptance, respect, and inclusion through advocacy, education, and support groups worldwide.

GLPCI programs include:

- Communication with the media to promote the reality of lesbian, gay, bisexual, and transgendered people as nurturing individuals who can raise emotionally and physically healthy children

- "Destroy the Myths!" a campaign to dispel misconceptions about homosexuality through networking, a speakers' bureau, press releases, and an information clearinghouse of organizations and published materials

- *Both of My Moms' Names Are Judy,* a ten-minute video and accompanying training manual designed to teach elementary school children about homophobia

- An annual conference that brings together gay and lesbian families from all over the country to attend workshops, seminars, and social events

- An annual Gay and Lesbian Family Week vacation in Provincetown, Massachusetts

- *GLPCI Network,* a quarterly newsletter, with features on gay and lesbian parenting issues, book and film reviews, gay and lesbian parenting news briefs from all over the world, and other articles of interest to gay and lesbian parents

- *Parents' Network,* a bimonthly online newsletter

- A directory of parenting groups from all over the world

- Workshops for teachers and school administrators

- Straight Spouse Support Network (SSSN), an international support network of straight spouses currently or formerly married to gay, lesbian, bisexual, or transgendered partners, cosponsored by GLPCI and PFLAG

- Publications and other resources for gay and lesbian parents

- Adoption resource directory

- Legal resources

- COLAGE (Children of Lesbians and Gays Everywhere), an organization for the kids

For more information, contact :

GLPCI
P.O. Box 50360
Washington, DC 20091
(202) 583-8029
E-mail: GLPCIN@ix.netcom.com
Web site: http://qrd.tcp.com/qrd/www/orgs/glpci/home.htm

whom we both enjoy a lot—in our lives without actually raising them from infancy to adulthood? Many lesbians and gay men are trying to make this same complex decision for themselves.

Amy Samonds and her partner Suzy Reno, who live in North Carolina, have already been down that road together and opted not to become parents. "We both love kids and love being around them," says Suzy.

"But there's this wonderful 'selfish' factor that comes in, and we love being together and being able to go [when and where we want to]."

The irony of the baby boom for lesbians in particular is that societal pressure on women to become mothers now extends even to us. "Society says, 'Why don't you want to be a mom? That's not normal. You're a woman, you're supposed to be a mother,'" Suzy observes. "Well, no. I'm a woman. I'm supposed to be a woman. That's enough." In addition, Amy and Suzy have access to an extended family of nieces and nephews, "so we can go and have fun with them and get the good stuff and fulfill some of that desire of parenting and shepherding," says Suzy.

Suzy has experienced outside pressure about being a mother, but Carolyn, who was raised Mormon, says she has felt a great deal of internal pressure to have children, which came out of her religious upbringing. "That's what a good Mormon girl does," Carolyn says. Though Carolyn and her partner Genelle's strict Mormon families are against them having children, Carolyn still grapples with the question, battling her own inner tensions. "The pressure kind of comes from the church," she explains. "This is what women do."

Doing the dad thing.

Marjorie Hill and Christine Edwards, both busy with demanding jobs and numerous activities in the lesbian and gay community, have also come to the conclusion that becoming mothers isn't in the cards for them. Though they have felt that, as accomplished black women, they probably *should* raise kids, "Children have so many needs," Marjorie points out. "In order to do it well, our lives would have to be so different. . . . And I'm not ready to make those kinds of sacrifices." Resisting internal and external pressures, they've acknowledged that parenting isn't in their future.

Because children never happen accidentally in same-sex relationships as they often do in heterosexual ones, we are, in fact, fortunate to be able to make informed and very serious decisions about parenting. Many lesbians and gay men who decide they want kids take years to do so, setting out a plan for revamping their lives to accommodate the dramatic changes children make in an individual's or couple's world. "It's something we've been thinking about for a long time," says Mark, who has been involved with Andy for eleven years. "I am the one who is pushing for this, but we did agree on a five-year plan. There are some things that we'd like to get done before we bring a child into our house—home remodeling, finan-

© Jonathan Elderfield/Gamma Liaison

cial considerations, and putting our lives in order so that we will have the most amount of free time."

"We're both workaholics," Mark's partner Andy explains, "so we have to get ourselves to a position where we can create space and time for a child." They hope to adopt an Asian child—Andy is Asian American, and Mark is white—though Andy is concerned about his child experiencing racial prejudice *and* homophobia. "The child would grow up in a loving family without a doubt," he notes, "but I know how cruel others can be." Mark and Andy have begun to attend seminars on gay parenting, "and they have given me hope," Andy concludes. Like many other couples before them, they'll try to figure out the best way to create their family. "And we'll be great parents," Mark says confidently.

> *"We're both workaholics, so we have to get ourselves to a position where we can create space and time for a child."*

And Baby Makes . . .

A lesbian friend of mine quips, "I always thought the two best things about being gay were (1) you didn't have to get married, and (2) you didn't have to have kids." But as lesbians and gay men become less marginal and more a part of the fabric of society, they are also seeking out the rights and privileges of marriage and family that straight people enjoy. Although it's a weighty decision, lesbian and gay couples and individuals are increasingly opting to become parents.

Adoption and foster parenting remain problematic because of homophobic restrictions on lesbians and gay men adopting. Many lesbians therefore are choosing to have children biologically, while gay men are coparenting with lesbian or straight female friends or seeking out surrogate mothers. Whatever avenue people use, it all adds up to a virtual baby boom right in our own community.

"Just My Darling Baby"—Terry and Rosemary

Terry Boggis and her late partner Rosemary,[5] who became a couple in 1983, decided early in their relationship to have children together. Rosemary had been married to a man for many years and had raised two children from that marriage. But she felt she had been too young and inexperienced to enjoy her daughters and wanted a second chance at motherhood. "She said, 'I'd like to do it right this time,'" Terry recalls. Terry herself had "back burnered" motherhood, but six years into the relationship with Rosemary, she felt they were ready. By the late eighties, more information about lesbian motherhood had surfaced in the community.

First, they explored coparenting with a gay male couple, placing classified ads in several newspapers and getting only two responses. "We 'dated' these two male couples for a while," Terry laughs, "everybody putting their best feet forward and trying to impress one another and hoping to get picked." They discussed important issues like the role of religion and extended family in their lives, public school versus private school—issues that would surface during childhood. Ultimately, Terry and Rosemary decided on another path to motherhood.

"We really became aware that it was a lot to negotiate between two people, let alone *four* parents," Terry observes. One gay male couple they met was quite wealthy, and Terry and Rosemary felt they'd be forced to compete with them. "Rosemary said that the kid would never want to be with us," Terry remembers. Gradually, they moved in the direction of using a sperm bank. They chose the Sperm Bank of California, where the child, at maturity, could learn the identity of his or her donor. (See the sidebar, "Sperm Banks.")

"We got a short, typed list of height, weight, hair color, eye color, ethnic background, blood type, and that was about it," says Terry.[6] "A friend of mine who's a pediatrician said, 'Pick your blood type, it minimizes complications.' So there were only two O-positives who would agree to be contacted [by the grown child]. One was a sociology major and one was a chemist. . . . Rosemary said, you can be stupid to get a sociology degree, but you can't be that stupid to get a degree in chemistry, so we're going with the chemist." In that fairly simple way, they got their donor. Though Terry was already in her mid-thirties and was told by her (lesbian) gynecologist that it might take a year, she was pregnant within two months.

Because she knew that lesbians were having more boy than girl babies, Terry wanted to know early on in her pregnancy if the baby she was carrying was male or female. She had never really been in tune or comfortable with boys when she was growing up and had not been a tomboy. As an adult feminist, she was leery of having a boy and expected that she'd have to get used to the idea. This, in fact, has been an issue for many lesbian moms-to-be who identify as feminists. (See also pages 250–252.)

"I wanted to know, to be prepared," Terry recalls. "I found out on

FAMILIES ONLINE

The Internet is both a great organizing tool and means of support for the many lesbian and gay families with access to it. Queer parent-focused Web pages provide needed information and help to ease the stresses and the isolation of raising children in a homophobic world. In addition, there are a number of mailing lists for lesbian and gay parents that can hook you up to a whole network of online families.

Some of the most useful online resources are:

Family Q—
http://www.studio8prod.com/familyq/

This is a huge Web site that provides information and networking opportunities for thousands of lesbian and gay parents. Family Q has links to organizations, news, chat groups, legal information, adoption and insemination resources, books and articles, and fun stuff for kids.

Clicking on "Starting a Family," for example, brings up helpful information about adoption (including resources and agencies that work with gay and lesbian couples and individuals), alternative insemination resources and agencies, fostering children, and surrogate mothering. The "Organizations" link leads you to a list of national and local organizations, as well as further links to other Internet resources and the personal Web pages of queer families.

Gay and Lesbian Family Values Home Page—
http://www.angelfire.com/co/GayFamilyValues/index.html

In the midst of the high-tech world of the Internet lives a cozy Web site that provides emotional support and encouragement to gay and lesbian families by presenting true stories of people who are doing it. Click on "Stories of Support" and read about Rick and Brian, two gay dads who are raising a couple of kids together. Meet Joel, a single gay man, and his son, Joshua. Seventeen-year-old Caitlin writes about what it's like to live with her father, his partner, and her two younger brothers in a nontraditional family. You can sub-

mit your own story or comment on the Web site at the guestbook.

The Gay and Lesbian Family Values Home Page is a touching, human argument for the acceptance of gay and lesbian families in our society. And gay and lesbian family members who visit this site will feel a little more connected.

Gay and Lesbian Parents at Parent Soup—
http://www.parentsoup.com

Parent Soup isn't specifically lesbian and gay, but it's got information, advice, and discussion groups on topics for parents of kids of all ages. You can get generally helpful tips about everything from diapering to choosing a college, and more specific gay- and lesbian-oriented information at the discussion group called, "Gay and Lesbian Parents." Recent postings included discussions about gay dads, progressive day care, books of interest, and gay and lesbian stepparents.

Lesbian Mothers Support Society—
www.lesbian.org/lesbian-moms

A valuable source of information on many different issues, including adoption, pregnancy and alternative fertilization resources, children's resources, legal issues, parenting articles, and more. There are also links to organizations and support groups for lesbian parents and their children, plus a list of camps for children of gays and lesbians and also camps for gay teens. The Web site also directs you to other Web pages that offer resources of general interest to lesbians.

Lesbian Moms Web Page—
http://www.lesbian.org/moms/index.html

A wonderful Web site with lots of information to help women who want to have babies through nontraditional means. The site offers information on a variety of topics including lists of doctors and sperm banks, donor considerations, general insemination information and terminology, health and diet factors, and insurance and legal issues. The files that are linked to each topic have been generated by the lesbian mom's discussion group (for mom wannabes and moms of the young and old alike) who have either used the services listed or have discussed the issues and want to share their experiences with others. There are also links to related Web sites.

Queer Resources Directory— http://www.qrd.org/qrd/www/index.html
This comprehensive Web site has close to 20,000 lesbian- and gay-related files, with worldwide links to other sites that address issues of concern to the lesbian and gay community.

There is an entire subindex on family issues, and a click on the link "Queers and their Families" accesses home pages for the Gay and Lesbian Parents Coalition International, Lesbian Mothers Support Society, Parents and Friends of Lesbians and Gays (PFLAG), as well as recent articles on same-sex marriage and gay and lesbian families that have appeared in magazines and newspapers all over the country.

Here's how to subscribe to a few lesbian and gay parents online mailing lists. A word of warning if you aren't familiar with mailing lists: Be prepared for an onslaught of daily e-mail messages.

Lesbian Moms
    Send to: majordomo@qiclab.scn.rain.com
    In the message area: subscribe moms Your Name <your e-mail address>

Gay Dads
    Send to: majordomo@vector.casti.com
    In the message area: subscribe gaydads Your Name <your e-mail address>

Queer Parents
    Send to: majordomo@vector.casti.com
    In the message area: subscribe queer-parents Your Name <your e-mail address>

Christmas Eve, 1987. They called and said, 'It's a normal boy.' And I said, 'That's an oxymoron.' " She laughs at the memory, because as soon as their son Ned was born, her feelings changed completely. "It was literally the second he was born," she says. "I saw his face, and it was like who cares. . . . The whole instant bonding thing completely kicked in. I didn't think of him in any kind of political way. He was just my darling baby."

"The Nicest Person on the Block"—Linda and Vickie

Former *Essence* magazine editor Linda Villarosa knew she wanted to be a mother even before she met her partner Vickie six years ago. Linda had been involved with a woman who had no interest in coparenting, and therefore the relationship hit an impasse. When it ended and Linda met Vickie, they started talking immediately about how they both liked children and about the idea of being parents. For Linda, that was a big point in Vickie's favor.

FOR YOUR BOOKSHELF

Just a decade ago, it wasn't easy to find resource material about lesbian and gay parenting. Now there are a number of fine books in print that can help you with your decision and give you the ins and outs of parenthood. The following are some standard and recent titles:

Katherine Arnup, ed., *Lesbian Parenting: Living with Pride and Prejudice* (Gynergy Books/Ragweed Press, 1995).

Robert L. Barret and Bryan E. Robinson, *Gay Fathers* (Lexington Books, 1990).

Laura Benkov, Ph.D., *Reinventing the Family: The Emerging Story of Lesbian and Gay Parents* (Crown, 1994).

D. Merilee Clunis et al., *The Lesbian Parenting Book: A Guide to Creating Families and Raising Children* (Seal Press, 1995).

Rip Corley, *The Final Closet: The Gay Parents' Guide for Coming Out to Their Children* (Editech Press, 1990).

April Martin, Ph.D., *The Lesbian and Gay Parenting Handbook: Creating and Raising Our Families* (HarperCollins, 1993).

Cheri Pies, *Considering Parenthood* (Spinsters Ink, 1985).

Jill Pollack, *Lesbian and Gay Families: Redefining Parenting in America (The Changing Family)* (Franklin Watts, 1995).

Sandra Pollack and Jeanne Vaughn, eds., *Politics of the Heart: A Lesbian Parenting Anthology* (Firebrand Books, 1987).

Wendell Ricketts, *Lesbians and Gay Men as Foster Parents* (Univ. Southern Maine, 1991).

Cindy Rizzo, ed., *All the Ways Home: Parenting and Children in the Lesbian and Gay Communities: A Collection of Short Fiction* (New Victoria Pub., 1995).

Lisa Saffron, *Challenging Conceptions: Pregnancy and Parenting Beyond the Traditional Family* (Cassell Academic, 1994).

They spent a few years talking seriously about parenthood, but disagreeing strongly about the "when" of it—a conflict that sent them to couples' therapy to work out the logistics. When they finally agreed on a time frame, they also decided that Linda would be the one to conceive first. "My biological clock was beyond the ticking point," she quips. "You could hear it in neighboring states!" She says she had always wanted the experience of conceiving and bearing a child.

Unlike Terry and Rosemary, they chose a known donor. "I have such a great relationship with my father," Linda notes, "and I wanted my child to have a similar relationship with someone." Linda's desire was also based on her friendship with a woman who grew up an orphan in the foster care system and spent a lot of time getting over the loss of her parents. "I felt like I didn't want to set up an experience for my child in which she was spending so much of her life searching for her missing parent."

Linda, who is black, strongly wanted a black donor. "Being light-skinned," she notes, "I had a problem throughout my life of people saying, what are you, what nationality are you, or, you're not black enough." But after interviewing almost twenty black men and not being able to find

SPERM BANKS

When lesbians decide to have children via alternative insemination, they have to make the decision of a known donor (a friend or in-law, for example) or an unknown donor. If they choose the latter, they'll need a supportive gynecologist as well as a lesbian-friendly sperm bank. Here are a few places to check out:

California Cryobank
1019 Gayley Avenue
Los Angeles, CA 90024
(800) 231-3373;
(310) 443-5244

CryoGam Colorado
805 E. 18th Street, 9B
Loveland, CO 80538
(970) 667-9901

Cryogenic Laboratories
944 Lexington Avenue North
Roseville, MN 55113
(612) 489-8000

Fenway Community Health
Center
7 Haviland Street
Boston, MA 02115
(617) 267-0900

Pacific Reproductive Services
44 DeHaro, Suite 222
San Francisco, CA 94107
(415) 487-2288

Rainbow Flag Health Services
43A 30th Street
Oakland, CA 94609
(510) 763-7737

Reproductive Resources
720 I-10 Service Road,
Suite 509
Metairie, LA 70001
(504) 454-7973

Sperm Bank of California
115 Milvia Street, 2nd floor
Berkeley, CA 94704
(510) 841-1858

This sperm bank maintains a list of donors who will agree to be contacted by their adult offspring.

one they really clicked with, Linda and Vickie chose Vickie's best gay male friend, Lorry, who is originally from Peru and had always wanted to have children, and who has become an active part of their family.

Linda found that her colleagues at *Essence,* most of whom were straight, were ecstatic about her pregnancy and full of helpful hints about parenting. "In fact, I became closer to a lot of people," Linda comments. "People who may have had a little problem with me being a lesbian got over it because they could relate to me better when I was pregnant. I had a great big shower [at work], which Vickie came to."

Like many other lesbian moms and moms-to-be, Linda found herself having to come out to people over and over again, beginning when she was pregnant—a process she describes as "uncomfortable," because she thought she had already come out to everyone who mattered. "Just thinking, 'Oh, can I conceal this a bit, just till I figure out something to say?' was upsetting. There are a lot of black people on our block and I was worried about how they'd feel about me and about the baby. I felt especially nervous about people of my race rejecting me." But people ultimately began asking who Vickie was—was she the nurse? Linda's sister? (Even though

Vickie is white.) It was a frustrating experience, and one Linda found she could deal with best by just being blunt.

"Now everybody on the block gets it," says Linda. But because she still worries about people's treatment of her daughter when she gets older, "we're probably the nicest people on the block!" Linda laughs. "I know we're probably going overboard. We have notes reminding us of the neighbors' names, which houses are theirs, who their pets are, who their kids are, because we want to be accepted." In fact, many lesbian and gay parents overcompensate in this way, trying to set an example as superparents to try to neutralize the prejudice their families may encounter from the outside world.

Linda notes with some surprise and relief that many of the fears she and Vickie had about how parenting would change their lives never came to be or else were less important when the baby arrived on the scene. Vickie, a music publicist, was concerned that the baby's birth would mean they would never be able to go out socially again or come home at two in the morning. "But the second the baby came, she became completely devoted to our family life," Linda notes, "not just to the baby, but to us as a unit. It really ended up bringing us together more."

Linda feared that the baby might alienate their childless friends—that "they'd think we were so boring," she says. But even a friend who claimed to hate babies did an about-face when their daughter was born. "Now she's one of the head baby-sitters," Linda laughs. They might not stay out until the wee hours these days, but when Linda and Vickie socialize with friends, they do often bring the baby along. "Our daughter was the first baby in our circle, but there are more coming," Linda says. "She's changed the way we're dealing with each other as a circle of people."

> "*Our daughter was the first baby in our circle, but there are more coming. She's changed the way we're dealing with each other as a circle of people.*"

The More, The Merrier

Linda and Vickie are coparenting with a gay male friend, who sees his daughter once or twice a week and spends occasional nights and most holidays at their house. His role, however, is a limited one. In Albany, New York, Siobhan Hinckley and her partner Anita Bobersky are also coparenting with two gay men, who see the kids about once a week. They drew up an elaborate coparenting agreement with the men in advance, which spelled out visitation rights and stipulated that the men have no financial responsibility for the children. "Essentially," says Siobhan, "they can develop an emotional and spiritual relationship with the children when they see them, but that's it." It's clear that Siobhan and Anita are the children's parents, while their gay male friends are "fathers" in a looser sense.

Some lesbians and gay men, however, have created cozier coparenting situations, in which they actually live and raise their children together. One gay man involved in such a family believes that it works because people come equipped with their own emotional baggage and "meshugaas" [craziness] and multiple parents can offset each other's foibles and quirks. While nontraditional in both the general populace and the lesbian and gay community, families like the Montclair, New Jersey, one of Anne Quinn, Joyce Weeg, and Terry McKeon are making it work.

The family started with Anne and Terry, who had become friends from their volunteer work and talked about having children together as early as 1988. Anne came to their discussion with a list of concerns and issues about raising children together—important things likes values, religion, discipline.

According to the original plan they devised, Anne would have the baby, then give it to Terry to be the primary parent. That plan went by the wayside quickly, though, and then they decided to live in the house Terry owned, with Terry on one floor, and Anne and the baby on the other. But that, too, soon changed.

"We just decided we would live together," says Anne. "I moved in during my second trimester." Daughter Emma was born in 1989, and because they wanted a larger family, Anne got pregnant again not long after—this time with twins.

They decided to move in together, says Terry, "because we realized we couldn't just be coparents, that we had to have something invested in each other's futures. It just couldn't be these two parents with this child. There had to be a family, and there had to be an interest on the part of both people in the family with each other."

At that time, both Anne and Terry were single, and they appeared to the straight world to be a heterosexual couple. "My family really got into it and loved it," says Terry. "Even though I was up front about it from the beginning—about who we were and what our plans were and that if people came into our lives, we were going to pursue them—they just didn't want to see that. They thought Anne and I were 'curing' each other of our homosexuality. So that was stressful. It wasn't just our families, it was the world. We really saw how much the world wants people to be heterosexual."

A year after twins Jordan and Kate were born, something happened that irrevocably changed the way the family looked to outsiders: Anne met and fell in love with Joyce, whose sister lived down the block and acted as matchmaker between the two. In January 1993, Joyce moved in, and the family of five increased to six. Nine months later, Anne and Joyce tied the knot in a backyard commitment ceremony.

Joining the family was an ideal situation for Joyce, who says that she "always wanted to have kids, but I really didn't want to be the one to give birth to them. There was this instant family . . . and I missed out on the time of the kids' life that I don't really like. I don't like babies. But you have to have babies to get kids!"

Joyce credits her own ability to mesh with a ready-made family with having been a middle child. "I really was and am able to fit in a lot of places that may seem unusual to others," Joyce says. The three now consider themselves equal parents to the kids, though Terry and Anne are the legal guardians.

"All of the schools, the pediatrician, basically everyone we deal with on a regular basis knows there are three parents in the household," Anne says.

Their family structure hasn't caused any problems in their middle-class community in northern New Jersey where, as Joyce puts it, "A family with a mom and a dad who both have the same name and are both biological parents is the unique family here." An accepting community—one that's not hung up on the Ozzie and Harriet version of family structure—is an important factor in the success of families such as theirs.

But another deciding factor is certainly interparent dynamics. When I asked Anne, Joyce, and Terry about the ups and downs of their arrange-

ment, they all agreed that there had been no real downs. The three-parents-to-three-kids ratio works well for them. "There's more time we can spend with the kids because there are three of us," Terry points out. "We each have more time to ourselves because there is always another parent available."

One possible down, he allows, would be disagreements about raising the children. But so far, they have been able to settle their differences to everyone's satisfaction. "I'm more into want-

Storytime with Dad.

ing the kids to have some kind of spiritual life," Terry gives as an example. "Anne and Joyce are not. So I've pursued joining the Unitarian Church with the kids, and I do that alone with them. And Anne and Joyce are fine with that. We have some issues and disagreements, of course, but not ones that could prove very serious for the family."

In Anne's mind, the biggest plus of a family with three parents is that "the kids get three different points of view. And they get incredibly different things from us." If it were up to her, she laughs, the kids would probably never leave the house, because she isn't good at and doesn't enjoy sports. But the kids get their fair share of physical play with Terry and Joyce. On the other hand, Anne is the family organizer, a classic "mom" who arranges all the play dates and doctor's appointments. The trio make a complementary set of people.

"If you put the three of us together," Anne notes thoughtfully, "we're like the perfect parent."

The Adoption Option

We live in a country with too many children who need homes and too many restrictions placed on those who are willing to be parents, particularly lesbians and gay men who are interested in pursuing adoption rather than conception. While only Florida and New Hampshire expressly prohibit lesbian and gay adoption, the laws of the other states are nebulous and often tricky to negotiate. A handful of states are definitely friendlier than others. But with a few southern states already gearing up to tighten their adoption restrictions, many activists believe that adoption will be the next big battleground for lesbians and gay men. (See the sidebar, "Adoption Overview.")

Adoption laws make it easier for a single gay person to adopt than for a same-sex couple to do so, though in late 1997 a New Jersey gay couple made legal history by obtaining a joint adoption. The concern about joint adoption seems to be that a lesbian or gay couple might exhibit openly sexual behavior in front of the child, increasing the child's risk of being "turned" into a homosexual. As ridiculous as this may seem, it is still the way too many people think, based on ignorance and fear. In a 1996 Harris poll, fully 61 percent of Americans opposed adoptions by lesbian couples; the percentage rose to 65 when pertaining to gay male couples.

Therefore, within many couples, one partner will adopt a child as a single parent, then his or her lover will seek a second-parent adoption. But this is only possible in certain states or in certain counties, depending entirely on sympathetic judges. It is also a costly and time-consuming process.

In 1992 in Los Angeles, I attended the second-parent adoption of baby Maggie by Nancy, her nonbiological lesbian mom. The adoption was handled by Mary Newcombe, who was at that time an attorney with the L.A. office of Lambda Legal Defense and Education Fund. Everything was in order; Newcombe expected no problems from the judge whom Nancy, her partner Joan (the biological mom), and Maggie would appear before. But at the last minute, Newcombe learned that the judge whom she had counted on handling the adoption was on leave. She told Nancy and Joan with a stricken look that meant she expected failure. "If we run into problems," she reasoned, "we'll just postpone it." We all stood in the hallway outside the judge's chambers, terrified that the adoption might not go through.

To everyone's relief, the presiding judge was also sympathetic to lesbian and gay parents and had approved several second-parent adoptions. While nine-month-old Maggie played on his desk, the judge signed the papers making Nancy her second legal parent. It was only the twentieth such adoption in Los Angeles County.

Too many lesbian and gay families have experienced setbacks and failure in obtaining second-parent adoptions. Without marriage, it is the only option that truly legitimizes the nonbiological parent's rights. The inability to obtain these adoptions can create a legal nightmare for many families, as happened in the case of Terry Boggis and her late lover, Rosemary. Though New York State's highest court issued a landmark ruling on second-parent adoptions in November 1995, making them available throughout the state, Rosemary was already too ill at that time to take advantage of the ruling. Sadly, she died before she could legally adopt their son Ned, making it impossible for Ned to collect the Social Security benefits he deserves as her son. (See the sidebar, "Our Ned Has Two Mommies.")

"Nothing Was Going to Stop Me"—David and Joshua

Increasingly, lesbian and gay singles are adopting and raising children on their own, outside of relationships, fulfilling personal desires they have had for a long time. David, a forty-year-old who lives in Oregon, recalls wanting to be a father from the time he was in high school. But he also realized about the same time that he didn't want a wife. "I didn't reconcile these two until I was twenty-one and finally accepted being gay," he says. Coming out for him, as for many gay men, seemed to push parenthood out of the picture. "At that time [the mid-1970s] single people, much less single men, much less gay men, were not considered appropriate placements for adoptive children."

Though he had no idea if this would ever change, David says, "I never

ADOPTION OVERVIEW

Lambda Legal Defense and Education Fund publishes a detailed survey of the adoption laws of all fifty states and the District of Columbia, including the standards state courts have used to make their rulings about lesbian and gay parents. You can obtain it by calling Lambda's New York City office (see appendix) and asking for the intake department. Here is a brief summary of their findings:

States that have permitted private and agency adoptions by individual lesbians and gay men:

California, Connecticut, District of Columbia, Illinois, Massachusetts, New Jersey, New York, Ohio, Pennsylvania, Rhode Island, Texas, Vermont, Washington

States that expressly forbid such adoptions:

Florida, New Hampshire

States that have approved second-parent adoptions* at the highest court level:

Massachusetts, New York, Vermont

States that have approved second-parent adoptions in lower courts and in individual counties:

Alabama, Alaska, California, Connecticut, District of Columbia, Illinois, Indiana, Iowa, Maryland, Michigan, Minnesota, Nevada, New Jersey, New Mexico, Ohio, Oregon, Pennsylvania, Rhode Island, Texas, Washington

* Second-parent adoption refers to the adoption by a lesbian or gay man of her or his same-sex partner's biological or adopted children.

gave up entirely on my dream." With one lover in the early 1980s, he began exploring the possibility of adoption, spurred on by some successful adoption attempts by gay couples. But that relationship ended and his next lover expressed no desire for children, so David's dream got put on hold again. "I knew I would have to choose between staying with Howard and adopting a child," David explains. "I chose Howard."

When the second relationship came to an end in 1993, David decided to pursue parenthood on his own. "My biological clock was ticking quite loudly," he quips, "and I knew if I were going to do anything, it had to be soon."

David went the route that so many lesbians and gay men travel, trying to decide exactly how to become a parent. "I considered artificial insemination with a lesbian in a coparenting situation," he recalls. "But a lawyer friend said it would likely result in many problems—differences in parenting style, custody time, and legal snafus. . . . I never really explored that option very much. Likewise, I didn't spend much time thinking about a surrogate mother either. I knew this would be a very expensive option, and I had limited resources."

Though he knew adoption might be costly, too, David decided it was

"Our Ned Has Two Mommies"

BY TERRY BOGGIS

ON NOVEMBER 2 [1995], the New York State Court of Appeals issued a landmark decision allowing the adoption of children by two unmarried parents—heterosexual or homosexual. My household, one of thousands headed by lesbian and gay parents throughout the state, rejoiced at the ruling.

What does it mean to us? Nearly thirteen years ago, when my companion Rosemary and I pledged to love and care for one another for the rest of our lives, we started talking about having children. Rosemary had raised two daughters with a husband years before, and, with lots of experience and a Ph.D. in psychology under her belt, wanted to try parenting again as a more mature adult. I was in my early thirties, and the vague desire I'd always had to be a mother was becoming more sharp and urgent. In July 1988, our son Ned was born.

As gay parents, we had to pay a visit to our lawyer practically before our first trip to the pediatrician. I had to specify in my will my intention that Ned be placed in Rosemary's care should I die. I had to prepare a guardianship agreement to reinforce my wishes. I had to provide Rosemary with medical power of attorney for Ned should I become incompetent.

Still, after all this paperwork—and more—was completed our attorney was required to inform us that my wishes could easily be challenged, in all likelihood successfully, by my blood relations. Regardless of the safeguards we had in place, no legal paperwork available to us could guarantee the integrity of our family. We would always be at risk.

As years went by, we were reminded of the fragility of Rosemary's legal relationship to Ned. Although he called her "Mama" and bore her last name, although she coached his birth, assembled his crib, painted his bedroom his favorite color, green,

the best option. He wanted an older child, something that worked in his favor. "The state had lots of kids in foster homes who needed placement," he points out, "and they often try to make adoption financially attractive, not difficult, in order to place these children. I had always sort of felt adoption was the 'right' thing to do anyway." He could give a home to a child who desperately needed one.

When I ask how long the adoption process took him, David quips, "I was pregnant for two years." That, he says, is counting from the first paperwork to the time his son Joshua was finally placed with him in October 1995. Throughout the process, David never tried to hide his sexual orientation. Though he thinks some agencies probably rejected him for that reason, he was ultimately able to work with Open Adoption, a gay-friendly agency in Oregon.

Joshua is now seven, and David has found the relationship both ex-

walked him through colicky nights, schlepped him to dentist's appointments, made him pancakes to order on Sunday mornings, played catch with him and taught him to ride a bike, and although he proudly claimed her daughters as his sisters and her granddaughter as his niece, he still wasn't "hers."

What we knew to be a good and true parental relationship was not recognized by the state. Rosemary could not pick Ned up from preschool without a signed consent form from me. She could not be with him after his tonsillectomy without waiving her medical power of attorney.

Now, thanks to last week's ruling, these extra steps and daily humiliations won't be necessary. We may proceed with Rosemary's adoption of Ned, feeling confident that it will be approved.

This is of immediate importance to us. When Ned was two, Rosemary was diagnosed with ovarian cancer. Our lives took a difficult and unplanned turn. The past five years have been hard, and along with medical challenges and terrors we've had the added worry of the absence of legal protection for our family in case of Rosemary's death.

There have been more trips to the lawyer, more papers, and the enraging realization that despite our best efforts and those of our attorney, there are limits to what we can do. In the event of her death, for example, Ned would not be able to collect the Social Security income to which he should, as her son in every genuine sense, be entitled.

We've tried not to think about these things. Ned and I have been working hard to "take care of Mama" (he is her stalwart hand-holder when she gets her injections). But now, we hope to be able to proceed with Rosemary's legal adoption of Ned as rapidly as Providence seems to be indicating we will need to.

We are grateful beyond words for this court decision. We'll celebrate when the paperwork is finished. But at last, after more than seven years, the law acknowledges what the three of us have always known in our hearts—that Ned has two parents who claim him and cherish him. That we are a family.

This article appeared in The New York Daily News, *November 13, 1995. Reprinted with permission of the author.*

tremely rewarding and challenging. Joshua is severely attention-deficit/hyperactivity disordered; so, for David, one of the best parts of parenting "is seeing your kid do well at something. Having him read entire books to you, when only a few months ago he could barely read his name." Then there are the things that make parents melt: "A hug for no reason. When he says, 'I love you, Daddy, more than anybody else in the whole world.'" David's greatest challenge is to not lose patience. "Joshua is very volatile," David says, "and the slightest upset to his routine or expectations may set off a torrent of hostile and disruptive behavior."

Being a parent also put a crimp in David's social life, but he says he was happy to remain single and expected to do so. Two years ago, however, David met Richard on the Internet, when he answered a personal ad Richard had placed for "someone to talk with." "I thought I would qualify," David says, and an online social life was about all his busy life as a single father would allow. Though he expected only friendship, the relationship blossomed, and now he and Richard are discussing marriage.

David has broached the marriage topic with Joshua, as one way of discussing gay relationships being on a par with other relationships. "I want him to view gay relationships as natural as nongay relationships," David says. When Joshua gets older, David knows he will have to prepare him for the homophobia he may encounter in the world, teaching him certain tools against intolerance. "Not doing so would be a disservice and poor parenting," David concludes.

Though the adoption process can be fraught with difficulties for lesbian and gay parents-to-be, David says he never let anyone or anything discourage him. "From the minute I began filling out the application forms," he says resolutely, "I knew that this was something that was really going to happen—that nothing was going to stop me."

"Real Family Values"—Deacon, Jim, and Justen

At the height of the baby boom, a lesbian friend of mine stated that she felt lesbians and gay men had a duty to adopt children and teenagers and not to procreate. "There are too many unwanted kids," she said, "and as outcasts ourselves, we should be making that contribution." Though many "boom" parents would disagree with her opinion, a growing number of lesbians and gay men, like David, have particularly sought out hard-to-place or special-needs children. In addition, many have been opening their homes to young queers who have been rejected by their families of origin.

Too many young lesbians and gay men find out the hard way that "family" is not the protective, all-caring unit the myths would like all of us to believe. Queer teenagers are often forced out of their homes or made so miserable by homophobic parents that they pick up and leave. As a result, lesbian and gay youth are particularly vulnerable to homelessness, drug and alcohol addiction, HIV infection, and suicide. Justen Bennett-Maccubbin,[7] the adopted son of Jim Bennett and Deacon Maccubbin of Washington, D.C., actually received death threats from his religious biological father—a chilling example of how "family values" can go awry when a child comes out as gay.

"Justen grew up in the rural Midwest," says Deacon, co-owner with Jim of Lambda Rising Bookstore, "and at sixteen, he told his parents he was gay." His mother's reaction was to ship him off to his father, from whom she was divorced. "His father said that, 'as a good Mormon,' it was his responsibility to remove homosexuality from the face of the earth,

ADOPTION AGENCIES AND SERVICES

If you are looking to adopt children, it's especially important that you have a professional in the adoption field who can help you navigate through all of the details—particularly one who is sensitive to the needs of the lesbian and gay community. The following list includes both organizations that can refer you to gay-friendly agencies in your area, and also a few agencies that have worked successfully with lesbians and gay men.

ASK America
(Adopt a Special Kid)
2201 Broadway,
Suite 702
Oakland, CA 94612
(415) 543-2275
(agency)

Americans for African Adoptions
8910 Timberwood Drive
Indianapolis, IN 46234
(317) 271-4567
(agency)

Center Kids:
The Family Project
The Lesbian and Gay Community
Services Center
208 W. 13th Street
New York, NY 10011
(212) 620-7310
(referrals)

Family Focus Adoption Services
54-40 Little Neck Parkway,
Suite 4
Little Neck, NY 11362
(718) 224-1919
agency; hard to place children)

Friends in Adoption
P.O. Box 1228
Buxton Avenue
Middletown Springs, VT 05757
(802) 235-2312
(agency)

Gay and Lesbian Parents
Coalition International (GLPCI)
Adoption Information
Wayne Steinman
171 Father Capodanno Boulevard
Staten Island, NY 10306
(718) 987-6747
(referrals)

Growing Generations
310 San Vicente Boulevard,
Suite 410
Los Angeles, CA 90048
(310) 475-4770
(agency)

PACT
3450 Sacramento Avenue,
Suite 239
San Francisco, CA 94118
(415) 221-6957
(agency dealing specifically with children of color)

Three Rivers Adoption Council
307 Fourth Avenue, Suite 710
Pittsburgh, PA 15222
(412) 471-8722
(agency)

starting with his own household," Deacon recounts. "He literally tried to kill his son."

Fortunately, Justen escaped and shortly after met Jim and Deacon while they were visiting St. Louis in 1992. A friend of theirs who works at the Gay Youth Group there introduced them. "But we didn't actually get to know each other that well until a year later," Deacon recalls, "when the March on Washington [for Lesbian, Gay, Bisexual, and Transgendered Rights] came to Washington. Justen had been living in Chicago and came for the march because he was the youth coordinator for it." The three spent a lot of time together and got to know each other very well. Soon after, Jim and Deacon arranged to adopt Justen.

"He was legal when we adopted him," Deacon says. "He was eighteen or nineteen. We did it because in his entire life, he had never really had a family. He calls them his biological genetic contributors—his original biological mother and father—because to him that's all they ever gave him. . . . And it was so important to him, even at that age, to have a family for the first time in his life. He never had a home before, because they didn't want him there."

Justen refers to Jim and Deacon as "Mom and Dad." "Jim is Mom, and I'm Dad," Deacon laughs. "If you knew us, you'd probably know why." He is now a junior majoring in political communication and journalism at George Washington University, and though he doesn't live with Jim and Deacon, he is close by and they see each other two or three times a week.

What do Jim and Deacon have to offer an already grown gay youth? "We're the first to offer him unconditional love," Deacon says thoughtfully, "to be there with advice or help when he needs us, to take pride in his accomplishments, or gently chide him and urge him to do better when he slips." And that, says Deacon, is what "real family values" are all about.

The Adoption Debate

The lesbian and gay community often has to thrash out thorny issues for itself, and one debate that is raging now and will continue to rage in the future is the question of transracial and international adoption. As is happening in the straight world, too, many white lesbians and gay men are adopting children from other cultures and countries. Sometimes they pursue transracial adoptions simply because of the long wait required to adopt white infants in this country, but sometimes prospective parents have a sincere desire to be open to children of all nationalities and races who need homes. Still, the politics of transracial and international adoption are complicated and often painful.

Besides being an expert in international adoption issues, lesbian activist Mi Ok Song Bruining was herself born in Korea and came to this country as a five-year-old, when she was adopted into a white, suburban family. As she grew up, she experienced racism that her white family was not able or willing to deal with, and a profound sense of loss of her cultural identity.

Bruining's experiences point to a major problem that may occur when white families adopt children of color. Many children of color find their cultural identities submerged into that of their white adoptive families. Even if those adoptive families are loving ones, problems may arise.

"I believe that many—not all, but many—white adoptive parents are not willing or interested in encouraging the cultural identities of their adopted children of color," Bruining maintains. "All the privileges I was given by being an adopted child, a U.S. citizen, and the daughter of white adoptive parents did not reaffirm my cultural identity, nor did it fill the emptiness I felt in not being Korean, not knowing who my birth mother was, and not knowing my mother tongue."

Bruining believes that international adoption becomes especially cruel when adoptees, as adults, seek to find their birth families and are prevented from doing so because the records are sealed. "Only a very, very small percentage of Korean adoptees who search [for their birth families] ever find them," Bruining notes sadly.[8]

Activist Carmen Vázquez is also critical of both transracial and international adoptions. "You're not just taking 'a' child into 'a' family," she says of white lesbians and gay men who adopt transracially. "There's this racist world around you. When you've got a little African American kid, for example, being raised in a white environment, no amount of love for that child is going to change the fact that that child lives in a racist world." Too often, as happened with Mi Ok Song Bruining, white parents do not make allowances for racism in their children's lives, nor do they try to instill in their children of color a sense of their cultural and ethnic heritage.

In fact, the community as a whole, says Vázquez, has not created services for these families. "These children," continues Vázquez, "didn't choose this. We chose. They were infants. So therefore we have a responsibility to create programs and institutions that are going to be able to address the needs of these particular families in the future."

Until those community services can be established, Vázquez has some common sense advice for white lesbians and gay men contemplating or involved in transracial adoptions. "Go spend some time living and breathing [the child's] culture," she suggests. "Go figure out what kind of food we're talking about. Go learn Spanish, or whatever language. Make it your business to know the culture before the baby gets here."

Indeed, the most successful examples of transracial and international adoptions are those in which the parents have made an attempt to both learn and teach the child about the culture from which they were taken. Elizabeth and Sara, a white lesbian couple in Denver, have raised five children, ages seven to twenty-six, only one of whom is white. Two of the kids are African American, and two are biracial. "Race is a *big* factor in our lives," Elizabeth says, with heavy emphasis on the word "big." To try to give the children a sense of their African heritage, "We all moved to Africa for a year to celebrate Nelson Mandela's election."

Though she admits that even her mother disagrees with her on this issue, Linda Villarosa says she has an accepting attitude toward transracial adoption, which has been influenced largely by a friend of hers, a black woman who grew up in foster care. "She would have been willing to have a white mother, a mother from any culture, rather than to have had the experience she had," Linda notes.

Linda also thinks that "the [white] people I know who are doing transracial adoptions are bending over backward to bring some sort of a cultural experience to the child or to get to know the culture through the child. If the parent is going to do that, I think these adoptions can work." She finds the lesbian and gay community, in particular, to have a lot more cross-racial socialization than the straight community. "I think that the experience [of transracial adoption] can be much fuller in the gay community. We can bring a lot of richness to the child through the relationships that we have."

In a different but also increasingly common situation, Perry and Hoa are an interracial couple—white and Vietnamese—who adopted a baby boy who is biracial—black and Chicano. Consequently, "Race tends to be an ongoing educational process for us," says Perry, when I ask how their family deals with racial difference. "We feel that multiculturalism is the only way to go [in this society]." To make sure that Julian, their son, would have access to his own cultures, Perry and Hoa worked with an adoption agency called PACT, which places children of color and helps adoptive parents and birth parents retain contact (see page 239). Julian's birth mother has become a part of their extended family, and Julian "will grow up knowing Momma," Perry says.

Perry likens their family to "an onion with many layers." Not only are they a gay couple, they're an interracial gay couple, an interracial gay couple raising a child, and an interracial gay couple whose child is of differing cultures than their own. "We have a whole melange of issues for the world to hold up and scrutinize, and you know they will," observes Perry. "We just want to be prepared and have our children prepared for what they are going to encounter."

Religious Aspects

The gayby boom has brought other issues to the fore besides race and cultural difference. Religion, as we have seen in other chapters, plays an important role in many lesbians' and gay men's lives. Consequently, the surge in the number of children in our community has forced lesbian and gay churches and synagogues to take families with children into account in their programming and long-term planning. "We're just now starting to think about a Hebrew school," reports Rabbi Sharon Kleinbaum of Congregation Beth Simchat Torah—something that never would have happened five years ago.

But even if lesbian and gay parents aren't particularly religious, having children together can raise the issue of religious upbringing. When both parents weren't raised in the same religion or are agnostic because of negative associations with organized religion, the question of religion in the family's life can be a perplexing one. (See the sidebar, "To Worship or Not to Worship.")

Many families try to find a "low-impact church," one that will help create a spiritual foundation for the family while being extremely gay-friendly. When they had their first son, Teresa and Lori decided to join a Unitarian church and have been loosely involved in several congregations since then. Why did they suddenly perceive the need for religion in their lives? "Religion plays an important role in validating our family," Teresa says. "We also feel the Unitarian faith will give our children a positive spiritual base from which they can grow."

Other lesbians and gay men find themselves creating alternative options to religion, just as they have created alternatives to the concept of "family." Karin Kaj calls herself a "lapsed agnostic," but she does feel she has a spiritual side. It is a sense of spirituality and a respect for different religious traditions that she and her partner Maria hope to instill in their son, Kelson. "I am hoping to raise Kelson with an open mind," says Karin, "one that's exposed to the best that many different faiths have to offer. I like the meaning of bar mitzvahs, all the trappings of Christmas, the nonviolence of Buddhism, and the common sense of treating Mother Earth as the only planet we have."

> "Religion plays an important role in validating our family. We also feel the Unitarian faith will give our children a positive spiritual base from which they can grow."

Though Karin and Maria say they've rejected Christianity, "it's certainly a little different with a child," notes Maria, "because now I'm responsible for deciding his belief systems." The moral guidance she wants to give Kelson seems simple and down to earth: "I want to make sure he's clear about right and wrong," Maria says. "I want to make sure he understands that there's nothing immoral about his parents." If he ever decides he wants a more formal approach to religion, she says, "I'm not going to stop him."

Like Karin and Maria, Carole and Jackie don't practice the religions in which they were raised. But their family does celebrate all the Christian

"To Worship or Not to Worship"

BY NELLSON MOORE

I NEVER THOUGHT THAT ADOPTING my son would have me reexamining the meaning of religion in my life. My partner and I talked endlessly about how having a child would affect our social lives. We knew that it would mean no more barhopping with our friends. We knew that we would have a lot more birthday parties to attend than Sunday afternoon brunches. We started making changes in our work schedules and habits so that we could devote more time to helping our son with early development. We knew that our lives would be changed profoundly, but we never anticipated that adopting our son would suddenly have us rediscovering the importance of our religious upbringing.

When we met, neither of us had been practicing our respective faiths for some time. My partner is Jewish. His family went to temple only on High Holy days, and even that only happened once in a while. He did go to Hebrew school for four years after his bar mitzvah, but that was motivated more by his love for learning than his devotion to his religion. He says that he has always loved the sacredness of the rituals, the perseverance of the history, but he never felt completely attached.

I was raised in a nondenominational Christian church that seemed awfully Southern Baptist in style. I was very active: the Junior Usher Board, the Inspirational Gospel Choir, and the Young People's Willing Workers. Then I started to fully understand who I was and what I was all about. The people who had held me in their bosom and suckled me to manhood were noticing a change. They were not pleased. I was not amused. They seemed to forget that I had grown up with them. What happened to love thy neighbor as thyself? Let's just say that I was disillusioned.

Given our ambivalence about religion, why were my partner and I seriously discussing how to bring organized religion into our son's life?

Despite our feelings (or lack thereof) about our religions, we had deep connections to our faiths in the belief that positive thinking, living, and action bring you closer in line with the rhythm of the

and Jewish holidays, learning the history behind each one. They've brought up their daughter Kristi to be respectful of all religions. "Kristi has been taught that each person is unique with her or his religious needs," says Carole, "so we never make fun, feel arrogant or superior. Each person is on their own path according to their own needs."

Joy and Carlena, who are currently trying to have a child together, have talked a lot already about the place religion will have in their family. "I believe that children should be raised with a spiritual background," Joy comments, "but I'm not into organized religion." When the time comes, she says, the family will try to find a nondenominational church, one that preaches against prejudice and narrow-mindedness. "We'll try to teach them love, acceptance, and tolerance of others," Joy says simply.

universe. Mine came by way of the I Ching and ethical culture, his by way of Asia and its mystical influence. We also had to admit to ourselves that through our association with the church/temple we had come into contact with people who were immeasurably positive influences on us. The foundation of our faith had begun with them. Because of these institutions we were, for the most part, surrounded by other young people whose parents were focused on the same things that ours were: education, sports, music, literature, etc. The kind of kids who stayed away from trouble. Serious trouble, anyway. We wanted that environment for our son. But whose religion do we use as a vehicle?

We found ourselves scrambling around finding books on raising children in interfaith relationships. We read books such as *But How Will We Raise the Children? A Guide to Interfaith Marriage* by Steven Carr Reuben, and *If I'm Jewish and You're Christian, What Are the Kids? A Parenting Guide for Interfaith Families* by Andrea King (U.A.H.C. Press, 1993). They were both very helpful in letting us know how common an occurrence this is today, and that every family has to do what is most comfortable for them.

Our son is African American, as I am. The fact that he and I would always have our African American heritage and rituals to share played a large part in our decision to raise our son to be Jewish. We both agreed that, even though we would expose our son to both religions, he should be indoctrinated into only one.

Earlier on in all of this my partner had said something that was still buzzing around in my head. He had been keeping quiet about his feelings of wanting to pass on his Jewish heritage to our son because he had assumed that since I was the "legal" parent I would raise him as Christian. It forced me to really think about how he felt not being the "legal" parent.

Our son should be a wonderful combination of both his parents. My son and I will always have our African American history, heritage, and customs to share. As a family we have our shared history of slavery, separation, persecution, deliverance, determination, and faith that makes the uniqueness of families formed like ours centuries old. *Asante sana,* shalom. Giving thanks, peace.

"To Worship or Not to Worship, and Which Religion, That Is the Question," reprinted with permission from Kid's Talk, *June 1997.*

Are Grandma and Grandpa Onboard?

Whether our children are biological or adopted, of the same race as us or different, girls or boys, there's an enormous obstacle facing lesbians and gay men who parent, one that most straight couples never encounter—the disapproval of their parents and family of origin. In fact, many straight couples feel pressured by their families to have children, since families are the backbone of society. The birth of the first grandchild takes on great significance and is cause for much celebration.

But when lesbians and gay men announce impending parenthood, the reaction from their families can sometimes be harsh and unaccepting. Because being homosexual is still widely misunderstood, lesbians and gay men are often stereotyped as child molesters or recruiters for their "lifestyle." It can be especially hard for those who come from religious families.

Mother, daughter, and granddaughter.

"My family has come around, slowly but surely," says Siobhan Hinckley, who relates that both her father and her partner Anita's father were outright cruel to her when she was pregnant. Siobhan was raised Catholic, and her own father wouldn't even speak to her during her first pregnancy.

"I think one of the things that [gay] people don't realize," Siobhan reflects, "is that if your family isn't already 'out' about your sexuality, once you have children they're forced to come out to a certain degree. Some families will accept the challenge and do it gracefully, some won't do it at all, and some, like my own, do it, but not gracefully. They do it kicking and screaming."

Some parents hold out false hopes that parenthood means their daughter or son has gone straight. When Barbara told her mother that she was expecting a baby, her mother asked, "Do you have a boyfriend now?" Barbara couldn't believe it—her mother had stayed with Barbara and her partner Dalia for two weeks the previous year and knew about their commitment ceremony, even though she didn't attend. But like Siobhan's father, Barbara's mother is now coming to a gradual acceptance.

"Initially she was pretty vocal about the alternative process of getting pregnant being 'disgusting,' " Barbara recalls. "Now she concentrates just on my state of health and seems to have come to accept it." Lesbian families like theirs, Barbara notes, are part of a new era. "It will be hard for a lot of people to accept the lack of secrecy around gay and lesbian relationships of the future," she observes.

Others report that their families of origin have surprised them by being very supportive of the decision to parent. After David's family got over the initial shock of his adoption plans, they were able to welcome David's son Joshua into the fold. "They love it when I visit and bring Joshua," says David. "My sister has asked me to send him to her for a week [in the] summer."

Linda Villarosa's mother was delighted at the news that her daughter was pregnant, especially after the baby arrived—she had been repeating "I want a grandchild" like a mantra, Linda laughs. Linda's father was happy too. It was Linda's partner Vickie's parents, however, who were the "big surprise."

"We didn't know how they'd react," Linda remembers, "given that Vickie isn't the biological mother, and that the baby is a different race [from them]." But Vickie's mother made a special trip to visit after the baby's birth. "The baby and I went to the airport," Linda relates, "and I had her in the baby carrier, carrying her in front. And [Vickie's mother] just grabbed the baby out of the carrier and hugged her and kissed her and said, 'I love you so much!' at first sight." Linda notes that Vickie's mother has remained active in their daughter's life and has bragged about the baby to relatives and friends. This has, in fact, helped her become more comfortable with Linda and Vickie's relationship, something that other lesbian and gay couples have noticed as well.

Family acceptance is one more thing, says Dr. April Martin, that a couple or individual should evaluate before having or adopting children. Added to questions like "Do we have the money?" and "Is our relationship strong enough?" should be "Do we have extended family onboard?" Raising children is hard work, particularly for lesbians and gay men, and the more support they can garner from family, the better. "At the beginning of the [children planning] process," suggests Martin, "two or three years before you're about to do it, is the time to say, 'We're thinking about having kids. How does that idea fly with you guys?' Give the whole family time to get onboard with the idea and to dialogue about it."

Facing the World

Though lesbians and gay men may know very well what "family values" mean, we often have a hard time convincing the rest of the world that the term includes us. In addition to all the other challenges of parenting, lesbian and gay parents have to steel themselves and their children for the homophobia they are very likely to encounter at some point, from some source, and to prepare their children for hostile reactions to their nontraditional families.

Lesbian and gay parents are often asked how they told their children about having two moms or two dads. But when children grow up in a gay household, "You don't have to tell your kids about your relationship," says psychologist April Martin. "Straight people don't tell their kids they're heterosexual. Kids understand love. Our kids [her son and daughter with her partner, Susan] came to understand that we loved each other and were committed to each other in the same way that any child in any family [does]. I think babies of a few months get the idea."

Carole and Jackie, a lesbian couple from California, have followed that advice. They have been together for fifteen years and have a thirteen-year-old daughter, from whom they have never hidden their relationship. "We have always been demonstrative in front of Kristi," says Carole, "so our relationship is natural to her."

While you may not have to instruct kids about love, it's difference and prejudice, continues April Martin, that lesbian and gay parents have to teach children about at an early age. "You have to educate them about family diversity in the toddler years," she notes. "And educating them about prejudice starts right about school age, when you have to let them know that there are some people in the world who have rigid attitudes, negative attitudes, frightened attitudes, and what that means for the family. How we deal with that. How we make sense of that."

Minneapolis moms and children get together for fun and support.

Perry and Hoa's son Julian is only three, but they are getting ready for the time when they'll have to address the subject of their "different" family. "We want him to have pride in his family structure," Perry says, "and know about how to present his family to others. We want to give Julian all the truths in his life, we can't deal with withholding information. This is his story, and he has a right to the truth."

The truth, though, can hurt, especially when playmates and classmates are not brought up to respect or honor difference. Though she didn't experience any negativity when her son was an infant and toddler, Terry Boggis has had to confront prejudice since Ned started school. "A father talked to me the first day of school last year in the yard," she recalls. "He was complaining about living on Christopher Street [in Greenwich Village, New York City, traditionally thought of as very gay]. It was all about 'them' and 'those people' and 'you don't want to live there.' And I said, 'Well, I'm gay, so it's fine.' " Since then, the father has not been keen on having Ned play with his sons. "So it happens even here, at a pretty liberal school," Terry observes.

Ned has also come home with stories of being teased about having two mothers. "I've said to him, 'if people don't believe it's possible to have two moms, just ask your friends or their parents to call me, and I'll be happy to talk to them about it.' This is my effort to back him up because I can't really be with him in those moments of challenge." She also wants to teach him how to field these kinds of questions on his own.

One day on the street, a classmate ran up to Terry and Ned and asked, "It's not possible for Ned to have two moms, right? How is that possible?" Terry was grateful for "a teachable moment," she says, "to be able to take the question and give Ned that support—let him see how I handled the question and how really unflappable I am at all times." Terry turned to the mother and asked, "Do you mind if I go there with her?" With the other mother's permission, Terry launched into a minilecture about how most women fall in love with men, but sometimes women fall in love with women, and that's what happened with Ned's mothers. Still, the little girl looked skeptical and asked her mother if it was really true.

The school years are the hardest on kids with lesbian and gay parents, but a few progressive school districts across the country are trying to educate children at a young age about different kinds of families. In the excellent documentary *It's Elementary,* filmmakers Debra Chasnoff and Helen Cohen show how homophobia is combated best with very young children; if it isn't addressed until middle school or later, it's much harder to influence ideas and confront biases that have already been firmly set. Teachers and administrators have to be educated not to think of families without including lesbians and gay men and their children. (See the sidebars, "It's Elementary" and "Steps to Help End Homophobia in Schools.")

"I have trepidation about the thought of the PTA," says Maria Kaj, whose son Kelson is only two, "and the first day of school or the first day when you call up the teacher and tell them what the situation is. That will not be easy but will have to be done." Maria expresses the opinion of most out lesbian and gay parents: We have to grin and do it for the kids. "We have to exude the confidence and assertiveness that this is how we want to be treated and how we want our son to be treated and that we will accept nothing less than dignity and respect. That's the best thing I can think of to teach [Kelson]."

Though lesbian and gay families do experience prejudice, most queer parents still concur that being out and open is the best policy. The straight parents and teachers they come in contact with will then be better able to foster tolerance in other children. "People respect the decision to have children and respect the work that goes into it," says one lesbian parent.

Chase, who is raising two adopted daughters with his partner Grant,[9] agrees. He has found that, even though they live in the Deep South, "We have not met anyone who blatantly couldn't 'deal' with us. Everyone we have met has treated us with respect."

Siobhan Hinckley has a son and daughter with her partner Anita in Albany, New York. Since the births of her children, she has seen "a lot more people accepting gays and lesbians that I ever would have thought before." Heterosexuals, she thinks, find parenting a way to relate to lesbians and gay men.

Another lesbian mom in upstate New York relates a story about bringing cupcakes to her son's school birthday party. The teacher commented that it was the first time any parent had thought to do so, and the incident fostered a positive image of lesbian parents and their commitment to their children in the teacher's mind and in the minds of the other pupils. "Cupcakes can change the world," the lesbian mother quips.

The stories of tolerance and acceptance are heartwarming and hopeful. They make us think that maybe the world *is* changing after all. Karin Kaj relates how she and her partner Maria were asked by a stranger whom their son Kelson "belonged" to. The woman never considered that Karin and Maria might be a couple, so Maria set her straight, so to speak. "Maria answered, 'He belongs to both of us. We're both his moms.' " They expected a horrified, or at least surprised response, but the woman only paused briefly. "What a lucky little boy," she replied, "to have *two* mothers."

Role Models

The world outside our families can be cruel, but sometimes it can just be perplexed. Rigid ideas about family and gender roles persist in our society and cause people to question our families. If two lesbians raise a son, won't he grow up to be "effeminate" (i.e., gay)? If two men raise a daughter, where will she get female role models?

The answer, of course, lies in the way lesbian and gay men have always created family—from a mixture of friends, ex-lovers, and family of origin. To raise a family, both gay and straight people need support systems, extended families that will be there to help out with baby-sitting and act as role models for the kids.

Most of the parents I interviewed were, in fact, very aware of needing help, and they had devised extensive support systems to help them with the awesome task of child rearing. Grant and Chase[10] rely not only on their families of origin for help with their two daughters, but also on what they call their "community family"—lesbian and gay friends, straight neighbors, and coworkers.

Anne Quinn—who is parenting with both her lesbian partner and a gay man—relates that they have a network of families who call on each other for help. Their kids have gotten very attached to a number of adults in the community. "There's a whole bunch of women on Joyce's rugby team that they call 'the rugby women,'" she laughs. "They're very excited when they go to a rugby game and play with these women. Our son Jordan especially loves grown-ups."

Peggy and Nancy Frantz-Geddes have a family of choice they refer to as "the tribe." Their two-year-old son, Carter, has an array of lesbian "aunties" who love to spend time with him. But what about male role models? "At this point," Peggy says, "Carter doesn't seem to need men on a daily basis," but he does have grandfathers, uncles, and a gay male couple in his life whom he enjoys being with.

Other lesbians express the concern that their sons—and many *do* have sons—have male role models in their lives, and so they have sought out relatives and friends to help. Though they believe the most important thing is having two loving parents, Renee and Jackie Griffin have invited a gay male friend of theirs to be a presence in their son Casey's life. Karin and Maria Kaj are concerned about having men around for their son Kelson to teach him practical "guy" things like how to use a urinal. But also, "I think it's important that Kelson have a male influence in his life that comes from reality, not television," says Karin.

Is this a real or imagined need? It seems to depend on the children, the parents, and their view of the situation. For Terry Boggis, "The male role model thing comes and goes as a concern for me." Terry's partner Rosemary did all the rough-and-tumble, traditionally "dadlike" activities with their young son Ned. But Rosemary became ill with ovarian cancer when Ned was still a toddler, and she died in 1996. After she passed away, Ned said sadly, "Now I'm not going to learn anything," because Rosemary was the mom who taught him to ride a bike, swim, and partake in other sports.

"I'm bad at the wrestling kind of play that Ned adores," Terry admits. "And while I don't think it's necessary for his development or sexual orientation or anything, I know that it's the kind of energy he misses and feels a lack of in his life." Terry and Ned, however, do have several male relatives and gay friends in their lives who are "guys' guys" and help fill in the kind of companionship that Ned seems to crave. "I try to make that happen for him," Terry notes. "But sometimes I just wish I could bring in Patrick Swayze!" (See also the sidebar, "Raising Sons by the Book.")

When Families Change

When Terry Boggis's partner Rosemary passed away, her death left a gaping hole in their family. "This family is too little," Terry's son Ned would periodically say in the months following his other mom's death.

Just as they do in other families, death, divorce, and new relationships can change the configurations of many lesbian and gay families. How we handle the complexity of those changes is an important piece of the lesbian and gay parenting story.

How, for example, do our families survive the breakups of same-sex parents? Much like straight couples—sometimes with success, and sometimes with difficulty. Lesbian and gay couples, however, don't have the legal backing that can assist straight couples in matters of custody and visitation, so many have had to work it out on their own. And then, how do we incorporate new partners or stepparents into our children's lives?

"A Bitter Breakup"

Nine years ago, Nora and Melinda brought into their family an infant girl, Toby,[11] whom Nora legally adopted as a single woman. In New York state, there was no possibility of coadoption at that time, and adoption by out lesbians and gay men was difficult if not impossible. Because Melinda had been initially less enamored of the idea of motherhood than Nora, they did not sign any written coparenting agreement. Over the next few years, though, Melinda did come to view Toby as her daughter.

But when Toby was a year old, her parents began to run into problems. "I don't think having Toby caused them," Nora reflects. "There were problems before, but now there were *serious* problems. I think having Toby exacerbated a lot of issues about feeling closed in, issues about time." Because neither of them wanted a stranger to raise Toby, Nora quit her full-time job and became a stay-at-home parent. Melinda was the "breadwinner," and the traditional roles the women were playing put an added

STEPS TO HELP END HOMOPHOBIA IN SCHOOLS

School should be a place for children to feel comfortable and safe. For gay, lesbian, or bisexual children, and the children of gay and lesbian parents, it often doesn't work that way. They may experience verbal and physical harassment and are sometimes without the support of the adults at school who are supposed to protect them.

What can lesbians and gay men do to help, even if they aren't parents? According to the Gay, Lesbian, and Straight Education Network (GLSEN), here is one proactive strategy:

1. If you identified as lesbian or gay in school or had a lesbian or gay parent, choose one or two teachers or administrators from a school you attended and write them detailed personal letters using your experiences at school to illustrate what homophobia does to young people. Ask for a reply that specifies what they will do to end homophobia in their school or classroom.

2. Send a copy of GLSEN's packet, "What You Can Do: Ideas and Resources for Educators Working to End Homophobia in Schools," to these teachers and/or administrators. The package is available free of charge from: GLSEN, 121 W. 27th Street, Suite 804, New York, NY 10001; e-mail: GLSEN@glsen.org.

---

strain on their relationship. Melinda began having an affair, and by the time Toby was three, Nora and Melinda had broken up.

"It was a very bitter breakup," Nora recalls. "Both of us were extremely concerned about the effect on Toby. Melinda was very, very scared because she had no rights. I was very scared because I had no money. And I had no rights to any money that Melinda had. I was faced with being a single parent with no money."

Because two women can't legally marry, Nora and Melinda had no structures to fall back on and nowhere to turn for help in sorting out their breakup. Amazingly, though they were both angry at each other and Nora was hurt by Melinda's infidelity—"I really hated her at that point"—the two women were able to work out a solution.

Though she admits she felt spiteful toward Melinda at that time, Nora says, "I felt it would be extremely harmful to Toby not to have Melinda in her life. And Melinda desperately wanted to be part of Toby's life. We had a difficult conversation in which I said something like, 'Well, I've got the kid and you've got the money. We have to work this out.' " So Melinda agreed to pay child support in return for visitation rights.

"The model we used is more or less the traditional one, with our own variations," explains Nora. In the six years since their breakup, Melinda's visitation time with Toby has gradually increased. Toby now stays with

RAISING SONS BY THE BOOK

As Jess Wells points out in the introduction of her anthology, *Lesbians Raising Sons* (Alyson Publications, 1997), lesbians who conceive via donor insemination have a 65 percent chance of bearing sons. While this may have caused trepidation in lesbian-feminist communities of the past, times are changing. Wells, who is herself the mother of a son, has gathered together a wide range of moving personal essays by lesbian mothers, among them Jenifer Levin, Robin Morgan, Lillian Faderman, and Minnie Bruce Pratt. These writers describe the rewards and the difficulties of raising boys and help shatter the myth that women without male partners can't raise "real men."

Melinda one night a week and every other weekend and also spends vacation and holiday time with her.

"Melinda has been incredibly there for Toby," Nora admits, something she wasn't sure would happen. Consequently, Melinda is now named in Nora's will as Toby's guardian.

Because lesbian and gay couples don't have legally sanctioned marriages, our breakups can be particularly devastating for us and for the kids. Though Nora and Melinda were able to reach a mutually agreeable solution, stories of lesbian ex-lovers fighting over their kids have become commonplace. In August 1997, Kate Kendall, the executive director of the National Center for Lesbian Rights, reported that her office's caseload of lesbian mothers in custody battles with each other has increased phenomenally—in fact, there are now more Lesbian Mom vs. Lesbian Mom cases than Lesbian Mom vs. Straight Dad ones. All too often, biological or adoptive lesbian mothers are even denying visitation rights to nonlegal mothers.

"It's not only that there's no legal recourse for these women [the nonlegal parents]," observes Terry Boggis, "but also there is no acknowledgment, even within the lesbian and gay community, of what these mothers have lost. It's kind of like, 'These aren't really your kids.' "

Even with coparenting agreements in place, lesbian and gay parents may find themselves shut out and not recognized by the courts. Second-parent adoptions have begun to be questioned, too, when parents move to states that don't grant these adoptions and then they break up. In one recent example, a lesbian couple had a child together, and the nonbiological mother obtained a second-parent adoption in Washington State. The couple subsequently moved to North Carolina and then broke up. In an incredible show of homophobia, the lawyer for the biological mother argued that the ex-partner's second-parent adoption should be declared null and void, because North Carolina does not grant such adoptions.

These examples all point to some of the reasons that access to legal marriage would greatly aid lesbian and gay families. "It's indisputable that marriage would be beneficial for the children who come from our households," says Terry Boggis, even though she herself is ambivalent about marriage. Not only are the legal and financial benefits important, Terry notes, "but it would help to have our unions validated for them. We tell them we're just as married as their friends' parents. But at some point, they start to realize that it's not quite the same."

The New Partner

Since her breakup with Melinda, Nora has been in one serious relationship. "I have found it extremely difficult to bring another person into the picture," Nora says, particularly if the person is someone who does not have experience with children. The change to being a parent figure was too radical for Nora's lover Shelley, who was used to living a certain way—that is, without having to think about kids. "I felt like I ended up in the middle," Nora says, "trying to satisfy everyone's needs."

"There were a lot of issues," Nora comments. Shelley didn't like to have Toby come into bed with them in the morning, but Nora didn't want to stop her daughter from doing that. "After a while, I preferred that Shelley not stay over, because I didn't like the hassle."

One positive thing was that Nora and Shelley ended up having an intense sexual relationship. Nora would go to Shelley's apartment, but "I didn't want to be out more than twice a week," says Nora. "That's not a lot of time. So we ended up having sex all the time we were together, because we knew we didn't have a lot of opportunity." She laughs at the memory and speculates that she had more sex during that relationship than she did when living with Melinda.

A mom and her teen.

Terry Boggis found herself in a different situation when she began dating again after her lover Rosemary's death. Her new lover, Rosalba, had been a friend of the family, and Ned, Terry's son, already knew and liked her—a big plus. Though Terry allows that bringing a new person into the family is always challenging, she says they have been extremely lucky.

"Ned had been in an unhappy house a lot of his life," she says, noting that Rosemary had been ill since Ned was two. "Rosalba was a breath of fresh air. She knew how to be with kids. She brought home CDs, and they would do the macarena in the living room together."

As Rosalba and Ned spend more time together, though, "the more parental she becomes as opposed to just being a really fun pal," Terry says. "Ned will say now, 'I think she's too bossy.'" But that, Terry allows, is just part of the stepparenting deal. Terry encourages Rosalba and Ned to spend time alone and to forge their own relationship independent of her.

Like Nora, Terry has had to weigh the need to be alone with Rosalba with Ned's needs. "It's a constant balancing act," Terry says. How will the child feel to suddenly find a lock on mom or dad's bedroom door? How can the new partner feel in control and not victimized by the needs of a child? As director of Center Kids, Terry fields questions like this almost every day, and both the questions from parents and her own experience have led her to start a stepparenting group.

"If you act secretive, people interpret it as shame."

When Jeremy Corry became involved with Richard Jasper, who had two young children from a heterosexual marriage, the adjustment was a pretty easy one. "I like kids and am good with kids," Jeremy explains, a real bonus in this sort of situation. "We got along fairly well from the time we met."

There were some rough patches with Richard's daughter—she was at first very protective of her relationship with her dad—but they eventually got smoothed over. Now, according to Richard, both kids adore Jeremy. "One day Emily threw her arms around Jeremy's neck and exclaimed, 'Oh Jeremy, you're just the best stepdaddy ever!' I think the J-man floated on air for about a week after that."

Dr. April Martin thinks it's imperative that the child or children's parent help define the role her or his new partner will play. Will that person just be "Mommy's partner" or "Daddy's boyfriend," or will she or he be part of the family?

"I've seen lots of family conflicts happen because that role was never defined," Martin says. "The children are never really asked to regard that person as a parent or somebody due parental respect. It can set off a whole chain of family dynamics." When lesbians and gay men take their relationships seriously, however, Mom or Dad's new partner can become a vital part of the family in much the same way that straight stepparents do.

Smashing Stereotypes

Lesbian and gay couples and families have been held up to enormous scrutiny in the last year. Public attention has focused on celebrities Melissa Etheridge and Julie Cypher having a child together and the Hawaii same-sex marriage case dragging on into 1998. In all of this, one simple fact has been largely ignored by straight society—that lesbians and gay men have created lasting relationships and families all along, without headlines, media hype, or the legal benefits afforded to heterosexuals.

In the September 1996 *Baehr v. Miike* trial (the Hawaii case), the lawyers for the defense argued weakly that same-sex couples should be denied marriage licenses because: (1) their unions don't naturally result in offspring; and (2) children raised by gay men and lesbians are bound to suffer adverse affects. The lawyers for the plaintiffs—our side—argued compellingly that (1) heterosexual couples who can't or don't want to have children are permitted to marry; and most important (2)

> *Defendant's position . . . ignores the reality that same-sex couples have children. They have biological children, stepchildren, foster children, and adopted children. Children of same-sex couples are in no way protected or helped by denying them the rights and benefits of the children of opposite-sex married couples. This, in effect, is discriminating against and punishing children because of the status of their parents. This does not protect the health and welfare of children.*
>
> *Defendant will attempt to prove at trial . . . that children are best raised by their parents or a married male and female living in a single home. . . . The evidence at trial will show that same-sex parents, foster parents, stepparents, and the parents of adopted children can be and are good parents who protect the health and welfare of their children.*

Lawyers for the defense failed to prove their feeble arguments, while lawyers for the three Hawaiian same-sex couples who wished to marry presented testimony by experts on lesbian and gay families. Charlotte Patterson, for example, a psychologist who has done groundbreaking research on children of lesbians and gays, convincingly demonstrated that these children grow up pretty much the same as children of heterosexual parents in terms of gender identity, gender role behavior, and sexual orientation.

One of the biggest disadvantages children of lesbians and gay men face, in fact, is that their parents can't legally marry. Without legal marriage and without access to second-parent adoption, these children are not only branded as "different," but they're denied basic rights and privileges afforded to the children of straight parents. "A child's interests are best served," states Lenora Lapidus of New Jersey's ACLU, "when both partners are legally recognized as parents."

And why aren't they? Because of widespread, lingering stereotypes. Gay people are child molesters. Gay people recruit. Sexual orientation is chosen. Homosexuality is a decadent "lifestyle." "Even people who are in favor of gay rights," points out Dr. April Martin, "start to balk when it comes to children. They'll say, 'I don't know about having them as teachers or pediatricians or adopting children.'"

One way to attack stereotypes, of course, is to come out, and the lesbian and gay parenting movement is providing us all with good coming-out role models. For many of these parents, coming out has become almost second nature. "You have to steel yourself to doing it over and over again," notes Maria Kaj. Though she's gotten used to it, it is never easy and she is always a little afraid.

When mothers in Siobhan Hinckley's son's play group asked her, "What does your husband do?" she swallowed her fear and responded, "Well, my wife works for . . ." Parenthood has forced a lot of lesbians and gay men to be ruthlessly honest about their sexual orientation, in a way they might not have been before. They know that anything less than total honesty will instill fear and shame in their kids, and the circle of homophobia will continue unbroken. "If you act secretive," Karin Kaj says simply, "people interpret it as shame." You don't have to be a parent to take a lesson from these words.

What is important to keep in mind as we continue to push for our rights is that as a people we have survived over many years of oppression and public ignorance. We've found partners and created relationships that are marriages in every way but legally. We've raised and are raising happy, healthy, normal children who have an appreciation of difference and an understanding of tolerance. We've forged families of choice to back us up when our families of origin have not. We've built a community to nurture and sustain us. There's no shame in any of that. It's been an amazing achievement, and one we should all be proud of.

Notes

1. Stephanie Grant, "Exes Are Forever," *Out* (August 1997): 103.
2. The Web site is accessible at http://userwww.service.emory.edu/~librpj/gaydads.html. It includes Richard's complete coming-out story, frequently asked questions about gay fathers, a list of resources, and a "Gaydads on the Internet" directory for networking.
3. Not his real name.

4. Dr. April Martin, *The Lesbian and Gay Parenting Handbook: Creating and Raising Our Families* (HarperPerennial, 1993), 5.

5. Rosemary died of ovarian cancer in January 1996.

6. At some banks, you can also find out interests, hobbies, medical history, and other types of information that can help in making a more informed donor decision. Ask the sperm bank what type of donor profile they do and how extensive it is.

7. His birth name was officially changed to this by the court at his request.

8. Letter from Mi Ok Song Bruining to author, June 16, 1997.

9. Not their real names.

10. Not their real names.

11. Not their real names.

Appendix

An Annotated List of Organizations and Resources for Lesbian and Gay Couples and Families

National Organizations

FAMILY-RELATED

Children of Lesbians and Gays Everywhere (COLAGE)
2300 Market Street, #165
San Francisco, CA 94114
(202) 583-8029
E-mail: KidsOfGays@aol.com

Children of Lesbians and Gays Everywhere (COLAGE) is an international organization for the children of lesbian, gay, bisexual, and transgendered parents. It offers the following services:

- Support groups for kids and young adults
- Advocacy to increase the visibility, rights, and acceptance of children of lesbian and gay parents by working with the media, providing fact sheets about custody cases, providing speakers for meetings, places of worship, and schools, sponsoring videos and theater productions
- An annual conference that brings together children of many different ages
- *Fun Pages,* a quarterly newsletter for young children filled with activities, stories, pictures, games, puzzles, reviews, and contests
- *Just for Us,* a newsletter written by and directed to teenagers
- *Second Generation,* a newsletter for the lesbian and gay children of lesbian and gay parents
- Pen pal service, which matches children all over the world
- T-shirts, pens, and books that celebrate gay and lesbian families

Gay and Lesbian Parents Coalition International (GLPCI)
P.O. Box 50360
Washington, DC 20091
(202) 583-8029
Fax: (201) 783-6204
E-mail: GLPCIN@ix.netcom.com
Web site: http://qrd.tcp.com/qrd/www/orgs/glpci/home.html

GLPCI is a source of support for the estimated four million lesbian and gay parents who face the extra challenges and joys of raising children. The organization transmits its message of love, integrity, and responsibility and works to gain acceptance, respect, and inclusion through advocacy, education, and support groups worldwide.

GLPCI programs include:

- Communication with the media to promote the reality of lesbian, gay, bisexual, and transgendered people as nurturing individuals who can raise emotionally and physically healthy children

- "Destroy the Myths!" a campaign to dispel misconceptions about homosexuality through networking, a speakers' bureau, press releases, and an information clearinghouse of organizations and published materials

- *Both of My Moms' Names Are Judy,* a ten-minute video and accompanying training manual designed to teach elementary school children about homophobia

- An annual conference that brings together gay and lesbian families from all over the country to attend workshops, seminars, and social events

- An annual Gay and Lesbian Family Week vacation in Provincetown, Massachusetts

- *GLPCI Network,* a quarterly newsletter, with features on gay and lesbian parenting issues, book and film reviews, gay and lesbian parenting news briefs from all over the world, and other articles of interest to gay and lesbian parents

- *Parents' Network,* a bimonthly online newsletter

- A directory of parenting groups from all over the world

- Workshops for teachers and school administrators

- Straight Spouse Support Network (SSSN), an international support network of straight spouses currently or formerly married to gay, lesbian, bisexual, or transgendered partners, cosponsored by GLPCI and PFLAG (see page 263)

- Publications and other resources for gay and lesbian parents

- Adoption resource directory

- Legal resources

- COLAGE (Children of Lesbians and Gays Everywhere), an organization for the kids (see page 261)

Parents and Friends of Lesbians and Gay Men (PFLAG)
1101 14th Street NW
Washington, DC 20005
(202) 638-4200
E-mail: info@pflag.org
Web site: http://www.pflag.org

PFLAG is a support group of parents, families, and friends organized in four hundred communities across the country. With over sixty-seven thousand members, its mission is to promote the health and well-being of lesbian, gay, bisexual, and transgendered people through support, education, and advocacy.

Project Open Mind, PFLAG's public education campaign to counteract gay and lesbian hate speech, included four thirty-second television commercials, speakers, public exhibits, and media interviews. Other PFLAG programs have included a conference for educators; local and national lobbying efforts against antigay and lesbian legislation; a campaign to reach out to Asian and Pacific Islander families; quarterly publications *PFLAGpole* and *Tips and Tactics;* Straight Spouse Support Network (cosponsored with the Gay and Lesbian Parents Coalition International); and a Web site.

PFLAG is a tremendous resource for the people who love you to gain insight, understanding, and support and to meet, mingle, and to feel connected.

Partners Task Force for Gay and Lesbian Couples
Box 9685
Seattle, WA 98109
(206) 935-1206
Web site: http://www.buddybuddy.com

Partners Task Force for Gay and Lesbian Couples provides information, support, and advocacy for same-sex couples. Through publications, surveys, videos, and a comprehensive Web site (featuring links to other Web sites of interest to same-sex couples), Partners Task Force is committed to ensuring that lesbians and gay men involved in long-term relationships get social and legal recognition, as well as emotional support. (See page 172 for a complete profile of Partners Task Force.)

LEGAL

American Civil Liberties Union
Lesbian and Gay Rights Project
132 W. 43 Street
New York, NY 10036
(212) 549-2500
Web site: http://www.aclu.org

The Lesbian and Gay Rights Project is a division of the American Civil Liberties Union that works to end antigay discrimination, reform sexual intimacy laws, help lesbian and gay families, and protect the rights of gay people to speak publicly and organize. To accomplish these goals the project concentrates on three areas:

- Impact litigation that tries cases the outcome of which are expected to have a significant effect on the lives of lesbians, gay men, and bisexuals

- Writing and promoting laws and policies that will help achieve equality and fairness for gay people

- Public education through books, position papers, articles, lectures, and media campaigns

Lambda Legal Defense and Education Fund

National Headquarters
20 Wall Street, Suite 1500
New York, NY 10005
(212) 809-8585
Fax: (212) 809-0055

Midwest Regional Office
1 East Adams, Suite 1008
Chicago, IL 60603
(312) 663-4413
Fax: (312) 663-4307

Western Regional Office
6030 Wilshire Boulevard, Suite 200
Los Angeles, CA 90036
(213) 937-2728
Fax: (213) 937-0601

Southern Regional Office
1447 Peachtree Street NE, Suite 1004
Atlanta, GA 30309
(404) 897-1880
Fax: (404) 897-1884

Founded in 1973, Lambda Legal Defense and Education Fund is the oldest and largest gay and lesbian advocacy organization in the United States. Lambda works to protect the civil rights of lesbians and gay men through impact litigation (test cases) and education in the interest of creating a society that fully recognizes and legally accepts lesbian and gay couples. Lambda's mission is to ensure that lesbian and gay families have access to the same social and economic benefits that heterosexual families enjoy, and to that end, it has become active in the fight to legalize lesbian and gay marriage.

In addition to its staff attorneys, Lambda maintains a network of volunteer attorneys to assist lesbians and gay men with litigation. Lambda's attorneys have recommended strategies in a wide variety of issues, including equal marriage rights, parenting and relationship rights, domestic partner benefits, public accommodations, and access to health care.

Although Lambda does not make attorney referrals, it will provide names of local attorneys who have indicated they are interested in working on gay and lesbian issues.

In its commitment to public education, Lambda dispatches its legal staff to speak at forums and professional conventions across the country and makes available a wide variety of publications on issues as varied as asylum, civil marriage, health care reform, and HIV and the law.

National Center for Lesbian Rights (NCLR)
870 Market Street, Suite 870
San Francisco, CA 94102
(415) 392-6257

Since 1977, NCLR has been the only organization in the country dedicated to defending and expanding the civil rights of lesbians. Every year, they offer assistance to hundreds of lesbians and their families in the form of legal representation and advocacy, advice and counseling, community education, and public policy work. NCLR works to change discriminatory laws and create new legislation in the areas of civil rights, employment, housing, immigration, partner benefits, child custody, donor insemination, adoption, foster parenting, lesbian health, and youth rights. To accomplish its goals, NCLR holds workshops and produces videos and publications. NCLR projects also include the Youth Project, a national, legal, and public policy resource center for lesbian, gay, bisexual, and transgendered youth.

POLITICAL

The Forum on the Right to Marry (FORM)
Box 8033, JFK Station
Boston, MA 02114
(617) 868-FORM
Web site: http://www.calico-company.com/formboston

FORM is a grassroots organization that engages in education and outreach on same-sex marriage rights, providing resources and training to other groups around the country. Some of the resources they offer at their extensive Web site include: a primer on the Hawaii marriage case; the legal history of same-sex marriage; a press kit; a same-sex marriage time line; and a list of newspapers that publish same-sex wedding announcements. FORM can also be accessed through the "onQ Gay and Lesbian Community Forum" (keyword: GLCF) on America Online, under the link "Home and Families."

Gay and Lesbian Alliance Against Defamation (GLAAD)
150 W. 26 Street, #503
New York, NY 10001
(212) 807-1700
Web site: http://www.gladd.org

GLAAD calls itself a lesbian and gay news bureau, but it is really much more. As the nation's only lesbian and gay multimedia watchdog organization, it actively monitors discrimination based on sexual orientation and works to improve the public's image of the lesbian and gay community. GLAAD believes that the most effective means of challenging discrimination is to promote fair, accurate, and inclusive media representation. Today, thanks to GLAAD's efforts, news about gay men and lesbians appears in mainstream press and gay relationships are portrayed on network television and in Hollywood-produced films.

GLAAD concentrates on encouraging the lesbian and gay community to react to media portrayals of lesbians and gay men both positively and negatively and works with the media and the public to provide education about the lesbian and gay community. GLAAD sees as its mission a general improvement in the understanding of lesbian and gay issues.

GLAAD has won important victories: In 1987 GLAAD was successful in getting the *New York Times* to agree to use the word "gay" as part of its editorial policy and in 1989, the organization convinced *Daily Variety* to list survivors of same-sex couples in its obituary column. More recent accomplishments include the campaign to have the TV sitcom character Ellen come out as a lesbian, which she did on April 30, 1997, and convincing Comedy Central, in 1996, to stop airing the antigay movie *Partners.*

From GLAAD's inception in New York City in 1985 and its initial protest of the *New York Post*'s offensive AIDS coverage that year, GLAAD has grown to eight chapters across the country. It hosts an annual Media Awards Ceremony, at which it honors those who have represented gays and lesbians most accurately and fairly, offers a variety of publications, and maintains an active Web site at http://www.glaad.org.

Plans for the future include more media visibility of lesbians and gay men, national media watchdog alerts to GLAAD members, the establishment of new local chapters across the country, an information clearinghouse, and educational seminars for the news and entertainment industries.

The Gay, Lesbian, and Straight Education Network (GLSEN)
122 West 26th Street, Suite 1100
New York, NY 10001
(212) 727-0135
Web site: http://www.glstn.org/respect/

The Gay, Lesbian, and Straight Education Network (GLSEN) is an organization of parents, educators, students, and citizens who concentrate their efforts on ending homophobia in our schools through the use of audio, visual, and text-based educational materials, training, and community programming. From its initial struggle in 1993 to ban antigay discrimination in the Massachusetts public schools, GLSEN has grown to a national network of more than forty chapters throughout the United States.

GLSEN works to accomplish its goals through the following programs:

- Resources for staff training and curriculum development (print material, videos, retreats, workshops, conferences)
- Lesbian, Gay, and Bisexual History Project
- Gay-Straight Student Alliances support programs
- Annual Back-to-School Campaign. Lesbian, gay, and bisexual adults are encouraged to write letters to their former schools urging them to change their attitudes and policies toward gay and lesbian students.

Gay and Lesbian Association of Retiring Persons (GLARP)
10940 Wilshire Boulevard, Suite 1600
Los Angeles, CA 90024
(310) 966-1500

This international, nonprofit membership organization is dedicated to enhancing the aging experience of gays and lesbians. It is an excellent resource for gay and lesbian retirement-related information and services. One of GLARP's goals is to raise money to develop gay and lesbian retirement communities, retirement resorts, and skilled nursing facilities.

GLARP membership benefits include:

- A quarterly newsletter that provides benefits and information relevant to the retirement needs of gays and lesbians
- Legal services at a reduced rate, for a low annual fee
- Financial planning
- Car rentals at reduced rates in the United States and Europe
- Cellular phones and services from Celluland
- Discounts for casket purchase

Hawaii Equal Rights Marriage Project (h.e.r.m.p.)
P.O. Box 11690
Honolulu, HI 96828
(808) 261-4568

The Hawaii Equal Rights Marriage Project (h.e.r.m.p.) is a volunteer organization that provides information to the public, as well as media and legislative bodies, about the test case in Hawaii that seeks to legalize same-gender marriage. h.e.r.m.p. has been instrumental in obtaining experts and resources for the legal team and works to educate the public about the civil rights issues involved.

Human Rights Campaign (HRC)

1101 14th Street NW
Washington, DC 20005
(202) 628-4160
Fax: (202) 347-5323
Web site: http://www.hrcusa.org

HRC is a national lesbian and gay political organization. With over two hundred thousand members and an annual budget of $10 million, HRC works to provide equal rights and safety for lesbians and gay men throughout the country through congressional lobbying efforts, campaign support to lesbian and gay and gay-friendly candidates, and public education programs. In addition to providing financial assistance to the same-sex marriage fight in Hawaii, HRC has hired a field organizer to assist in the struggle to defeat that state's proposed constitutional amendment against lesbian and gay marriage.

International Lesbian and Gay Association

81, Kolenmarkt
B-1000 Brussels Belgium
Phone: 32 2 502 24 71
E-mail: ilga@ilga.org
Web site: http://www.pangea.org/org/cgl/ilgae.htm

The International Lesbian and Gay Association is a federation of lesbian, gay, bisexual, and transgendered groups from all over the world. Founded in 1978, ILGA works to end gay and lesbian discrimination and promote human rights by hosting world and regional conferences; publishing an international lesbian and gay news magazine; providing information to academics, lawyers, and students; and lobbying international institutions on the behalf of lesbian and gay rights. ILGA has contributed to the successful effort to eliminate homosexuality from the list of World Health Organization diseases, in gaining acceptance of "prisoner of conscience" status for gay men and lesbians imprisoned for their sexuality in Amnesty International's policies, and in passage of the European Parliament's "Resolution on the Equal Rights for Homosexuals and Lesbians in the European Union."

ILGA's extensive Web site has information about worldwide gay and lesbian conferences, international legislative updates, and partnership, immigration, and asylum laws for countries around the world.

Latino/a Lesbian and Gay Organization (LLEGO)

1612 K Street NW, Suite 500
Washington, DC 20006
(202) 466-8240
Fax: (202) 466-8530

LLEGO is a national nonprofit organization that addresses issues of concern to gay and lesbian Latinos/as on the local, state, regional, national, and international levels. LLEGO acts as a supportive network for gay and lesbian Latinos/as through conferences that explore strategies for organizing and strengthening the movement, formulation of a national health agenda that recognizes the impact of AIDS on the gay and lesbian Latino/a community, and the creation of a forum for advocating for the legal rights of gay and lesbian Latinos/as.

The Lesbian and Gay Immigration & Asylum Rights Task Force

P.O. Box 7741
New York, NY 10116
(212) 802-7264
Web site: http://www.lgirtf.org

Until lesbians and gay couples are granted the right to marry, they are excluded from the benefits of the U.S. Immigration and Nationality Act which guarantees the spouses of U.S. citizens the right to legal immigration. In fact, many lesbian and gay couples endure emotional and financial hardships, suffer trauma, and face real dangers just to stay together, since U.S. immigration law provides no recourse for same-sex partners. In addition, despite the widespread persecution of lesbians and gay men all over the world, only a handful of U.S. courts have recognized persecution on the basis of sexual orientation as grounds for granting asylum.

The Lesbian and Gay Immigration & Asylum Rights Task Force is committed to political and social activism to change these laws and practices with the eventual goal of gaining full legal recognition for lesbians and gay men.

The Task Force's objectives include:

- Mobilization of support from the lesbian, gay, bisexual, and transgendered communities for reform of U.S. immigration law

- Education of immigration lawyers, authorities, and resource groups

- Creation of resource information about local organizations that provide legal representation and social services for lesbian and gay immigrants

- Dissemination of information on immigration laws

- Elimination of immigrant bashing and discrimination against immigrants on the basis of sexual orientation, race, national origin, and other unfair biases

The Task Force has chapters in Chicago; Columbus, Ohio; Los Angeles; Philadelphia; New York; San Francisco; Seattle; St. Louis; and Washington, D.C., that sponsor legal clinics, conduct outreach efforts, and work to raise awareness of gay and lesbian immigration issues. The Task Force actively collects personal stories written by gays and lesbians to help document the hardships caused by current immigration laws. The stories will become part of a collection of affidavits that make up the backbone of the legal argument for reform.

National Association of Black and White Men Together (NABWMT)

1747 Connecticut Avenue NW
Washington, DC 20009
(800) NA4-BWMT
Web site: http://members.aol.com/nabwmtocc/index.html

With chapters across the country, NABWMT sponsors educational, political, cultural, and social activities that deal with racism, sexism, and homophobia. Members of NABWMT have the opportunity to attend regional gatherings and an annual convention; receive newsletters and a quarterly journal; participate in antiracism workshops; and be in a supportive atmosphere that encourages personal development and free expression.

National Association of Lesbian and Gay Community Centers

c/o Lesbian and Gay Community Services Center
208 W. 13th Street
New York, NY 10011
(212) 620-7310
Web site: http://www.gaycenter.org

In June 1994, representatives from more than thirty lesbian, gay, bisexual, and transgendered community centers gathered for an all-day meeting at the Lesbian and Gay Community Services Center in New York City and began the formation of a national network of community centers. This association works to foster the growth of lesbian, gay, bisexual, and transgendered (LGBT) community centers around the country and share ideas and program models. A listing by state of all the community centers nationwide can be found at the association's Web site. Besides being great places to meet friends and lovers, community centers provide vital support to lesbian and gay families and couples, often offering social service programs and counseling projects and referrals.

National Black Lesbian and Gay Leadership Forum (NBLGLF)

1436 U Street NW, Suite 200
Washington, DC 20009
(202) 483-6786
E-mail: NBLGLF@aol.com
Web site: http://www.nblglf.org/

Founded in Los Angeles in 1988, NBLGLF seeks to empower black lesbians, gay men, bisexuals, and transgendered people by:

• Increasing visibility

• Advocating for the interests of the community

• Developing and supporting strong leaders for the future

NBLGLF is the only national organization dedicated to the nation's 2.5 million black lesbians, gays, bisexuals, and transgendered people. Programs include an AIDS Prevention Team; a Brother-2-Brother Men's Program, which empowers black men by providing a safe space to explore issues of identity, sexuality, health, and masculinity; and a Women's Health Program, providing black women with education and awareness presentations everywhere from the church to substance abuse facilities, as well as safer-sex socials.

NBLGLF has just converted part of its office in Washington into one of the first black lesbian and gay community centers, featuring free community space and an archive, which contains books, manuscripts, videotapes, photographs, posters, and other records of black lesbian and gay history open to all. The new National Field Program empowers black activists and will soon provide resources, skills, and technical assistance for local organizations. A new youth program will help to develop leaders with annual scholarships and a National Mentoring Project that connects youth with positive role models.

National Freedom to Marry Coalition (FTM)

Freedom to Marry Coalition
120 Wall Street, Suite 1500
New York, NY 10005
(212) 809-8585 ext.205
Fax: (212) 809-0055
Web site: http://www.ftm.org

> FTM is an organization dedicated to winning the fight to legalize and recognize same-sex marriages in every state. Through committees that meet regularly across the country, FTM advocates via public relations and education campaigns, speakers bureaus, and lobbying efforts to give lesbians and gay men the right to take advantage of civil marriage wherever they live in the United States.

National Gay and Lesbian Task Force (NGLTF)

2320 Seventeenth Street NW
Washington, DC 20009
(202) 332-6483
Fax: (202) 332-0207
Web site: http://www.ngltf.org/

> NGLTF is a progressive civil rights organization that has supported grassroots organizing and advocacy since 1973. In all its efforts, NGLTF helps to strengthen the gay and lesbian movement at the state and local levels while connecting these activities to a national vision of change.
>
> NGLTF serves as the national resource center for grassroots lesbian, gay, bisexual, and transgender organizations that are facing a variety of battles at the state and local level—including the struggles for domestic partnership laws and for same-sex marriage rights. It offers a wide range of low-cost

publications, maintains an exhaustive Web site, and sponsors an annual conference for exchanging ideas among activists, called Creating Change.

PUBLICATIONS

The Advocate
6922 Hollywood Boulevard, 10th floor
Los Angeles, CA 90028
(800) 827-0561
Web site: http://www.advocate.com

The Advocate calls itself "America's indispensable gay and lesbian news source." Founded in 1967, it has the longest life of any lesbian and gay magazine in the country. The magazine is published every two weeks and contains news, celebrity interviews, entertainment news and reviews, essays, and polls for and about the lesbian and gay community. Reading *The Advocate* is a good way to keep on top of what's happening with issues such as same-sex marriage, adoption rights, and domestic partnership.

BLK
P.O. Box 83912
Los Angeles, CA 90083
(310) 410-0808
Fax: (310) 410-9250
Web site: http://www.blk.com

In publication since 1988, the award-winning *BLK* magazine has become the black lesbian and gay community's publication of record. *BLK* includes in-depth feature articles, profiles, interviews, analysis, controversy and commentary, as well as news from across the nation, the arts, a media watch column, and a gossip column. *BLK*'s Web site holds a wealth of information, including extensive links to people of color organizations across the country, a national calendar of events, and a marketplace for selling black products. It also provides an online classifieds section, featuring services and personal ads for the queer black community.

In the Family
7302 Hilton Avenue
Takoma Park, MD 20912
(301) 270-4771
E-mail: Lmarkowitz@aol.com

A quarterly magazine that started in 1995, In the Family bills itself as "a magazine for lesbians, gay, bisexuals, and their relations," and it is the only one that deals specifically with issues of interest to lesbian and gay couples and families. Most articles are written in an accessible style by therapists and psychologists who deal with LGBT issues in their practices. Topics dealt with in the past have included: how commitment ceremonies change couples; what makes successful, long-term couples; negotiating a breakup; revitalizing your erotic relationship; and deciding to become an adoptive parent.

OUT

110 Greene Street, Suite 600
New York, NY 10012
E-mail: outmag@aol.com

A slick, high-gloss monthly magazine, *OUT* features a little bit of everything—the occasional in-depth article on topics like lesbian and gay families and the court case in Hawaii; brief, *People* magazine–like celebrity profiles; fashion layouts and travel stories; and a consistently good Op-Ed column by Michaelangelo Signorile. Though the quality of the magazine's content varies from month to month, *OUT* provides a good overview of what the community is thinking and talking about.

RELIGIOUS ORGANIZATIONS

Unitarian Universalist Association

25 Beacon Street
Boston, MA 02108
(617) 742-2100
Web site: http://www.uua.org/

The Unitarian Universalist Association is a liberal progressive religious denomination with historical roots in Jewish and Christian traditions. It represents the interests of more than one thousand congregations across the country and prides itself on welcoming participation from a diverse population without regard to race, color, sex, disability, affectional or sexual orientation, age, or national origin.

Although members of the UUA clergy have been marrying same-sex couples since the 1970s, in 1984 the church officially sanctioned these ceremonies with a formal resolution authorizing their ministers to perform them.

UUA also produces a planning guide for same-sex weddings with nine sample ceremonies as well as a premarital counseling guide to help its clergy give support to same-gender couples. The church's premarital counseling sessions offer couples a sense that after marriage they are not alone. The message is that if they do experience problems along the way, ministers are available to help.

UUA maintains the Office of Bisexual, Gay, Lesbian, and Transgender Concerns that works to foster acceptance, inclusion, understanding, and equality for bisexual, gay, lesbian, and transgender persons—both within the UUA and in society at large. OBGLTC helps confront homophobia and affirm the inherent worth and dignity of persons of all sexual orientations. Resources include educational, ceremonial, and program materials; consultation; workshop leadership; advocacy; information and referral; and conflict resolution.

UUA ministers have publicly supported rights for same-gender couples through speeches and congressional testimonials.

Unity Fellowship Church Movement

5149 West Jefferson Boulevard
Los Angeles, CA 90016
(213) 936-4948

Founded in 1985 by Bishop Carl Bean of Los Angeles, the Unity Fellowship Church Movement—a Christian black gay church—has spread rapidly, establishing fellowships in cities across the country. As Elder Zachary Jones of Unity in Brooklyn, New York, puts it, the aim of Unity is "to live and exist openly as lesbian and gay people of faith in our community, among our families, neighbors, and friends." As of spring 1997, the following were Unity Fellowship churches:

Unity Fellowship New York
230 Classon Avenue
Brooklyn, NY 11205
(718) 636-5646

Liberation in Truth Unity Fellowship
P.O. Box 20043
Riverfront Plaza 07102-0308, Riverfront Plaza Station
Newark, NJ 07102
(212) 228-3329

North Dallas Unity Fellowship
P.O. Box 190869
Dallas, TX 75007
(214) 521-5342 ext. 226

Inner Light Unity Fellowship
400 I Street SW
Washington, DC
(202) 554-6588

Uplift Unity Fellowship
P.O. Box 617547
Orlando, FL 32861
(407) 297-5709

Sojourner Truth Unity Fellowship
8326 49th Avenue South
Seattle, WA 98118
(206) 632-4775

Full Truth Unity Fellowship,
4458 Joy Road,
Detroit, MI 48204,
(313) 896-0233

Divine Truth Unity Fellowship
3645 Locust Street
Riverside, CA 92501
(909) 684-9025

Unity Fellowship of Christ Church
P.O. Box 55340
Atlanta, GA 30308

United Fellowship of Metropolitan Community Churches Mother Church

8714 Santa Monica Blvd.
West Hollywood, CA 90069
(310) 854-9110
Fax: (310) 854-9119
E-mail: mccla@aol.com
Web site: http://www.ufmcc.com

The Universal Fellowship of Metropolitan Community Churches (UFMCC) began in 1968 as a group of twelve men and women meeting in a living room in Los Angeles. It has grown to over thirty-five thousand members and friends, worshiping in over three hundred churches worldwide. Since MCC's Revered Troy Perry performed the first same-sex religious marriage ceremony in U.S. history in 1968, MCC has been a major supporter of such ceremonies, and performs approximately two thousand such unions a year. Metropolitan Community Churches are inclusive. All persons are welcome at services, regardless of sexual orientation, sex, race, or previous denominational affiliation. While the primary outreach is to the gay, lesbian, bisexual, and transgendered community, MCC's doors are open to all. Here are some local MCC churches in some major U.S. cities:

474 Ridge Street NW
Washington DC 20001
(202) 638-7373

7701 SW 76th Avenue
Miami, FL
(305) 285-1040

5757 South University Avenue
Chicago, IL 60637
(773) 288-1535

Cathedral of Hope
5910 Cedar Springs
Dallas, TX 75235
(800) 501-Hope

Golden Gate MCC of San Francisco
1508 Church Street
San Francisco, CA 94131
(415) 642-0294

World Congress of Gay and Lesbian Jewish Organizations (WCGLJO)
P.O. Box 23379
Washington, DC 20026
Web site: http://www.wcgljo.org/wcgljo/

The World Congress of Gay and Lesbian Jewish Organizations (WCGLJO) is an international group of over sixty-five synagogues, Jewish community centers, social groups, and other gay and lesbian Jewish organizations in North America, Latin America, eastern and western Europe, South Africa, Australia, and Israel. WCGLJO's mission is to represent the worldwide interests of lesbian and gay Jews through the sponsorship of conferences and workshops. WCGLJO held a World Conference in Dallas, Texas in July 1997 at which more than one thousand attendees had the opportunity to participate in fifty workshops on topics such as gay parenting, aging, coming out, women's issues, AIDS, the Holocaust, activism, and Judaism.

WCGLO maintains a Web site with links to its member organizations and other information of interest to gay and lesbian Jews. Some of the member organizations in the United States are:

Bet Haverim
P.O. Box 54677
Atlanta, GA 30308
(404) 642-3467

Bet Mishpachah
P.O. Box 1410
Washington, DC 20013
(202) 833-1638

Beth el Binah
P.O. Box 191188
Dallas, TX 75219
(214) 497-1591

Beth Rachameem Synagogue
c/o Unitarian Universalist Church
19 N. Arlington Avenue
St. Petersburg, FL 33701
(813) 839-4911

Congregation Ahavat Shalom
P.O. Box 14392
San Francisco, CA 94114
(415) 752-4979

Congregation Beth Simchat Torah
7 Bethune Street
New York, NY 10014
(212) 929-9498

Long Beach Community Center Lesbian and Gay Havurah
801 East Willow Street
Long Beach, CA 90815
(562) 426-7601

Some Landmark Local Organizations

Center Kids
The Lesbian and Gay Community Services Center
208 W. 13th Street
New York, NY 10011
(212) 620-7310

Center Kids, a program of the Lesbian and Gay Community Services Center in New York City, works with over two thousand families and offers support groups, networking and socializing opportunities for both parents and children, recreational programs, forums, financial planning seminars, advocacy, and *Family Talk* (formerly *Kids' Talk*), a monthly newsletter and calendar.

Center Kids also provides services for lesbians and gay men who are considering becoming parents. Through adoption and artificial insemination support groups and Center Kids' affiliation with adoption and educational associations, members of the community can explore parenting options.

A Different Light
8853 Santa Monica Boulevard
Los Angeles, CA 90069
(310) 854-6601

489 Castro Street
San Francisco, CA 94114
(415) 431-0891

151 W. 19 Street
New York, NY 10011
(212) 989-4850
E-mail: adl@adlbooks.com
Web site: http://www.adlbooks.com/~adl

Some of the best resources on gay and lesbian marriage and parenting are books, many of which are hard to find in mainstream bookstores. If you're having trouble locating a particular book, contact A Different Light, a pioneer in alternative literature retailing.

Fenway Community Health Center (FCHC)
7 Haviland Street
Boston, MA 02115
(617) 267-0900

FCHC serves the health care needs of the lesbian and gay community of New England as well as the residents of the local neighborhood.

FCHC operates an extensive alternative insemination program coordinated by FCHC's Family and Parenting Services. The staff provides education on ovulation prediction and self-insemination, support groups, laboratory testing, and a health exam, and makes arrangements for donor screening and ordering sperm from three sperm banks. The sperm banks quarantine sperm for six months while the donor is tested for HIV antibodies. The sperm banks ship the orders to FCHC, which stores them in liquid nitrogen until it's time to inseminate. Participants in the program can expect to spend about $800 for startup services and the first insemination. FCHC charges extra for each additional office insemination.

FCHC's Family and Parenting Services also offers support, information groups, and workshops for lesbians and gay men who are considering becoming parents biologically and through adoption, and for women who are currently involved in the inseminating process.

Other FCHC Family and Parenting Services programs include:

- Information for men and women who are planning to be sperm donors and recipients but do not plan to parent together

- Childbirth classes for pregnant lesbians

- Adoption referral

- Lesbian and Gay Family Day, held once a month, which provides networking opportunities for parents and child care for their children younger than seven years old

In addition to the Family and Parenting Services, FCHC offers the following:

- Primary care

- HIV care, treatment, counseling, testing, support, and research

- Women's health

- Holistic health care, including acupuncture, chiropractic, and polarity therapy

- Counseling and mental health therapy

- Addiction services

- Multicultural outreach
- Victim recovery for lesbian and gay victims of violence, harassment, rape, and battering
- Gay and Lesbian Helpline/Peer Listening Line

Gay and Lesbian Advocates & Defenders (GLAD)
294 Washington Street, Suite 740
Boston, MA 02108
(617) 426-1350; (800) 455-GLAD

GLAD is to New England what Lambda Legal Defense and Education Fund is to the rest of the country. The nonprofit legal organization maintains a full-time staff based in Boston and interfaces with a network of attorneys in New England to provide litigation, advocacy, and educational work in gay, lesbian, bisexual, and HIV civil rights issues. GLAD's services include:

- Legal representation, consultation, and referral
- Speakers bureau
- Written material
- Amicus (friend-of-the-court) briefs

GLAD helps thousands of people every year in Maine, New Hampshire, Vermont, Massachusetts, Rhode Island, and Connecticut. Its services are provided free of charge to all clients, regardless of their financial circumstances.

Hetrick-Martin Institute
2 Astor Place
New York, NY 10003
(212) 674-2400

The Hetrick-Martin Institute is a nonprofit social service, education, and advocacy organization that serves more than seven thousand lesbian, gay, and bisexual youth annually through six programs:

- After-School Drop-In Center
- Individual and family counseling
- Project First Step homeless services
- Training and resources for adults who work with lesbian, gay, and bisexual youth
- National Advocacy Coalition on Youth and Sexual Orientation (NACYSO)
- The Harvey Milk School in New York City, established in 1985 as the nation's first alternative high school for lesbian, gay, and bisexual youth. A joint project of the New York City Board of Education and Hetrick-Martin, a nonprofit social service, education, and advocacy organization that serves lesbian, gay, and bisexual children, the Harvey Milk School

offers these youngsters a safe environment conducive to learning and free from antigay harassment. Since its inception, the school has served over 230 students, helping them achieve positive feelings of learning and academic success and has become the model for other programs and alternative schools throughout the country.

New York City Gay and Lesbian Anti-Violence Project (AVP)
647 Hudson Street
New York, NY 10014
(212) 807-6761

The New York City Gay and Lesbian Anti-Violence Project (AVP) was founded in 1980 in reaction to neighborhood incidents of antigay violence and the failure of the criminal justice system to respond.

AVP serves gay and lesbian victims of domestic violence, sexual assault, bias crimes, HIV/AIDS–related violence, or other forms of victimization by offering free and confidential assistance in the form of therapeutic counseling, advocacy within the criminal justice system and victim support agencies, and provides information for self-help and referrals to practicing professionals and other sources of assistance. It is AVP's goal that through these services victims will be able to regain their sense of self-respect, identify options that are available to help them, and learn to assert themselves and understand their rights.

AVP is also proactive in that it serves the community through efforts to educate the public about hate-motivated crime. By raising public awareness about inadequate official response to these crimes and their victims, AVP aims to hold law enforcement and social service agencies accountable to their social and moral obligation for impartial service. AVP is working to change the public attitude of apathy toward hate-motivated violence and to promote public policies designed to discourage such violence.

Senior Action in a Gay Community (SAGE)
305 Seventh Avenue, 16th fl.
New York, NY 10001
(212) 741-2247

Senior Action in a Gay Community (SAGE) was founded in New York in 1977 to serve the social and political needs of older lesbians and gay men. SAGE offers support groups, counseling, a drop-in center, women's events, AIDS and seniors programs, education, community outreach, and a national conference to teach interested individuals how to establish similar centers in their areas. If you cannot locate a senior lesbian and gay center in your area, call the SAGE's executive office in New York for help locating one near you.

Index

Achtenberg, Roberta, ix-x
Adoption, 233-42
    agencies and services for, 239
    legal overview of, 235
    transracial and international, 240-42
Advocate, The, 20, 273
AIDS, gay marriage and, 183
Alcoholism and recovery movement, 18
Alternative insemination, 217, 218-19,
    224-30
American Civil Liberties Union Lesbian
    and Gay Rights Project, 263-64

Baker, Jack, 80
Banaszak, Rob, on widowhood, 35
Barbara and Dalia, 34-36, 54, 57, 104-5,
    217-18, 246
Barbee, Naomi, 180
Barnes, Patrick, 36-38, 48, 49
Bars, gay and lesbian, 17-20
Bechdel, Alison, 129
Belinda and Terri, 159
Bennett, Jim, 90-91, 238-40
Bennett-Maccubbin, Justen, 238-40
Berger, R. M., 44-45
Berkowitz, Lori, 55, 98, 107, 134, 210
Berzon, Betty, 38, 141
Beverly and Jamie, 107, 145, 155-56, 161,
    171-72, 182
BLK, 273
Bobersky, Anita, 156, 230-31, 246, 249
Boggis, Terry, and Rosemary, 118, 219,
    224-27, 236-37, 248, 251, 255
Boykin, Keith, 72

Bram, Christopher, 1
Bruining, Mi Ok Song, 240-41
Buckmire, Ron, 55
Buddhism, 34-36, 104-5
Burns, Richard, 7-8, 54-55, 62, 166,
    189-91, 192, 202, 211

Calderwood, Brent, on gay prom, 8-9
Calhoun, Carlena, 57, 130, 156, 209, 244
Carole and Jackie, 243-44, 247
Carolyn and Genelle, 32-34, 151, 223
Carranza, Ruth, 49-50, 181
Casey and Dakota, 22-25, 87
Catlett, Pat, 159, 171
Center Kids, 219, 277
Ceremonies, marriage. *See* Weddings
Children. *See also* Parenting
    adoption of, 233-42
    alternative insemination for pregnancy
        and, 224-30
    custody battles for, 51-52, 82, 254
    divorce and, 252-55
    religious education of, 242-45
    school experience of, and "out" parents,
        249-50
Children of Lesbians and Gays Everywhere
    (COLAGE), 261
Chris and Deb, 64, 133-34
Clare, Harriet, 123, 124, 131
Cohabitation, decision for, 44-56
Cohen, Richard, on gay marriage, 108-9
Cole, Sylvia, 7
Coleen and Ava, 216
Coming out, 153-60

to families, 168-69
jobs and, 135, 156-60
as lesbian and gay family, 247-50
to vendors, 93
Committed same-sex relationships, 41-73.
    See also Marriage, same-sex
    cultural context of, 71-73
    decision to live together in, 46-56
    overview of phases in, 44-46
    proposals and engagement in, 45, 64-71
    ring exchange as symbol of, 56-64
    terms for participants in, 41-44
Community activism, 26-31
Community centers, gay and lesbian, 3, 189
Congregation Beth Simchat Torah, 78, 95
Contreras, Guillian. *See* Zoe, Melise and
    Guillian
Cook-Daniels, Loree and Marcelle, 194-96
Coparenting arrangements, 230-33
Corry, Jeremy, 130, 184, 214, 256
Courtship. *See* Meeting potential partners
Cox, Gregory, 47, 150, 160, 184
Cromey, Robert Warren, 86, 88-89
Curtis, Diane, 51-52, 82-83, 155
Custody battles, 51-52, 82, 254
Cyberspace, meeting people in, 22-25. *See
    also* Internet

Dahir, Mubarak S., 43
D'Amico, Antonio, 192
Dating, 5-9
Dave and Skip, 216
David and son Joshua, 234-38, 246
Death of partner, 142, 192-94
    new relationships after, 35, 36-38
Defense of Marriage Act (DOMA), 125,
    198
DeGeneres, Ellen, 31
DiDonato, Paula, 63, 78, 86, 106
Different Light, A, 277-78
Divorce, 188-91
    parenting and, 252-55
Domestic partnerships, 114, 116-19, 158,
    159
Domestic violence, 185, 186-87
Donovan, Jim, 58, 96-97
Doug and Jerry, 145
Dubin, Murray, 193

Edwards, Christine, 38, 45, 90-94, 98, 176,
    223

Elizabeth and Sarah, 241
Elliott, Jo Ellen, 119, 165
Employment, 135, 156-60
Ensig-Brodsky, Ellen, 112-13, 199

Families-of-origin, gay and lesbian
    relationships with, 141, 161-68
Family(ies), 205-59
    R. Achtenberg on lesbian and gay, ix-x
    adoption and creation of, 233-42
    alternative insemination and
        coparenting in formation of, 224-33
    cultural and social pressures on lesbian
        and gay, 247-50
    divorce and new partnerships affecting,
        252-56
    expanding concept of, 205-8
    friends as chosen, 208-12
    "gayby" boom of same-sex couples
        having children and creating, 218-19
    Internet resources for, 226-27
    parenting children from past
        relationships in, 213-18
    religious aspects affecting, 242-45
    role models in, 250-52
    smashing stereotypes about lesbian and
        gay, 257-58
    support from parents and families-of-
        origin for, 245-47
Fenway Community Health Center
    (FCHC), 278-79
Finances, 140, 146-50
Fiol-Matta, Liza, 28-31, 62, 117, 177,
    215-16
Forum on the Right to Marry (FORM),
    265
Frantz-Geddes, Peggy and Nancy, 58, 155,
    251
Friends as chosen family, 208-12
Fure, Tret, 61-62, 129, 172-73

Gay, Lesbian, and Straight Education
    Network (GLSEN), 266-67
Gay and Lesbian Advocates & Defenders
    (GLAD), 279
Gay and Lesbian Alliance Against
    Defamation (GLAAD), 266
Gay and Lesbian Association of Retiring
    Persons (GLARP), 201, 267
Gay and Lesbian Parents Coalition
    International (GLPCI), 222, 262

Gay and lesbian relationships. *See* Relationships
Gigi and Sandy, 212
Gingrich, Candace, 29, 66
Goldstein, Fran, 42, 60, 77, 164, 175
Gomez, Jewell, 178-79
Graff, E. J., 168-69
Grant, Stephanie, 211
Green card, obtaining, 54-55
Grief and death of partner, 35, 36-38, 142, 192-94
Griffin, Renee and Jackie, 103, 155, 217, 251

Hadash, Brendan, 93, 154-55, 175, 212
Happel, Aaron and Eric, 103, 118-19
Harrison, Linda F., 220-21
Hawaii, same-sex marriage case in, 55, 125-28, 257-58
Hawaii Equal Rights Marriage Project (h.e.r.m.p.), 267
Heche, Anne, 31
Hetrick-Martin Institute, 279-80
Higdon, Jennifer, 83-84, 165
Hill, Marjorie, 38, 45, 80, 91-94, 98, 130, 176, 223
Hinckley, Siobhan, 156, 230, 246, 249, 258
Homophobia
    "family values" and, 205-8
    religious fundamentalism and, 31-36
    in schools, 249-50, 253
    shifting away from, 68-69
Honeymoons, 98
Hultquist, Alan, 93, 154-55, 175, 212
Human Rights Campaign (HRC), 268

Ian, Janis, 116, 174-75, 185, 212
Iannozzi, Maria, 180
Immigrants, problems facing lesbian and gay, 54-55
International Lesbian and Gay Association, 268
Internet
    meeting people and romance on, 22-25
    resources for same-sex couples on, 6, 127, 226-27
    Web sites, 3, 6, 127, 173, 226-27
    In the Family, 272-73
    It's Elementary (film), 249, 250
Ivanish, Gary, 122-23

Jackie and Betty, 52

Jackson-Paris, Bob and Rod, 188
Jacobowitz-Cain, Paul and Kurt, 131, 212
Jan and Mary Lou, 196-97, 198
Jasper, Richard, 130, 184, 213-14, 256
Jill and Randi, 145, 150-51, 172, 188
Joan and Elaine, 47-48
Joeline and Sandy, 102, 131, 165, 185
Johnson, Fenton, 152
Jones, Oscar, 47, 130, 150, 160, 184
Jones, Zachary, 77, 78, 79, 85, 90
Jones-Mack, Edward, 47, 106-7, 210
Julie and Wendy, 48-49, 52, 77, 81-82, 147, 160

Kaj, Karin and Maria, 5-6, 53, 59-60, 131, 133, 146, 153, 154, 162, 173-74, 207, 243, 250, 251, 258
Karen and Lisa, 63, 149-50, 184
Kazan, Zoy, 68-69
Kendall, Kate, 254
Kleinbaum, Sharon, 78, 79, 85, 87, 95, 194, 243
Kowalski, Sharon, 151

Lagon, Patrick, 125-28, 174
Lambda Legal Defense and Education Fund, 127, 234, 235, 264-65
Latino/a Lesbian and Gay Organization (LLEGO), 269
Lawson, Cheryl, 83-84, 165
Legal documents required to protect same-sex relationships, 130, 131, 148-53
Legalization of same-sex marriage, xiii-xiv, 72, 255
    in Hawaii, 55, 125-28, 257-58
    on-line resources for, 127
    statement on, by Association of the Bar of the City of New York, 120-22
Lesbian and Gay Community Services Center, New York, 3, 18, 189
Lesbian and Gay Immigration & Asylum Rights Task Force, 268-69
Lind, Tracey, 42-43, 60-61, 77, 86, 164, 175
Liz and Judy, 13-15, 159
"Love Makes a Family" photo exhibit, 209
Lucas, Craig, 36-38, 48, 49
Lynne and Esther, 19-20, 147

McConnell, Mike, 80
MacCubbin, Deacon, 90-91, 238-40
McKeon, Terry, 231-33

Mack-Jones, Timothous, 47, 61, 106, 210
McQuay, Bekki, 51-52, 82-83, 155
Mano and Andrew, 145, 157, 176, 183
Marianne and Marie, 82
Mark and Andy, 63-64, 113-15, 139, 145, 151, 170-71, 223-24
Marriage, opposite-sex
    benefits and perks of legal, 119, 120-22, 132-33
    historical overview of, 75-76
Marriage, same-sex, 75-203. *See also* Family(ies))
    ceremonies for (*see* Weddings)
    controversy and popularity of movement toward legalization of, 129-34
    domestic partnerships and, 114, 116-19
    in Hawaii, 55, 125-28, 257-58
    historical marriage and, 75-76
    legalization of (*see* Legalization of same-sex marriage)
    long-term commitments and concept of, 134-37, 197-200
    as political act, 119-25
    proposals for, 45, 64-71
    relationships with families of origin and, 161-68
    as sacrament, 88-89
Marshall, Vanessa, xiv, 57-58, 105-10, 142-43, 165, 169-70, 209
Martin, April, 5, 15-17, 42, 46, 72, 79, 141, 188, 200, 218, 247, 248, 256, 258
Martin and John, 11-13, 134, 151, 170, 198-99
Mazurkiewicz, Christine, 58-59, 162
Mediation, 189, 191
Meeting potential partners, 1-9
    in bars, 17-20
    at community events, 26-31
    after death of partner, 35, 36-38
    earlier difficulties of, 9-17
    on Internet, 22-25
    in personal ads, 20-22
    "type" casting and, 38-39
Melillo, Joseph Kealapua, 125-28, 174
Metropolitan Community Church, 32, 85, 87, 275-76
Molina, Santa, 57, 105-10, 165, 170, 209
Monogamy, 141, 181-84
Moore, Dave, 58, 96-97
Moore, Nellson, 244-45

Mormon Church, 32-34
Munisteri, Ben, 147, 152, 192, 193
Murray, Louise, 28-31, 62, 117, 177, 214-16

Names
    last, in same-sex marriage, 101, 103
    terms for relationship partners, 41-46
Nancy and Alicia, 97-99, 156-57, 212
National Association of Black and White Men Together (NABWMT), 270
National Association of Lesbian and Gay Community Centers, 270
National Black Lesbian and Gay Leadership Forum (NBLGLF), 170-71
National Center for Lesbian Rights (NCLR), x, 265
National Gay and Lesbian Task Force (NGLTF), 271-72
National Freedom to Marry Coalition (FTM), 271
Nelson, Joy, 57, 130, 156, 207, 208, 244
Nelson, Judy, 190
Newcombe, Mary, 233-34
New York City Gay and Lesbian Anti-Violence Project (AVP), 186, 280
Nora and Melinda, 252-54
Nora and Shelley, 255
Nurturing same-sex marriages, 168-88

On-line resources. *See* Internet
Organizations
    landmark local, 277-80
    national family-related, 261-63
    national legal, 263-65
    national political, 265-72
    religious, 273-77
Out, 273

Parenting. *See also* Children
    adoption and, 233-42
    of children from former straight relationships, 213-18
    coming out as family and, 247-50
    decision for, 220-24
    divorce and, 252-55
    "gayby" boom, 218-19
    with new partners, 255-56
    pregnancy and birthing, 224-33
    religion and, 242-45

role models in, 250-52
of sons, by lesbians, 254
Parents and Friends of Lesbians and Gay
Men (PFLAG), 161, 263
Parents of gays and lesbians, 31-32, 161-68
support for lesbian and gay families by,
245-47
Partners Task Force for Gay and Lesbian
Couples, 4, 44, 172-73, 182, 263
Patterson, Charlotte, 257
Paul and Craig, 61
Pearse, Martha, 24-25
Pela, Robert, 41
Perry, Troy, 85, 87, 91
Perry and Hoa, 242, 248
Personal ads, 20-22
Piazza, Michael, 5
Political act, marriage as, 119-25
Political and community activism
meeting potential partners in, 26-31
weddings as, 119-25
Powsner, Steven, 147, 152, 192, 193
Pratt, Kris, 29, 66
Price, Deb, 116-17
Pride Senior Network, 199, 200
Project Connect, 18
Proposals of marriage, 45, 64-71
Publications, 272-73

Quinn, Anne, 231-33, 251

Race, class, and culture
adoption and considerations of, 240-42
in same-sex relationships, 176-81
Real estate agents, 53
Relationships, xiii-xv
adjusting to transitions in, 194-97
age and role modeling of, 200-202
coming out as in committed, 153-60
committed (see Committed same-sex
relationships)
concept of ideal "type" in, 38-39
death of partner in, 142, 192-94
difficulties of building, in earlier times,
9-17
divorce in, 188-91
domestic violence in, 185, 186-87
families based on (see Family(ies))
fundamentalist religions and prejudice
against, 31-36
marriage and (see Marriage, same-sex)

new, after death of partner, 36-38
nurturing, 168-88
self-defined roles in, 139-45
"settling down" phase of, 143-53
stereotyped cultural perceptions of, 1-9
ways of meeting potential partners and
building, 17-31
working to create lasting, 168-88
Religion and parenting, 242-45
Religious fundamentalism, 31-36
Religious organizations, 87, 273-77
Rene, Norman, 36, 37
Reno, Suzy, 66-67, 72, 222-23
Resources for gays and lesbians
books, 6, 10, 46, 51, 77, 143, 183, 228,
254
community centers, 3, 189
on marriage rights, 127
on-line, 6, 127, 226-27 (see also
Internet)
on parenting, 222
on retirement, 201
for teens, 6
for transgendered people, 196
Retirement, 201
Rieman, Walter, wedding of, 108-9
Rings, exchange of, 45, 56-64
Role models
for long-term relationships, 200-202
parenting and, 250-52
Roles in same-sex marriage, 139-45
Roman Catholic Church, 31-32
Rotello, Gabriel, 183

Samonds, Amy, 65-67, 72, 222-23
Scarpitta, Tom, 122
Schibley Schreiber, Paul and Mark, 94-96
Schmiege, Karen, 159, 171
Schools, reducing homophobia in, 249-50,
253
Senior Action in a Gay Community
(SAGE), 201, 280
Shahar, Robin, 135
Shapiro, Diana, 55-56, 98, 107, 134, 210
Shernoff, Michael, 39, 136, 140, 141, 142,
170, 182, 192
Signorile, Michaelangelo, 201
Snow, Melise. See Zoe, Melise and Guillian
Snyder, Pat, 116, 174-75, 185, 212
Spannbauer, Nancy, 112-13, 199
Sperm banks, 225, 229

Stereotypes about gays and lesbians, 1-9, 157, 257-58
Steve and Ric, 20-21, 111-12, 145, 174, 182-83
Stoddard, Tom, wedding of, 108-9
Stratton, Susan, 119, 165

Teal, Pamela, 59, 162
Teens, gay and lesbian, 6
    gay high school prom, 8-9
    homeless, 9, 13, 238
Teeven, Judy, 63, 78, 86, 106
Teresa and Lori, 243
Terri and Belinda, 59
Terri and Debbie, 216-17
Thacker, Becky, 123, 124, 131
Thompson, Karen, 151
Tim and Mario, 21-22, 60, 178, 209
Transgender relationships, 194-97

Unitarian Universalist Association, 123, 243, 273-74
United Fellowship of Metropolitan Community Churches Mother Church, 275-76
Unity Fellowship Church, 78, 85, 92, 210, 274-75

Vazquez, Carmen, 119, 136, 166, 191, 241
Vendors, 59, 93
Versace, Gianni, 192
Villanueva, Noli, 18-19, 50, 179, 192
Villarosa, Linda, and Vicki, 7, 50, 129, 140, 177, 227-30, 242, 246-47

Walker-Smith, Shawn and Robert, 26-28, 67-70, 98, 136, 175, 176
Walton, Pam, 49-50, 181
Wanda and Mildred, 163, 210
Ward, Joseph, 42, 98, 135
Ward, Mary, 213
Warren, Patricia Nell, 132-33
Web sites, 3, 6, 127, 173, 226-27. *See also* Internet
Weddings, 76-80
    new rituals for, 99-110
    private ceremonies, 81-84
    as religious ceremony, 87, 88-89
    secular, 110-15
    traditional public, 85-99
    vendors for, 93
    vows and blessings in, 97, 100-101, 102, 106-7
Weeg, Joyce, 231-33
Wicca handfasting ceremony, 102-4
Williams, Lamont, 42, 98, 135, 180
Williamson, Cris, 61-62, 129, 172-73
Wishing Well, The, 20
Wolfe, Maxine, 213
Wolfson, Evan, xiii, 127, 128
Woodworth, Robert, 18, 36, 50, 179, 192
World Congress of Gay and Lesbian Jewish Organizations (WCGLJO), 276-77

Youth. *See* Teens, gay and lesbian

Zoe, Melise and Guillian, 98, 100-102, 103, 155, 165